Communicating When Your Company Is Under Siege

Communicating When Your Company Is Under Siege

Surviving Public Crisis

MARION K. PINSDORF

Third Edition

Fordham University Press
New York
1999

Copyright © 1999 by Marion K. Pinsdorf
All rights reserved.
LC 98–38612
ISBN 0–8232–1783–3 (*hardcover*)
ISBN 0–8232–1784–1 (*paperback*)

Library of Congress Cataloging-in-Publication Data

Pinsdorf, Marion K.
    Communicating when your company is under siege : surviving
public crisis / Marion K. Pinsdorf.—3rd ed.
        p.   cm.
Includes bibliographical references and index.
ISBN 0-8232-1783-3 (hc. : alk. paper)
ISBN 0-8232-1784-1 (pbk. : alk. paper)
    1. Corporate image.   2. Public relations.   3. Crisis management.
4. Business communication.   5. Strategic planning.   I. Title.
HD59.2.P55   1998
659.2—dc21   98-38612
                                                                    CIP

Printed in the United States of America

Dedicated to
two chief executive officers,
pragmatists who communicated
with candor and conviction:
Henry A. Walker, Jr.,
Amfac, Inc.
and
the late John W. Hill,
Hill and Knowlton, Inc.

Contents

Preface/Memo

To: CEO and Senior Operating Officers
From: Marion K. Pinsdorf
Subject: Communicating During Corporate Troubles

Besieged as you are by the production breakdowns, stiffer global competition, and just plain keeping our company profitable, corporate communications may seem soft and ancillary, draining profits rather than producing them.

Communications is soft, all right: the soft underbelly of our business, vulnerable to losses not only of money, but of that ephemeral yet critical public perception. Many companies (but fortunately not yet ours) have been pounded by expensive events that came winging in from the outside. Think what Tylenol cost Johnson & Johnson— and that was a public success! Or Bhopal, Union Carbide. Or the sexual harassment and discrimination charges against many organizations. Or even that relatively simple explosion at our competitor's plant. Granted: how well we respond to such challenges depends largely on how profitable and strong we are internally, but we must recognize and plan for external public relations problems, particularly those that erupt without warning.

Maladroit communications can create and deepen many corporate calamities; destroy markets, financial strength, and reputations; cost a company its existence and you, your job. In its wake it leaves protracted investigations, litigation, and expensive fines. Millions are spent on advertising, product liability, or reputation management. When E. F. Hutton speaks now, the SEC listens, not its customers. Had Hutton understood a cardinal rule of communications—that there are no secrets—it might be flourishing instead of sullied. We can learn how to survive from such very expensive communications lapses of others.

You all have as many good reasons as would-be dieters for not developing a communications strategy. A few compelling arguments dictate the contrary. First, in an age of techno-hubris, when we universally depend on machines to do our thinking and attempt to quantify everything, it's hard to measure communications. Seldom can it produce numbers to prove its contribution and utility. Communications is a very diffuse corporate function. And how those public relations types go on and on when they have a case that does quantify their value!

Then there's the department itself. Too often, it's used as the dumping ground for corporate losers, burn-outs awaiting retirement, or ill-trained, unfocused, but bright liberal arts graduates. They are consigned to communications, where, supposedly, they can do less harm than if they were running a plant. High schools put football coaches and driver education teachers in history departments with the same rationale. Oh yes, it's also been the corporate EEOC token, where women and blacks get their first shots at senior management. That's all very risky.

The communications officer carries these stigmata as well as the burden of being a Janus manager—charged with knowing our business well, but also scanning the world outside for elements, hostile or advantageous, which influence our operations. It's a damn delicate role to caution about dangerous specks on the competitive horizon or to warn that you are being carried away by your enthusiasm for that pending merger or acquisition. Often the communications officer is thrust into the uncomfortable role of corporate conscience, pointing out how much cost overruns on government contracts or a polluted stream are going to cost, not just in good will but in dollars—lots of them. We are all more civilized than the Greeks, who simply beheaded a bearer of bad news; instead, we tune him out, relegate him to impotency, or, if he's too persistent, fire him.

And he must cope daily with your *bête noire*—the media. When you are immersed in operating problems, nothing annoys you more than the press emphasizing the negative or searching out the sensational. They're not behaving as corporate types do, and exercise news judgment very different from yours. Some of these adversarial relations are understandable: your aims and knowledge are often different. But well-trained, good reporters do share your goal of honestly telling your corporate story to the public. Should a headline or television news segment be unfair or damaging, however, it's the communications officer who must bring it to you and explain. Too often he's blamed for whatever the reporter wrote.

The most effective, even profitable, communications is embedded in the matrix of our business and the general economic, social milieu, not positioned atop Mount Olympus as a staff function. Communications can counter the wishful thinking so endemic today: that somehow next year will be much better than the dismal one just past. Communications can be a valuable correcting device, a very loyal, questioning devil's advocate and corporate gyroscope. It keeps shaking your shoulder, telling you to look out the window at a wider world. The rest of us are just too pressured with the details of running the business to do this, although we all know we should. Insular thinking in executive offices bodes trouble—always.

All of us who have awakened in anguish at 3 a.m. because of the crunch of corporate pressures smile at the panacea peddlers with their simple nostrums and one-minute easy how-to-dos— entertaining corporate fairy tales. We know the reality is much tougher, but also gives a much deeper sense of accomplishment. Too often, technology is grasped as a panacea, with little thought to its downside—instantaneous transmission of information, correct or damaging sans much corporate control. One need not be a neo-Luddite to see dangers or to recognize the dilemmas, stylistic and conceptual aspects of communications.

Read on if you want to think, and to pick my thoughts, which have been trained in journalism and history, then battle-tested in the trenches of communications counseling and senior corporate management. Most recently, my most skeptical audiences—and soon yours—are an enterprising, tough breed of young managers.

Acknowledgments

Polynesians customarily thank everyone. When distilling a lifetime of thought and professional experience in a field as ever changing as communications, it is difficult to do otherwise.

Did the learning start with demanding historians—Professors Robert Brunhouse of Drew University, John Fagg of New York University, and the late Carl Bridenbaugh of Brown University—who kept me constantly searching for the biases, intentional or unconscious, in the fabric of writing and decision-making? Or the psychologists—Professors James A. McClintock of Drew and Ferdinand Jones of Brown—who heightened my understanding of how vulnerable and noble leaders can be?

But before the educators was journalism. One editor, infected with *Front Page* style, profanely bellowed every mistake and stupidity of a scared sixteen-year-old across the city room. The late Pulitzer Prize winner William A. Caldwell taught us journalists to think widely and deeply, even on the police beat.

Coming into communications in the 1960s, I was fortunate to learn from two pioneers in corporate communications, and in counseling: the late Milton Fairman of Borden, Inc., taught with all the cussedness of his early Chicago newspaper days, and the late John W. Hill, founder of Hill and Knowlton, Inc., with indefatigable curiosity and collegiality. The bridge from counseling to corporate officer was crossed with the encouragement of Edward Starr, retired Hill and Knowlton executive vice president, and Henry A. Walker Jr., CEO and chairman emeritus of Amfac, Inc., who has the unique gifts of listening sensitively, implementing swiftly, and appreciating worlds much wider than most business executives.

As a corporate officer myself, I learned from the chairmen I served: the impact of high national visibility from G. William Miller and Robert P. Straetz of Textron; the quicksand of merger from Ralph A. Saul of INA (now CIGNA); the practicality of Japanese ideas from Henry Wendt of SmithKline Beecham; the importance of Brazil from

Augustine R. Marusi of Borden; the wisdom and productivity of participatory decision-making from Dr. Sidney Harman of Harman International; and the wisdom and patience of Portuguese traditions from Nelson Vieira, former director of Brown University's Department for Portuguese and Brazilian studies, where I taught for a decade.

During the best of corporate times and the worst, an intelligent, compassionate circle of confidants have cared. Their titles and accomplishments are impressive, but their greatest gift to me has been their friendship over many years, miles, and job changes, through successes and pain. They are: Robert Ames, James Baar, Chester Burger, Robert L. Dilenschneider, William Ford, Robert K. Gray, Bert Heffner, John Leo, Ellen Magnin Newman, Daniel Picard, Albert Ross, and Larry M. Speakes. And the personal friends: Joan (deceased) and Martin Ainbinder, Nessa Forman, Roberta Jacobs-Meadway, and Lily G. Spierer. My Amfac colleagues, directors, and officers translated *aloha* as supporting and enthusing.

Leonia is a special little town, long ago dedicated to artistic and creative achievement. You work with the sense of the outstanding people who once made their homes here. Some years ago, two then neighbors, Bob and Mary Ludlum, encouraged my dreams of writing. Edward Brewer at his harpsichord took the lonely edge off writing. Sushil and Veena Chadda, and Harriet Maneval were always caring. Harold Ficke, director of the public library, and his staff found any book I needed.

All these people are both prologue to this book and very much a part of it. My specific thanks are extended to Dave Dyer, then associate editor of the *Harvard Business Review*, who started it all by introducing me to Bruce Katz, who became a supportive, sensitive editor and friend for the first edition—and to the people who shared ideas and experiences generously: Karen Berg of Commcore; Harold Burson of Burson-Marsteller; Richard Cheney, Richard Hyde, and Robert Taft of Hill and Knowlton; William Dobbins of Reliance Group Holdings; Phillip Fried then of Monsanto; Kirk O. Hanson then at Stanford Business School; Harry Matte and Robert Ozaki then of Amfac; Allan E. Shubert of *Fortune*; Michael Tabriz of Philip Morris; and many others over the years who thought analytically about communications.

From each I have learned that the fun and accomplishment of a

career comes not on a mill pond, but in surviving the waves and troughs of turbulent waters.
To each, *mahalo*.

1987

Stasis is impossible in disciplines as dynamic and ever volatile as public relations and business. Instantaneous, constant communications only speeds the velocity of change. Personally, stasis drains verve and adventure from life. In the years elapsed since the first two editions, many new ideas, supportive, sharing colleagues and friends have enhanced my writing, teaching, and life. Most of those acknowledged earlier are still encouraging greatly and generously. But there are new ones.

Fluke and happenstance, vital to understanding and practicing public relations, put me in an MBA classroom. After completing the first *Communicating* manuscript I spent two weeks chewing on a lean diet, but rich conversations. During one, Arthur Taylor asked: "Want to teach?" "Sure," and not long after I was in a classroom at Fordham's Graduate School of Business. Arthur, then its dean, now President of Muhlenberg College, encourages still. He, President Joseph O'Hare, S.J., and Dean Ernest J. Scalberg found ways to keep me in the classroom. And Robert Wharton encouraged my research in many ways. The MBA students, hard-working, intelligent, and amazingly generous despite great stress, assuage any despairing about the future. Not only did two particularly insightful graduate students, Scott Morcaldi and Sarah Hunt, hone perspectives, but Sarah worked diligently and long to produce this edition.

For constant conversations about public relations from which I always learn a great deal, I thank Keith Anderson of Travelers; Linda Bock of the International Insurance College; George Glazer of Hill and Knowlton; Douglas Hearle, president of Hearle and Company; Bob Stone of The Dilenschneider Group; Susan Hullin; Jim Lane; Gary Lavine of Niagara-Mohawk; Ray O'Rourke of Burson-Marsteller; and members of the Page Society. Two Drew University friends bridge communications and the academy. Cindy Moran was its communications officer; and Scott McDonald, its interim president.

Academic friends widened ideas and interests: Patricia Ramsey, management systems; Katherine Combellick, acute literary insights; Joyce Orsini, Deming management; Fred Carstensen, business history; Bob Gilbert, communicating presidential health; Linda Menton, Hawaiian ethnicity; and Richard L. Rubenstein, so gifted in seeing specks of trouble or opportunity before anyone else. He foresaw redundant people long before corporate "right-sizing." Evelina Kelbetcheva, Todor Petov, and Nicholai Genov I met teaching in Bulgaria. As public relations of necessity becomes more cross-cultural, I reach back to my Brazilian family and to my classmate Noriko Arima Kashiwagi. U.S.-born, she has for many years sensitized me to her Japanese heritage.

Two military officers encouraged analyzing military strategy to gain insights into business management. One is kin. Vincent Davis, director emeritus and professor at the Patterson School at the University of Kentucky, in his military life is Captain USN retired. After conversation during an endless flight across the Pacific Ocean, Lieutenant General Stephen Silvasy invited me to the Army War College. There I understood how much the army learned from its public relations mistakes in Vietnam and vowed never again. In the Gulf War that showed. How many companies need to suffer the beneficial, albeit tragic cauterizing of a Vietnam to communicate more wisely?

Friends are vital during solitary, sedentary writing. And Doctors Marian and Paul Bernstein, Felix Kloman, Ruth Cohen, and Yolanda Murphy each opened exciting new avenues with intelligence and caring. And, once again, Chet Burger and Harriet Maneval read the manuscript with caring wisdom.

To each again, *mahalo*.

Leonia, 1998

For the Third Edition

Communicating When Your Company Is Under Siege

1

Turbulent Times

The Kaleidoscope of Corporate Communications

Corporate communications is a kaleidoscope of ever-changing functions, talents, and crises that do not so much proceed as crystallize anew each time. With each turn, each event or crisis, a different configuration forms. What worked previously helps in understanding the new cluster, but, in truth, each serious public crisis is different. Tunnel vision—looking down the tube at the kaleidoscope's always changing colors—reveals only surface happenings at a given moment. Absent are the lingering shadows of events long drained of their power or the shifting new elements presaging the future. Communications decisions, often solidly rooted in quicksand, as a result pose greater-than-usual challenges and risks to operating executives—who must depend upon and evaluate the function—and, most of all, to the communicators themselves.

To be effective—or of any use at all—communications must be intimately, intelligently interwoven with the sobering realities of the times and the business it seeks to serve. It cannot be a cosmetic attempt to gussy up ugly or dishonest facts with a false, pretty face. Realities in the late 1990s mean understanding shrinking rather than expanding markets, the demassing of the economy. Some of the elephantine corporate structures no longer function effectively and profitably. They are proving dysfunctional as technology flattens corporate pyramids and transforms once orderly channels of communications into a centipede with many legs—and, yes, fangs. Reality means managing across many cultures and countries, coping with instantaneous communications.

Managers must motivate a new breed of employees: less loyal and more demanding, impatient and justly scared for their futures. They are seeking more individualism; gathering information more from sight, sound, and each other than from traditional print sources; some are stuck below what they were taught to expect.

Companies must face tougher off-shore competition. Some warn that the United States is in danger of becoming a service island in a manufacturing world, of consigning very educated people to slinging Big Macs—life after corporate right-sizings. Often overlooked is the penchant for naïveté and wastefulness. A military example illustrates a corporate problem. Tom Mangold and John Penycate, writing on the Vietnam War, describe how well Americans lived above the Tunnels of CuChi and how poorly the Vietnamese existed below. But the obvious disadvantages to the Viet Cong were balanced. The Americans used large numbers of support soldiers and fighters, required many supplies, and were hobbled because they returned to base every night. They were hobbled, too, by retrieving their wounded. Underneath, the Vietnamese listened, fought, and supplied themselves on U.S. leftovers and discarded food and arms. In stark contrast to regular troops, Americans who eventually became tunnel rats themselves were very cool, calculating, and careful with their supplies and opportunities.

Corporate changes are swift, unforgiving, and hidden until announced. Many examples could be chosen, but the decline of Chesebrough-Pond's will illustrate. Though it was heralded by *In Search of Excellence* as one of the best-managed U.S. companies, its growth quickly turned anemic. The company was plagued by rapid management turnover, maturing markets, a dearth of new products, and excessive debt. Like many managements today, Chesebrough-Ponds preferred buying products to growing them. Too often, research and development, long-range planning fell victim in the 1980s battles against acquisition predators. The future, like eating one's seed corn, pales in the struggle for survival. Polaroid let good practices grow undisciplined. In other companies guaranteed employment mutated into a civil service attitude of sinecure. Once-innovative employees became overpaid and undermotivated, with little understanding of long-term goals or, more important, the changed competitive climate.

Although change hits with increasing velocity and force, many miss signals crying for mutation and modification until the old ways require surgery. Highly innovative, productive ideas, such as IBM's guarantee of lifetime employment, often lapse or harden in nonproductive sinecures. Thomas Watson, Jr.'s *Father, Son, and Company* poignantly details how his father's firm belief that nepotism was good for business, IBM's cult-like atmosphere, and vest-pocket management style silenced "too many good people." It dammed up change. Assuming control, Watson, Jr., faced "the classic position of a company that gets tunnel vision because of its success and asking the wrong questions."[1] He feared "IBM would explode like a supernova and end up a dwarf" while he had "to ride a runaway horse, expanding on a scale that no company had ever matched."[2]

In his study of the insular world of the *Philadelphia Gentleman*, E. Digby Baltzell saw "an excellent example of a business aristocracy which too often placed the desire for material comfort and security above the duties of political and intellectual leadership."[3] That discouraged outsiders, essential change, even keeping up with the times. For example, the Pennsylvania Railroad, an early model of management, *The Saturday Evening Post*, and other Philadelphia creations withered like the cut flowers they were. A poignant picture of such painful change can be found in the two portrayals of Willy Loman in Arthur Miller's *Death of a Salesman*. In the 1950s, Lee J. Cobb played a big, bluff salesman huckstering American goods to hungry markets. He dreamed big, but failed tragically. In the mid-1980s, Dustin Hoffman played Willy as a shuffling shrimp who started smaller than Cobb and ended up defeated even in modest aspirations. Instead of buoyant expansion, he was, as one reviewer noted, "The graduate who can't even make a killing in plastics."

Once all institutions were perceived—incorrectly, even in boom times—as everlasting, always expanding, and supportive. Now, as Peter Drucker points out, they are brittle and staid; they must limber up. Comparisons of the top 100 companies fifty years ago with those today document just how brittle companies are under the press of changing technology, markets, and competition. A survey by Patrick–Douglas Outplacement in Cleveland reported that about one quarter of the CEOs in *Fortune 500* companies were replaced between 1983 and 1985, about forty-one percent of financial chiefs, and about twenty-seven percent of human resources officers. More activist boards and demanding pension fund managers only whipped up more churn. Researchers don't keep count of communications chiefs, but you could guess that their turnover rate would be even higher. Loyalty has been sundered up and down—even with golden parachutes. "Operational restructuring," reengineering, new competitive factors, technology, buying, selling, or consolidating businesses have displaced and discouraged millions of workers. Employee morale and loyalty have declined, almost disappeared, most dramatically and seriously among managers.[4] Your young management won't tell you they've tuned out messages from the chairman.

COMMUNICATING ON CONSENT OF CONSTITUENCIES

With all the imperative business and personnel problems, it is all too easy for the pressured executive to consign communications to the back burner. But this book will demonstrate that such relegation is done at great peril and expense. When "fat" corporate staffs were cut, PR was excised beyond bare bones. Huge departments shrank to two or three professionals augmented by extensive outsourcing. Trace lines of concern are apparent to academics and businessmen alike. George Cabot Lodge of Harvard Business School writes of companies being able (even allowed) to operate in the future only by consent of their constituencies—a commercial application of Lockean theories of government by consent of the governed. Battle-scarred executives lament that activists have done a better job than business in allying themselves with the world's resentments, then calling those resentments into battle against multinationals. To counterbalance this, one executive advises:

> Think politically. Overcome a natural aloofness and protectiveness. Become aware of the concerns of others. Reach out for ongoing dialogue with many new publics. The goal, very bluntly, is survival.

> Think in advance, strategically, of the consequences of closing a factory, or of not renewing a mining concession or a contract with a farm owners' association. Think through the effects on individuals, families, communities, and, yes, companies themselves of surgical cuts in employment and operations. Explain candidly the reasons for actions or nonactions—their immediate and long-term benefits or their costs, and why they might have to be borne by local interests. When necessary, companies under public criticism may be forced to open their files to show continuity in policies and responsibility to consumers and other publics. Most of all, in every action executives take they must indicate that they are truly aware of the world outside

the executive suite. Only in that way can companies justify continued existence, the privilege to create wealth for themselves and others.[5]

These statements come from a business school classroom and from Nestlé's painful encounters selling their baby formula in Third World countries.

To executives still unbloodied by public crises, such advice may seem extreme. The initial banality and repetitiveness of danger sometimes lull even the wary. However, the prudent manager considers the powerful, expensive impacts external events have had on companies in just the past few years—the oxygen of publicity. In the decade to come, communications, internal and external, will be the catalyst of early warnings and solutions—the canary of the corporation—if it is understood, respected, and encouraged to function as it should and can. As will be demonstrated several times, the event in itself may not be as expensive as the public aftermath: the "but I didn't inhale" of media management.

When President Bill Clinton was asked about pot smoking, he answered so little so often, he made a continuing story and a folklore joke out of nothing. When Vice President Gore was asked the same question in his own 1988 quest for the presidential nomination, he said yes he tried it, didn't like it, doesn't anymore. By 1992 did anyone remember? The difference is a story with legs and lasting, and a one-shot.

Many trends and external conditions must be factored into running a company, particularly its communications. Too often myopia creates walls between a company's operations and the way the public perceives them; between operating managers faced with harsh realities and staff assuming process is invulnerable. During a day-long brainstorming at a large multinational, public relations people, despite drastic changes in operating and competitive environments, prattled on with clichés thirty years stale, invoking corporate deities in support of their irrelevant positions. Nostalgia is fun, comfortable, even intelligent, but not functional. Knowing yesterday and just what is comfortable is simply not enough, even dangerous. Many business failures and damaging public performances are the fault not simply of limited resources and unscrupulous competition. Rather, it is poverty of imagination that keeps a manager from breaking out of traditional modes; that restricts solutions to the manageable and thinkable—thinking within the box, in current business jargon.

When trouble hits, constantly shifting tactics, personal strength, and resolution will count for far more than all the jejune communications plans ever written. It is sheer hubris to even think public crises can be controlled. Financial executives and strategic planners look for quick, predictable solutions. The best a battle-scarred executive can hope for is damage control—countering outrageous criticism and telling the truth day after day until it gets across. Never doubt the resourcefulness or tenacity of your adversaries, or the willingness of the public to believe the worst of the best companies.

For some executives, the worst shock is being thrust from private, structured corporate life into the volatility of high public visibility. Whether as individuals, heads of their companies, or the company itself, such an experience is chilling, surprising, and can produce nasty, expensive mistakes.

Such a transition was a culture shock, "like suddenly moving to a very foreign country," for W. Michael Blumenthal, former chairman and chief executive officer of Bendix, then Burroughs and Unisys, who served as Secretary of the Treasury under President Carter. In a *Fortune* interview, "Candid Reflections of a Businessman in Washington," he explained the major differences he experienced. Today they would be even more powerful and dangerous to reputation. An important change to Blumenthal was between appearance and reality. At Bendix, financial reality—the bottom line—determined whether someone succeeded or failed. The executive report card. In government, which lacks a bottom line, you can be successful if you appear to be. That image is largely determined by how the press perceives and reports on you. Blumenthal also counseled expressing yourself very carefully, building a defense against being misquoted or misunderstood. No stronger argument can be made than two words—"irrational exuberance"—imbedded in a long 1996 speech by Federal Reserve Chairman Alan Greenspan that caused global market trembles. Some code words you must avoid, Blumenthal counseled. Others you can use to state a certain proposition. Eventually, you learn how to use public statements to shape, influence, and enunciate policies.[6]

Former Mobil president William P. Tavoulareas crossed from private to public very differently–with media allegations that he had used Mobil resources to establish his son in a shipping business, which resulted in legal actions, and a book, *Fighting Back*. Although known as a hard-nosed trader, Tavoulareas was shocked by *The Washington Post*'s intransigence, by the impact of the publicity on his personal life and his son's—and by his legal expenses. Business executives would do well to think of the public scrutiny and damage done to politicians.

Catching trends vital to any business is as elusive as trying to hold quicksilver in one's palm. In addition to the many techniques discussed elsewhere in this book, two general important ones are:

- Looking back to succeed ahead—analyzing corporate or general history as a competitive tool is overlooked when the immediate is slighted to concentrate on the future.
- Developing ways and people to look at established structures from a different point of view.

In her foreword to *The Distant Mirror,* Barbara Tuchman sees reflections of the fourteenth century in our own—parallel phenomena to the aftermaths of the Black Death of 1348–50 and World War I. She lists economic chaos, social unrest, high prices, profiteering, depraved morals, lack of production, industrial violence, frenetic gaiety, wild expenditures, luxury, debauchery, social and religious hysteria, greed, avarice, maladministration, and the decay of manners. We now have, she concludes, a greater "fellow-feeling for a distraught age" whose rules were breaking down under the pressure of adverse and violent events, a kinship with "a period of anguish" when there is no sense of an assured future.[7]

The Disney Corporation's failure to look back at its own mistakes at Euro-Disney, derided as a cultural Chernobyl, or to the overbearing confidence of Union forces at First Manassas, brought a needless defeat of a proposed theme park (Disney "rode" into Virginia with the same visions of early victory as northern troops). Or, had Michael Milken studied the career of an earlier change agent, Daniel Drew, also a symbol of his age, his unexpected great fall might have been mitigated.

A different viewpoint also gives new insights. Through his drawings, artist David Macauley forces us to look up at New York from the tangle of subterranean pipes and tubes, or to study a modern motel as an archeological site. What was that votive altar those ancients all faced and worshiped in motel rooms? A television set, stupid. Journalist Joel Garreau, by dividing North America functionally into nine nations, reveals communications and marketing opportunities obscured by conventional state lines—and thinking. MexAmerica obliterates the U.S.–Mexican border. Function, migration, businesses, and language make lines on a map irrelevant. Post-industrial America gives insights into the plight and perhaps the rebirth of New England. Each of these nations forces a very valuable exercise in analyzing afresh.

COMMUNICATORS AS CRYSTAL-BALL GAZERS

A broad-thinking communications officer, properly heeded, can be that alternative view. In that spirit of taking a fresh look, the following trends will be important to companies generally and to their communicators.

First: power and wealth are shifting from the European Museum and eastern United States to the Pacific Rim. The twenty-first century will be dominated by strong Asian economies and the U.S. West Coast. There will be new conflicts, entrepreneurs, and questions of cultural relationships. Communicators will face racially, linguistically, and nationally mixed labor and management. U.S. citizens will be working for managers and companies from other nations. Press relations will become more complex. Overseas media, often government-owned and -controlled, may be more tendentious than ours.

Second: the new breed of workers will be as driven by their projects as the computer experts in *The Soul of a New Machine* (or they may be hackers—adventurers on the Internet, visionaries, risk-takers, and artists—who infuse the marketplace with a new ethic). They will seek unlimited access to information, to anything that is useful or that can teach them something. Mistrustful of authority, they will espouse decentralization. Telling the troops anything won't work anymore. Even genuine candor may not be believed. Disaffected and discouraged, workers may drop out. Many lack the common bond of information and skills on which motivation could be built in the past.

Third: we suffer an overdose of information, but a paucity of understanding. Everyone will have unlimited access to the glut, but few will understand the material, take time to analyze or verify it, much less put it to work. Donald Rumsfeld likens this to trying to drink from a large fire hose. Richard B. Madden, former chairman and CEO of Potlatch, warns that too much information produces a fascination with manipulating numbers at the expense of other important goals, such as quality. You can become too remote from the shop floor, he says, if you're sitting behind a large electronic console trying to solve every problem with a new and very expensive by-the-numbers resolution.[8] (Or, I might add, if you are operating like a corporate ostrich, with your head hidden in a very comfortable corporate suite.)

Fourth: can any executive doubt, after Bhopal, Tylenol, Perrier, Dow-Corning breast implants, and the Dalkon Shield, that liabilities—legal, public, and product—will increase? Many cases in this book demonstrate that the most effective way to mitigate the risk of this trend at its flood is to ask again, and again, and again, what a particular flaw or fault would took like if publicized widely; to question information before rushing to action and orders. Operations and executives must be squeaky clean. This advice is not the last gasp of a Puritan ethic, but a sensible means of protection and profitability, even survival. Chester Burger, who has counseled many companies through crises, warns that public opinion will always believe the worst about you unless you tell your side honestly, completely, and very quickly.

Fifth: as business continues in the public spotlight, executives will not be able to hide anything from searching investigations conducted by government agencies, the media, lawyers, or their own increasingly activist boards of directors.

Sixth: as broadcasting and, to a lesser extent, the print media become show biz, sheer entertainment, business must learn to work within those parameters, no matter how distasteful and mindstretching. Corporate performers must learn to compete, cosmetically at least. A television appearance can spell disaster for an executive who does not appear sartorially perfect and in charge, or who wants to convey anything more than a single, noncontroversial point.

Seventh: can so many lemmings be wrong? Yes! Whatever the industry trend, too many think only, "Me too." When the fad was to acquire companies, everyone who could, did. When sell was the cry, it was difficult to avoid that cliché. Or to downsize with nary a question to human cost, public image, or operational wisdom. If everyone else is overcharging on government contracts, we can too. Right?

Wrong, as several defense contractors discovered. Procedures and administrators change. The press gets on a hot topic, such as military contracts, white-collar crime, environmental abuses, and suddenly the once widely acceptable becomes headlines—many and very damaging.

Eighth: problem-solving will be more complex under greater public scrutiny. Stonewalling questions on rampant management turnover, maturing markets, a dearth of new products, and large layoffs won't work. Nor will public and investor attention be deflected easily by the razzle-dazzle of a new acquisition and management fad. That strategy is a bit like Argentina's and England's going to war over a cluster of remote islands, partly to distract attention from inflation and terrorism at home. It worked, but only briefly. The difficulties resurfaced, compounded by more debt and the war casualties.

Ninth: "entrepreneurism" has been overused into imprecise meaning. But Peter Drucker sees entrepreneurism as a major turning point. It puts greater sinew and innovation into communications, particularly among employees, and has forced convincing explanations of the boom-and-bust of some products and bright star performers. Increasingly, it is seen as the antidote to foundering giants and the need to adjust quickly to new global opportunities.

Tenth: current business turbulence should be viewed as natural, creative, and eventually productive of stronger organizations. Dr. Rollo May writes that necessary creative chaos must be worked through, as old forms crack and new ones either have not emerged or are not recognized for what they are. As painful for many as job insecurity, or the "creative destruction" espoused by economist Joseph Schumpeter, executive revolving doors, and rapidly shifting corporate sands are, they can perhaps be viewed as a renewal. The past two decades have brought extreme turbulence: disappearing or diminished corporate giants, the collapse of smokestack industries, unwilling acceptance that the United States is no longer the preeminent economic power. Competition is global. Money, the most highly valued workers, and information respect no borders. Communication is instant and almost uncontrollable. Do these factors spell creative chaos? Operating executives must demand their communications officers or outside counsel interpret these and other emerging business and social trends. Where do public dangers and opportunities lie? Important trends specific to communications are:

Increasingly mobile, disaffected professionals, particularly the best and brightest, must be better motivated. Unenlightened self-interest at the top—huge salaries and bonuses for failure or during layoffs—won't wash anymore.

Weasel words and spinning bad news are just simply tuned-out or, worse, scorned. The most senior communicators don't listen to the troops. Just what won't your junior manager tell you? Lots!

Images are all. Corporate executives may hope to change a false public image with the truth or their facts. When audiences don't know, don't care, and don't listen, image rules. With greater anonymity, faster transmission of more, ever more information, and fewer who question, image is much more difficult to change. Fight false image with your image. Raymond O'Rourke, crisis guru of Burson-Marsteller, sees Exxon's using words to fight nightly damaging visuals of oil-coated wildlife pulled from Prince William Sound after the oil spill from its supertanker *Valdez* a major PR mistake.

Stonewalling the press, or, even worse, eeling around major questions only arouses suspicions that worse is to come. Rumors, usually worse than the facts, fill the vacuum. "But, I didn't inhale" represents eeling at its most damaging.

Cut the techno-babble. Speak to employees, public, and the press in intelligent lay language—not as a put-down, but as dialogue. When reporters don't understand nuclear physics, i.e., Three Mile Island nuclear insident, or sophisticated chemistry, i.e., the Bhopal plant explosion in India, human interest, sometimes damaging to the company, will fill the news void.

Few observers have watched public relations as long and as thoughtfully as Harold Burson, chairman of Burson-Marsteller. Once, he notes, the principal requisites for public relations were a typewriter, mimeograph machine, mailing lists, and knowledge of newspaper, magazine, and wire service contacts. As others point out, the PR person was looked upon as the official mouthpiece and cheerleader, not the skeptic he should be. Often he was a newspaper writer "who sold out for money," denigrated as a flack.

In the 1960s, Burson explains, public relations became less focused on the press and more oriented toward television. Society and news became more complex. The stereotypical newspaper man was replaced by specialists trained in a broad spectrum of disciplines—

environment, health care, law, and finance. They gravitated toward problem-solving and pragmatic analysis. Companies moved away from blatant advocacy toward a more sophisticated total communications strategy.

According to Burson, economic forces are driving corporate change. Clients are not interested in doing good and getting credit— the dominant aim of the gray flannel suit practitioners. Today, realistic, pragmatic, cost-effective, and less ideological executives focus on nothing less than survival. They eschew warm fuzzy communications, for what it can it do for them. They want results, not systems or platitudes. They don't want to talk about employee communications, but about how that contributes to production. Or about glossy, expensive annual reports, but how they affect stock value and the ability to raise funds. Or about marketing public relations, but about products moving off the shelves or out of dealer showrooms. Or about government relations except as a means to an end. Contrary to Marshall McLuhan, Burson concludes, the *act* is the message. What we do communicates more clearly than what we say.[9]

Another trend, which seems to fly in the face of all practical considerations, is executive refusal to be interviewed, even for favorable articles. When the news is bad, how many managers are on long business trips or otherwise unavailable? Although each stonewaller undoubtedly has good reasons, he still risks having his company's story told poorly, adversely, or not at all by those far less informed or favorably disposed toward the company. In the absence of CEO comment, financial analysts increasingly are sought to comment and analyze actions. It behooves a company more than ever to keep analysts *au courant* with strategies, executive succession, and product developments.

The third trend important to communicators is the spreading use of weasel, pallid, rubber, or outright deceptive words. The linguistic equivalent of junk food, weasel words, which each manager can define as he likes or to his benefit, end up subverting original thoughts and instructions and killing credibility. Buzz words not only irritate through their overuse (think how many times "bottom line" is used by those without any inkling of what it means); they also pollute already muddy waters. Whatever happened to speaking plainly?

And ,finally, as will be discussed in the next section, some communicators—who should be moving ahead of the times, standing terror watch, and doing preventive analysis—are shooting themselves in the foot. The communications officer must be the harbinger of change, demonstrating in a farsighted way how changes and trends will affect his company. He may find himself the designated scapegoat, particularly in media relations, but that risk comes with the turf. Only those battle-tested in corporate warfare or in the more treacherous and dangerous areas of public perceptions can even begin to guide managers safely across the mine fields laid by constituencies, media, advocates for many causes, and sometimes disgruntled employees. If the communicator is looking backward or viewing the future as more of the same, his counsel will be worth little.

Endangered Communicators, Or, The Lawyers Will Get Them If They Don't Wise Up

Is PR too important to be left to PR people? Yes! Every employee must be involved. Gary Lavine of Niagara-Mohawk is in a unique position to ask—and answer—the question. A lawyer by training, he is Senior Vice President, Legal and Corporate Relations, for the Syracuse, New York, utility. He counters three canards. First, that PR practitioners were "innocent of clannishness," "quite receptive" to him. Second, he sees PR as "a true profit center for a corporation." Third, PR is central to leadership.

His point of view is born of basic realities—corporate, regulatory, and political—that scuttle any idea of command and control of any constituencies, internal or external. Such groups must be communicated to, educated, persuaded, cajoled, and bargained with. Competing agendas must be reconciled. This is the essence of both executive leadership and public relations management. They are one and the same.

"The fundamental role of public relations is to protect the credibility of the corporation and its CEO. Because challenges to that credibility are significant, pervasive, and unending, the PR professional has to be an analyst and interpreter, interlocutor and intermediary." Lavine views the CEO as the chief political officer and "the corporate philosopher who helps employees and public alike to understand corporate polices and actions with the least possible distortion." As his chief public relations officer, Lavine sees himself as functioning somewhat like a campaign manager: "We are responsible for the perceptions of our company held by our stakeholders. Success depends almost entirely on how well we manage the thousands upon thousands of quiet, private, daily interactions between Niagara-Mohawk people and our company's stakeholders."

"That means relying on PR professionals—and outside counsel—for objective analysis and advice, and for creative approaches to our problems and opportunities," Lavine explained. "However, for us to succeed, all 11,000 employees must be engaged in our public relations effort and fully committed to keeping Niagara-Mohawk's promises—explicit and implicit—to customers, investors and regulators. It is a job too important to leave out anyone at Niagara-Mohawk."[10] Ironically, Lavine's cogent comments illustrate the lawyer–PR tussles and the cosmic–reality split.

During the public relations boom years in the late 1950s and 1960s, practitioners navigated by unjustifiably rosy crystal balls, foreseeing only further growth and enhanced power. They disdained reporting to anyone but the CEOs. They felt that writing a news release, or even an annual report, was beneath their professional dignity. Press relations was a grubby task to be delegated to a yeoman, a specialist, or a recent convert from journalism. Superstars counseled—whatever that meant.

Several strategic mistakes undermined prestige and profit. Instead of studying management, finance, law, and industry marketing trends, the "professionals" caviled endlessly about how management did not understand or appreciate communicators. Such a we/they stance only predetermined that "they" would win and "we" be consigned to irrelevance. It is self-destructive for anyone reporting to or in senior management not to learn how peers talk, think, and plan; not to immerse oneself in the very spirit of the company.

Second, as communication needs and techniques, companies, and competition were changing drastically, so-called professionals prattled on about accreditation and professionalism, and whether New York City dominated the Public Relations Society of America. Annual society meetings became mostly fluff and puff. Job hunters hounded the senior practitioners who showed their faces. Students bounded around, assuring everyone that they really liked people—the most often cited and most useless reason for seeking a public relations job.[11] Ignored were the meat and thrust of the job today and in the future. Ignored, too, were the growing number of executives from other disciplines taking power in communications.

Lawyers, financial types, MBAs, and human resources staff are demonstrating they know how to communicate effectively, hence winning the hearts and minds of senior management. Communicators boxed themselves into a defensive position, leaving the field open to the apparently more savvy and forceful connivers. A recent spate of booster books, speeches, and articles touting the public relations boom only proves the axiom that when something is shouted about, it's usually no longer vital.

Communicators must recapture respect and demonstrate anew their unique skills and effectiveness. Otherwise, some cussed-minded and farsighted communicators predict a splintering of functions that were formerly centralized: investor relations to finance, employee communications to human resources, press relations to the legal department, and speech writing to one specialist—perhaps a do-all assistant to the CEO. With constant integration with operations, outsourcing looms. When other skills, extra hands, or precise expertise is needed, outside firms will be hired.

These difficulties have surfaced dramatically. Communicators lost the most ground in corporations, where salaries, prestige, and power are the greatest. Takeovers, mergers, and the downsizing of corporate staffs translated into dramatically smaller staffs. Killing off the glossy company magazine or dropping image advertising gets the austerity message across very quickly.

Troubles among formerly high-flying high-tech companies—particularly in California's Silicon Valley, GE's reduction of its once large and greatly respected news bureau network, IBM's slash at its PR department—meant the loss of many more corporate and counseling jobs. Acquisitions and mergers among public relations firms, some into large multinational conglomerates such as Saatchi and Saatchi and WPP, both London-based, further reduced opportunities. Merging of public relations firms with advertising agencies under the ill-conceived rubric of total client service or synergy usually meant the advertising tail wagged the PR dog. And some firms were afflicted by the very woes they counsel against—public troubles.[12]

It is ironic that at the same time as companies are suffering badly from mangled media relations and bungled public opportunities, trained PR practitioners are either shooting themselves in the foot or nattering away as if nothing has changed. Courageous communicators are still trying to alert management to possible bad news and public liabilities, sometimes successfully. The best are demonstrating the sinew and value of communications as an integral part of management, as a way of achieving business goals and controlling damage. Many tell compelling war stories to demonstrate the high cost of not managing public image well. Informally, many senior practitioners are meeting over dinner to share wisdom, lick wounds, and get ready intelligently and pragmatically for a tough tomorrow.

WHAT'S IN A NAME:
DISAGREEMENT AND SEARCHING

A name, broad yet precise enough to encompass the myriad ways a corporation communicates, internally and externally, is very difficult to agree upon. The search itself often fails and confuses rather than illuminates. Some names reflect little more than a current fad, are too restrictive, or connote the worst rather than the best that communications can offer management.

One illustration documents the dilemma. The 1984 Hill and Knowlton annual report cover lists thirty-five separate experiences—many of them multiple—to explain the services a counseling firm offers clients. They range from the mundane and expected—proxy solicitation, shareholder list analysis, and merger and acquisition/takeover communications—to the more exotic: satellite services and audio-visual productions, destination marketing, initial public offering, and leveraged buy-out communications.[13]

"Corporate communications," narrow and confused as it can be, with telephone systems, computer software, even body language, is used increasingly by major companies. It is probably more complete and clearer than other choices. Public relations, once the standard term, is being supplanted because of its narrowness, its less-than-professional connotation among some executives, and its old-fashioned feeling.

Edward Bernays, acknowledged as a founder of the business, encouraged use of "public relations counsel" to connote both two-way communications (publicity was one-way) and expert counsel. He at-

tempted to capture some of the legal counsel's authority and prestige. (Some are still trying today.) Bernays considered PR counsel
the giving of professional advice to clients, regardless of whether or
not such advice resulted in publicity. Bernays used "engineering of
social consent" as a definition of public relations generally. Limited
as that is, I've not found a better one.

Not everyone defines public relations so benignly. H. R. Haldeman
understood it as the use of techniques to badger, bully, bribe, entice,
and persuade people to your side; this could be accomplished only
by organizing, orchestrating, and hammering away. William Safire
notes that Nixon aides called their brand of news management public relations, but "As a professional PR man, Haldeman was merely a
good ad man."[14] Even harsher critics call PR an enterprise roughly
synonymous with calculated deception or manipulation. Practitioners themselves worry about the "dumbing down of PR"—
uncritically including advertising, sales promotion, direct mail, even
party going. They urge PR for PR. Its first great victory was getting
major publications such as The Wall Street Journal to banish the
offensive "flack" unless in a direct quote.

"Public affairs," often synonymous with government relations, is
not broad enough either and carries a whiff of sensuality. Public
information or liaison, popular among nonprofit organizations and
government offices, excludes a company's important internal audiences. To some the term seems Orwellian. Marketing, advertising,
and investor relations are too specific, unless a department is restricted to those functions. If so, it cannot fully supply all the communications needs important to management. Finally, business is
too sophisticated and competitive today to return to the name or
the practices of press agents, who, like Bernays, began by slipping
juicy tidbits favorable to their clients to newspaper columnists.

By default—until a better name emerges—"corporate communications" will be used to describe activities most vital to senior management and directors. These generally include comprehensive
strategy, positioning the company with its many constituencies,
planning for major crises, and fostering favorable, accurate public
perceptions. These broad goals are implemented by a number of
activities, such as the communications officer's counsel with peers
in senior management, media relations, internal and external publications, financial public relations, speech writing, and monitoring

key external individuals and events. To succeed, communications must be embedded in the company's business plans, strategy, and marketing, and be sensitively aware of the trends and needs of our times.

Three topics—employee communications, advocacy advertising, and government relations, or lobbying—will be discussed only generally. Employee communications is a specialized challenge, increasingly sensitive as workforces, even middle managers, become more mobile, cynical, and less loyal to a lifetime employer. As workers seek more information from visual rather than traditional print sources, television monitors replace bulletin boards. In-house newspaper megapapers emulate *U.S.A. Today*, which combines many photographs with small amounts of print and snippets of stories. E-mail and in-house closed-circuit television have become major ways to reach employees. But with all the fancy technology and messages, the most believed, effective communication comes from the immediate supervision. Relationships are shifting among an employee, his manager, and his company. V. R. Buzzotta in a *New York Times* column ("A Quiet Crisis in the Work Place"), noted that takeovers and mergers are undermining job satisfaction and producing a deep disaffection, most precipitously in managerial ranks. A quiet frustration is festering "in the collective heart of our work force."[15] Peter Drucker warns frequently that the unrealistic wish to retire at the earliest possible moment, despite increased longevity, is the greatest indictment of management today.

Experts working in industries with traditionally strong labor unions see a new relationship emerging. As labor becomes more multinational and less secure, it seeks more participation in decision-making, asks "why" more frequently. Bitter news of layoffs, more competitive off-shore labor, health hazards, the economic push for greater productivity are all difficult stories. To convince they must be told candidly and well.

Advocacy or issue advertising—distinct from product advertising—advocates a particular company point of view, or rebuts one inimical to its interest.[16] Such advertising often rides a chairman's pet hobbyhorse. It also is used widely during tender fights to explain acquisition or spin-off strategy, to address strikes and legislation, or actions being taken to counter a disaster. Mobil and United Technologies are perhaps best known for their advocacy advertising. While

Herbert Schmertz was Mobil's chief communications officer, advertising countering criticisms or proselytizing for positions important to Mobil appeared frequently on *The New York Times* op-ed page. Under former CEO Harry Grey, United Technologies's image-advertising took a more personal, folksy-moral tone. The Singer Company used such ads to augment other media to explain its shift from a well-known sewing machine company to a high-tech one. Although effective only if intimately linked with general communications, advocacy advertising is specialized and not needed in every corporation.[17]

Finally, relations between government and corporations, is a vital interface. It may encompass lobbying, nationally or at the grass roots, preparation of executive and material for appearances before government bodies, and, yes, access.

NOTES

1. Thomas Watson, Jr., *Father, Son & Co: My Life at IBM and Beyond* (New York: Bantam Books, 1991), p. 200.

2. Ibid., pp. 271, xi.

3. E. Digby Baltzell, *Philadelphia Gentlemen: The Making of a National Upper Class* (Philadelphia: University of Pennsylvania Press, 1979), p. 5.

4. V. R. Buzzota, "A Quiet Crisis in the Work Place," *The New York Times*, September 4, 1985, p. A27.

5. Rafael D. Pagan, Jr., "Carrying the Fight to the Critics of Multinational Capitalism: Think and Act Politically," *Vital Speeches*, July 15, 1982, pp. 589–591.

6. W. Michael Blumenthal, "Candid Reflections of a Businessman in Washington," *Fortune*, January 29, 1979, pp. 36–46.

7. Barbara Tuchman, *The Distant Mirror: The Calamitous Fourteenth Century* (New York: Alfred A. Knopf, 1978), pp. xiii–xiv.

8. Richard B. Madden, "A Key to Management in the 1990's," given at the *Business Week* Conference on the Future, White Plains, New York, April 30, 1985.

9. Harold Burson, "A Decent Respect to the Opinions of Mankind," given at the IPRA World Congress, Amsterdam, June 1985.

10. Gary Lavine, "Is PR Too Important to be Left to PR People?" Remarks to the Page Society, April 1991.

11. "I like people" is the most often-cited reason for seeking a public relations position. "That is not a decisive grace," rebuts John Hill.

12. From various 1985 issues of *Jack O'Dwyer's Newsletter*.

13.The complete list is revealing: Financial Relations Counseling; Media Relations; Individual and Institutional Investor Communications; Banking and Financial Institution Communications; Merger and Acquisition/Take-over Communications; Proxy Solicitation and Shareholder List Analysis; Initial Public Offering and Leveraged Buy-Out Communications; Agricultural Business Communications; Marketing Communications Counseling; Sports and Recreation Marketing; Destination Marketing; Medical Products and Services Marketing; Editorial Services; Entertainment Communications; Food and Nutrition Communications; Corporate Events Production; Product Introduction Communications; Communications and Staff/Function Audits; Professional Service Firm Communications; Satellite Services and Audiovisual Productions; Industrial/Scientific/Advanced Technologies Communications; Interview, Speech, and Confrontation Training; International Economic Development Communications; College and University Relations; Public Issues/Public Policy Counseling and Communications; Japanese Business Communications; Legislative and Regulatory Monitoring and Analysis; Crisis Communications Counseling and Training; Environmental and Consumer Affairs; Corporate Design and Corporate Identity Services; Energy Affairs Communications; Employee, Labor and Organizational Communications; Strategic Information Research/Opinion Surveys; Research and Information Services; Domestic and International Government Relations.

14. William Safire, *Before the Fall: An Inside View of the Pre-Watergate White House* (Garden City, N.Y.: Doubleday, 1975), p. 290.

15. Buzzotta, "Quiet Crisis in the Work Place," p. A27.

16. There are many differences in approach. Selling products is not analyzing the gamut of public perceptions; convincing people is different from buying a way to their pocketbooks. The public, however, often confuses advertising and public relations.

17. Television will not accept this type of advertising, even accompanied by the offer to pay for equal time.

2

Bottom Line *vs.* Front Page

Corporate Relations with the Media

Journalism is an extraordinary and terrible privilege.

—Oriana Fallaci

Senior executives often come to media relations either bloodied or virginal. Few understand or even want to know how the media works, the pressure journalists face, and how differing judgments about what is news create adversarial relations. "Sue the bastards," "Stonewall them," the ubiquitous but potentially damaging "No comment," and "Why are they hounding me?" are uttered frequently by despairing executives. Others entertain the naïve hope that the press can be controlled, ordered about like subordinates. Too few today—on either side—display trust and good intentions. Media complain of lack of access (particularly to the CEO), less-than-complete candor, delayed or no response to queries, talking only in good times, and blatantly building a case for the company. Executives counter with "They don't understand our business," "Don't even try to," "Look only for the sensational so miss the important."

Yet, there is common ground; opportunity for understanding does exist. The best-trained reporters share with the most progressive corporate leaders the aim of providing the most accurate possible public portrait of the company, its operations, and future prospects. Individuals on both sides are under intense pressure, vulnerable to paying mightily for just one mistake. Both worlds are small. Experiences can be shared intimately and intelligently only with those who have sustained the same defeats and rejoiced over the same successes. Some executives and journalists are high-flying successes, well-known names; others are the unsung, unappreciated grunts doing a good job. Both view the other as all-powerful, aloof, and shielded from the pressures and pains of ordinary mortals. Both are, of course, wrong.

MEDIA AND BUSINESS: A COMMON GROUND?

Despite verbal sniping across the barricades, media and business share many concerns and interests. Senior business executives and well-known journalists explored them at a meeting in Princeton, New Jersey. Participants Joseph A. Califano, Jr., and Howard Simons noted that the antagonism boils down to "business builds up; media tears down."[1] Business always hides its wrongdoing, only the media penetrates the stone wall. Business, concerned with its public image, is eager to put its best foot forward; the press wants a good story. Executives may complain about shallow, superficial, biased coverage, but that doesn't mean they really want comprehensive, thoughtful, fair coverage. Every large organization or person has potentially embarrassing secrets.

Media criticize business for stonewalling, unavailability, giving just the agreed-upon company line but no more, and elusive executives, who seem to live private, privileged, sheltered lives. The perceived difference in earnings, perks, power, and lifestyles is an unspoken irritant. Once reporters led a modest life financially. Watergate changed all that. Now superstar reporters, and, even more, anchors and talk show hosts, live very well on salaries, books, and lucrative but ethically questionable lectures.

Complaints come from both sides, some bred of half-knowledge, others better founded. Business leaders call the media too powerful and sensational. They accuse it of writing about the bad news, never the good. They charge that reporters oversimplify or just don't understand what they are writing about.

Executives at the conference wished aloud that reporters knew the difference between a stock and a bond, net and gross; and that those covering economic matters had taken a course in economics—and passed it. Many reporters cared or knew little about the company they were covering. Until the 1970s, foreign affairs and politics, even sports, were the sought-after reporting jobs. Unattractive, below even show biz, was business reporting. The losers were stashed there. Some business reporters on local newspapers also sold advertising space. That all changed in the 1980s. The big stories were business and economics: inflation, unemployment, investment incentives, major bankruptcies, deficits, giant takeovers, and trade pacts. The drama of hostile takeovers and colorful figures—Carl Icahn, Mad Dog Beck, Ronald Perleman, Henry Kravis, and many others— transformed business into a prestige beat. Reporters demonstrated much better, wider knowledge. Many held MBAs. They were regularly assigned to one large company or industry, rather than assigned to general beats. The old tradition that any mention of a company is free publicity died. Executives fret when a fire, strike, giant layoffs, a Bhopal-type disaster is widely covered. They fuel the criticism that the press emphasizes the negative. But good news is no news.

Louis Banks, a former *Fortune* managing editor, asked the press, "why do they hate you out there?" Banks cited careless news stories, chronic negativism, and "ignorant reporting that tangles business complexities into erroneous conclusions or ducks complexities in favor of power struggles and personality clashes, real or imagined."[2] In the urge to simplify, the press may fasten on a single, obvious, but not necessarily important quality of a public figure: the grandeur of a John Gutfreund contrasted with the straightforward simplicity of a Warren Buffet or the arrogance of Alexander Haig. Television, with its relentless time constraints, suffers from this problem even more acutely. CNN, with global 24-hour news, only enhances the rush to coverage. Criticism, once directed solely against newspapers, has been deflected by television. Its equipment is intrusive and potentially dangerous in a factory setting. Even a complex story must be restricted to 30 to 90 seconds on the air. A good, fair, talented journalist finds it difficult to probe a controversial, complex subject within sound bytes.

Many difficulties are systemic to all journalism: deadlines, limited news space, competition with other media, and personal quirks. Lewis H. Young, for many years the editor of *Business Week*, explains that the business view is often out of focus because it understands neither the reporter's job nor how to play up to media needs. Misperceptions spring not from inaccuracy alone, but from genuine differences as well. "As outsiders, journalists are . . . immune to the internal vested interests—the politics, history of a decision, especially the prejudices, biases and pressures on decision-makers."[3] This feeds some executives' belief that journalists are biased against business, ignorant of industry, sensation-seeking, and fundamentally unfair.

Another area of conflict is news judgment. Young's criteria for a good business story are: a company does exceptionally well or poorly; conflicts surface between companies, business, and government, or among executives; a breakthrough development or striking new idea is announced. But rather than understand what motivates the media, its strengths and weaknesses, many executives carp or turn cynical, bite their tongues, or try to foist company-serving stories as news. Other businessmen learn to work with the media as successful politicians do. This requires developing a thick skin to withstand criticism and a willingness to learn from each encounter. The rewards? Young lists better investor relations, increased sales, higher employee morale, and fewer labor problems.

Neither side seems to accept that what is good for the goose is good for the gander. One issue—disclosure of interests—illustrates this. Business is both private and public. Financial interests, board appointments, individual or corporate positions in other companies, family ties, and stock holdings must be made public. But reporters have cried foul—often and loudly—at any attempt to determine whether they hold stock in a company they are covering or whether a family member stands to gain financially. Professional and personal lives should be kept separate, except when they influence news. Just a few questionable examples. A reporter and a source, each an avaricious careerist, are linked romantically. Information traded in pillow talk shows up in newspaper headlines. When that's unavailable to competition or to the subject of the story, or is raw and damaging data, then that relationship is fair game for questions and revelation. R. Foster Winans was convicted of profiting from information gained by writing The Wall Street Journal's "Heard on the Street" column. His roommate was a factor. It was so reported by the Journal.[4]

When journalism professor John C. Behrens began contacting well-known reporters for interviews, he found paranoia common. Some never answered his calls at all, and others only after repeated calls. One shunted Behrens to his lawyer. Most questioned him closely about the reasons for his interest. Although eager to ask others about income, journalists don't entertain questions about their

own and its sources from speaking, newsletters, and syndicated columns.[5] Do lucrative fees from, say, trade groups, influence what they
report and what they don't? Such questions are rudely declared out-
of-bounds. Recent abuses, charges of buckraking, are creating restrictions and impetus for greater disclosure.

Such double standards cloud the issues of confidentiality and
competition. Revealing sources of information is an issue a journalist
would risk jail to protect—and some have. But the press leaps eagerly
on business or government secrets. During the Princeton meetings,
a television executive said that he would not wait a day or two to go
with a story about a CIA agent, even if it cost the agent his life; a
competitor might scoop him. How would the press react if a pharmaceutical company rushed a product to market to beat its competition?

Until recently, businesses operated under considerably less scrutiny than today. They were often shadowy powers in their communities and foreign countries. Often CEOs played *éminence grise*. Some
newspapers were company-owned: Anaconda owned papers in Mon-
tana; DuPont, in Wilmington, Delaware. United Fruit published
several newspapers in Central America. Even large newspapers once
ran company handouts. It was great sport among the public relations
people, often put down as hacks by reporters, to compare releases
issued by a major counseling firm against "news coverage" in the
next day's business pages.[6] President Lyndon Johnson, no fan of the
press, was convinced that reporters were merely transmission belts
for shrewd public relations people.[7] But journalistic Prufrocks, mea-
suring their lives in handouts, are discredited by the best of their
peers.

Despite important differences, both sides share interests. Business, as it operates increasingly on the consent of its various publics,
must assume the risks of heightened exposure and accessibility. It
must argue its position vigorously and confidently, not shrinking
from controversy. Conversely, reporters and editors need to know
about economics, international competition, the mechanics of doing
business, large organizational structures, and ways of decision-making. A truly fine newspaper cannot be a public relations operation, a
business blotter, or a booster for the community, but it should be
accurate and fair.

WATERGATE: A SEA CHANGE

Journalism once was slow moving and tradition-bound. It refused to budge until shoved by some irresistible external force. The shove came: competition from electronic media, change in reporting techniques, dying newspapers, plus a burst of new technology, which explosively speeded up the transmission and processing of information. Every minute, every way, everywhere.

The once-vaunted objectivity in reporting began to be criticized as a guise for superficiality, even mindless neutrality. Anti-objectivists argued that trying to be objective could slant a story, give a minor aspect more attention than was justified. Relativists in journalism and history shunned *veritas* as impossible. But the very striving for objectivity is key, the necessary discipline. Some reporters began to feel caged by old formulas—each story had to have a neat point and start with hard news, even if based on some phony staged event. It had to impose some meaning, however superficial or spurious, on often insignificant, mysterious, or downright absurd happenings.

A bias developed toward negative news, toward conflict and controversy. This distorted coverage far more extensively than the frequently discussed ideological slants, such as automatically being anti-business. Some reporters, swept away by the passions of the moment, rushed past or ignored important, more complicated issues and ideas. The old, tight pyramid structure—a first paragraph or lead with 5 w's and an h (who, what, when, where, why, and how) followed by news in descending importance—was dumped. Soft feature style replaced it.

Columnist Georgie Anne Geyer explained the changes induced by Watergate. In the late 1950s, as a reporter for Chicago's feisty *Daily News*, she covered fires, murders, or investigations. "We did not write columns or inject our personal interpretations on the news page," she noted. It was a "much straighter," much more "honest job" than it is now. Staff reporters competed brutally with other papers, but not with each other, unlike *The Washington Post*, where everyone was pitted against everyone else. Reporters worked for prizes, not for the readers.[8]

Information-gathering changed. As a young reporter, this author covered fires by asking officials—fire and police chiefs usually—how the fire started, damage estimates, family displacement, and any suspicions of arson. Too often today, reporters begin not with such a *tabula rasa*, but with preconceptions. The fire was arson, so the reporter looks for—and in the worst cases creates—only facts to complete that story.

This sea change also reflects in history, a parallel discipline to journalism. Thomas J. Archdeacon, in his review of David Hackett Fischer's *The Great Wave: Price Revolution and the Rhythm of History* writes:

> Fischer, an un-deconstructed empiricist, believes that objective evidence exists and can reliably be brought to bear on the search for answers to properly framed questions. He accepts quantitative analysis as an essential tool in that search. . . . Expertise in handling both quantitative and qualitative evidence exemplify the historian's craft. Those attributes reflect the style of training that assumed historians must possess the integrated corpus of knowledge and skills that sets apart a profession. . . . Mr. Fischer criticizes the deductive "knowing–believing" paradigm dominant in the social sciences, in which research *begins* with the assertion of a theory with potentially universal application. He favors the approach of the French *Annales* school: investigation begins with intensive empirical description and the compilation of data. It then advances inductively through a series of open-ended questions carefully set in a specific cultural and historical context. . . . The logic of historical thought is a process of adducing answers to specific questions, so that a satisfactory explanatory fit is obtained.[9]

Geyer notes another change. We were reporters, not journalists—and certainly not media celebrities. "Nobody came into journalism for power." Some came because they wanted to write. Others were attracted by a view of life or by the excitement not afforded elsewhere, a chance to be not quite participants in, but not completely observers of, either, the high drama of life. The new breed of journalists became "arbiters of truth," moralists who mistook relative judgment for absolute moralism. They began to "judge and criticize, to take it upon themselves to reform, if not the world," at least their own evil country. They saw "goodness everywhere but at home." They began a love affair with advocacy, which hit government first, but did not leave the private sector unscathed.[10]

Watergate coverage glorified the gumshoe drudgery of leg-work, fact-gathering. Many reporters succumbed to an almost detective-like cloak-and-dagger fever, ready to probe the murky depths of clandestine corruption. Some young journalists, especially from television, tended to skip over telling the reader just the facts—a straight recitation of what happened—to concentrate on the more exciting speculation about backstage maneuverings, personalities, and often specious predictions. In their defense, frequently the backstage and publicly obscured is ultimately more important. Henry Kissinger's publicly announced illness in India covered his precedent-breaking covert trip to China. Likewise, bland announcements of corporate departures obscure protracted struggles and personality clashes.

Gradually, walls separating news from advertising, reporting from opinion or just plain propaganda buckled, then disappeared. Max Frankel, writing in *The New York Times Magazine*, noted "Something Doesn't Like a Wall":

> Self-respecting news organizations used to pride themselves on the sturdy barriers they maintained to guard against all kinds of partisan contamination. Inside the office, they built a high wall between those who reported and analyzed events and those who offered opinions about them—between the newsroom and the editorial page. A second wall separated both the news and editorial departments from the commercial ambitions of the business office. And an especially thick wall was erected around the entire enterprise to keep out the pollution generated by politicians and advertisers.[11]

Now politicos "change identity faster than Clark Kent," with little pause, embarrassment, or comment. Frankel cites the most recent: George Stephanopoulos and Susan Molinari, preceded by Bill Moyers, David Gergen, William Kristol, and DeeDee Meyers.

If Watergate produced important changes, Vietnam brought others. To Geyer, writers covering the war assumed the right and duty to make the most astonishing judgments to change society through their writings—not merely to report or reflect, but to redeem it. She views this shift as dangerous, nearly destroying truth in journalism. Other writers became heavily influenced by movements: environmentalism, consumerism, feminism, and Naderism. Many of these journalists routinely assumed that these groups were right, hence government and business were wrong.

Actually, the changes were a mixed bag. In his study and interviews of "Typewriter Guerrillas," John C. Behrens outlines qualities typical of the best of the post-Watergate reporters. They cajole, compromise, berate, badger, and hassle people; can be insufferable asses, unintelligible mystics, and tough adversaries.

But, Behrens warns, the tough exterior is vulnerable. Although outwardly abrasive, strident, and moralistic, the best must also have unusual sensibilities and intelligence, curiosity, and a high degree of skepticism. They must be able to bluff their way to information. Tenacity and perseverance are needed to get information from someone who does not want the reporter to have it. Long-term investigations, distinct from straight reporting, are very lonely work, devoid of the camaraderie and instant gratification of seeing a story appear immediately that sustain other reporters. Some reporters approach a story with swift, almost hurricane force. Others use the telephone as deftly as an expert surgeon wields his scalpel. Still others, such as the late I. F. Stone, discover important stories by laboriously reading every document issued on a given subject.

Only when a business spokesperson understands where the journalist is coming from, and the pressures and competition he faces, can the communicator stand a good chance of getting his company's message across effectively. Or, possibly, at all.

One *Fortune* 100 CEO, hounded, bewildered, raked over by some of the toughest investigative writers, and deeply troubled by what intense national media visibility was doing to his company and its management, exploded: "Why are they doing this to us?" To supplement the painful insights inflicted on the public battlefield and from his own management group, his communications officer gave him three cautionary tales in press relations.

First he read Heinrich Böll's novel *The Lost Honor of Katharina Blum*, a chilling account of a young German woman falsely accused and defamed by the sensationalist press. "The reporters were relentless," the CEO reacted. Precisely the point! Granted: Böll's account is highly dramatized; however, it illustrates the possible harassment not only of a target, but also of every associate and family member. The police leak information gathered during investigations to the press and delve into intimate details. Alarming changes in Katharina's behavior take place. She becomes almost totally apathetic— bombarded by epitaphs from neighbors, pornographic mail, and unpleasant propositions. Few question the newspapers' slanders, lies, and distortions, even as they altered the lives of the otherwise rational people around Katharina—such as her employer, who wanted to rig up a Molotov cocktail to toss through the newspaper's windows. Eventually, after avoiding them, she agrees to meet the photographer and reporter for an exclusive interview. She kills them. When the film version was shown in New York City, one audience clapped. As Louis Banks has warned the press, they hate you out there.

Individuals never the target of media harassment may deem Böll's tale overdrawn. But is it? Mary Cunningham in *Powerplay* describes her feelings of being hunted and betrayed while she was in the eye of a media blitz. Every telephone call zings; every public appearance is a cat-and-mouse game. Tragically, deaths can result from sensational, distorted coverage. The essentially private business executive, unlike public figures more inured and accustomed to visibility and criticism, withers and worries with exposure. Even seeing words quoted accurately in headlines or broadcast for millions can sting and disconcert. They are so public.

Neophytes who become the cynosure of press attention always make damaging mistakes. Without a staff savvy in media relations or a communications strategy, they damage themselves early on—and never recoup. The case for preparation is made by comparing Katharina Blum and Richard Jewell, caught unprepared by a media circus, to the superbly prepared military during the Gulf War. Although damaging stories of smart weapons that weren't and secrets of troop exposure to dangerous elements are emerging now, during the war itself generals and briefers understood and manipulated the press.[12]

HERO TO DEMON TO TALK SHOW

Böll's fiction anticipated by decades the real-life saga of an obscure, private person, Richard Jewell, thrust into a media feeding-frenzy. Until one is sucked into such a maelstrom, one cannot believe the intrusions, loss of any shred of privacy, and the serious circus of unwanted attention. Friends and neighbors are invaded. Many so subjected use "imprisonment"—correctly. Jewell's 88-day ordeal is a cautionary tale that it can happen to anyone—swiftly, unexpectedly, easily, unfairly, and all encompassingly. He is far from unique.

Now-retired Los Angeles Detective Mark Fuhrman gained wide

attention through his role in the O. J. Simpson criminal trial. To shield his family, Fuhrman moved them first to northern California, then to Sandpoint, Idaho. The press pursued. The Fuhrmans explained they felt "like prisoners . . . unable to venture outside the house without cameras and reporters besieging them." They hoped reporters would respect their wishes not to expose their children, both under five. The media didn't. One day a camera was jammed up against the windshield of the family car. Another time, the children sneaked out a side window to a concert. Speeding cars were used as decoys. Some neighbors resented the reporters just as much; another rented space to a television crew, so they had a good vantage point to "shoot" the detective's house.[13]

Proximity is reason enough for intrusions. The Boulder, Colorado neighborhood of the Ramsey family, following the murder of their 6-year old daughter, and the Merrick, Long Island one of Amy Fisher suffered, too. Interest in Fisher, involved in a messy, sensational saga, resulted in television crews staked out to capture any possible pictures inside the Fisher home. "Curiosity scavengers became their jailers." Neighbors kept a bitter tally of cars cruising their once quiet cul-de-sac—from 10 a year to 20 daily.[14]

Jewell's words, anguish, and "imprisonment" reflect all such cynosure of media attention—except his was worldwide. The incident during the 1996 Atlanta Olympics raises many disturbing questions of the FBI's performance, jurisdictional disputes among law enforcement groups, and the use of profiling based on little factual experience, then restricting the search to fit the profile. More than two years later the search for the bomber continues still. Unlike Böll's character, Jewell fortunately had a buffer between him, investigators, and the press: a lawyer friend. Ironically, Jewell viewed himself as part of law enforcement, talked the lingo. He had been so certified by Georgia authorities, and so had understood the procedures. Despite these important issues, comments will be limited to media/communications aspects.[15]

The presence of an estimated 10,000 reporters and television crew members, worldwide interest in the Olympics, a concern for safety prompted by previous Olympic bombings and deaths, the *Atlanta Journal Constitution*'s aim to restore its journalistic reputation by Olympic coverage, and the coalescing of flukes, egos, and rush to judgment inflamed an already hyper milieu.

The incident began with a call to 911 warning of a bomb at Centennial Park. The explosion killed one person, contributed to the death of another, and injured 110 more. Jewell, working as a security guard for AT&T, was initially cheered as a hero for clearing the area around the suspected bomb. The bending of facts to fit a better story began immediately. AT&T sought media exposure on television for its hero guard. Jewell was reluctant, but agreed. He wore an AT&T tee-shirt. When he became a suspect, these efforts were attributed to him, a publicity hound looking for face time and visibility.

Now, his 88-day travail began. The plight of Jewell is dramatized by *New York Times* headlines and photographs between August 26 and December 10, plus Max Frankel's reflective "An Olympian Injustice." With acknowledgments to John Dos Passos, the headlines read:

August 20, 1996:
"Atlanta Bombing Suspect Mostly Just Stays Home, Many Eyes Glued on Him; If it's not the FBI in pursuit, then it's camera crews, or sometimes both."

The accompanying photograph shows a cameraman, comfortably staked out, camera at the ready for any possible sightings of Jewell or his mother.

The next day:
"Lie Detector Clears Atlanta Bomb Suspect, His Lawyers Say"

August 27, 1996:
"Focus on Bomb Suspect Brings Tears and a Plea, Fighting Back Against the Glare of Cameras and Public Scrutiny"

The photograph shows Barbara Jewell breaking into tears as she spoke at an Atlanta press conference of the strain.

September 22, 1996:
"Agents Find Little to Link Suspect to Olympics Bomb, But Park Guard Remains Focus of Inquiry"

The story, which notes Jewell is neither charged nor cleared, is highly critical of the fruitless investigation, conducted under the unrelenting glare of publicity and intense pressure from superiors, of the behavioral profile of a potential bomb planter; it even questions the legal grounds for the search of Jewell's apartment. Jewell is pictured reflecting his limbo.

October 27, 1996:
"Guard Isn't Bomb Suspect, Government Says"
"He Felt Much 'Like a Hunted Animal,' Cleared Atlanta Bombing Suspect Attacks FBI and News Media"

Jewell and his mother still looked fearful in a photograph as they left a news conference where they described "88 days of hell." A sidebar proclaimed, wrongly as it turns out: "Lawsuits by Guard Would Face Obstacles."

October 28, 1996:
"A Man's Life Turned Inside Out By Government and the Media" headlines a front-page story and sidebar inside. The lengthy profile features not only a recap and analysis, but such quotes as "there will always be a shadow," "non-healing scar," and "the news media just jumped on it like a piranha on a bleeding cow [sic]"–only if the cow is in the water; piranha are fish. But the thought is clear. "A Story Where the Telling Itself Has Raised Many Questions" Jewell is pictured, even then, still surrounded by fuzzy-headed microphones, cameras, and print journalists.

The next day *The New York Times* editorial "The FBI's Latest Lapse" began "If the Federal Bureau of Investigation is lucky, the debate over the hounding of Richard Jewell will focus on press coverage of the case." After detailing the recent history of Bureau abuses, the editorial concluded that the FBI had committed the "real abuse."

Three final *Times* headlines:

October 30, 1996:
"FBI's Interview in Bombing Is Investigated by Justice Department"

December 10, 1996:
"FBI Posts a Big Reward in Olympic Bombing Case, Asks Public for

Photos Shot on Night of Blast; With leads drying up, investigators call for help"

"NBC Pays to Avert a Suit by Ex-Bombing Suspect"

Behind these headlines lies a frightening saga of details. The FBI questioned Jewell under somewhat dubious explanations. With the issuance of the August 3 search warrant, 40 agents with dogs spent 9 hours searching the small apartment he shared with his mother. A special agent pulled 50 hairs from Jewell's head. Unwittingly the searchers created images and comments strikingly effective to the general public: Jewell sitting forlornly for seven hours on the steps of the apartment house while the search went on and on, "the most famous image of the summer"; messing up Mrs. Jewell's once spotless, orderly kitchen; taking all the Tupperware, Disney tapes, and other personal items. In later interviews both Jewells asked the FBI to return the Tupperware. Mike Wallace asked about the Tupperware on *60 Minutes*. When returned, it was covered with pen markings. Who would use that? Who would eat anything from that? lamented the Jewells. Those appeals everyone can relate to. They aroused powerful public sympathies.

Now that he was a suspect, the harassments and intrusions began in earnest. He began receiving 1,000 calls daily. Someone had "thoughtfully" listed his mother's telephone number on the Internet. Sound trucks were parked around the middle-class neighborhood where Jewell's mother lived. As reporters "peered" into the apartment, Jewell peered out. One hundred to 150 reporters camped on a nearby hill. When he appeared in a hotel auditorium, cameramen yelled "Showtime. Showtime." Sound trucks and reporters awaited every appearance. A trip to buy a pizza included an entourage of chase vehicles—media and law enforcement. Once he sensed a plane low overhead. One newspaper called it a strike force. The Jewells felt like prisoners in their own apartment, unable, because of the anticipated commotion, to visit a dying friend.

Marie Brenner in her long *Vanity Fair* profile quotes some of the Jewells' understandable responses: "I don't want to be around reporters right now"; "They are animals"; "I hope and pray that no one else is ever subjected to the pain and ordeal that I have gone through."[16]

Most characterizations of Jewell were hurtful, exaggerated, or just plain wrong. The 34-year-old was described as having "an open face, a bland pleasantness and an eagerness to please."[17] A Baptist, he had a reverence for authority. Yet he was perceived and described as a hapless dummy, a plodding misfit, a Forrest Gump, a child-man, a mama's boy, and a beefy wanna-be policeman. Given the national obsession with weight, Jewell's heft was roundly criticized.

Two tangential events complicated Jewell's life. According to Marie Brenner, the *Atlanta Journal Constitution* had become something of a journalistic joke first for a noisy, messy firing of a top editor, but more for its editorial style. In addition to its "Voice of God tone, it featured 'chunklets'—short bits in a soft-news style known as eye candy." "The paper intended to set new standards in its hometown during the games."[18] Instead, it set questionable practices. The rush to closure that dominated both law enforcement and media was led by the *Atlanta Journal Constitution*. After some debate about using Jewell's name, the paper decided to run with the headline: "FBI Suspects 'Hero' Guard May Have Planted Bomb" followed by copy saying he fit the profile of the lone bomber, itself based on data questioned later. Some experts said Jewell failed to fit the cobbled-together profile.

How the name got to the *Journal* may never be known. Reporters guard zealously and go to jail rather than name sources. Now, like a genie out of a bottle, other news channels used the *Journal* story, showing its headlines or quoting it in their own coverage. Tom Brokaw, anchor of the NBC *Nightly News*, and, ironically, one of Mrs. Jewell's favorites, said on air: "They probably have enough to arrest him right now, probably enough to prosecute him, but you always want to have enough to convict him as well. There are still holes in this case."[19] Only *The New York Times* did not pick up the *Journal's* story. CNN weighed the ramifications of using the name, but eventually did.

As coverage intensified, the stories got nastier. He was called a village Rambo, a big fat stupid guy, an enraged homosexual, a cop-hater, and a Unadoofus, and was compared to serial killer Wayne Williams. Secondary considerations arose as well. The landlord threatened to rescind the apartment's lease. The manager's son was out selling pictures he took of the Jewells.[20] In psychological limbo, Jewell was followed by swarms of FBI agents and the press wherever he went.

When the FBI finally admitted in a highly unusual letter that he was no longer a suspect, the tables were turned—Jewell and his lawyer began suing and winning cash settlements from NBC and other media. News executives began rethinking their news policies, particularly at the *Journal*, which was criticized for sloppiness and lack of sources.

Another suit was against Piedmont College, where Jewell once had worked as a campus security guard. Some colleges are reluctant to admit troubles, even serious ones, on campus. It would spoil their images, hurt recruitment and alumni donations. Was Jewell's heavy-handed enforcement at Piedmont overzealousness or a threat to its image? Both? He had been nudged to leave. In analyzing any public relations problem, especially one as intense and hyper as Jewell's, one must constantly look at the milieu, such as the *Journal*'s journalistic standing and aims, as well as the flukes, hidden agendas, and needs. Piedmont's President Ray Cleere illustrates this.

Brenner describes how Cleere, now head of a rural Baptist mountain school, had once been Mississippi's commissioner of higher education. "He was said to feel he had suffered a loss of status in the boondocks, out of the academic mainstream." Associates said he loved the limelight, wanted public attention, the very trait he reportedly ascribed to Jewell.[21]

Against a colleague's advice and complaining that no one locally would pay attention, Cleere called the FBI in Washington himself. The link to Jewell was made, triggering a complex set of circumstances. The FBI gathered extensive quotes from students, largely negative of Jewell, of course. "The FBI took Cleere at his word." But rather than leading to Jewell's arrest, it got "them both in a bunch of trouble."[22]

Even before Jewell was cleared, Max Frankel surveyed the media frenzy, "the hellish limbo to which the media lynch mob consigned" Jewell. Too easily overlooked, "among all the athletic and political entertainments," was "the careless abandon with which this uncharged 'suspect' . . . was identified, vilified, stalked and stigmatized before the entire world without a shred of evidence."[23] Frankel noted that "cameramen and interviewers practically crushed Jewell as he tried for a day or so to carry on his life." "Reporters dug up embarrassing, but by no means criminal information about his past." Although he criticized chronic leaks from law enforcement true or false, deliberate or accidental, or to prove competence quickly before the impatiently watching world, Frankel wrote that media's duty is to "just say no" and not yield, despite the temptation of competitive pressures. "Whatever the source of suspicions about Jewell, he was owed respect and privacy at least until formally charged, let alone convicted. . . . [Instead] American media committed an Olympian injustice."[24]

The Centennial Park story that began with a bang ended with whimper. After 88 days, the FBI, in a letter delivered to his attorneys at dawn, told Jewell he was no longer a suspect. No media hype there. Despite the suits and his own media appearances, Jewell says repeatedly, he cannot get his good name back. He will always be known as the former suspect in the Olympic bombings. How true. During a *Larry King Live* interview, Jewell made exactly that point. After a commercial break, King reintroduced his guest as, that's right, the former suspect. "Excuse me, Mr. King. That's exactly what I'm talking about."

The "media establishment [began] falling prostrate before him," Jeffrey Toobin commented in *The New Yorker*.[25] The media would rather think of themselves as "speaking truth to power than as spreading falsehoods about the powerless." However, the round-the-clock stakeout made the media look far more massive than responsible. "Reputation is more easily wrecked than rescued. When a private citizen comes up against the armored divisions of the networks it isn't exactly an even match."[25]

Although Jewell's story ended rather happily, it failed to instill caution. The rush to decision, the failure to check, the vulnerability of the famous was rerun with Michael Irvin and Erik Williams of the Dallas Cowboys. An accusation of sexual assault was blared in headlines. When the "victim" was herself charged with filing a false police report, Irvin said what many other victims wish they could: "Rerun it [the charge], reprint it—just like you did, with the same intensity that you did."[27]

The Jewell syndrome has passed into the language as a rush to judgment. But in the most important sense it is a cautionary tale that you, too, a largely unknown, private citizen can get caught in the crosshairs of conflict—quickly, sometimes innocently, but always painfully. Think the worst, then devoutly hope it never happens.

What other lessons can corporate communicators learn from Blum's and Jewell's predicaments?

- Be prepared. Know how the media pursues a human-interest story of high drama, such as a revolutionary involved in the case of Blum, global exposure in Jewell's.
- Put a buffer—a spokesperson, experienced friend, or lawyer —between you and the press. Jewell's attorney did this successfully, although he was not media-wise. Perhaps a healthy sense of the absurd helped him. Experienced and skillful as he is with the media, President Clinton probably should have used a buffer when he was surprised and deeply grieved by the suicide of long-time friend Vincent Foster.
- Do a risk assessment of associates and family members the press may seek out. Prepare them. Tell them the issues. What is the press expected to ask? Should you answer or stonewall? No one ever does a good job when surprised and unprepared.
- Protect the vulnerable. In Blum's case reporters, misrepresenting themselves, found her gravely ill mother in a hospital and interviewed her. At a minimum, the mother's room should have been protected, her identity hidden under another name.
- Know your hot buttons and vulnerabilities. What will cause anger? Make you blurt out damaging sound-bytes? In Blum's case, reports of a one-night assignation and a messy apartment wounded her privacy and German sense of neatness. A word or image once spoken or captured on T.V. can never be recalled. Rather than spinning ex post facto, exercise discipline.

INVESTIGATIVE AND HERD JOURNALISTS

The second book the CEO tackled, Carl Bernstein and Robert Woodward's *All the President's Men*, details step-by-step how the authors sleuthed information on Watergate. One of their tactics, important to corporate media relations, was to approach lower-level employees—particularly executive secretaries—who had important information and were willing to talk. Bernstein tells of knocking on the front door of a small tract-house in suburban Washington. He thought the resident, a bookkeeper, might know a great deal. She worked for Maurice Stans, Republican Party fund-raiser. Many so approached were not willing to talk, but enough did to give *The*

Washington Post reporters their story. Watergate itself, the two reporters' techniques, and their subsequent stardom produced a sea-
change in how news is gathered and reported.

Resulting implications important to corporations include:

- The rise of tough, well-financed investigative reporting. Of course,
  all reporting involves investigation, so the term indicates more jargon than change. However, it meant teams of reporters, usually not
  just one, who dug, dug, and dug for information. It was not a benign
  hunt, but aimed at exposé and stardom–power–riches for the reporters. With tighter profit margins, the emergence of lawyers as
  "final editors," and legal action against careless reporting, investigative journalism has diminished, but not enough for any corporation
  to relax.
- Don't overlook *any* employee as an information source, a leaker.
  Those who disagree with corporate policy or action, the downsized,
  disgruntled, physically injured, or ideologically driven are most
  likely. When Texaco downsized an executive, did they ever think he
  would turn over tapes of damaging racial remarks?
- Know exactly what the reporter's and his media's biases are. Don't
  expect objectivity from Green Peace if your plant is polluting a
  beautiful bay.
- Be careful when you talk to reporters. Late at night, at home, after
  a drink or two is neither opportune nor prudent.

The CEO's third cautionary tale came from *Boys on the Bus*, Timothy Crouse's account of reporters covering George McGovern's
1972 presidential campaign. The book illustrates the competitive,
bone-wearying pressure-cooker in which reporters work. Often surface and reality are contradictory. A giddy camaraderie mixes with
fear and low-grade hysteria. The dangers are great. If reporters file a
story late or make a glaring factual error, they risk losing everything.
"When it came to writing," Crouse observes, "they were as cautious
as a diamond cutter."

The bus's womb-like ambience, the closed circles of high-powered
journalism, produced what Crouse calls a "notorious phenomenon-
pack [herd or fuselage] journalism." Trapped on the same bus or
plane, reporters ate, drank, gambled, and compared notes with the
same colleagues week after week. Off the bus, socially, they saw the
same people, used the same sources, belonged to the same background groups, swore by the same omens. "They arrived at their

answers just as independently as a class of honest seventh graders using the same geometry text—they did not have to cheat off each other to come up with the same answers." Of course, the same charges of exclusivity and insularity are often brought against corporate management.

Neither a participant nor a bystander, an insider-outsider, the journalist always sees in greater depth and earlier than the average person. But some of the most insightful information never reaches the news columns. It is shared among reporters over drinks or, according to Crouse, sent as memos to senior editors as grist for their cocktail circuit.[28]

Crouse and others also comment on the tendency to blame the reporter an executive sees rather than the invisible editor whose power and role he may not fully understand. One communication executive relates how a major business magazine reporter wrote an exceedingly positive story on the repositioning of his company from a dirt-floor, rust-belt manufacturer to high-technology. Normally, reporters fiercely refuse to let any outsider review their story before it appears. (Caution: asking even an outwardly friendly reporter for the right to review courts big trouble. It simply isn't worth the risk. Offering to check facts is sometimes O.K.) Company executives didn't see the copy. Imagine how stunned they were when a very critical, almost damaging story appeared. How could it happen? An editor, unknown by the company, edited without knowledge or checking back with the reporter. Olympian editors, detached from the story, create problems.

As a young reporter, the author saw these played out—tragically. A police officer in the county seat died of gunshot wounds. Although some facts indicated a possible suicide, no officials would say so for attribution. The reporter had no choice. The copy desk chief flicked his pencil and changed the lead to suicide, then handed it to a woman copy editor recently converted to Roman Catholicism. She was unusually sensitive to the impact on the officer's Roman Catholic family. The senior editor, even with her insistence, refused to check with the reporter, only a few feet away. He knew. He never thought of his journalistic responsibility or the pain he could cause. When the first edition appeared—unfortunately, it circulated in the county seat—copy editor and reporter protested to the city editor. The front-page story bore her by-line. The story was changed back.

Too late. Several weeks later, a cub told the municipal reporter a high school classmate wanted to see her. A highly unusual visit for a newspaper city-room, but she agreed. No nostalgia, no small talk. The visitor asked: "Why did you write my husband killed himself?" The reporter took her to the offending editor. Forced to face the effect of his arrogant flick of a pencil, he retreated to First Amendment press freedoms. How dare she face him down. She was just emotional. But he never forgave the reporter for making him face the consequences.

Few corporate stories are as intimate or tragic, but the unseen editor and reputation of the publication must be considered as much as, even more than, the highly visible reporter. The editor rides in the reporter's psyche to any assignment. Journalists self-censor in anticipation of an imaginary showdown. They second-guess a cautious editor, know that they must justify a lead different from a competitor's or the wire services'. Although reporters may appear rash, bold, or frivolous to a corporate type, they often must play it safe, following the pack, current fads, and cant. Just forget about the fight for scoops, the drive for exclusive information, fresh approaches, or leads. Paraphrase; paraphrase *The New York Times* and you're safer. That's driving sameness and repetition in news.

As a reporter matures, he often develops doubts about his work, questions how he is using his power. How can he bridge the difference between the reality he witnesses and what he reports? Reporting, perhaps even editing, is a young person's job. Not just because of the physical pressures—relentless deadlines, irregular hours, constant travel, and junk food—but because a reporter must jump from one subject to another, without time to be immersed in any. Watergate and the extension of the beat system from geography and turf to subject has somewhat mitigated this concern.[29]

Some individuals view the press as an aggressive monolith. Remember competition! Reporters, even on the same newspaper, compete fiercely among themselves. Television competes with print, cable with networks, news services with each other. When television people first appeared on the McGovern press bus, older newspaper reporters regarded them with outright loathing, considered them dilettantes, glamour boys, and know-nothings. Exacerbating these feelings was the dramatic growth in impact and financial strength of television while newspapers were dying. Today the enmity still exists, albeit muted, but critics still cavil about highly paid "rip-and-read heads." (Translation: attractive men and women who rip stories written by someone else from various sources and read them on camera.)

Without question, television and cable have changed news-gathering, image-making,and the way reporters interact with their subjects.[30] Vermont Royster, who for almost fifty years wrote for *The Wall Street Journal*, detailed how the presidential press conference evolved from the relatively intimate format of FDR's chats with a few reporters in the Oval Office into today's instant visual drama. Some 200 reporters, cameramen, and technicians jam into a conference room competing to become the stars of the action. Sheer numbers and visibility have replaced free-wheeling conversation with confrontation.

Instant transmission has robbed the President—or anyone on live television—of the chance to "think out loud," perhaps rephrase or hone his words. "He must live in constant fear of a slip of the tongue; awkward, damaging phraseology beyond recall or correction."[31] Spin and instant rebuttal are the only redress. So a President hesitates to be frank and open, or share his thought processes. If relations between President and press are contentious and the questions tough, spokesmen ooze answers, limit press contacts to controlled photo-ops or "not hearing" over helicopter rotors.

Such press relations are vastly different from what corporate leaders experience. Though no CEO enjoys television networks or reporters eagerly awaiting his every word, some parallels and lessons apply to both. For all their power, no President ever had prolonged success at muzzling the press. Even former President Richard M. Nixon, who experienced the most antagonistic relations, eventually learned one crucial lesson: give them lots of news doled out at just the right amount at the right time. The alternative is damaging coverage or reliance on ill-informed, possibly even hostile sources.

What Does the Media Want?

When business bothers to ask this question, the press is quick with suggestions. Carol Loomis, a member of *Fortune*'s board of editors, makes six:

- Staff media relations with bright, pleasant people.
- Make sure they return phone calls from the press promptly, without fail. Saying "no" isn't the ultimate sin; not responding within a reasonable time is.
- Get to know the editors and writers most likely to be involved in a company story. "People on my side of the fence are as susceptible to flattery as everyone else." (Some fault the press for being pushovers for access to powerful and articulate officials.)
- Be helpful on stories, even general industry or trend articles.
- Encourage senior management to be candid and honest with all its audiences, particularly the press. This may seem naïve, a bit Boy Scoutish, but once one is caught in a cover-up or an outright lie, the damage is always worse.
- Open meetings with security analysts to the business press.[32] Although this sounds simple, analysts often resent the intrusion of the press, thinking it would restrain comments or focus them more generally than financially. Journalists and analysts compete for exclusive information. Some companies compromise and hold a special press briefing or interview session immediately following the analyst meeting.

Other business editors suggest better contact, particularly access to CEOs, and understanding of deadlines. Some corporate people try to be cute by calling in a major story at 6 p.m. when they think deadlines will preclude thorough research. Round-the-clock news and multiple editions in different time zones, such as the *Asian Wall Street Journal*, make hiding or timing bad news almost useless. Others bother editors with too much junk, failing to understand there must be a good reason for a story: a news peg, not yours, theirs. At times the fault is silence—not telling editors about unusual stories or mistakes, or being reluctant to release financial information on subsidiaries or percentage of market share. This information, business people point out, can be useful to competitors or raiders looking to pick off a highly profitable division. Both are valid reasons. However, one company refused to give the age and sex of its top six officers, even though such information is routinely available in most annual reports and all 10-Ks. Withholding such routine information only stirs more suspicions than necessary.

Adroit and open corporate communication often can turn coverage to a company's advantage. When Hoffman-LaRoche in northern New Jersey announced substantial layoffs, management was cooperative and very forthcoming with local reporters. They invited reporters to talk with employees and participate in out-placement and other meetings. This positioned the layoffs in a positive light and may have deflected probing stories of long-term problems.[33] What management lapses, for example, made such lay-offs necessary?

Walter Guzzardi, Jr., a member of *Fortune*'s board of editors, has other words of advice on the politics of the press. There is no place to hide, he counsels. If the press is going after you for a story and you duck, many outside sources—disgruntled former employees, hostile competitors, and others—not all favorably inclined toward the company or up-to-date may give the story an undesirable cast.

Guzzardi views the business–press relationship as wary, not adversarial. Mutual needs surmount different perspectives, objectives, and interests. To Guzzardi, distrust exists largely because of deficiencies on both sides. Many in the press are enormously self-important. They think life should be organized to suit them professionally, even personally. They enjoy the enormous power they wield. Also, the dramatic organization of a story requires extremely pointed ways of making arguments, which inevitably shadow the truth. On the other hand, corporate executives expect too much: that copy appear as they have written it. That's unrealistic. They, too, have an ego screen. "The process of becoming a CEO," comments Guzzardi, "is an enormous ego-feeding experience."[34]

WHAT "NO COMMENT" REALLY MEANS

Unfair, yes, but "no comment," like taking the Fifth Amendment after the McCarthy hearings of the 1950s, connotes at least something to hide. At worst, guilt. Hence, it must be used as sparingly as a pungent spice in a delicate stew. At times, during registration for a new stock offering, mergers and acquisitions, legal action, or when the full information collection is incomplete, silence or diversion may be necessary. Even then, communicating no comment without saying the actual words is prudent.

Presidential spokespersons must be particularly inventive. At times lying may be unavoidable. Jody Powell, press secretary to President Carter, was confronted directly in April 1980 with the question "Are we attempting a rescue mission in Iran?" He knew "no comment" would reveal the deal. So he lied. Once the mission was over, he revealed that he had. The press didn't hold it against him.

Larry Speakes notes: "There are 10,000 ways of saying 'no comment.' . . . Day in and day out I dealt with top-secret information and avoided spilling the beans. A press secretary can use a variety of tactics to avoid a direct answer: "I'll get back to you" or "physically ducking the press for as long as necessary." Go underground. Keep your door shut. Tell staff "I just cannot take any calls today."[35] Corporate spokespeople, when talking to the press in difficult situations, may not be forgiven as quickly as when issues of national security are at stake.

Writing in the *Journal of Corporate Public Relations*, Bernard Charland takes a traditional view: when a company responds to media inquiries with "no comment," it "usually reflects disorganization or disregard for the media and the public interest." Charland argues, however, that several companies have used "no comment" as a planned response "for a more balanced approach to the all-or-nothing mentality." No matter how a company refuses to provide information to the press, what words it uses, "the act's the same." Yes, but. . . . Euphemisms don't seem to wave the same inflaming red flag.

The PR canon, to Charland, is very clear. "Not commenting is a mistake that damages [press] relations and negatively impacts a company's reputation." "It usually indicates a lack of strategic management information . . . and flies against the premise of corporate responsibility." Satisfying media's want to know and the corporate agenda is a delicate balancing act for the practitioner.

Key variables—strategic and situational—help categorize degrees and circumstances when companies withhold comment:

Strategic:

- Is it intentional?
- Is refusal consistent or selective? Are just some publics stonewalled?
- Is all or only some information withheld?
- Are means other than the media being used?

Situational:

- What are the specific circumstances—a legal dispute, inherently negative issue, timing, executive pique?
- Is there a potentially legitimate reason behind the refusal?

- Is the company private or public? (Public companies must observe the "material" rule, meaning any news that can affect stock value, such as a CEO's firing, must be announced promptly. Private companies have more latitude legally.)
- Does the company enjoy a reputation as a forthright and honest source?

Since companies rarely "stifle or ignore" a positive story, no news is often interpreted as bad news.

To expand and illustrate his thesis, Charland cites four case studies—Wal-Mart, Mars, Olympia & York, and NASA—"egregious examples of media stonewalling." His analysis, however, cites just communication aspects, not the operational or historical.

Wal-Mart's press shyness traces back to its founder, Sam Walton, who was reluctant even to have his picture taken by *Fortune* for its prestigious Hall of Fame. It hadn't hurt him personally or the company. His successor's press experience was neither pleasant nor productive. The operational lapses of Wal-Mart's "Buy America Program" (the garments were made overseas) or Sprawl-Mart impact on small-town main streets would take master spinners to explain away. Charland attributes Wal-Mart's media shyness to its focus on "retail and business customers at the expense of other shareholders." He concludes: "Wal-Mart's reluctant and antagonistic stance toward the press has likely contributed to its deteriorating image with media, investors and the public." An expected conclusion from a communicator, it omits natural cycles following the death of a founder, operational difficulties, and overlooked damaging details in promotions such as "Buy America."

Mars too has its reasons. Charland describes the leading candy manufacturer as "a notoriously secretive, family-owned corporation." Though successful financially, "Mars faces some serious marketing problems, challenges and rising criticism . . . exacerbated by its tendency toward a go-it-alone strategy." Some observers describe Mars's silence as arrogance; others, as "an enigma inside a mystery tied up in a bright candy wrapper." Like many consumer-product companies, Mars advertises widely, but is tight-lipped about corporate and family matters. Has this really hurt Mars? Again, Charland notes the inability to "effectively manage external communications" which allows outsiders to fill the information vacuum. Hurt profits? Not really.

Also taken to task is Olympia & York, once one of the world's largest property-owners, privately held by the Reichmann brothers of Toronto. The company symbolized the spend-and-grow mood of the 1980s. "When the real estate bubble burst in the early 1990's, the empire crumbled," and most of its assets were liquidated. According to Charland, a "main factor in the downfall . . . more specifically in making its recovery unlikely, was its secretive nature." "For years, the company provided little or no information to the press, investment bankers or lenders." Even potential investors were only reluctantly allowed to glimpse its financial statements. Media relations "were sparse, strained and even hostile." Olympia & York sued *Canadian Life* for libel after a tough, critical exposé of the Reichmann family. The resulting court battle "sent a chill through the Canadian press." Would open, good press relations have made a difference? Probably not. Operations speak louder than words. But certainly Olympia & York could not expect help from a long-ignored press when they needed it.

The fourth instance, NASA, especially the Challenger 10 explosion, showed not so much NASA's stonewalling of the press as its total inability to reverse publicity from its long-standing good, positive news. The media had failed to question the dangers of space exploration. Instead, it accepted copious PR that touted milk-run safety. "NASA, once known for its superb public relations machine, destroyed its stellar reputation by responding to the disaster with a siege mentality" and prolonged silence, Charland comments. "The Challenger fiasco resulted in a lengthy investigation of NASA decision making and a loss of prestige and credibility. . . . Almost 15 years of accumulated goodwill, positive image and credibility can be destroyed by one instance of stonewalling." Just stonewalling, not the seven deaths and the end of uncritical hype and glory?

Charland assesses the communications risks, short- and long-term, of "no comment":

Short-term impact:

- Perception of guilt
- Suspicion and hostility among affected stakeholders
- Negative image and relations with the media
- Vacuum of information filled by uncontrolled speculation
- "No comment" reputation clouds good business stories

Long-term impact:

- Negative implications for crisis management and public support
- Limited credibility
- Lessened ability to manage messages for general public
- Potential difficulties with government officials and regulators (who dislike secrecy) or nasty surprises.

Media relations isn't a simple question of tell all, tell nothing. Considerations of confidentiality, competition, public safety, and humaneness are factors. Announcing deaths or, worse, letting the press do so before families are notified is infinitely worse than delaying—but not too long—the announcements. Previously, lawyers urged a say-nothing strategy, fearing liability, but now some advise: "Assertiveness is a more prudent tack than stonewalling. . . . Companies might have to disclose some normally confidential information to bolster their candor and credibility."[36]

As in so many PR situations, the practitioner is left with a conundrum addressed by the specifics of event, company, and practitioner.

COSMETICS COUNT

Senior executives, even male, are increasingly sensitive to physical presentation. That's what all those dye jobs, cosmetic surgeries, and pumping for impressive pecs are all about. PR charm schools teaching executives how to appear most effectively on television or before congressional committees are flourishing. These do not automatically translate to fully appreciating the full impact of television on employees, customers, and corporate image. Too many executives dismiss television as "shallow and sensational," not important, while most Americans are glued to the tube six hours daily.

Merrie Spaeth, a Texas-based counselor, advises: "Executives need to be students of TV communication skills" even if "they never expect to see a camera in their office." Television has shaped expectations of how "we communicate and present ourselves." Television anchors, Spaeth points out, "have set a standard employees, shareholders and other key constituencies expect. If [an executive's] style of communication differs drastically from theirs, the executive risks appearing unprepared, uninteresting and, worst of all, untrustworthy." Teachers at all levels face the same judgments.

In a *Wall Street Journal* column, "What You Can Learn from Brokaw & Co.," Spaeth lists five lessons:

- *Tell a story*. Whether it's budget figures, a pitch for a new market, or to a new client. Transmitting only isn't good enough. Consider your audience.
- *Maintain critical eye contact*. Know where to look, "create a one-on-one bonding." "Untrained executives often appear uncertain and hesitant. Good eye contact is deliberate and slow-paced. Look at an individual long enough for him to realize you're talking to him. Such eye contact translates "directly to whether a person can be trusted."
- *Look as if listening*. Spaeth's firm has trademarked the term "listening face . . . what someone's face looks like when he's waiting or listening." Too often its "very grim instead of animated or pleasant," giving "the impression we don't want to be there."
- *Use a variety of visual elements to heighten interest*. Spaeth cites the example of a reporter doing a story on the price of a popular children's cough medicine. Props included a "bottle of medicine, graphics (showing the labeling and circling parts that had changed) and a video clip of a mother who felt misled." Spaeth advises at least two visuals, such as slides and props, regardless of the audience.
- *Make presentation seems spontaneous, even if it's been prepared and rehearsed*. "Get comfortable with a TelePrompter" which displays text written for the ear, not the eye. The distributed text "will not have pauses, half sentences and repetitions, asides and self-deprecating lines" of the spoken version.[37]

MIKE FRIGHT: THE WARFARE OF INTERVIEWING

Leave a note on any corporate executive's desk reading, "Mike Wallace called about a *60 Minutes* interview," and pangs of genuine anxiety ensue. Although Wallace has mellowed recently and the program attacks business less forcefully, he was the *bête noire* of executives for many years.

"Mike fright" demonstrates many techniques used in interviewing—some would say entrapment—and the evolution of television journalism. Wallace explains the aims of *60 Minutes* and its forerunner, *Night Beat,* in his *Close Encounters: Mike Wallace's Own Story,* written with Gary Paul Gates. Modestly, Wallace explains that the programs became enduring models of thorough preparation and of insistent probing to get at the face behind the mask, the elusive truth behind the nervous evasion. The aim: to stimulate, not avoid, controversy. Guests were thoroughly and painstakingly researched. The formula and staging—often klieg lights glaring over the interviewer's shoulder in the guest's eyes—forced interviewees to come clean and blocked their retreat into amiable reassurance. *Night Beat* used searching, tight close-ups to record tentative glances, nervous tics, and beads of perspiration. Wallace developed techniques not needed in print—brusque interruptions, exaggerated facial gestures, the cigarette as a weapon—as part of his performance.

Anyone who did not prepare himself in background or techniques, who expected an easy, cordial, almost insouciant mood, a light workout, was in for big trouble. One guest who worked the *60 Minutes* system well, according to Wallace, was H. R. Haldeman. He was unfailingly courteous, displayed a highly selective memory, and deftly parried attempts to pin him down on Watergate. He answered vaguely and tentatively, yet conveyed the impression of a man trying to be cooperative and forthcoming. Even his evasions seemed credible. He took a difficult or provocative question and smothered it in a morass of detail or hair-splitting qualifications, resulting in confusion or tedium. Haldeman understood that a dull, imprecise interview suited *his* purpose and sabotaged Wallace's. He projected, according to Wallace's assessment, a manner and tone of sincerity that made him credible. By contrast, his colleague John D. Ehrlichmann sweated and came across as angry and uptight.

Wallace sees television journalism as successor to the muckraking journalism at the turn of the century. He admits that sometimes *60 Minutes* got carried away in the excitement of the quest, and wound up with stories that conveyed more heat than light, more theater than substance. Television tends to raise disposable issues; topics come and go. Fresh diversions change with the seasons and the ratings. To others television thrives on the popular culture, the new, not unlike traditional retailing or theme restaurants.

Two *60 Minutes* interviews of particular business interest involved San Diego Federal and Coors. Dick Carlson, senior vice president of Federal, said he would participate only if his own video crew taped the interview. (One of the most persistent and telling criticisms against the program is its highly tendentious film-editing and -splicing.) Wallace agreed, never imagining he would be hoist on his own petard. During a halt, while the 60 *Minutes* tape was being changed, Federal cameras kept rolling, and caught Wallace's ethnic expletive. When he learned of it, he asked to have the tape erased, but later backed off. Carlson was amused that the master of ambush was caught off guard by his small California savings and loan company.

Joe and Bill Coors decided that they had two choices when the 60 *Minutes* staff approached them: tell them to go away, or accept the challenge and open the entire brewery. During the research and interviewing, the crew found that Coors was a victim of a systematic campaign by labor to discredit the company—and they reported it.

Ironically, the unpleasant encounters and fights Wallace and his crews created, the potential damage to some companies and their images, forced business leaders to train for television appearances, to learn how to work the medium. This has spawned a thriving charm school business: firms teach executives how to talk and parry tough questions, how to dress and appear effectively on television, and how and when to utter the positive sound-byte.

Interviewing techniques for questioner and subject are at the heart of such training. Wallace, Georgie Anne Geyer, and Oriana Fallaci—all with differing styles—explain their approaches to interviewing. The most adroit, successful interviewer—but also the most dangerous to the neophyte—is the openly friendly and empathetic reporter. Caught off guard or lulled, the subject may make damaging, emotional, or embarrassing statements. Who can forget Henry Kissinger talking about the Lone Ranger diplomacy to Fallaci, or Newt Gingrich's mother coaxed to confide her unflattering assessment of Mrs. Clinton to Connie Chung and millions of viewers? Perhaps this was the grasp too far—the Gingrichs had tea at the White House with Mrs. Clinton; Connie Chung disappeared from network news.

Geyer explains the woman interviewer's advantage. She believes in empathetic immersion, basically a psychoanalytic term meaning immersing yourself: listening intently, sympathizing with the interviewee's perceptions, then extracting truths from what was heard or said. Women seem to put men at ease, Geyer writes. "Sooner or later, everything pours out. Men forget they are with a journalist" and so respond as they always have to women as listeners and comforters.[38] (Men often will talk in front of women colleagues with the same openness, as if they were invisible and surely no competition or threat.)

Geyer's style contrasts greatly with the more confrontational Fallaci, the Italian journalist. Fallaci considers herself not a cold recorder of what she sees and hears, but a participant, intently observing, as though the matter concerned her personally and required her to take a stand. She approaches her subject not with detachment, but armed with provocative questions. Despite all her preparation, she fears being "a worm hidden in the wood of history"—not having enough eyes, ears, and brains to understand. With the powerful who have been her subjects, she has had to exert herself to keep them talking. "It became a game to reach the truth." She sought to draw out the moral drama, the truths never before revealed in public. Some of the comments she elicited made news in themselves.[39]

Wallace uses confrontational tactics also, provoking subjects and attempting to trap the innocent with his friendly manner—between you and me (and millions of viewers). The subject confesses and, zap, Wallace is on him. Even pallid answers to provocative questions reveal the interviewee's character and personality. Wallace considers an interviewee's appearance on television license to probe beneath the carefully constructed layers of public image.

In interviewing, in all media relations, lack of immediate rapport and veracity must be analyzed. The reporter must ask himself: Why are you telling me this? Are you attempting to cover a problem? Hype stock? Promote a career? Speaking for someone hiding from the press for a variety of reasons? Reporters know, for example, that short-sellers on Wall Street cultivate the press—probably more successfully than most investors. (They're using the Internet, too, as several recent incidents illustrate.) Highly competitive reporters seek the kind of hard-hitting, insider information the shorts appear to be peddling. Leaking is part of sourcing. Journalism's mythology requires knowing powerful people who leak information for their own or a superior's advantage. Reporters must examine the dynamics of the leak and be judicious using a tip. If a reporter becomes known as a conduit, he jeopardizes his position with other sources and his publication.

BATTLING POOR PERCEPTIONS:
NAVISTAR AND IACOCCA

Businessmen are most reluctant to protest poor reporting, even though many in the media say they welcome reasoned, honest responses. Some executives fear future problems or second- and third-day articles that only drag out the event or bring it to the attention of even more people. The echo effect—continuing stories on the same or similar subject—magnifies the visibility and damage. When a situation is protracted and seriously damaging or unfair to a company, business leaders feel increasingly forced to take the offensive.

Influencing the public toward your company, its products, even its problems demands innovative approaches tailored to the situation. Many look only to the top, visible players, thus overlooking grass roots influentials. Mary Ann Pires, president of a public affairs/public relations counseling firm, urges attention to these "real influentials," particularly as a part of an overall grassroots effort—a "value-added" dimension to the total campaign.

Calling this Third Party Ally Development, Pires notes that, if handled strategically, it shows returns on the investment from the beginning. It is "incremental investment that pays greater dividends toward maturity!" Although public relations is by nature incremental, some practitioners make "episodic approaches to their alliances and coalitions. Is it really more cost-effective to 'gin-up' a few fast friends" for each major policy issue, Pires asks, than to rely on relationships of trust you've already developed?

Granted: ally development "can by a real budget-buster in the hands of inexperienced or unscrupulous consultants." For hefty fees they build a "bogus coalition" for the moment, but when the legislative or regulatory push is over, they're gone. "The only good news about this abuse," Pires points out, "is that front groups are beginning to wear out their welcome. Increasingly, they're being 'outed' by ligitimate activists. And clients are getting smarter."

Pires offers guidelines to public affairs to avoid "either overlooking a third-party piece in their public affairs planning, or resorting to the cheap imitation brand of coalition:"

- Would our position be greatly enhanced if others, with no connection to our company or industry and not vested in the issue, agreed with us. Wouldn't the company be best served by support from legitimate, long-standing, public-policy–savvy organizations rather than by more "marginal"—or sometimes fictitious—ones?

- Is the company's position so intellectually bankrupt that no one but those whom we have to co-opt would agree with us?
- Isn't it prudent to build relationships beyond a specific issue.
- Has the agency being considered developed third-party allies? Has it truly motivated other groups to act, or is it merely name-dropping?
- Will the firm hired "take the pledge" not to benefit from this assignment at the expense of our potential allies?

Pires concludes that reputable third-party groups will be around—and influential—for a long time. They have staying power. An adroit one-time strategic investment in building sound relationships with them will provide substantial returns.[40]

Donald D. Lennox, when chairman and CEO of the International Harvester Company (now Navistar), talked publicly of reckless reporting that first worsened his company's ordeal, then unfairly ignored its turnaround. Harvester apparently was having a banner year in 1979: a record $369 million in profits and revenues of $8.4 billion. The future looked bright, at least to the outside. Despite the fact that Harvester was a high-cost producer and other sour signals, management continued to be optimistic—too optimistic as it turned out. Measured against the reality of Harvester's performance, Lennox explained, this optimism was creating credibility gaps with customers, lenders, vendors, and the media, which "recorded the unfolding drama in meticulous, if not always accurate detail." Negative speculation was increased. Caught in a perception bind, Harvester had to make corrective actions abundantly apparent. First, the CEO Archie McCardell resigned. Drastic measures were taken: severe cutbacks in plant production, sales of assets not deemed critical to ongoing business, furloughs, and layoffs. In spring 1982, the media saw news in this saga of a deteriorating giant. "Unfortunately, their research was weak," comments Lennox. "They went beyond reporting facts," injecting their own reactions. Competitors used the quotes to sell against Harvester. Vendors began to question open-account terms.

Harvester's management felt that the media had pushed them virtually to the wall, only to ignore their nascent turnaround. "Financially troubled," "ailing," or "failing" seemed inseparable adjectives to Harvester's name. "They left us high and dry, our reputation in tatters and our credibility all but lost." Many publics important to Harvester were being hammered by adverse publicity. The company decided its only option was to counterattack. First, they committed scarce dollars and management time to the first corporate advertising campaign in Harvester's history, "On Track . . . and Moving Ahead," supported by supplier newsletters, employee communications, and word of mouth. Executives visited lending institutions, company locations, and major vendors. Lennox concluded that, although the price was high in terms of time, dollars, employee morale, and customer confidence, Harvester finally could tell market and customers, "The commitment is forever."

What did Harvester learn? Lennox cites mistakes in what was said and how. "For too long our public forecasts were overly optimistic; we should have been more realistic. We were not as candid, forthcoming or accessible to the press as was in the company's interest." However, the executive also noted the almost cavalier treatment dished out by large segments of the press, seemingly obsessed by writing the company's obituary. "When the patient did not die, we became a non-event, left by the media publicly bruised and battered." Lennox concludes, "When the media reports speculation of coming events as facts, when they imply inside sources when it is pure speculation, I believe they have assumed an irresponsible position. Corporate management must be factual, honest, and forthright, make certain they keep the media informed. . . . I believe the media assumes the same responsibilities when they enter into the dialogue."[41]

In January 1986, Harvester changed its name to Navistar: the final proud recovery. The new name, necessitated by a divestiture of the farm equipment business to Tenneco, Inc., was heralded by an advertising blitz. Ads spoke of crises past: "we weathered one of the most difficult series of crises any American corporation has ever faced." They complimented employees as magnificent, responding to every adversity with hard work, determination, savvy, and guts. After citing financial accomplishments, Navistar pointed out that all the experts had predicted imminent doom. Bankruptcy had been a specter.

Although Lee Iacocca gained phenomenal positive attention for both his management successes and his autobiography, he assessed media coverage of Chrysler's financial troubles much as Lennox did. First, the press jumped the gun by leaking the announcement of his switch to Chrysler from Ford before he had accepted the new position. Then, press coverage of the financial bailout offered much silly advice. Tom Wicker of *The New York Times* suggested that Chrysler devote its energies to building mass transit equipment instead of automobiles. Great cosmic thinking, but what about market and overseas competition? Editorial cartoonists had a marvelous time. *The Wall Street Journal* called the loans "Laetrile for Chrysler" in one headline. Editorially, the *Journal* urged that Chrysler "be put out of its misery," "let them die with dignity." Angered by what he considered abusive freedom of the press, Iacocca in a letter to the editor accused the *Journal* of running every single item of bad news, but none of the more hopeful.

Even loan guarantees did not convince *The Wall Street Journal*. "We had enough money," were a restructured company, with a new management, the right product, and quality, still the *Journal* kept pointing out that the economy could get worse, as could car sales: "Chrysler, having cut muscle as well as fat, is still in a weak state."

Given such coverage, Iacocca argued, it was not surprising the public had trouble understanding what was going on. Even the terms confused: "bail out," although better than handout, implies an inadequate crew that needed help. "We were portrayed as a big monolithic company that did not deserve help." Actually, Iacocca countered, Chrysler was an "amalgam of little groups—suppliers, dealers, and small businessmen, not fat cats, that needed a helping hand, not a hand out. Many people thought we were asking for gifts, or had received $1 billion in cash in a brown paper bag and never had to repay it."

To control public damage and explain Chrysler's new resolves, Iacocca reluctantly became the spokesman for the corporate advertising campaign. He feared—unnecessarily as it turned out—that the external pitchman wears out his welcome in a disposable society, fickle about its heroes. Actually, Iacocca's caution was prudent. Tying a product or corporate image too closely to any one individual, CEO or celebrity, is risky. The Marlboro Man model died of lung cancer. Victor Kiam's pitches for razors suffered from inept remarks about women athletes. Hertz canceled its long association with O. J. Simpson when he was indicted for murder. And think of poor David Thomas. How will his heart surgery impact his advertising role for Wendy's hamburgers? Seemingly very little. Iacocca, advertising visibility, and the respect he gained for successfully turning around a large company beset by difficulties in a very competitive market and a soft economy, prompted another theme in *The Wall Street Journal*: his hankering for public office.[42] Despite many wooings, he never did run.

In 1996, an MBA student looked back at public relations' role in Chrysler's recovery, nay survival. His analysis started in the late 1970s when Chrysler teetered on the edge of bankruptcy. Years of management miscues resulted in inefficient manufacturing that fostered massive overproduction. Adversarial labor relations had exacerbated an already high cost-structure, "ill advised acquisitions of second-rate auto producers in Europe, South America and Asia had drained scarce resources needed for new product development."[43]

Not only did its competitors, General Motors and Ford, enjoy a lower cost-structure, but Chrysler's product-line focused on larger gas-guzzling cars, including RVs, vans, and large passenger cars. Staggered by two economic shocks in 1979, the fall of the Shah of Iran followed by an oil crisis, then the U.S. recession of 1979–80, consumer confidence and auto sales plummeted. Rumors began to circulate of an impending Chrysler cash shortage and possible bankruptcy.

"Chrysler effectively used myriad public relations and communications tools to elicit the support of its core constituencies, including its employees, unions, vast dealer network, the political establishment in Washington D.C. and the general public." Chrysler first turned to its employees to reduce its financial burden. To stem the red ink, the company laid off approximately 15,500 employees in 1979 and 1980 for a total annual cost-savings of $500 million.[44] Iacocca handled most of the firings of senior people himself, explaining forthrightly the company's reasons. A weak financial condition muted criticism from employees and the press. "The company was portrayed as having no other choice."

Despite past tooth-and-nail negotiations with the UAW, Iacocca addressed its leadership committee twice. "He spoke in a relaxed, easy-going fashion and connected with his blue-collar audience by using 'filthy epithets.'" He presented Chrysler's condition using easy-to-read charts and graphs. To head off criticism that he and other senior executives were not making any sacrifices, he agreed to cut his own salary to $1 per year from well over $300,000 and reduced executive salaries by 5 to 10 per cent per year.[45] Iacocca won the union leaders over. In a move unique at the time, Union President Douglas Fraser agreed to join Chrysler's Board of Directors.

"Once the wage cut backs had been implemented, Iacocca went to every Chrysler manufacturing plant to speak directly with the workers. He worked each like a local politician, thanking workers for their support."[46] "Such direct and adroit communication from senior management, and Lee Iacocca, helped Chrysler effectively communicate with employees being let go, with union leaders, and with the workers in plants."[47]

Iacocca viewed dealers as a vital link to the car-buying public. Dealer relations were already poor. Not only did they have virtually no say in the cars, but poor quality and a dismal repair record created resentment among dealers, who bore the brunt of consumer complaints. Iacocca asked dealer spokesmen to list complaints and areas where Chrysler's activities created hardship. "At a week-long grievance session, Iacocca laid out the grim picture at Chrysler, acknowledging its failures with the dealers, and outlined solutions to each complaint. To boost morale, he showed slides of the 1980 Chrysler car lineup and explained features that would make them marketable."[48] In an inspirational plea for teamwork, Iacocca used various sports analogies. One dealer said, "He had us mesmerized. We were hypnotized. . . . We were ready to go out and slay the dragon."[49] Iacocca also improved dealer relations by hiring a trusted dealer-relations expert, listening to dealer concerns and responding quickly, and using emotional and inspirational appeals to win concessions.

Even with streamlined operations and staff, and with employees and dealers aboard, Iacocca still needed financial guarantees from Washington. The company continued to plunge toward bankruptcy in mid-1979. A bipartisan political media consultant, Ken Duskin, positioned Iacocca not as a car salesman, but as a leader, responsible for saving thousands of Chrysler jobs. "By extension, the public would be convinced that by buying a Chrysler, they too would help save these workers' jobs."

Conscious of image, Duskin scratched early commercials showing Iacocca behind a desk. Now he was on the factory floor, an auto assembly line manned by serious hard-working employees in the background. "Carefully, the image was crafted of Chrysler as an underdog fighting for its life with the automotive heavyweights, GM and Ford." Ads implored Americans to test-drive a Chrysler before they bought a competitor's car. As Chrysler and Iacocca grew more confident, the message became bolder. *'If You Can Find a Better Car—Buy It!'* A patriotic tone was introduced by subtle use of flag imagery and patriotic background music. It tracked a distinctly more pro-American theme used successfully in President Reagan's 1980 campaign. By wrapping itself in the flag, Chrysler rode this wave of patriotism to convince the public that buying a Chrysler was tantamount to a vote in favor of America and the American worker.

Lars Larsen, Iacocca's hand-picked Vice President for Public Affairs, decided Congress and the country would not act until Chrysler staged a calculated morality play. In August 1979, not only was Chrysler's reputation dismal in the popular press, but the conservative business press opposition was especially fierce. Larsen's job was to help Iacocca counteract negative press and sway both public opinion and public sentiment in Chrysler's favor. He used standard PR techniques most effectively. He coached Iacocca to testify before the House and Senate Committees on the loan guarantees: Keep your temper in check; be direct, honest, and forceful; demonstrate that not only are 150,000 Chrysler jobs at stake, but that 2 million Americans and the country would be severely impacted by the ripple effect; argue that there is precedent for loan guarantees to other major industrial companies.

Iacocca also highlighted his strong free-market beliefs, that government regulation was a main cause of Chrysler's precarious situation. Adroitly, he did not mention that other auto producers faced the same regulations, but were not in Chrysler's condition. Nearly 2,000 dealers were brought to Washington, D.C., to lobby congressmen from their home districts. Each dealer was briefed on the day's message—talking points to coordinate the overall message. Each congressman received hard data documenting his or her district's economic ties to Chrysler—jobs to be lost and the economic impact. "These proved to be very effective in convincing the congressmen of the 'dire' need to vote in favor of the loan guarantees."

Nor did Iacocca scant the public, who had seen months of bad press in major newspapers. To counter the negative stories, full-page newspaper ads gave Chrysler's position succinctly in a plain, direct style. Questions raised included:

- Would America be better off without Chrysler?
- Does the loan guarantee set a dangerous precedent?
- Does Chrysler have a future?
- Is Chrysler's management strong enough to turn the company around?

Essentially advocacy advertising, they sought to elicit support for the "New Chrysler," not to implore a product purchase. Iacocca personalized the ads first by signing each ad, inviting the public to write to him with questions and comments, and eventually appearing as spokesman in television advertising. These efforts successfully shifted public opinion in Chrysler's favor. The final and successful effort was to gain President Carter's support. "In late 1979 all of these efforts paid off. Chrysler got a $1.5 billion loan guarantee, the largest in American history." However, the company was not yet out of the financial woods. It had to transform its image with the car-buying public and address weak car sales.

Iacocca's ad agency, Kenyon & Eckhardt, urged him to take his message to television. A nationwide campaign featured Iacocca. Today when CEO's regularly tout their products and companies, it is difficult to appreciate the debate. Some feared the plan would backfire, "that Iacocca's positive spin would appear false in the face of negative images of Chrysler in the general media." They were protective of Iacocca's personal image. A general consideration, then and now, was tying public image exclusively to one person. Should that individual leave or die, or his reputation be tarnished, the good messages are negated. (Helmsley Hotels advertised the queen, Leona, until she went to jail.) Iacocca was a great success. He sought to convince the public that Chrysler was not going bankrupt, the quality of its products was improving, and management was innovative. At first, ads tacked Iacocca onto the end of traditional car ads. "I'm not asking you to buy one of our cars on faith, I'm asking you to compare."[50] Soon advertising was changed to position Iacocca more politically, appealing to patriotism. Each sale of a Chrysler became a "vote" for its chairman.

The advertising/public relations efforts eventually became much more than an appeal for loan guarantees. It convinced the nation and its top leaders that Chrysler was a company that deserved a second chance. Its survival would benefit the U.S. economy. Had

Chrysler not used many forms of public relations and communications effectively to gain support from its core constituencies, employees, unions, dealers, the political establishment in Washington, D.C., and the general public, there is little doubt it would have gone bankrupt. Iacocca became such a national personality that he was considered as a candidate for senator from Pennsylvania, even President.

CREATING IMAGES: FOLLOWING FADS

Media relations are often used and sometimes abused in creating images of companies, countries, and their leaders. The persona created for presidents and other political leaders are much more visible and much better documented than the quiet work of corporate communications people. However, there are principles and techniques in common.

In *The Splendid Deception*, Hugh Gregory Gallagher explains how the press, secret service, staff, and family cooperated in presenting Franklin D. Roosevelt as vigorous and physically fit—a carefully constructed and artfully maintained image. Throughout his presidency, photographs of FDR being carried, crawling, or fallen were banned. Someone, usually a family member, always bore his weight or helped him rise and locked his heavy leg braces, which were blackened so they would not be obvious.

Just before his death, the President's few public appearances were carefully arranged, widely publicized, and heavily photographed. His skillful press secretary, Steven Early, made full use of releases, statements, short press conferences, and radio talks. Roosevelt continued to dominate the war news, but far from the public eye and the press, who saw only what he wished them to. More recently, it was a well-hidden fact that President Jimmy Carter—in contrast to the poor peasant farmer image he projected—was a millionaire, personally worth $5 million as an agribusiness corporate executive.[51]

In business, a known and controversial image-creator and fad follower was automobile executive John DeLorean. He spun such a convincing legend that even as his automobile company unraveled, most reporters were still reluctant to look at him closely and critically.

Only his arrest on cocaine charges sparked critical attention. (He was ultimately acquitted.) Until then, DeLorean had crafted well.

Early in his career, he spoke to 1960s sensibilities, espousing corporate social responsibility, minority employment, and the "ethical" car. Customers would get not only a car, such as the GTO or, later, a DeLorean model, but also a part of his personal Horatio Alger dream. The automotive executive excelled in selling the American Dream back to the country. Meanwhile, he molded himself to the current fashion in appearance and personal life. In looks, he played the classic corporate nonconformist. In a day of Brooks Brothers uniforms in corporate suites, he tended to wear turtleneck sweaters, bell-bottom jeans, and a peace symbol on a chain around his neck. However, he disclaimed the maverick role. Professionally, DeLorean left the less-newsworthy field of engineering—many attest that he was an extremely talented executive, a highly skilled engineer, and marketing manager—for the more fertile and faddish fields of finance and public relations.

He became a feast for the news-hungry press. *The Detroit Press* found him unusually accessible and always good copy. He came across as brash, egotistic, energetic, and optimistic. His departure from General Motors was portrayed as high moral principle: a gutsy career change and a conquest of midlife crises, immortalized by Gail Sheehy in *Passages*. He could discuss the Beach Boys, quote Montaigne, or mention ruminations on human misery by social historian Peter Gay. DeLorean listened intently and turned encounters with reporters into casual conversation. The press was caught up with his idea of producing an ethical car. Reporters did not check easily verifiable facts—such as patents granted—or look for the substance behind the bold rhetoric. Investors and reporters alike were sucked in. Much about DeLorean could blind the most cynical eye.

The maverick auto engineer was too compelling to be deflated by tough journalism. His impressive stack of press clippings was a potent weapon. (Clips are impressive, but usually a meaningless indication of effective publicity. How many reached target audiences? Told your story accurately? What are the demographics?) No other entrepreneur in business history used publicity as well to amass capital. His pristine façade began to crumble. Court documents in lawsuits against his company—and later against him personally—filed across the nation told the other story. They ran alongside laudatory media accounts "like photographic negatives."

Foolishly, DeLorean came to believe his press, became a prisoner of his own outsized vision. Any executive is headed for big public trouble when he believes the publicity he's paid for. Like the Wizard of Oz, DeLorean scrambled behind a curtain to maintain his credibility, with little concern about the methods he used to keep his reputation and investment intact. But the glamour he cultivated made him prime meat for the media. Periodicals, previously circumspect about his car company, began recycling negative stories. Industry executives who once had only kind words or silence about DeLorean circulated anecdotes. Even DeLorean's careful cosmetic presence was falling away. Boarding a transport bus in a blue prison jump suit, manacles on his hands and legs, did little for his image.[52] As John Hill counseled wisely many years ago, public relations is not a cosmetic; it cannot put a pretty face on a bad situation or an untruth.

Even when broke, divorced, and under indictment, DeLorean still cleverly promoted his image. In an interview in San Francisco, where DeLorean was promoting his book, a reporter described him as craggy, the image of a macho national treasure. In maintaining his innocence, DeLorean comes across as a modern-day Job, who must endure, persevere, and survive—a scrapper, down but not out.[53]

JOURNALISTS CRITICIZE THEMSELVES

One reason the media falls for the DeLorean fad and others is lack of rigorous self-criticism. Analytic members of the press do call peers on the carpet. Tom Goldstein, dean of Columbia University's School of Journalism, did in *The News at Any Cost: How Journalists Compromise Their Ethics to Shape the News.* He points out that reporters chasing a citizen down the street with cameras rolling paints a false picture that no subsequent explanation can eradicate. Reporters can entrap the unwary, ambush the unsuspecting, and assume false identification to gain access and gather information. Reporters have gained employment in plants, nursing homes, and elsewhere to research abuses otherwise cloaked from their view. Fair? Responsible journalism? The debate rages both among journalists and executives and in the courts. Some reporters justify the ambush interview when requests for a formal interview are either turned down or are expected to be. Surprise, however, yields dramatic footage, catches the subject saying something he might not have or might have stated in a less damaging, less headline-grabbing way. The camera allows no qualifiers. Little damage control. Large cash settlements may chill these tactics. Will Tom Brokaw be so quick to label after NBC paid Richard Jewell an estimated $500,000? And Jewell's lawyer plans more suits against the media.

Gotcha journalism backfired for ABC's *Primetime Live*. This technique—where reporters insinuate themselves into the belly of some beast and discover something shocking or newsworthy—had become an accepted staple of T.V. news, until Food Lion. It raised questions such as: Do the news hounds go too far? Have they crossed the line from protecting the public interest to getting scoops? Reporters for *Primetime Live* finagled their way into Food Lion stores for a report that accused the supermarkets of selling spoiled meat. In January 1997, a North Carolina jury decided that ABC had gone too far and awarded Food Lion more than $5.5 million in damages. Interestingly, the food store chain neither sued for libel nor disputed the findings, but because producers submitted fake résumés of network employees to get jobs.[54] Although some media mavens dismissed the trivial complaints, others foresaw a definite chill on investigative reports. The main issue, particularly for smaller T.V. stations and newspapers with very slim profit margins, is: even if you win, the legal and image costs may threaten your survival.

Aggressive reporters use other durable—sometimes dubious—techniques: secret taping of the unwary, reconstruction of an event long after it has occurred, use of undercover reporters, lulling the subject by faking note-taking or taking none at all; appearing very sympathetic to tease out information; reading memos on unattended desks, even borrowing them for photocopying. During a highly visible time for one company, the chairman's secretary returned to her desk to find a reporter with a highly confidential telephone log in his hand. The important lesson here is: rather than argue, it is easier to be secure. Keep sensitive documents out of sight and accompany reporters while they are on the premises. Presidential Deputy Press Secretary Larry Speakes created an amusing piece of mischief when he left memos directly concerning press corps arrangements lying around on staff desks. The press found them and howled.

As Goldstein also points out, sometimes reporters just plain go too far. "They advise politicians, assist prosecutors, fabricate quotes and events, and, of course, make mistakes, then refuse to admit error."[55] One criticism of television coverage of the 1985 TWA hostage crisis was that the journalists seemed to be conducting diplomacy by network; they had become actors rather than observers.

Reporters cannot withdraw empty-handed. Nor can they fully understand an event without direct observation: seeing, smelling, touching, or talking to participants. Reporters themselves and their training pose other problems. Until Watergate, and to some degree once again, journalism schools did not attract the best and brightest. Working journalists tend to be young and inexperienced, first working on a newspaper well away from their home or college towns, and then anxiously moving on (and hopefully up) several times in quick succession. They have little time to fully understand a locality, or even a major subject, before they are off on a new adventure.[56] And one becomes a journalist when one declares it. Little formal control exists over the "profession"—there are no entrance requirements, no explicit or really enforceable code of ethics, and no system for weeding out incompetents and scoundrels. Even the U.S. Congress gave up attempting to define "journalist."

Mistakes creep in through time pressures and differing interpretations of news. Editors can override reporters: most of the *Time* information damaging to Israel's Defense Minister Ariel Sharon (basis of his suit) was sharpened or changed in New York. To be fair, some mistakes are difficult for a reporter to detect. Sources lie. People genuinely misunderstand each other. But reporters compound these problems when they do not try to understand or do not dig hard or deep enough for facts. The cardinal sin lies in deciding in advance what the story line will be and then finding the facts to fit the theme, or, as in the case of Janet Cooke's *Washington Post* "Jimmygate," (a series on a "created" child involved in drugs), inventing them.

Newspapers are reluctant to admit when they are wrong or don't know. They equivocate, bluster, alibi, and hide behind technicalities, secretaries, or lawyers. Edward R. Murrow once said that the press does not have a thin skin—it has no skin at all. Although newspapers make a great fuss about running minor corrections—address, first names, or letters to the editors—more substantial corrections are rare. And they never catch up with mistakes. If made at all, the correction straggles in days or weeks later, usually in an obscure section of the newspaper.

Perhaps the most frequently asked question is how to correct a very damaging, important media mistake. Here are several ways:

- Monitor the news, always, constantly. Some large corporations and trade associations watch Internet and newswires at all times. a tedious and difficult job, but a necessary first step.
- If the mistake is purely factual, respond immediately. The more often a mistake is repeated, the more data banks it's in, the more damaging it is. This is why politicians have "truth-squads" following their opponents. Correct or spin statements before the next news cycle.
- After anger is slaked, think if correcting the mistake is worth the possible reactions. For years, PR people counseled: "Don't pick fights with people who buy ink by the barrel." Maybe.
- Talk first to the reporter. Even if you know his editor or publisher, don't go over the reporter' head. Build your case on details, facts, financials, not emotional press-bashing.
- If all else fails, seek the newspaper's ombudsman. Larger news organizations, such as *The Washington Post*, designate a respected, usually senior, news person to investigate complaints and report findings in an attempt to reach an equitable resolution.
- One final caution: research your facts before mouthing off. Corrections can be more damaging than the original stories if reporters dig further and find more. One retailer—thinking his image would cloak all—was infuriated by a very critical front-page story in an important business publication. He demanded a meeting with the editorial board. The result? One very mean correction and much tougher coverage ever after.

How reporters precipitate events or watch immolation or other deaths is much discussed, more in the public arena than in business. In Japan, the media sent out platoons, overwhelming the alleged mastermind of an elaborate scheme to sell bogus gold certificates. The press stalked him, waiting for something to happen. It did. He was murdered in his apartment while newspaper reporters and photographers jostled each other for a better peek through cracks around the door. They did not call the police. The incident created a great deal of soul-searching over the essential tension between being a human being and being a professional observer. Should journalists, or, even more, photographers, intervene during wartime shootings or immolations? To prevent a killing on the street? Even when former Senator Robert J. Dole tumbled off a stage during the 1996 presidential campaign the question was raised: should a photographer help break the fall or get the picture? One helped, another got the shot.

New Journalism, which burgeoned after Watergate—intermingling fact with fiction—further complicated these problems. Writers embellished quotes, burrowed into a character's interior thoughts, created scenes that might have happened, but in fact had not. Characters were composites of several people, laced with imagination. Some of the best-known journalists and novelists were involved: Thomas Wolfe, Gay Talese, Norman Mailer, Truman Capote, and Gail Sheehy. These authors argued that since perfect objectivity is impossible, their only choice in these either/or times is to abdicate to absolute subjectivity. The reporter became the center of interest rather than the real world he was supposed to be picturing or interpreting. Farther afield still are those who make up quotes and scenes. The wall between advertising and editorial has crumbled, too. How much air time, particularly on local news shows, is devoted to shilling for books, records, movies, plays, or celebrities? Seldom are viewers warned.

More stringent editing and requests for sources, an ombudsman to adjudicate the aggrieved inside or outside the city room, and diminishing the star system would ameliorate these abuses. Attention must be paid soon. Studies consistently report that the media ranks very low in the public's confidence.

NOTES

1. Howard Simons and Joseph A. Califano, Jr., eds., *The Media and Business* (New York: Vintage, 1979), p. ix.
2. Ibid., p. 2.
3. These comments were gathered from various writings and published speeches of Lewis H. Young, including comments at the *Media and Business* sessions and in "The Distorted Image," *Financial Executive*, April 1985, p. 18.
4. Some criticized *The Wall Street Journal*, noting that it had a hammerlock on information and used techniques to protect its image. It broke

the story and was credited with coming clean when actually there was no choice. Also, Winans's wrongdoing, distrust, and betrayal were stressed. The *Journal* was portrayed as a trusting victim, with no question of supervision or the paper's mistakes. See Jeff Blyuskal and Marie Blyuskal, *PR: How the Public Relations Industry Writes the News* (New York: William Morrow, 1985), pp. 178–179.

5. A complete discussion of Behrens's difficulties in getting information can be found in John C. Behrens, *The Typewriter Guerrillas: Closeups of Twenty Top Investigative Reporters* (Chicago: Nelson-Hall, 1997).

6. In their book, *PR*, Jeff and Marie Blyskal cite an estimate that 45 to 50 percent of the business news appearing in *The Wall Street Journal* on a given day was generated by press releases, merely rewrites of stories initiated by public relations people. Even worse are food pages, "a PR man's paradise," entertainment, automobile, real estate, home improvement, and living style pages (p. 28).

7. George E. Reedy, *Lyndon B. Johnson: A Memoir* (New York: Andrews & McMeel, 1982), p. 61.

8. This discussion is distilled from Georgie Anne Geyer, *Buying the Night Flight: The Autobiography of a Woman Foreign Correspondent* (New York: A Laurel/Merloyd Lawrence Book, 1983).

9. Thomas J. Archdeacon, "The High Cost of Living," a review of *The Great Wave: Price Revolutions and the Rhythm of History* by David Hackett Fischer, *The New York Times Book Review*, January 5, 1997, p. 29.

10. Geyer, *Buying the Night Flight*.

11. Max Frankel, "Something Doesn't Like a Wall," *The New York Times Magazine*, January 19, 1997, pp. 18, 20.

12. Readers interested in greater detail of Gulf War media relations should see the author's "Image Makers of Desert Storm: Bush, Powell, and Schwarzkopf" in *The 1,000-Hour War*, ed. Thomas A. McCain and Leonard Shyles (Westport, Conn.: Greenwood Press, 1994) or a longer, unpublished paper "The New PR Pros: The Generals and the Pols."

13. H. G. Bissinger, "The Detective's Story," *Vanity Fair*, February 1997, pp. 114–119, 140–146.

14. Diana Jean Schemo, "Hidden and Haunted Behind the Headlines," *The New York Times*, June 12, 1992, pp. B1,7.

15. Readers interested in a full, very troubling account are directed to Marie Brenner's "American Nightmare: The Ballad of Richard Jewell," *Vanity Fair*, February 1997, pp. 100–107, 150–165, and to Kevin Sack's lengthy report, "A Man's Life Turned Inside Out by Government and Media," *The New York Times*, October 28, 1996, pp. A1, B7.

16. Brenner, "American Nightmare," p. 103.

17. Ibid., p. 104.

18. Ibid., p. 152.

19. Ibid., p. 159.

20. Ibid., p. 162.

21. Ibid., p. 154.

22. Ibid.

23. Max Frankel, "An Olympian Injustice," *The New York Times Magazine*, October 20, 1996, p. 60.

24. Ibid., pp. 60–61.

25. Jeffrey Toobin, "Courtroom vs. Newsroom," *The New Yorker*, January 21, 1997, pp. 5–6.

26. Ibid.

27. Ibid., p. 5.

28. This discussion is drawn from Timothy Crouse, *The Boys on the Bus* (New York: Ballantine, 1972).

29. Formerly, reporters were assigned to cover a police beat or a geographic district; now, in addition, some journalists are assigned to special subjects, such as the environment, or business.

30. An electronic news release—a technique that is increasingly important, but seriously debated within the news industry—is a television segment, usually produced by major public relations firms for a client and then widely distributed free to local stations. The spots carry subtle messages of corporate or national interest. Many foreign nations use them to influence U.S. public opinion on a specific issue. The reporter's voice is recorded separate from the video track, so stations can use their own anchorperson or tailor the script to local interests. Some stations use them entirely without change; others use only portions; still others won't show them at all. Although the technique is not new, wider use and much more sophisticated messages are raising questions of fairness in labeling sources for viewers. Proponents argue that electronic releases merely modernize the written press release—a public relations stock-in-trade for years—and that they provide national and international coverage that smaller stations cannot afford. Pro or con, both sides agree that it's an expensive, although effective, means of getting a message across.

31. Vermont Royster, "End of a Chapter," *The Wall Street Journal*, March 5, 1986, p. 30.

32. Carol Loomis, "Six Handy Rules for Dealing with the Media," *Crosscurrents in Corporate Communications*, No. 14 (New York: Fortune, 1985), pp. 65–68.

33. Elizabeth Podd, business editor of *The Record* in Hackensack, New Jersey, shared these comments with the author in conversation.

34. Walter Guzzardi, Jr., "The Politics of the Press: How to Deal with It," *Crosscurrents in Corporate Communications*, No. 14 (New York: Fortune, 1985), pp. 68–70.

35. Larry Speakes, with Robert Pack, *Speaking Out: Inside the Reagan White House* (New York: Charles Scribner's Sons, 1988), p. 156. A risky tactic, but the only one possible under the circumstances.

36. Material excerpted from a long discussion by Bernard Charland, "No Comment: Moving Toward a Measured and Managed Media Response," *Journal of Corporate Public Relations*, 1996–1997, pp. 91–115, augmented by the author's own valuation of "No comment."

37. Merrie Spaeth, "What You Can Learn from Brokaw & Co." *The Wall Street Journal*, January 6, 1997, p. A12.

38. Geyer, *Buying the Night Flight*, p. 98.

39. Oriana Fallaci, *Interview with History*, trans. John Sheply (Boston: Houghton Mifflin, 1976), pp. 9–12.

40. Mary Ann Pires, "Time to Cultivate Real 'Influentials,'" *Impact*, December 1996, p.1.

41. Donald D. Lennox, "Reckless Reporting: The International Harvester Ordeal," in *Crosscurrents in Corporate Communications*, No. 14 (New York: Fortune, 1985), pp. 60–64.

42. Lee Iacocca's comments were distilled from *Iacocca: An Autobiography* (New York: Bantam Books, 1984).

43. George M. Dugan, "The Role of Public Relations in the Recovery of Chrysler Corporation," as partial requirement for an MBA at the Graduate School of Business, Fordham University, Winter 1996.

44. Iacocca, *Iacocca*, p. 189.

45. Ibid., p. 229.

46. Dugan, "Role of Public Relations in the Recovery of Chrysler Corporation," p. 6.

47. Ibid., p. 15.

48. Ibid., p. 20, and Iacocca, *Iacocca*, p. 156.

49. David Abodaher, *Iacocca: A Biography* (New York: William Morrow, 1987), p. 138.

50. Dugan, "Role of Public Relations in the Recovery of Chrysler, p. 22.

51. Ron Nessen, *It Sure Looks Different from the Inside* (New York: Playboy Press, 1978) p. 299.

52. This discussion was developed from various press reports, conversations, and Hillel Levin's *Grand Delusions: The Cosmic Career of John DeLorean* (New York: Viking, 1983).

52. *San Francisco Examiner*, October 29, 1985, pp. 1, 6.

54. "The Gotcha That Backfired," *The New York Times*, News in Review, January 26, 1997, p. 2.

55. *The Wall Street Journal*, August 21, 1985, p. 1.

56. A poll taken among journalists in the fall of 1985 reported a greater lack of credibility toward younger journalists, who were described as tran-

sients who frequently shuffled jobs and had fewer community ties. More than their older counterparts, they were likely to shrug off credibility problems as inevitable and were less inclined to fault the press for lack of public confidence. These journalists tended to be younger, better educated, less religious, and somewhat wealthier than the public. See *The New York Times,* October 30, 1985, p. A13.

3

Planning the Unplannable
Surviving Communications Crises

A good P.R. program is like a guardrail on a cliff, not an ambulance at the bottom

—ARLEN SOUTHERN

Episodes that get people and instituitions in trouble are not always objectively the most important.

—JAMES FALLOWS

When kidnapping corporate executives was providing fun and funds for Latin American terrorists some years ago, a senior international executive, home from South America for a business meeting, asked his CEO what the company would do when he was kidnaped. The CEO, who looked as if he thought his trusted colleague had taken leave of his senses, replied: "Don't you mean 'if?' " "No, 'when'—it's just a matter of time."

Exactly right. Business crises are no longer the exception, but to be expected, even inevitable. Crises fanned by the oxygen of publicity are more visible and severe, arouse greater concern than ever before. They can damage, even terminally, a company and individual careers. When not well handled, they produce interminable legal suits and government investigations that disrupt operations and absorb management time for years. A more aggressive media, a volatile economy, weakening of respect for business organizations and those who run them, and quickened global competition signal danger. But the unimaginative think it, like automobile accidents, will always happen to the other guy.

Reality may be sobering, but it still has not convinced some managers to think of disaster and failure, not just success. While speaking to parents, then Brown University President Vartan Gregorian cautioned that students must be prepared for defeats, not just victories. Historians who dissect why the British Empire succeeded would learn far more from studying why Spain failed. Positive mindsets almost determine a manager to fail. He does not know, much less imagine, what he will face. Without planning, he finds himself coping with an all-out disaster that he might have managed and contained when it was a mere disturbance; planning is akin to catching a cancer before it metastasizes and threatens life. In both vigilance and early diagnoses are vital.

Despite war story after war story, and costly examples in any day's news, planning is surprisingly difficult to inculcate in a bureaucracy. Possible future concerns, which may never come to pass, deflect the time, attention, and priorities of busy managers. Operating executives trained in an immediate, pragmatic, can-do attitude, find planning for amorphous contingencies a mind-stretch. They find it even more difficult when forced to accept surprise, disorderliness, lack of control, and a good, quick solution. If the communications officer attempts to drum up interest in contingency planning, he is often put down as being a doomsayer or as trying to establish a power base.

Assessing the Risk

Risk and magnitude, visibility and liability vary enormously from crisis to crisis, from industry to industry. Some wounds are self-inflicted: tenders, plant closings, executives departing abruptly or staying too long. Others—plane crashes, oil spills, chemical leaks, and product defects—burst violently on a company.

Gerald Meyers, former CEO of American Motors Corporation, groups business crises into nine categories: changes in public perception, sudden market shifts, product failures, management succession, cash drain, labor strife, outside attack, adverse international events, and regulation or deregulation of an industry.[1]

Several factors escalate or minimize the risks. First, the quality and thoroughness of a company's preparation. Developing a philosophic base and a personal psychological gyroscope determines success infinitely more often than those eternally suggested checklists of opinion leaders, food service, and other basic how-to-dos best delegated to staff. The Johnson & Johnson credo, for example, provided a shared foundation for action by all the executives involved in Tylenol recalls. Other practitioners gain objectivity and support from a circle of battle-tested confidants.

The where, when, and who involved in a given event often determine the intensity and intelligence of media coverage. A plane crash into a remote Andean mountain peak, in which no Americans are killed, warrants a paragraph—if that—tucked away somewhere in the newspaper, and little or no television coverage, unless some spectacular pictures are available. Television feeds on dramatic visuals.

But if the crash occurs near the commuter rush on the Fourteenth Street Bridge in Washington, D.C., with several prominent people aboard, television crews will flock in. Proximity of a television station and a film crew heightens the chance of coverage. The San Francisco earthquake of 1989 was widely and quickly covered. The crews were at Candlestick Park to cover the World Series. So does the hour: close to the evening news. So do English-speaking news sources. The Air Florida crash in 1983 occurred in just such circumstances, and illustrates how abundance of human interest in accidents, hostages, or corporate struggles can obscure important news. The heroics of badly injured people struggling in the ice-caked Potomac River, others sacrificing their lives, and dramatic helicopter rescues pushed aside news coverage of possible faulty de-icing of the aircraft's wings and other weak operational procedures during a heavy snow storm. The 1996 crash of TWA Flight 800 illustrates how location, time, media markets, dramatic shots of flames off Long Island Sound, and human interest escalates coverage. When politicians and families became the focus of news coverage, the investigation was adjusted to their demands—a powerful but dangerous portent for future investigations, mostly media-driven.

Air disasters also illustrate differing cultural reactions. When a Japan Air Lines plane crashed on a mountaintop in 1985, the company's president apologized in person to the families of the dead and offered to resign. The maintenance chief, after dealing with relatives of survivors day after day, committed suicide. This is quite different behavior from that of the president of a United States airline, who might feel equally responsible and grief-stricken, but who probably would not visit the crash site, much less the families of the dead and the survivors. To succeed, PR must address the culture of country and company.

Location also determines how much attention a crisis gets and for how long. When a major oil spill occurred off Santa Barbara, California, the news media and influential people—particularly fervid environmentalists—were nearby. Night after night, shots of ever-encroaching oil spills and birds, their feathers slicked with ugly black oil, were broadcast. No lives were endangered and within a year the ocean would have washed away the oil, but the pollution was made to appear life-threatening and permanent. *Exxon Valdez* was not the worst or largest oil spill, but Exxon's tardy media relations, lack of CEO visibility, and the beautiful Prince William Sound ensured damaging, extensive, and prolonged coverage.

Who is involved matters greatly also. The Bhopal disaster was reported widely, but imagine the coverage if the tragedy had happened at a sister plant in Institute, West Virginia. It offers reporters relatively easy access, modest travel expenses, and no language barrier.

"When" weighs in exposure, too. One reason Union Carbide's continuing troubles gained so much attention was August. News holes—the space newspapers allot for editorial material—must be filled. When many good stories compete, some are sacrificed or cut severely. But in August, normally a slow news month, reporters must dig for stories. Hence, Union Carbide's continuing saga was a godsend for reporters who could milk a different aspect every day and fill space. So are hurricanes over holiday weekends and fires when the President is vacationing.

The news lull between Christmas and the New Year is another unfortunate time for the subject of bad news. In December 1983, Charles Z. Wick, then director of the U.S. Information Agency and a friend of President Reagan's, was reported to have taped numerous conversations with major administration figures. Each day another aspect was reported: William Safire of *The New York Times* wrote several columns commenting on the taping.

Time of day and day of week influence coverage also, but less than many communicators hope. Releasing news just before deadline, on the theory that reporters will be too harassed to ask searching questions, doesn't work anymore. Once corporate communicators would release bad news late Friday afternoon. With the stock market closed, the financial impact might be delayed or softened. Who reads the Saturday papers? Faultless in theory, but wrong in practice. Surveys show that day, even season, affect serious business readership very little. Another illusion: by Monday *The Wall Street Journal* will have fresh stories to crowd out the old old news. Maybe. The *Journal* doesn't neglect weekend news. Its readers willingly wait to read financial and business interpretations.

The wise executive knows whether his operations and industry are hot topics: extractive, petroleum, and exploration companies; electric utilities (particularly those operating nuclear plants), transportation, food and drug manufacturers, and chemical industries rate the highest. If media attention has already been drawn to an operation, particular care and sensitivity must be given to it. When the press is watching chemical leaks, sexual harassment, and bank failures closely, it behooves any executive to be absolutely sure his company is squeaky clean, or to correct abuses before they go public.

The most damaging crises are often concealed in deceptively trivial routine occurrences. One assumes and doesn't question or check. When the devil wears horns, he's not dangerous. You know exactly what you face.

Putting an incident in perspective when all around you are seeking sensation or seeing disaster is not easy, but essential. Frequent spills or minor fires in a factory, which the company knows are ordinary and unthreatening, may alarm a lay public and reporters, even if they are carefully explained, but surely will if they are not.

Usually the early signals of trouble are ignored or played down, thus allowing the problem to reach a boiling point. Even when a crisis goes public, insiders uncritically try to minimize its importance, to relegate it to a passing blip on corporate radar. One bank in serious trouble took the most leisurely route—mailing press releases even to important local newspapers. It said nothing at all to customers, employees, civic leaders, and financial analysts. Opinions were formed and the battle just about over before the bank's message was heard. The window of opportunity for a company to get its message out shrinks as communication speeds up. Currently, it's about 8 to 12 hours. After that, few people are listening. Opinions have been formed. When the import finally is banged home, too many executives react with impatience, seeking a quick fix, slashing at the Gordian knot; or they may say nothing, overreact, or adopt a siege mentality.

Corporate reasons to remain silent may be compelling internally, but pose serious difficulties externally. Lawyers worry about the liability involved in talking. Sometimes there's disagreement about who should speak. That should be settled long before trouble hits. Some executives are simply scared to face a hostile press for the first time. Others talk tough but carry a wet noodle.

Modern technology complicates crisis management. Machines supply an abundance of information—fast. Its very bulk and immediacy leave no time for reflection or for broader decision-making. Such loss of command and control downgrades individual judgment and evaporates wiggle room. When facts, photographs, media, and peers all are clamoring for a decision, it must be made—hasty, incomplete, and incorrect as it may be. Imagine the CEO who responded to queries with, "I want to think about that."

Keeping your head while all around you are tense, afraid, or looking for the dramatic is key. So are careful, realistic assessments. Is the crisis created or deeply rooted? Will it fade away or escalate? Has the company done all it reasonably can? Should it stay in the fight? Or is it a no-win situation in which the company should cut its losses? One lawyer wisely advised his client to drop his suit, after he was involved in an auto accident. He had run a red light, hit a car containing three nuns, and the judge's name was O'Leary.

WHO PLANS? AFTER THE DAMAGE OR BEFORE?

Despite all the horror stories daily in the business news, many companies and their executives are still abysmally unprepared. Many palm off crisis planning to the communications department and then forget to ask what became of it. If the communicator pushes the project, he probably won't be listened to and will be ignored when the inevitable happens.

In June 1984, Western Union commissioned a study by Burson-Marsteller Research to discover who plans, how and when, among *Fortune 1000* industrial corporations and 500 service companies.[2] About half the respondents (53 percent) had plans, many established in the past five years in response to previous troubles. Industrial accidents ranked first among motivations, followed by environmental problems, investor relations (in some ways this ranking is surprisingly high), hostile takeovers, rumor suppression, strike notices, proxy situations, product recall, and government regulatory problems. Also mentioned by respondents were data communications breakdown, natural disaster, fraud or embezzlement, bankruptcy, and industry or service risks. Understandably, four out of five companies (81 percent) handled crises themselves, although outside counselors may have assisted in the planning process.

Normally, planning is divided into two levels. The first involves noncatastrophic, usually local, often mechanical problems, such as water main breaks, commuter train breakdowns, or power outages. More extensive plans cover a widespread, sudden catastrophe—a large plant explosion, transportation accident, or bank failure—that must be handled with great urgency and speed.

Important as plans are, many are as desiccated as toy soldiers on a papier-mâché battlefield under glass in a museum. All the *Sturm und Drang*, the blood and personal pain, are drained. Such plans prepare a manager, psychologically or operationally, for a major crisis about as well as the recruiting sergeant prepares an enlistee for combat.

Among "important" details listed in the Western Union survey are: a phone index to reach key people 24 hours a day, travel agents, a 24-hour food service, a laminated wallet-sized card of crisis team members, sufficient corporate news release paper and envelopes, potential press conference sites, and keys to all supply rooms. Important as these details are, they are just routine mechanics. Managing a public problem needs much, much more.

Battle-experienced managers and counselors urge extensive preparation and greater realism—even if it is simulated. Many plans do not fully prepare the media spokesperson or point man for leaks, incessant media barrage, disloyalty in the ranks, the emotional shock of damaging headlines, tapped telephones, defeat despite best efforts, and even death.

Some companies—but more frequently counseling firms—attempt to give managers a preview of such realities. Executives arrived at a consultant's office for day-long media confrontation training. Stepping out of their limos, they anticipated a genial oozing into the sessions. Instead, when they got off the elevators, they were besieged by a barrage of bright lights, demanding television reporters, and blocked access. The first lesson of the day, although play-acting, was searing.

Another executive had just survived a session of role-playing in handling industrial disasters. As he was packing up, the "widow" of a man supposedly killed in the accident called, blaming the executive personally for her husband's death and all the agony her family would face. The tough executive broke down. Brutal scenarios, but not unrealistic.

Untested managers aim to control crises; experienced managers settle for coping day by day, detail by wearying detail. They hope all their planning and experience and their gut reactions will prevent a communications or financial disaster. Sometimes, the disaster lies not in the event itself, but in its public, media-shaped aftermath. Maladroit or unplanned company responses increase these risks substantially.

What Three Mile Island Taught

Two Hill and Knowlton officers have advised others and lived through their own share of crises. Robert L. Dilenschneider, then president and CEO,[3] and Richard C. Hyde, executive managing director, counseled Hyatt Corporation during the fatal collapse of a hotel skywalk in Kansas City and Metropolitan Electric after the Three Mile Island incident.[4]

Plan for the unplanned, they counsel, no matter how uncongenial that may be for highly structured organizations. Companies thrive on lack of surprises, orderliness, and chain of command. Crises are abhorrent because they break through, unscheduled, unannounced, and often violently. Only with superior, realistic planning and execution, spiced with lots of luck, is there any chance to control damage. Sometimes adversity can even be turned to the company's advantage. The two counselors suggest four steps:

- Identify potential problems—existing situations, particularly those endemic to the industry, and past incidents that may recur.
- Identify affected audiences—employees, media, customers, government agencies—then develop appropriate spokespeople, messages, and actions.
- Organize a response team, assisted by written plans and checklists of contacts and actions. When a situation is chaotic and fast-moving, this ensures that subordinates will cover the essential steps. But the plan cannot be too rigid or specific; it must be flexible enough

for executives to apply their common sense and experience to volatile situations.
• Make sure the company speaks with one voice, someone who is cool,
level-headed, and articulate and who knows how the media works
and can make swift decisions, sometimes on insufficient knowledge.

Not only do hydra-headed messages—conflicting stories from several people—confuse; they may imply that the company isn't in command, doesn't know what it is doing. Smart reporters can use even
differences in nuances to pry out material. All this is difficult when
speed, tempered by accuracy, is paramount.

Conversely, mysterious silences, evasive answers, and absence of
information only goad reporters to dig harder. Often they assume
they'll find more detrimental news than appears on the surface. Alternative sources are available—always. One used frequently today is
a financial analyst who follows the company or its industry. This is a
good reason for keeping analysts well informed and favorably disposed toward the company. But there are risks. With fewer analysts
covering more companies, their information may not always be fresh
and precise—but they will never not answer. Even those close to the
company may not know changes in strategy or internal dynamics,
particularly among personalities.

The worst problem during the Three Mile Island (TMI) incident,
according to the Hill and Knowlton counselors, was caused by the
conflicting reports generated by overzealous media that lacked
enough information. It was a technical story, difficult for the untrained to understand. In addition, nuclear terms in themselves
often create fear. Confusion may be inevitable in such dynamic situations, but that's no reason for the company to contribute to it.
"Reporters told us they really didn't know how to cover the story. It
was difficult, technically complex, even scary. Some reporters,
frankly, did not want to go on location, fearing they would be exposed to radiation," Hyde explained.

But TMI posed other problems for reporters. First, television at
best is an intrusive medium. Rural Pennsylvania, where the reactors
are located, simply was not able to handle hundreds of media people
and their equipment. Reliable information was scarce; facts kept
changing. Reporters claimed un-cooperativeness from the utility

company, secrecy, and a confused federal bureaucracy. For all these reasons, and because of their lack of background, the press deserted the technical to focus on human interests. Not only does this sell newspapers, but it avoids the need to seek out the subterranean, complex issues that are much more difficult to cover. Reporting of the 1985 TWA hostage crisis concentrated on people and never explained the tangle of political, religious, and military rivalries in the Middle East that created the hijacking.

The Kenny Commission Report on TMI soberly concluded that the incident's risks did not warrant the hysteria and melodrama of the on-scene reporting. TMI was not journalism's finest hour.

The accident illustrates another media trend: narrowly focusing issues. In addition, coverage of TMI took the question of nuclear energy out of the hands of specialists and bureaucrats and placed it squarely on the political agenda and in emotion-laden meetings. Exactly the same process occurred with TWA Flight 800's explosion off Long Island in July 1996.

TMI illustrates an emerging management problem—crisis without frame, no definite beginning and an unknowable end. A more acute example is the Chernobyl nuclear incident, when people were not told when it really began and may not know for generations when its genetic and other health effects will end. Yale sociologist Kai Erikson interviewed victims for his book, A New Species of Trouble. His findings remarkably confirm what PR counselors have been advising for years. Go to the scene. Show human empathy. Don't ring yourself with lawyers or blame the victim.

The greater human and public danger, according to Erikson, is produced by human hands, not explained (seldom successfully) as acts of God. These incidents involve some type of toxicity, and blur the line between acute and chronic problems. Such events contaminate rather than merely damage, pollute, befoul, taint, and penetrate human tissue. They scare people.

TMI and Erikson also illustrate the pitfalls of little credibility in authority. An evacuation-shadow phenomenon develops—a gap between the official wisdom and words, and what people at profound risk and deep dread did. Although widespread evacuation at TMI was not needed, some drove hundreds of miles before they questioned why they did so.[5]

POISONING INFORMATION WELLS

Another crisis management problem is the poisoning of information wells. Phillip P. Fried, experienced public relations counselor, tells the following story, of another chemical company. A tank car of vinyl chloride, derailed in a small Southern town, began to burn with acrid smoke. Civil defense people, after checking a manual, decided that burning polyvinyl would produce poisonous gas. They called the company's New York office to check this and to report that the National Guard was evacuating people in a 25-mile radius. What did the public relations contact advise? After checking with company scientists, he called back, assuring civil defense that the smoke posed no danger to anyone or anything. No poisonous gas would be produced. The civil defense people said, "Thanks for the assurance, but what about all the dead cattle around the tank car?" The company man could only wonder, to himself, if his own scientists had lied. When the stakes are this high, subterfuge among colleagues, politicking, or leaving the point man out there vulnerable to lie or respond with insufficient information results only in damaging headlines or serious community problems. Such strategies don't do much for credibility or corporate spirit either.[6]

Almost every experienced public relations practitioner has one cardinal rule, particularly when public safety is involved: Tell it all and tell it fast. Not only does this minimize fear because the general public is informed, but it means that the news makes headlines once. Dribbling out information disquiets people, because they always fear that more and the worst are yet to come. Perhaps more damaging, this policy also drags out coverage for days, magnifying the event in the public's mind. Lawyers, financial advisers, and media-burned managers often disagree. One instance when silence was far from golden occurred when the Canadian Broadcasting Company accused the Canadian subsidiary of Star-Kist Food, Inc., of shipping 1 million cases of "rancid and decomposing tuna." Throughout extended coverage the company kept mum. The result? They were massacred in the press. Profits plunged 90 percent. A brutal shock to Star-Kist and its parent-company, H. J. Heinz, but totally predictable.

One besieged corporate lawyer sought to release as little information as possible to a very persistent, powerful investigative journalist. Colleagues urged him to answer at least some of the reporter's questions. He declined. Without benefit of any company cooperation, the reporter developed a story on his own, which appeared—to the company's detriment—on the very day they were wooing financial analysts.

Even more cynical executives say that if someone asks a question you think is out of line or not in your best interest, just plain lie. Not smart in the long run. As one business journalist explains. "I'm only human. They lie to me just once and I won't believe anything they say, ever again." Faced with internal intransigence, particularly from superiors, the corporate communicator is left with the perilous choice of trying to convince the boss he's wrong, only to have a damaging story appear later. To press his point, the communicator may dredge up expensive war stories of how lying works only once and mortgages credibility, or how stonewalling and debating the public can unseat the most powerful, as it did President Richard M. Nixon.

Conversely, telling everything may pose liabilities unless the company presents its case very carefully. Which phrases are natural headline grabbers? Which will confuse? Dilenschneider gives this example from TMI. A telephone company technician remarked that the phone lines might "melt down" because of call volume. The comment, a natural headline, was heard—garbled—and became the source of needless and ill-founded concern.

Hyde, who tussled with a multitude of communications problems at Metropolitan Electric because they were not prepared for the magnitude of TMI, suggests that the following factors be incorporated in any plan:

- Speak with one voice.
- Cover all bases, all important subjects, to the fullest extent possible.
- Provide regular updates.
- Accept that in an increasingly technological world, a more complex society, more can go wrong.
- Understand that the less people know about what is happening, the more they fear the consequences.
- Get management involved early in crisis communication planning.

Tylenol: A Credo Worked When Planning Couldn't

Surely few companies have had a crisis burst upon them with the speed, ferocity, visibility, and tragedy that struck Johnson & Johnson

(J&J) and its subsidiary McNeil Consumer Products Company, maker of Tylenol.[7] In the fall of 1982, a still-unknown criminal poisoned the pain relief capsules with cyanide, killing, almost instantly, seven Chicago-area residents.

Tylenol, J&J's single best-selling product line, in 1981 produced more than $350 million in sales and held 35 percent of the total analgesic market. With such spectacular successes, no company executive could imagine a cloud when Chairman James E. Burke, just three weeks before the first death, asked his senior management to anticipate worst possible scenarios. What if something happened to Tylenol, he asked? It seemed almost an unnecessary question.

Individuals, in business or government, often cannot envision the ultimate horror. In developing scenarios for events in Iran when the Shah seemed all-powerful, for example, advisers advanced actions that could be controlled and managed—tepid extrapolations from what already was occurring. Their poverty of imagination—perhaps even of knowledge—prevented them from foreseeing the rise of a religious zealot, militant in his faith and in his opposition to modernization as exemplified by the Shah and the United States. Could a small Scottish town, Lockerbie, imagine parts of a 747, baggage, and bodies raining down from the skies? At Johnson & Johnson imaginations did not stretch to cyanide-laced capsules and murder.

Tylenol intrigues as a success story, unusual in public relations, but, even more, for the unique cooperation between press and corporation. Media relations more often resemble a chess game between what the company knows or wants to tell and relentlessness of the media demanding more, more, more. It does not diminish J&J's accomplishments or the complexity of Tylenol problems to note that the company had everything to gain by the widest possible press coverage as a means of saving lives, preventing panic, accomplishing a product recall quickly, and reasserting its outstanding reputation for product safety. That coincided with the media's need for the most accurate, up-to-date information that the company was gathering. It resulted in much closer media relationships than J&J had traditionally maintained. When a company may gain less and risk more through complete disclosure, the issue of media relations is much less clear-cut and more controversial.

For some years J&J's corporate planning groups had included crisis management and disaster plans. Conventional public relations practitioners talk of lists, friends, and control systems. But to Lawrence Foster, then Johnson & Johnson's vice president for public relations, who has survived the media firestorm, none of that was enough. Events were so atypical, unpredictable, and eruptive that instant improvisation was the only conceivable action. Devising or following a plan carefully sculptured beforehand was dysfunctional.

Aside from the success of Johnson & Johnson's candidness and openness, the case is unique in the strength executives found in a credo developed forty years before by Robert Wood Johnson. The credo established the company's priorities and defined its responsibility to its constituencies. Such credos usually are treated like Boy Scout oaths: put on the shelf unread, honored but not heeded. J&J's provided a cohesive direction for decision-making, a solid footing when the sands seemed to be shifting dramatically almost every minute.

The credo looks deceptively simple and modern. Back in the 1940s, Robert Wood Johnson noted that institutions, public and private, exist because people want them, believe in them, or at least are willing to tolerate them. "The day has passed when business was a private matter—if it ever really was." George Cabot Lodge, in his *New American Ideology*, echoed this idea of consent, writing that companies can no longer continue to operate without the consent of their constituencies[8]—the Lockean concept applied to the marketplace.

Johnson listed four specific constituencies:

- consumers and medical professionals using company products
- employees
- communities where the company's people work and live, and
- stockholders.

He considered these guidelines as being not only moral, but profitable as well.

The Tylenol saga started slowly, with several press queries about problems with the product, then reporting the first death at 9:30 A.M. (CST) on September 30, 1982. Despite the increasingly macabre news coming in from Chicago, despite the numbing disbelief, despite the horrible fear that someone had screwed up in the plant, calm decisions had to be made. The natural orderliness of corporate life was thrown into painful, engulfing turmoil. It seemed like a death in the family. Executives, attempting to learn what was happening, soon realized their first response required methodical analysis, not shooting from the hip.

Almost immediately, the public relations staff, with management's total support, decided to cooperate fully and candidly with the news media. Only later did they realize the decision had been made without a meeting—a surprise, but totally efficient. Telephone calls from pharmacies, physicians, poison control centers, press, and panicked consumers began to pour in, as well as false alarms, crank calls, and good advice. One weary executive felt that he could manage the crisis, but not all the well-intentioned good advice offered by callers. Television and press coverage was staggering—eventually, 2,500 press calls, 125,000 clippings. It was the most extensive coverage since President John F. Kennedy's assassination. During the first eight days, as much as 20 percent of one network's news time was devoted to Tylenol.

The damage was immediate. Within a few days the stock dropped seven points. Tylenol lost 87 percent of its commanding market share in two weeks. Recall costs alone totaled more than $100 million, pretax. Product reintroduction was expensive. (No exact amount was announced.)

As events progressed, several aspects became clear. Given the staggering levels of poison in the victims' blood, the cyanide could not have been put into the capsules in the plant, only at the distribution point. Although corporation and media focused on the immediate story, the wider concern was whether consumer trust in all product purity was jeopardized by mindless and anonymous terrorism. Were the benefits of self-medication at stake? The most routine everyday purchases suddenly seemed threatening. Even those who knew better hesitated before taking a Tylenol capsule. Copycat tampering was another general threat.

Early on, Chairman Burke formed a seven-member strategy group that included senior executives, those responsible for McNeil, the general counsel, and the public relations officer. They met twice daily to make decisions on rapidly changing events and to coordinate company-wide efforts. Their attention now centered on damage control and communication.

During the tragedy and in its aftermath, Johnson & Johnson established a number of communication vehicles:

- Toll-free consumer hotlines that, through November 1982, handled 30,000 calls
- Full-page newspaper advertisements in major cities, offering consumers the opportunity to exchange capsules for tablets
- Letters updating employees and asking for their continued support and assistance, which they gave generously; videotaped special reports for employees and retirees
- Interviews with senior executives in major print and electronic media
- Thirty-one million bottles of Tylenol were withdrawn and destroyed; eight million individual capsules were tested; eight bottles were tampered with; seventy-five capsules were contaminated. This massive effort helped convince the public of J&J's concern for product purity and safety
- Television spots telling consumers that Tylenol capsules would soon return to the marketplace in tamper-resistant packaging
- Every one of the 3,000 letters of inquiry and support was answered.

Following total product-recall and public opinion sampling, the company decided to restore its reputation by fighting back against public paranoia and against damaging public images such as the television graphic that showed the product next to a skull and crossbones. J&J would stay with "Tylenol." A new name might suggest guilt. New packaging would be tamper-resistant in three ways: a sealed box, a protective collar on the bottle, and an inner seal.

Just six weeks after the first death, a second media blitz, this one company-sponsored. A 30-city press conference via satellite announced the product's comeback and introduced the triple-safety-sealed package. The media gave the story wide coverage, despite the death of Soviet leader Leonid Brezhnev, announced the same day. Under normal circumstances, important international news would pre-empt product coverage—a measure of the Tylenol interest.

Not only customers, but the company and media seemed pleased with how the story had been handled, an unusual agreement. Editorials commented on a new level of corporate responsibility, on how a gap had been bridged between the news media and corporate public relations. The company was called candid and contrite, committed to solving the murders and protecting the public.

With government agencies, media, and business cooperating, two additional bottles of Tylenol capsules containing cyanide were returned, preventing other possible deaths. Most persons involved agreed that responsible, open public relations policies carried out at all levels helped minimize the spread of rumor and misinformation and provided valuable guidance to the public.

Chairman Burke had the first prescient word of warning about serious product difficulty and the word of summary: "When the public is watching carefully, they make incredibly smart decisions." The public had seemed eminently fair in assessing what had happened.

By early 1983, the product had recaptured almost 70 percent of its previous market share; eventually it regained the entire pre-crisis 85 percent. Despite the enormity and visibility of the tragedy, Johnson & Johnson's image "as a socially conscious business remains undiminished." Nor was a single negative letter received from a shareholder, despite the cost of $100 million. Even now the "antiseptic horror" slayings remain a mystery.

In early 1986, Tylenol capsules were back in the news with another cyanide death. This time J&J made the dramatic and expensive decision to remove all over-the-counter capsules from the market. Chairman Burke was highly visible, explained the decision on news programs and talk shows. But many persons were disquieted: another death, another serious breakdown of trust and, this time, almost overexposure of Burke in the media.

Today, Tylenol is generally accepted as the benchmark against which other companies and product-recalls are judged. A factor in Perrier's failure to react swiftly when benzene was found in its water, touted for its purity, was not understanding the U.S. public's expectation for total product-purity and -recall when dangerous elements were found. News media, too, sought the dramatic visuals of product being removed from shelves. When syringes were discovered in Pepsi cans, some media attempted to push both the FDA and Pepsi for total recall. It was not necessary. Videos of the filling process demonstrated speed made insertion of a syringe impossible. Danger could be avoided completely by pouring the Pepsi into a cup. And incidents were spotty, followed no pattern.

MANAGING DURING TURMOIL

In public turmoil a manager cannot enforce territorial imperatives and survive. All must trust and support with all available skills. Communicators must handle the news-gathering, legwork, drive for accuracy and completeness. The required analytical abilities, the eruptiveness, and the relentless deadlines reflect a newsroom ambience more than a corporation's. But communicators must consult constantly with the legal department to determine what can be told. To whom? How can the company answer the newest charge? Operating officers involved must be asked for facts to confirm or refute charges. Senior officers must understand the strengths and weaknesses of certain public words and positions. Under pressure, the tendency is to take shortcuts, to exclude, but taking the time and effort to do the job completely avoids many surprises and costly mistakes.

Sometimes this is a bit like walking through a minefield. Many executives expect their responsibilities to be relatively risk-free publicly, leaving them vulnerable when communicating with angry, downsized employees, for instance. When Earl Shoriss wrote *The Oppressed Middle: Politics of Middle Management, Scenes from Corporate Life*, some reviewers condemned him as an enemy of business and called the book "odd," "provocative." Few accepted his tales of middle management misery, of fatal caprice, exile, secrecy, planned divisiveness, programmed fear, and toadyism. Some executives are fortunate enough not to have experienced such clammy frights. More likely they have been taught to forget. The few senior executive women sometimes are more candid in acknowledging the formless terror, exclusion, and ostracism.

Success in crises means that a manager must be prepared to deal with the dark and sometimes destructive underside: distressing calls at midnight checking on media rumors; the accidental death of a very senior executive that arouses press suspicions—incorrectly; many nights consumed by debriefing the brain of the day's events and preparing for fears of the next morning's struggles.

How can a manager prepare to fight a media firestorm?

- First, know how reporters work: understanding their needs, particular interests, biases, fierce competition, and relentless deadlines is basic.
- Second, organize for turmoil as you would develop a strategic plan. This good mental exercise should never become an operational straitjacket.
- Third, attempt to get mentally outside the corporate cocoon to view

the company as others do. Historians are trained to bring as little of themselves as possible into an analysis or an event. Only by screening out biases inherent in a late twentieth-century purview and U.S. college training can they even begin to understand, for instance, the economy, strategic importance, and labor hardships of sixteenth-century silver mining in Potosi. Even with the best of intentions, many executives view the world from a highly selective slice of experience, reinforced by peers who think the same way.

- Fourth, encourage loyal devil's advocates, who question conventional wisdom and blind spots,.who see events differently from the way you do.
- Fifth, be sure your corporate house is clean and in order. If not, clean it up—fast. Tell the truth up front. Concealment, which never works in the long-term, only heightens media coverage and skepticism.
- Sixth, maintain a healthy personal balance, objectivity, and, if possible, a sense of humor and the absurd. Stress, anger, haranguing the press or lecturing associates, great impatience—all endemic during pressure and turmoil—are self-defeating.

SNATCHING ADVANTAGE OUT OF DISASTER

Although downside risks must dominate a manager's thoughts and actions during a crisis, later he can use his experiences to produce positive results. Even those who have suffered through tender fights and other assaults on their corporations admit that their ordeals forced them into long-overdue restructuring, shrinking operations, particularly of corporate staffs, and taking a very hard took at business actions shelved during more optimistic times.

According to Michael Tabriz, veteran of Love Canal, *60 Minutes*, and chemical industry public affairs, post-crisis analysis can produce the following advantages for the communications department:

- Elevating the public relations function (in many companies it's looked upon as soft and fuzzy, not as the guts of reality, especially not in the face of trouble)
- Focusing public attention on matters of critical concern and reaching audiences otherwise unavailable
- Building credibility

- Forcing an organization to review all policies relating to social responsibility.[9]

Conversely, big bucks and reputations can be made in crisis management. It's a hot ticket right now. Many besides communicators, lawyers, investment bankers, and outside specialists are competing for the action. Companies in deep trouble often chuck conventional budgeting and ways of doing things to hire savvy, tough street-fighters, with lots of connections, documented successes in corporate conflict, authoritative auras, and a zest for battle. Even the language used—war rooms, scorched earth, raids, and white knights—is martial.

Lawyers often take over what was once the communicator's strongest suit: media relations. They are becoming effective advocates and spokespeople for their corporations. Lawyers grandstand their victories. The late Melvin Belli once rang bells in his San Francisco law offices. Lawyers talk with the press, sometimes daily, during a case, feeding background and other useful information. Many lawyers fight their battles in both courts of law and personal opinion. Thoughtful leaders in both law and communications are concerned with the way public hoopla influences juries, public opinion, and the law itself, but it is a reality now.

Ultimately, the most dependable guides when a company's financial and operational future, even survival, is at stake, are executives who have overcome similar turmoil. However, their experiences cannot be adopted uncritically as a template. Despite some common elements, each high-pressure crisis is unique; the details always differ. In the end, a manager is thrown back on his own resources and those he develops under pressure.

NOTES

1. Meyers, in addition to his business career, taught crisis management at Carnegie-Mellon University's Graduate School of Industrial Administration.

2. "Crisis Communications in American Business," prepared for Western Union by Burson-Marsteller.

3. Robert Dilenschneider now runs his own firm, The Dilenschneider Group.

4. Information was drawn from both correspondence and conversation with Hill and Knowlton officers and Richard C. Hyde's untitled remarks to the Counselor's Section of the Public Relations Society of America in Chicago, October 9, 1979.

5. These ideas are drawn from Kai Erikson's general conclusions, including TMI in his book, A New Species of Trouble: Explorations in Disaster, Trauma, and Community (New York: W. W. Norton, 1994).

6. From conversation with Philip Fried and from his lecture material.

7. Material for the discussion in the Tylenol section was gathered from Johnson & Johnson's public relations department, newspaper accounts in The New York Times and The Wall Street Journal during both episodes, evaluations with various communicators, and conversations with Lawrence Foster.

8. George Cabot Lodge discusses the absolute need for business people in the future to understand and speak to the concerns of their various constituencies.

9. From lecture notes and conversations with Michael Tabriz.

4

Supplying Your Own Banana Peels

Troubles Companies Cause Themselves and Others

> The fault, dear Brutus, is not in our stars,
> But in ourselves.
>
> —*Julius Caesar*, Act I, Scene 2

> Authorities ought to know that a careless word can bring
> down the greatest empire.
>
> —Ryszard Kapúscinski

> Talk lots, deliver little.
>
> —Cantinflas

Angry, publicly embarrassed, defeated executives rage against the culprits. The whipping boys of choice are the media—uninformed, lazy, or tendentious. Thieving, incompetent subordinates, whistle-blowers, bureaucrats virgin to realism, unkind fates, unlevel playing fields, and rules changed in mid-stream are blamed as well—but always after the fact.

Analysis of public relations crisis after public relations crisis reveals, however, that the fault more often lies within the executives' own personalities, management styles, or insensitivities. They made their own trouble. They supplied their own banana peels, on which they slipped and slid.

When clumsy vaudevillians slipped and wobbled on real banana peels strewn about a stage, it was great, slapstick fun. Substitute business, political, and even sports leaders for vaudevillians, and the fun turns to dismay, cynicism, and derision.

A 1993 *Guardian Weekly* cartoon shows President Bill Clinton completely off-balance, his agenda a carton of eggs about to go smash. In a corner former Senator Robert Dole sits against a box labeled "Dole Bananas. Eat within the first 100 days." Dole is commenting: "What the Clinton program lacks is balance."[1] Self-generated problems create battles and dilemmas within each manager. He must respond with self-examination and skeptical foresight, battle rigid priorities and natural optimism, and suppress the urge to hide or falsely explain away problems. Like any communications problem, successful managing of the self-inflicted depends upon the quality of media relations, the CEO's and spokesperson's credibility, and whether the problem is acknowledged or hidden.

The following four chapters focus on the analyses of communications in individual cases—some generic and others prominent, some successes and others expensive disasters. Even in supposedly objective organizations, personalities still can dominate and damage. It may be a woman executive—new, alone, and vulnerable in the executive ranks—who does not understand that appearances can decide more than facts. A CEO may court unnecessary liabilities and criticism by being very visible and available (as Warren Anderson of Union Carbide at Bhopal) or absent during disaster (as William J. Catacosinos of Lilco, a Long Island, New York, power utility, during a massive power failure). Angry customers/residents surely didn't help Lilco's appeals for rate hikes or problems with nuclear power plant approvals.

Public announcements of messy senior management arrivals and departures usually are sanitized into personal reasons or other business pursuits: cover-up illusions as revealing as the emperor's new clothes. But power fights often go public. The boss won't leave (Harry Gray of United Technologies) or won't let his heir take charge (Harry Gray, Harold Geneen of ITT, and Dr. Armand Hammer of Occidental Petroleum). Or the company creator hangs on until he is unceremoniously pushed out. The celebrated battle between Steven Jobs and John Sculley for control of Apple Computer continued with their successors. And now, ironically, Jobs is back at a badly foundering Apple. Communications strategy in these cases is a Hobson's Choice. No clear-cut, satisfactory solution exists, except to stop making more trouble for yourself. The risk of making enemies and inflicting long-festering wounds is great. Sophisticated, patently bland explanations arouse skepticism and curiosity about the unrevealed real reasons. But airing corporate dirty linen and personality conflicts in public has liabilities as well.

Most of the troubles that companies cause themselves, however, spring from not monitoring operations closely enough for possible public liabilities; from trying to hide wrongdoing even when it is uncovered, then stonewalling; or from lying to the press. Managers who would consider it reckless to present a business plan without solid marketing, financial, competitive, and legal research, neglect to factor in public considerations. At other times a company takes the public rap when others are more culpable, as Hooker Chemical Company did at Love Canal. (See case study below, pp. 246–254.)

Sometimes reason dictates minimizing the possible effect of well-based or ridiculous rumors. But rumors can seriously damage. Procter & Gamble had to pay the devil his due to quell an off-the-wall rumor that their products were doing the devil's work.

But the most profound self-inflicted troubles are the great games of tenders and mergers played by white knights and raiders. Many such corporate wars founder on less-than-candid communications and cultural conflicts. The melding of INA and Connecticut General into one still-floundering insurance giant, CIGNA, illustrates these pitfalls—particularly in promising employees too much and later terminating them in the name of cost-avoidance.

One word, one brand name not researched can cause great troubles or humor. The classic case, cited in every marketing class, is the Chevrolet Nova in Spanish-speaking countries. Just what self-respecting Puerto Rican would want to drive a no-go car? More recently, Reebok tripped on its own laces by naming a women's shoe "Incubus." No one realized, until an Arizona newspaper reader pointed it out, that "an incubus is an evil spirit that in medieval times was thought to prey on sleeping women, having sex with them." Reebok, red-faced, asked retailers to black out the name on boxes. It did not appear on the shoe.[2] Two problems linger, "incubus" follows CEO Paul B. Fireman's public arrogance and unresponsiveness. Also, the gaffe raises questions: one-time flop or another example of the "poor communications and coordination for which Reebok was once famous"?[3]

EVERY DAY BRINGS NEW SLIPS

Strict adherence to company policies may make great bureaucratic sense, but result in unwanted attention. Two of the following examples demonstrate how absence of commonsense application made their enforcers look not only foolish, but highly visible. Lying to the press is guaranteed to be dangerous, especially when the topic is a hot-button issue such as abortion.

Not thinking how incongruous actions will look to others ensures wide coverage, jokes, and censure. From many examples a recent one is chosen. Catch a thief, act out of concern for a customer's safety, win an award for increasing sales and controlling costs. Sounds like a career fast-tracker—to being fired. Not only the actions, but the sequence: catch a thief, be fired because it is against company policy to interfere with anyone stealing or holding up a store, then make the award. Three days from hero, to unemployed, to hero again to the city of Houston. The employee, Wiley Berggren, became a martyr to West Texas media and the talk-radio circuit.

The police, acknowledging the matter was between Berggren and his 7-Eleven Southland employer, "Called him a hell of a manager." Berggren explained he simply relied on his instincts: "I feel like, in my heart, I had an angel on my shoulder and I did the right thing." His employer responded: "He violated the cardinal rule for dealing with criminals: not to confront them." You don't stand in the doorway as they're trying to escape, grab them, then "tie them down with a trash bag," a company executive explained. Regrettably, "we may be losing a valued employee, but if you have a policy, you have to stick by it."[4] Even if you look silly, get nationwide coverage, and disrupt a career. Wouldn't it be wonderful if the competition hired him!

Create a self-admitted public relations disaster by demanding Girl Scouts pay royalties for songs they sing around the campfire. Eventually, the American Society of Composers, Authors, and Publishers (ASCAP) recanted, called it a PR debacle, but that didn't stay stories and jokes about the big, bad bully, or headlines such as *The Wall Street Journal*'s "The Birds May Sing, But Campers Can't Unless They Pay Up," or T.V. broadcasting of scouts dancing the Macarena in silence.

Lying to the press is absolutely the best way to cause trouble—

lots—for yourselves and everyone affected. An issue as sensitive as abortion only makes it much worse. So does another source revealing and capitalizing on the lie. A recent case involves an abortion spokesman who said he lied. *American Medical News,* published by the American Medical Association, and *Media Matters,* a T.V. program funded by the Corporation for Public Broadcasting, reported leaders of abortion industry associations and other pro-abortion groups misled the press and the public regarding late-term abortions.

Ron Fitzsimmons, executive director of the National Coalition of Abortion Providers, which represents about 220 abortion clinic owners, told the medical publication that "leaders of the abortion rights movement tried to defeat the Partial-Birth Abortion Ban Act by telling press and public the procedures were done very rarely and only in extreme circumstances. . . . The pro-abortion movement knew these claims were untrue."

Fitzsimmons admitted that he had "lied" during a November 1995 appearance on ABC's *Nightline* "when he said the procedure was used rarely and only on women whose lives were in danger or whose fetuses were damaged." Compounding the misinformation, journalists "did little original reporting," accepting "information from pro-choice sources—which turned out to be inaccurate."[5]

No one country, company, or individual has the exclusive on flailing about. An analysis of Standard Chartered, a London-based bank, notes its valuable assets don't balance out against its banana peel factor. "Oh dear, oh dear!" an irreverent British journalist wrote. "Standard Chartered just cannot seem to manage a year without finding a banana skin to tread on." The peels include important but unavailable data and bowler-hat managers who hadn't seen a training program for twenty years, as well as a majority of senior executives from the outside, impatient with the "old-fashioned account manager selling a bit of lending product." Management began eliminating the peels. "Our strategy is to be very, very profitable," executives explained. Okay, but watch out for new banana peels.[6]

Count the Ways They Slid

How, why, do executives make their own trouble? The most common and costly ways include:

- Naïvely trying to keep secrets in this time of tell-all blabbermouths. Investigative reporters, and trouble-seeking lawyers who dig, dig, dig, question, question, question. Disgruntled, discharged, or even merely mistreated employees are anxious to give public airing to their grievances. Secrets perversely come out at the most inopportune times and in the most expensive ways.
- Ignoring or trying to hide potentially damaging complaints or research data. Small, easily corrected problems are allowed to metastasize into institution-threatening crises.
- Minimizing the first trace-lines of trouble; ignoring the clustering clues.
- Hyping a really good story past the point of credibility or ignoring conflicting details until hype engulfs the positive. Wal-Mart's "Buy America" promotion and Volvo's advertising illustrate a good story gone too far.
- Living too well or arrogantly, and failing to detect attitude shifts court revenge by angry shareholders, regulatory agencies, even voters. What woes extravagance brought Empire Blue Cross and Blue Shield, United Way, and televangelist Jimmy Bakker!
- Dreams of a lifetime disappear when superstars think they can get away with anything, lie, use and then duck the media. Did Pete Rose gamble away his chance to enter the Baseball Hall of Fame?
- Getting caught in the crosshairs of change may not always be a self-inflicted wound, but brashness can hasten trouble, as it did for former New York City Schools Chancellor Joseph Fernandez.
- Sticking to a strategy even when its going very wrong or when the major element of success, such as surprise in the ATF raid on the Branch Dividian compound in Waco, is lost.
- Treating a corporate culture only as an unmitigated good, never as a straitjacket on critical thinking. In this day of imageology, executives who begin believing the publicity they've paid for, or let their image diverge too far from reality, court invisibility. Reality always wins, even if it takes time. Where are executive glitterati John Gutfreund, once of Salomon, and James Robinson III, once of American Express, today?
- Perhaps the most ubiquitous banana peel, endemic but not exclusive to politicians, is foot-in-mouth, saying too much, too soon, too carelessly, that returns to haunt the speaker.

Each of the following illustrations, ranging from Texas politicians to scientific researchers, from high-living, overzealous executives to companies damaged by self-induced media frenzies, demonstrates how to supply your own banana peels.

CREATING A CULTURE FOR DISASTER

Building a corporate culture is touted uncritically as positive and progressive. It will unify operations, strengthen the organization, inspire and build esprit de corps. Everyone will think along—and follow—the same party line. Seldom is the downside of such homogenization or stifling of criticism considered. Heaven forbid that the culture can become a carapace.

A dominant corporate culture can screen out essential dissenting voices and ideas. One large firm of public relations counselors, renowned for having its fingers on the pulse of the times, missed completely the conflict, internal and external, and the damaging publicity that taking on a highly controversial client produced. Its culture dictated being eternally busy. Never think. Never look outside corporate suites. Never watch wrangling on the evening news. That collective mindset proved very costly. The PR firm needed PR counsel.

The Salomon Brothers culture, uncritically mired in an '80s brashness that was bragged about and lived very visibly, ended one regime and brought in another.[7] Former CEO John Gutfreund and Michael Lewis's *Liar's Poker* illustrate the destructive milieu that White Knight Warren Buffett cauterized. cleaned up, and disciplined.

Gutfreund set a very public fast-pace of high living and business high jinks. Trainees were encouraged to come to work each day ready to "bite the ass off a bear." The compensation system—traders paid on the basis of the profits they produced—encouraged a selfish, money-hungry, do-anything-to-be-on-top spirit. Terms such as "human piranha," "vitriolic profanity," "we are the market" were tossed about with admiration and envy. Glossy, slick annual reports, press coverage, and adulation of outsiders fanned the venality. Amid such intense pressure and chaos, lines blurred between legal and illegal.

Greed and ambition, gross jokes were badges of honor. Staggering debt for companies and countries simply meant more money for the traders. In this modern gold rush, Salomon was king of the traders— "the epicenter . . . that helped define an age. But it leveraged the United States."

Lewis's account of the training program reads more like the antics of the movie *Animal House* than the actions of sober, sedate Wall

Streeters'. In one chapter, "Learning to Love Your Corporate Culture," he describes total absorption in the job. Money never sleeps. He depicts the trading floor as a jungle, the education of trainees as "incestuous." Such hooliganism ensured anarchy—bad drove out good; big swamped small; brawn, brains. Any refinements of personality and intellect that trainees brought to Salomon were shed to accommodate the culture.[8]

Did any Salomon officer even consider the possibility of a great downfall? Lewis saw exactly the opposite in the training—brainwashing, uniform attitudes, the million little rules to obey, protective coloration, and the shunning of any personal loyalties. In this, a marine boot camp for elite MBAs, the best and the brightest accepted the yoke, victims of The Myth.[9]

Such group-think missed mounting questions about the damage that unbridled leverage, acquisitions, and eight-figure bonuses were inflicting. Drexel Burnham Lambert, Michael Milken, H. Ross Johnson, and the movie *Wall Street* were fueling outrage against Wall Street, huge bonuses, and unbridled behavior. Multi-mergers involving household names and products piqued the interests of Joe Six-Packs not normally concerned with great corporate dramas. All were missed or discounted by high-stakes players.

And then the inevitable happened. On August 9, 1991, Salomon Brothers publicly admitted to illegal bidding in the February and April Treasury auctions. This was bad enough, but initial inaction by senior executives only exacerbated the crisis. Silence greeted bewildered, disillusioned, fearful employees. Silence is not a public relations virtue.

But the sharpest contrast is between the CEO who scattered the banana peels and the CEO who cleaned them up: Gutfreund and Buffett, Mr. Conspicuous Arrogance and Mr. Clean. Many on the Street thought the abuses inevitable.[10] Dubbed the "King of Wall Street" by *Business Week*, Gutfreund cut a swath for thirteen years as Salomon CEO. He encouraged a macho mystique, a big, bad, bold culture. He both set Salomon up for a great fall and guided it to global eminence. With the Treasury auction scandal, the firm's reputation, motives, and internal controls, its trust and respectability, the oil that lubricates the machinery of Wall Street, were endangered.

Once the Oracle from Omaha, Warren Buffett, arrived, he acted decisively to save Salomon from the fate of Drexel. He quite simply changed the company's entire persona. Buffett ordered an independent outside audit, proclaimed in advertisements that he was now chief compliance officer, and set up a tough internal compliance committee. He promised that Salomon would set a new standard for ethical behavior in the industry. Unlike his predecessor, he shunned public attention. He instituted new reality and legal checks. Eventually, he used publicity to apologize for misdeeds, explain corrective actions, and promise a cleanup.

Although Buffett was already famous for his blunt, plain Berkshire Hathaway, Inc., annual reports, the 1991 Salomon report was classic. It reflected the firm's newly subdued style, explaining without bombast where the company was heading, and, unlike many Wall Street high-flyers, recognizing the human toll.

How did Buffett succeed where Gutfreund had failed? First, Buffett's strategy spoke to public sensitivities, recognizing the fact that the tide had turned against Wall Street excesses. Gutfreund conducted business as usual. Buffett realized his folksy, prudent image was in, and played it up with all constituents. Gutfreund was oblivious that personal greed was now bad. Buffett admitted mistakes— easier to do, because they weren't his—then preached and publicized his corrective actions. Ultimately, what did Buffett blame for the debacle? Mostly cutthroat culture. "I don't think the same thing would have happened in a monastery."[11]

Perhaps the most widely touted and profitable culture today is Nordstrom. Like most effective communications, the culture is based on two very simple sentences: "Use your good judgement in all situations. There will be no other rules."[12] How this translates into action is more diverse. For true Nordies—and they are reputed to know if they'll fit in or not within hours—it marks the beginning of a long-term, profitable relationship. Those who leave see relentless demands, persistent pressure to reach "a ceaseless series of goals," and the need "to do virtually whatever it takes to satisfy the customer." This supplies the Nordstrom mystique.[13] Great for customers, but a universal good for the company and all its employees?

Nordstrom's customer service is the benchmark against which others measure themselves. Surely, Nordstrom's has become the darling of trade and general press. A pastor once praised the department store for "caring more then we sometimes do in church."[14] Praise from management gurus and imitation by competitors are no less fulsome.

But no culture is without a downside. Some critics cited call the "urgency to compete and conform ferocious," not for the faint-hearted. It "incites employees to prey on each other." Off-the-clock expectations—delivering   merchandise   to   customers,   for example—plus the open/closed, union shop issue—dims the brilliant story.[15] Standards are non-negotiable. One Seattle journalist likens the family to Mount Rainier, as the epitome of the Northwest. If imitation and attention from business press and gurus are the yardsticks of success, Nordstrom has made it. The first store in a new area drives change and improvement among competitors. It did noticeably when Nordstrom moved into Paramus, New Jersey, mecca of retailers. Articles, scholarly and trade, even books such as *The Nordstrom Way* by Robert Specter and Patrick D. McCarty, praise and explain for those who want to do likewise. The store even won praise in a poem:

> of all the stores
> Nordstrom was best.
> They gave a husband
> a place to rest.[16]

FOOT-IN-MOUTH MEDIA RELATIONS

When former Texas Governor Ann Richards quipped, "Poor George. He can't help it. He was born with a silver foot in his mouth," she was describing many corporate executives as well as politicians. Caught up in the euphoria of success, or, more frequently today, panicked by impending disaster, they rashly make promises that return to haunt them. One need only remember the words of Richards's target, former President Bush: "Read my lips: no new taxes."

Talking to the press looks like great fun, a heady ego-trip until the executive is taped, trapped, and caught in the tangle of misinterpretations and "mis-speaks." One CEO, puffed up by visions of a highly successful merger, promised, in the face of contradictory facts, that all employees would have much greater, not less, opportunity. When the reality of rightsizing—getting fired—rolled in, no employee ever believed him again . . . ever. His promises were a pattern, not an exception.

Timing is another foot-in-the mouth problem. Some IBM employees took umbrage at Louis Gerstner's first-day gush—the same day his signing bonus was announced and 1,400 mainframers were discharged.

In talking with the media, executives too often think off-the-record really is, but the reporter may not have precisely agreed, or doesn't honor the arrangement. One CEO thought that once the television crew began packing up the interview was over. That's when he was most candid, uttering the zingers that, predictably, surprised him as features of the interview. Public figures wound themselves frequently with the unguarded word. Just consider the number of persons prominent in sports who have been fired, fined, or consigned to obscurity for one racially pejorative remark.

There is nothing really new about lacerating and defeating with one's own tongue. Civil War General Joseph Hooker's caustic tongue—known as Hooker's opinions—embittered the atmosphere in every camp. Nor is this welcome in any organization that does not care for criticism, that prizes harmony above energy, sometimes even at the sacrifice of results. Unlike what happens today, Hooker's "opinions" carried their own antidote. Repetition dulled their cutting power. Those who knew Hooker overlooked his words because of his deeds.

With General Eisenhower, the opposite, apparent caution, caused the problem. As President, Eisenhower was criticized roundly for seemingly muddled language and mangled syntax. He surprised almost everyone in post-presidency interviews. Sentences parsed. Comments were straightforward and incisive. Had the critics known he was once General Douglas MacArthur's speechwriter, or looked behind his "hidden hand presidency,"[17] they would not have been surprised at all. Military orders must be precise, quickly understood.

Unlike other politicians, Gary Hart and Clayton Williams most visibly, Eisenhower understood the power of the ill-chosen word to wound himself and others, to defeat his programs. To accomplish his objectives, he jettisoned the "precisely etched prose" he was eminently capable of to use the emotive, inspirational, or purposely ambiguous. "Verbal expression was his instrument,"[18] sometimes used as much to obscure as to clarify. In some press conferences he seemed uninformed, when in fact he was purposely being ambiguous. To deflate an issue, he often deflected a media question to a cabinet secretary or subordinate. Sometimes he simply remained silent.[19] Imagine any politician or executive trying that today.

Williams did just the opposite and got into exactly the trouble Eisenhower avoided. Even more than barbing Bush, Richards was unwittingly describing the foot-in-mouth disease suffered by Texas politicians. Essentially, Richards won a tight governor's race because her opponent, Clayton Williams, said too much, too maladroitly.

Texas journalist Molly Ivins said of Williams: "If they'd just shut him up in a box for the duration of the campaign, he'd be governor today."[20] Going into the race, Williams had a 30-point lead, a $10 million war chest, and the "best television ads anyone had ever seen." He was likable and had the big issue: drugs.[21] He blew it all by not sensing shifts and repeatedly putting his foot in his mouth over rape, prostitutes, handshakes, income taxes, and not knowing what he was voting for.

Being an anachronism, fighting change as zealously as a Luddite, is the surest way to lose. Williams, like many corporate executives, fell into the fault line between the way things were and the way they were becoming. He represented old Texas to the bone; Richards campaigned for "The New Texas."[22]

Williams did not seem to understand that he represented a vanishing Texan—white, macho, rich, who wore cowboy boots and hat all the time, who worshiped John Wayne and believed the world was simple. "If they tell you it can't be done—tell them they haven't met Clayton Williams." More positively, he was open-handed, sentimental, and gregarious.[23] His greatest gaffe: he didn't recognize the change in women, even Republicans. They saw him as a throwback to the old Texas stereotypes they sought to change with good deeds and new images. Richards got a great deal of political mileage out of Williams's "joke" comparing bad weather to rape: "If it's inevitable, just relax and enjoy it!" Richards responded: "It's time we had a governor who knows the difference between a joke and a violent crime."[24]

Two of her opponent's gaffes involved prostitutes. Allegedly, he bragged about "honey parties," for which he hired prostitutes, had them hide on his ranch, then let his guests hunt them down. Reporters found nothing conclusive, but the damage was done anyway. To add further insult, he claimed going to Mexico to be "serviced." As Ivins noted, Texas women "don't think of themselves as a service station."[25]

If he angered women with old times, he angered Texas men by forgetting traditional courtliness—refusing to shake Richards's out-stretched hand. An open mike caught his "Watch this." Television cameras replayed the slight again and again. Reaction was uniform: "Loses cool"; "The dumbest thing" ever seen in politics; "Texas men are gentlemen."[26] Richards took the offensive, goading her million-aire opponent to fight like a man, release his income taxes, and de-bate her. Williams's timing was impeccably bad and insensitive. Just days before the election, he finally reported not paying any taxes in 1986 because he had had a bad year.[27] Unfortunately, this crossed a hot topic. Congressional deadlock over the budget had focused attention on taxes. Kevin Phillips's book *The Politics of Rich and Poor* linked the growing income disparity to the Republicans.[28]

Williams wasn't finished scattering banana peels. When ques-tioned how he had voted (by absentee ballot) on Proposition One, he was aware neither of its contents (curtailing certain gubernatorial powers) nor of how he had voted. "I just voted the way my wife told me." That. too, was media fodder, played again and again.[29] Only too late did his handlers try to isolate him from the press. Desperate, handlers canceled local hotel rooms for reporters, forcing them across the border to Mexican hotels that lacked telephones.[30]

The governor's race opened the door to an even sadder foot-in-mouth event—Lena Guerrero. When she became Richards's politi-cal campaign director, Guerrero was already the darling of Texas Democrats. She had won her seat in the state legislature against five male opponents and chaired the Texas Women's Political Caucus. Touted as a comer, a "threefer—a woman, a minority and young— she was also aggressive, even abrasive, willful, articulate, tough and excitable."[31] And, as a "roaster" of Governor Richards, she was very, very funny. But her rapid rise from relative obscurity to high visibility ultimately defeated her.

Richards did the unthinkable when she named the 33-year-old Guerrero to the three-member, powerful Railroad Commission that sets oil prices in Texas. As chair, Guerrero donned the mantle of a reformer. In July 1992, she addressed the Democratic National Con-vention. *USA Today* began speculating that Guerrero might be the first woman President. Then it all ended, because she gilded an already dramatic story. She hyped too hard.

So many accomplishments so young were not enough. Nor were summers as a migrant farm laborer with her eight siblings. During her campaign for a six-year term as chair of the Railroad Commission, false claims, made twelve years earlier, that she was a Phi Beta Kappa graduate of the University of Texas, ended it all. College transcripts showed she was a semester short of the degree and had failed six courses. Then she threw down two more banana peels. Instead of admitting she had made a mistake and apologizing, as politicians do almost too frequently these days—they're wearing out the technique—she made inept excuses and tried to laugh it all off. Humor did not work. Too late, only in the last two weeks of the campaign, Guerrero ran a commercial, "The Apology." Voters considered it just a desperate political play. She lost the election, but won obscurity.

The all-time foot-in-mouth prize for scuttling one's own career must go to Gary Hart. Pressured repeatedly by the press about his personal life, Hart couldn't stay silent. He had survived an earlier flap about believing in "reform marriage," but throwing down the gauntlet to reporters sank him this time.

The grounds and interests of his major constituency had shifted dramatically between 1972 and 1987. The "bulge in the bell curve," "the boom generation," wanted everyone, especially presidential aspirants, to "march to their tune." They were almost puritanically serious about their second marriages, about no messing around. (Ah, that's changed again.) They now sought the very safe security of convention that Hart was so dedicated (still) to undermining. Womanizing was the trap Hart fell into, with a *New York Times Magazine* profile written by E. J. Dionne. Denying rumors was not enough; Hart had to prove himself to reporters. They staked out. He entertained Donna Rice. The press reported it.[32] Even newspaper friends thought that the feeding frenzy would go away. Hart knew it wouldn't. It didn't; he did. Isn't Governor Richards's quip a cautionary tale for those risking foot-in-mouth defeat? "We knew he [Williams] was going to blow it,"[33] she concludes.

The competition is keen for the most frequent and egregious foot-in-mouth gaffes. But can anyone match Prince Philip of England's long record? Each time he misspeaks, his record is updated and repeated. The most recent, in December 1996, involved an "offhand analogy to cricket" during a broadcast opposing handgun legislation. Repeating the argument that not guns but the people who fire them are responsible, he alluded to the Dunblaine, Scotland, massacre of 16 school children and their teacher. It not only traumatized Britain, but gave rise to the very legislation Philip was opposing. He said: "Look, if a cricketer, for instance, suddenly decided to go into a school and batter a lot of people to death with a cricket bat, which he could do very easily, I mean, are you going to ban cricket bats?"[34]

Even his qualified apology did not stem the criticism of "crass," "insensitive," and "stop blundering into politics." Worse, it "enhanced" his reputation for boorishness, a heavily starched obliviousness to how others live, and a litany of other gaffes, which include:

- At the height of the 1981 recession he said: Everybody was demanding more leisure. "Now they are complaining they are unemployed."
- During a royal visit to China in 1986, he described Beijing as "ghastly" and told Scottish undergraduates studying in Xian, "If you stay here much longer, you'll all be slitty eyed."
- He told a Briton he met in Hungary in 1993, "You can't have been here that long; you haven't got a pot belly."
- Commenting in a television documentary on the fiftieth anniversary of D-Day on stress counseling, he said: "We didn't have counselors rushing around every time somebody let off a gun, asking, 'Are you all right, are you sure you don't have a ghastly problem?' You just got on with it."
- Told that an Indian photographer covering a royal tour had broken a leg, he said, "A shame it wasn't his neck."
- In 1994 he declared that "absolute poverty" no longer existed in Britain.
- In 1995 he asked a Scottish driving instructor, "How do you keep the natives off the booze long enough to pass the test?"[35]

No comment!

COSMIC THINKING

"Important" executives hurry after the really big picture, the bottom line, the cosmic issues. They skip chains of command and standard procedures—not always a bad idea—and delegate details to "unimportant" subordinates to free themselves to think lofty thoughts. The trap is that success is in the detail.

Poisoning or subverting the protective systems opens the executive to many avoidable gaffes which either damage his public image or create avoidable problems. A senior executive with a defense contractor noted that if he could trust investigations, no matter how slow, cumbersome, and nit-picking, he felt somewhat secure. He—and this author—as a result consider Gary Aldrich's *Unlimited Access: An FBI Agent Inside the Clinton White House* a very important cautionary tale.

Conversations with former First Ladies, secret hotel trysts, generational irritation about young staff's dress, mien, and office decorum allowed Aldrich's book to be dismissed as merely sensational. They obscured the important messages. Despite fairly successful attempts to keep both the book and the author from wide national exposure, the book stayed on the bestseller list for months.

Why? What can an executive suffer from casual, slow, or absent FBI checks? Lots! Even before post-election revelations, Aldrich warned that laxity in procedures and security checks "threatened national security" and "honesty of the political debate." The Zöe Baird and Lani Guinier appointment debacles, the Rose law firm, FBI files and Craig Livingston, unvetted visitors—all created large, damaging brouhahas. It behooves corporate executives, especially communicators, to understand that what you don't know hurts you big time in public. And, once silence is broken, troubles mount even when the initial problem is already fixed. One mistake is damaging enough. A constantly growing cluster destroys credibility.[36]

Some cosmic thinkers display arrogance very young and never change. As a young reporter who learned her journalism on beats and streets, not in school, this author listened to newly minted degree-bearers fuss about having to cover that carpenter-mayor, a theater fire, or highway accident. How demeaning. They aimed to cover the world events, the movers and shakers. Sometimes they would settle for discussions of the First Amendment, trendy typefaces, or how the paper should be redesigned.

Foolishly, one thought that reality would cuff pragmatism onto them. Editors, politely but more often profanely, told the neophytes that learning to cover a community accurately, understanding the carpenter-mayor, and facing the consequences of their writing were basic to any news story, no matter how mundane or important.

But as this author moved into corporate management, the same grandiose contempt of detail became evident. When conglomeraters were riding high, the conventional wisdom was that managers could be managers anywhere—one day helicopters, the next lingerie. So what if they didn't know the business. Number-crunching was all. Reputations of individual or institution were counted on to obscure any glitches, quiet any criticism. Image-making would counter and conquer all. All wrong. All embarrassing. All counterproductive, as high-powered business executives and scientific researchers would learn.

The greatest personification of managing from on high by numbers alone, and the most damaging, is Robert McNamara. Imbued with the superiority of quantification in college and at Harvard Business School, he practiced quantification, while in the military, at Ford Motor Company, in the Pentagon during the Vietnam Conflict, and, finally, at the World Bank.

Even then, this was only flying in the face of participatory management and Dr. W. Edwards Deming's stress on quality control, or the worker-producer level. Unlike McNamara's Ford, Volvo under Per Gyllenhammer organized around pods of production. Workers, organized in teams, built a car, spoke up, and were heeded. Numbers can never substitute for knowing and caring.

In her biography *Promise and Power: The Life and Times of Robert McNamara*, journalist Deborah Shapley describes him as the epitome of a bean-counting manager who understood little about, for example, engineering or selling cars. Nor did he deem innovation important. All controls were from the top down, essentially disenfranchising manufacturing foremen and plant managers. No need to know the process; figures were enough.[37]

The mortal danger of this is demonstrated in retired General H. Norman Schwarzkopf's *It Doesn't Take a Hero*. If the boss wants numbers, he gets numbers. If he wants good numbers, inflate body counts. Compete with other services for the highest and the best. Schwarzkopf, who served two tours in Vietnam, leaves no doubt of his disgust with the practice. He describes a call from a staff officer for an enemy body count. Schwarzkopf replied, "I haven't the slightest idea. We didn't stop to count . . . we were fighting through them trying to get back to camp."[38] Asked for a "best estimate," he guessed at 150, explaining he had "no confidence in that number. We pulled it out of a hat." When it was officially reported, Schwarz-kopf writes, he felt he'd "been party to a bureaucratic sham."[39] He had.

Later, a 1970 Army War College report described how military management was subverted by "incompetent commanders" who distorted figures to get ahead, and by the Army's obsession with "meaningless statistics," particularly body counts. Later, officers admitted that they "simply inflated their reports to placate headquarters."[40] By Grenada, where Schwarzkopf was deputy commander, he refused to allow individual services to guesstimate body counts. "Don't you realize now much grief there was over body counts in Vietnam?"[41] When numbers are all, great mistakes are made. More ironically, accurate quantitative measurements would have signaled trouble, even possible defeat, in Vietnam.

Shapley writes that to McNamara, "EVP" (executive vice president) of the United States, numbers symbolized his supposedly detached, objective approach to policy. He embodied statistics-driven management. That was power, a voice of reason in a dangerous world. Detached even from the battlefield, he made decisions with no staff work outside the Pentagon. While sycophants applauded, others saw the weakness. Former Senator Barry Goldwater called McNamara "an IBM machine with legs."[42] The problems, the banana peels, were self-hypnosis, the unawareness of a gestalt, of the battlefield realities. The defense secretary dismissed this even when pressed on him by combat veterans. No dissident fact, not even a dissident figure, was allowed to function as a managerial gyroscope altering direction to a more realistic course.

Such attitudes contributed to two key mistakes—not understanding the enemy and imagining that bombing runs were balance sheets. Rolling Thunder aimed for escalation, but Ho Chi Minh would not react like Americans to such a massive attack. He would fight, and did, despite any escalations or pain.[43]

Later, as president of the World Bank, McNamara applied the same yardsticks. He forced the bank to meet statistical targets— money lent, miles of roads repaired, irrigation works completed. Local social and political factors, critical to success in many areas, were simply bypassed. Word of troubles had difficulty reaching the top.[44]

Both McNamara's great strengths and his tragedy were cosmic. Shapley wrote that he viewed the huge institution below him as too small in relation to his always-growing sense of what human will can achieve. He became, in essence, a big banyan tree under which little banyan trees couldn't grow.[45]

Why did he fall? His impatience and vision were equally great. He felt, according to Shapley, that he could transform his environment and invent the future by sheer will power.[46] All it inspired was lack of trust and corruption of the military command system, and it may have mired the very countries he genuinely tried to help in debt too great for them to handle.

Nor is academic science free of the quickstep spirit—a rush past checkpoints to finish research and publish. In the rush to publish, authors sometime neglect to examine critically the quality and sufficiency of data, or fail to seek out possible errors that other experts would surely find and criticize. Others assume reputations of scientists and institutions will cloak the problems or at least forestall questions. In business, many executives think they can skate by. No one will notice; fewer will care. The more prestigious the leader, the fewer who dare to question him. Once mistakes begin to surface, a preemptive strike is often staged. Attack and attempt to silence critics. When the critic is an outsider, all the easier to discredit and control him/her. Checks, reexaminations, and corrections are hurried and delegated. Superstars involved move on to greater glory, but not for long.

Many leaders today, totally convinced of their brilliance and invulnerability, assume a problem will never escalate into a damaging, embarrassing public brouhaha. But secrets are impossible to keep. There is too much scientific competition. Too many computers keep track. Too many aggressive reporters. Too many eager lawyers. Too many disgruntled, discharged, or mistreated employees angry enough to talk. Increasingly, moving on, rushing past explanations is risky. It can result in congressional investigations with substantial press coverage, lengthy and costly litigation, and loss of public credibility. Whistle-blowers may be the bane of universities, corporations, and superiors, but they are the darlings of the press.

Grasshopper managers flourish because they promote themselves as panaceas in the face of escalating stresses and temptations. As Paul Doty, Malincroft Professor of Biochemistry at Harvard University, notes, "the growth of the [scientific] enterprise itself with its accompanying bureaucracy, the near cut-throat competition" for grants, the "possible corruption . . . of peer review, the growing number of cases of deception in scientific papers, scientists' acquired sense of the increasing avoidance of meaningful review . . . all contribute to the pressure to compromise."[47]

Sometimes such a rush in research and publication, even when that lessens scrutiny of details and checking, is understandable. AIDS sufferers themselves say "Hurry, look at the big picture, we're desperate, we're dying." That can result in errors, as in the case described below. It embarrassed scientists at two prestigious institutions—Massachusetts General Hospital and Harvard Medical School. As Dr. Lawrence K. Altman wrote in *The New York Times*:

> The error, in a theory justifying a novel drug therapy for H.I.V., . . . illustrates the enormous pressures on AIDS scientists to publish quickly while maintaining traditional scientific standards. And it points up the risks run by scientists and Federal health officials when they rush into clinical trials on the ground that a lethal disease justifies greater speed. In the Harvard case, a national trial began without independent confirmation of preliminary research findings, illustrating the risks in taking such short cuts.[48]

Management's oversights compounded serious medical lapses. Altman notes "a surprising degree of sloppiness in the quality of bench research," publishing "without repeating the crucial steps to verify ambiguous data," failure to detect "a fifth mutation in the virus," failure of the "much-heralded peer review system" designed to weed out problems, "to detect the flawed research," although there were suspicions of flaws early on.[49] Did enormous enthusiasm, desperate need, and prestige permit the rush to trial?

Language has a curious way of revealing more than is intended. On the great tide of initial enthusiasm, the Harvard team issued a press release touting its research. "May have found the 'Achilles heel' of HIV." But, instead, research and "out of hand" publicity revealed Harvard's Achilles heel.[50]

More banana peels have been spread by public bragging, by saying too much too soon, too brashly, and without being sure that operations, research, and personalities are squeaky clean. Secrets and mistakes always win out. The public brouhaha discredited the researchers, who eventually had to admit their mistakes. Dr. Altman's conclusion is just as valid for business executives as for scientists: "Anyone can come up with a theory." The distinction between science and "armchair theorizing" is evidence. In businesses, supervising by shoe leather provides the evidence. Leaping "from laboratory to human experiments without such evidence" invites trouble.[51]

When Appearances Create Reality

Business and journalism alike pride themselves on being fact-driven, on solidly grounding their decisions on statistics and hard information. In reality, appearances—accurate or misleading—may be decisive. What people believe—fact or fiction—dictates their actions. Why else would disinformation be so successful? Why are images so carefully crafted?

Perception gaps should concern any senior manager. The public and media often act on what they see or believe, which is not necessarily the truth. Women executives, in particular, ignore appearances at even greater personal peril than male colleagues. Not fair, but the reality. Understanding this power of image and media interests could have drawn much of the sting and attention out of the celebrated, over-publicized Mary Cunningham–William Agee–Bendix Corporation brouhaha. (Later they gave an encore performance at Morrison-Knudsen). They unwisely gave the media a news peg, freeing reporters to print what previously had been only rumor. Also, they were so disliked that leaks from dissident directors, fired executives, disgruntled competitors, and family kept popping up as snippets in gossip columns, even in business reporting. When former White House Chief of Staff John Sununu became the butt of Air Sununu jokes for misusing official transportation, reporters couldn't use all the leaked stories. He was that disliked.

Cunningham, despite her Harvard MBA, was naïve in her understanding of how others would perceive her zeal for strategic planning and her relationship with male colleagues, particularly her mentor, Agee, at that time Bendix's CEO. Agee escalated the risks by promoting her to too much power too soon and by putting her in the greatest flack-catching position in a company: vice president for strategic planning. Even under ideal conditions, planning is extremely sensitive; it redirects markets, kills off products, suggests sale of subsidiaries, and enhances or downgrades careers. At Bendix, the appointment was inflamed by Cunningham's age, sex, attractiveness, and business inexperience, but mostly by her perceived relationship with Agee.

Cunningham showed her contempt for communications from the very start. She yearned for the guts of operations. She did not want to be "side-tracked" into writing or rewriting Agee's speeches, although she did this and far more menial chores. She wanted to steer clear of public relations or personnel—admittedly a ghetto for corporate females—but accepted the vice presidency for corporate and public affairs when Agee offered it to her.

Her media problems started locally, when a *Detroit Free Press* reporter asked, "Isn't it unusual for a woman like you to be in so high a position?" Cunningham assumed he was referring to her academic background—a major in philosophy and ethics. Agee made matters worse by commenting to her, "Don't worry about him. He is just an ass. He doesn't mean a thing." Any business executive that far off target—not understanding what the reporter was asking—is in for trouble. Good or bad, giving any member of the media the brush-off, particularly a hometown reporter, is dumb.[52] Conversely, treating even the friendliest journalist as family, a kindred spirit, or attempting to philosophize when all the reporter wants is facts, courts difficulties. Too much proximity and access are risky. Allowing a reporter from *Fortune*, or any other publication, to spend days with interviewees, as Cunningham and Agee did, is highly desirable for the writer, but a potential minefield for the subjects. Just who can be so disciplined and guarded hour after hour, particularly under great business pressure?

Most public relations people urge companies to tell all, fast, but this counsel has downside risks. Spokespersons must be sure that the information is complete and honest, must constantly consider all the ramifications while under unrelenting deadline pressure. A loose lip can sink the cause. An innocent quote today recycled later, out of context, hurts too. Bendix fell into all these media traps.

Damaging press coverage was triggered by Agee's "Western candor" at a routine annual meeting with Bendix employees. (Some press reports gave the impression this was a special meeting called to clear up Agee's personal situation.) He commented, with invited press present, that "Mary is a very close friend of mine and my family." Why raise this with employees, press, or board of directors? It became the news peg which allowed the press to write publicly about what had previously been only a private matter.

A Bendix public relations manager had advised addressing the issue publicly and had encouraged inviting the press to the meeting. This prompted Gloria Steinem to ask Cunningham later whether the manager was a friend. Steinem later commented: "I hope to God that you . . . are having an affair, because you're sure paying the price for it."

As the drumbeat of press coverage intensified, Agee and Cunningham encountered picture problems—that pictures can lie and mislead. One, taken at a business meeting, was cropped to appear as if they were gazing into each other's eyes. Another, in *People*, showed Agee on his knees before Mary sitting on their bed. These illustrate the classic mistake of not thinking critically enough about a photo-op, much less how the picture will appear in print to those unfamiliar with the situation. Dirty tricks in photographs—airbrushing, cropping, taking people out or putting them in, even total faking—change meaning, sometimes completely. But that's nothing new. Fabricated photographs have been around a long time. Some of the more infamous tricks include Charles A. Lindbergh parading past the Arc de Triomphe in 1927 (he didn't), posed models, duplicated events to supply shots photographers had missed, even superimposed heads. A sensationalist New York City tabloid ran a "picture" of Rudolph Valentino entering heaven. Usually, photographs are cropped or airbrushed for vanity or as gags, but some alterations have serious political or personal implications. The most humorously tragic was removing plumes of smoke from Chernobyl photographs to convince residents there was no fire at the reactor. It didn't work. It only destroyed the government's last vestiges of credibility at home and, to a large extent, abroad.

Another tactic is taking a picture that clearly tells a story—but falsely. Ron Nessen, press secretary to former President Gerald Ford, cites a picture taken of campaign chairman Rogers Morton looking bleary-eyed and dismayed in front of a batch of empty liquor bottles and beer cans. Reporters had helped consume the booze, but the photograph gave the impression that the "Ford campaign was drowning its sorrows."[53]

The print media were reveling in "Executive Sweet" and "Bendix Abuzz" stories. Such attention is to be expected. Outsiders invest corporate executives with power far beyond the realm of reason. When an attractive, highly placed woman appears in this predominately male preserve, it is rare—great news. Finally, the more easily understood and salable reports of human interest, mergers, tender and ego battles crowd out the mundane and difficult to understand stories on finance and operations. A journalistic Gresham's law dictates that spicy news pushes out the sound and sober.

In her account, *Powerplay*, Cunningham notes that "things surged ahead with the inexorable speed of events that precede something very good—or very bad. . . . We were actors being asked to read increasingly more difficult lines—but someone else was writing the script." Not completely; in their maladroit handling of media relations, the principals were ensuring unsympathetic coverage.

Naïvely, Cunningham still hoped the attention would subside. Naïvely, she trusted Gail Sheehy, who had interviewed her at length three years earlier for *Pathfinders*. The best reporters, and the most lethal, act as confidants and friends. During the brouhaha, Sheehy called, assuring Cunningham that she knew what an ethical, honest person Cunningham was. Even though burned and wary of the press generally, Cunningham still agreed to a twenty-minute interview. Sheehy also talked for half an hour with Agee, alone. When her five-part series, syndicated nationally in newspapers, was about to appear, Sheehy again assured her subject that it was businesslike. "Don't worry. It's very sympathetic. You'll love it." However, Sheehy had pulled deep background information from the confidential interview for *Pathfinders*: alcoholic father, dead brother, upbringing by mother and a Roman Catholic priest. The story incorporated pop psychology with what Cunningham noted were many inaccuracies.

One of the great strengths of *Powerplay*, a cautionary tale for any executive involved in media frenzy, is the vivid description of the overwhelming pressures of having every word and action reported upon. Of being recognized everywhere and harassed in person and on the telephone. Of hiding out. Most corporate leaders are essentially very private people—some almost shy—operating in a very protected, orderly world. Being the cynosure of press attention shocks and bewilders—always.

Even after Cunningham resigned, explaining that the "unusual convergence of events beyond my control has substantially impaired my ability to carry out my responsibilities as a corporate officer of Bendix," the "vultures and voyeurs" were active; of course, they saw a good, continuing story. Even her 91-year-old grandmother was approached. Life became corporate soaps. No article on Bendix, even in respected business publications, was complete without titillating references to Cunningham. She invited more comment and coverage by going for a prolonged retreat with Agee to his Idaho home. By the time Cunningham gave her well-received Commonwealth Club speech in San Francisco, both she and Agee had learned to field questions more adroitly. Neither wanted to create any more media events. When discussing her childhood and music preferences with a WQXR host, Cunningham spoke with the extreme caution of one badly burned by exposure. Agee became gun-shy even on relatively routine corporate matters.[54]

However, caution did not prevent the couple from embarking on another highly visible corporate adventure bound to excite more press coverage: Bendix's attempt to acquire Martin Marietta. This produced far more drastic consequences for Bendix and for Cunningham and Agee personally than had the media circus surrounding their supposed relationship. Any hostile merger invites great risks as well as great rewards. Concentrating on financial and legal aspects while ignoring communications increases the risk; that's exactly what Bendix did. The major appearance mistake was including Cunningham (now Agee's wife and a Seagram vice president) in merger meetings. Dick Cheney, then veteran tender and mergers specialist for Hill and Knowlton and Bendix's outside public relations counsel, warned how damaging her presence could be. She was not a Bendix employee. The press would focus on her participation. She would stiffen the machismo resistance of Martin Marietta management. She went. She did.

This merger battle, which ended with Martin Marietta still independent, Bendix absorbed into Allied Corporation, and Agee losing his job, illustrates several communication weaknesses. Cunningham lists three distinct press-generated impressions. First, that she functioned as a Lady Macbeth, whispering evil stratagems into her husband's innocent ears. (Actually, her very presence at meetings was more damaging than any advice given.) Second, that Bendix was a big, bad wolf out to gobble up poor harmless Martin Marietta for its own greedy ends. (It certainly looked that way, although Martin Marietta was far from harmless.) Third, that Agee's actions were bad for business, bad for the country, even bad for the American way. (Whether to buy assets rather than create them, or to pour millions into mergers rather than produce products. is a question troubling many executives and economists.) "All three are neat and tidy apothegms, but untrue," Cunningham concludes.[55]

She views herself and Agee as victims, scapegoats. She is still angry at being deserted by people who she feels should have known better than to swallow the media point of view. The press, she writes, forced a false personality and history about her, one she was compelled to defend or counter, again, and again, and again. "Being blind-sided shakes your confidence to the core," she wrote. You become paranoid, looking for reporters and photographers everywhere. Maybe that's realistic, reminiscent of a poster popular some years ago that read: The fact that you're paranoid doesn't mean people aren't out to get you.

The media—and its audiences—likes nothing better than simple human-interest stories and simple tags for prominent personalities and complex situations: Alexander Haig as arrogant, Rosalynn Carter as the iron magnolia, Harry Gray of United Technologies as the finisher, and Bill Clinton as Slick Willy.

Like Cunningham, many people would be much more comfortable if the press admitted to being a business that operates under the same rules and the same profit-and-loss risks as any other commercial enterprise. In the media's world, "If it's true, that's nice, but if it sells, that's even better."

Trial by media makes private concerns and vendettas public, pressures and intrudes upon individuals, and may focus on the dramatic at the expense of the important. To avoid damage, executives must learn to not feed the press exactly what will produce the dramatic but damaging headline or story, to accept that the relationship can never be one of family or philosophizing. For women—caught in the double standards of executive suite and media coverage—ignoring appearances invites pain, misunderstanding, unwanted attention, and often business defeats.

But after slipping seriously on banana peel after banana peel, doesn't the executive learn not to slip again? Agee–Cunningham didn't. After some years in relative corporate obscurity, Agee went home to Idaho as CEO of Morrison-Knudsen, and self-inflicted another stunning, but financially lucrative, defeat upon himself. His most dubious honor is running himself and four major corporations into public and financial mire.

EGOTISM: THE VICTORIAN SECRET OF BUSINESS

In his book *Managing*, Harold Geneen, former CEO of ITT, fingers egotism as any corporation's hidden, costliest disease. It is far more damaging in dollars and effort—particularly for the communications department—and to public perceptions, yet is far less acknowledged than alcoholism. Any manager with a drinking problem, no matter how senior or important, will be confronted by the liabilities of his illness. Not so with egotism, which remains as hidden as sex was in Victorian lives.

Egotism demands a heavy price of communicators. The sensitive relationship between a communications officer and senior management, often based more on chemistry than on demonstrated accomplishment, and his role as conduit to the public, make him the most vulnerable manager in the company. One counselor who advises many fired executives says that a CEO's megalomania intimidates subordinates, distorts reality, and damages employees more than any other management defect. It also prevents him or his company from taking full advantage of public relations. Though such managers may say they want to be told the truth, he points out, they damage, demote, or dismiss the bearers. They begin believing their own public relations, discounting a contrary word from the press or anywhere else. They seek personal stature even at the expense of the company.

Symptoms of egotism are highly visible, rampant, and expensive. The countless and costly printing charges involved in producing that vanity piece of the company, that albatross of any communicator— the annual report—is just the tip of the narcissistic iceberg. (Although the annual report serves many audiences—financial analysts, stakeholders, potential employees, government and community leaders—internally it too often evokes sheer ego. Who is pictured?

Whose operations are featured?) Other ego symptoms include: prestigious speaking opportunities before peers, press, and politicians;
memberships in the Business Roundtable or New York Economic
Club; doctoring photographs; transforming internal publications
into family albums; offices of pomp and panoply. Airbrushing photographs is expensive. No matter. Cover the chairman's bald pate with
hair. Take out the wrinkles. Put a more attractive head on the president's shoulders.

A few war stories document the extent of the disease. Many will
smile and say, "I don't do that." "Amusing, but that doesn't happen
here." Just wait, look, and ask an objective associate or spouse.

Woe to the trusting communications officer who thinks all is resolved when annual report photographs are agreed upon. Second-,
even third-guessing is standard operating procedure. One annual was
delayed to assuage an executive's wife, angered because her husband's picture was not scheduled to appear. Loud, numerous complaints at a company party resulted in another photography session,
redesign of several pages, delays, more costs, and the soothing of
egos of peers still not pictured. Another communications officer relates the nightmare of senior executives demanding extensive
changes on blue lines, the last process before printing. This money-
and time-consuming procedure dramatically increases the risks of
costly mistakes and delays. Regardless—"mature" executives hag-
gled over every comma, every "the" to "a" change, the size of signa-
tures. In despair, the communicator began assigning arbitrary,
expensive price tags. Want to remove that comma? It will cost fifty
dollars and one day. The running tally soon reached a staggering
amount, twice the total estimated printing budget. That finally
quelled the rampant egotism.

Another communicator suspects that he got his job on the possibility that he could secure a peer-generated invitation to the Business Roundtable for the chairman. But perhaps the apogee of ego is
recounted by a Washington-based counselor. A client CEO asked if
his daughter could meet the President the next day while she was in
Washington working on a college political science paper. Facetiously,
the counselor asked if the daughter would like to lunch or dine with
the President. The response: "Gee, that's great. I'll ask my daughter.
If her schedule permits either, I'll call back."

Media relations and internal publications suffer from executive egotism, too—an ever-growing appetite as addictive as any narcotic. When Thomas McCann presented the coup of coups—a long, positive *Fortune* story—Eli Black was dissatisfied; he wanted the cover. Black's zeal for maximum vanity publicity transformed United Fruit's internal publication into a family album dominated by his photographs, cover paintings by his wife, and spreads of his visits to company operations and cavortings with Central American dignitaries—a classic ego trip. Nothing undermines a publication's credibility and usefulness faster than overuse as a personal ego prop or as a platform for the company's position, with nary a nod to employee concerns or interests. A corporate vanity of vanities, *The World of Armand Hammer*, is 255 pages of the late Occidental chairman pictured with movers and shakers, the perks and props of power. *The New Republic* called it "executive porn," part of the gray-flannel fantasies that business publications feed their readers. Recent revelations of Dr. Hammer's many lives and covers raises the question: camouflage or ego?

Image creation is a never-ending story. Once revealed, it angers, shocks, but, hopefully wises up those taken in. Armand Hammer, when chairman of Occidental Petroleum Corporation, strode across business, diplomatic, and art worlds for years. Behind the highly visible was another, murky world. Personal life, philanthropy, health, business, and relationships with leaders of his native Russia were not all what they appeared. In the latest of many books on the intriguing Dr. Hammer, *Dossier: The Secret History of Armand Hammer*, Edward Jay Epstein portrays the "audaciously manipulative opportunist's" self-inventions as widely accepted with little question until his death in 1990.[56] Eventually secrets will always out.

Executives forget that the more visible they make themselves, the more they grandstand corporate financial strengths and cultural contributions, the more vulnerable they become. Everyone wants to topple the big-mouth.

George Reedy, in the *Twilight of the Presidency*, relates the dangers of ego-feeding and isolation in high office. His thesis: office neither elevates nor degrades a man. Rather, it provides a stage upon which all his personality traits are magnified and accentuated. Egos, Reedy writes, must face daily clashes with similarly strong peer egos; must pay obeisance to reality; must cultivate an environment where fools can be called fools. Where sycophants can be duly observed, discounted, and weeded out. Where a devil's advocate can be encouraged. No man is wise enough to play his own. But high office too often prevents even old, trusted friends from telling a leader "go soak your head." Certainly Reedy did not feel free to say that to his long-time associate Lyndon Johnson once he became President. We have become fearful, Reedy concludes, of disputatious personalities and clashing ideologies. The press is the only external uncontrollable force that can tell the President what is really happening. Even the press does not enjoy the free exchange that it once did. In chasing after personality rather than policy issues or in just plain pandering to the powerful they diminish their power as counter-weights.[57]

COVERS OF HUBRIS

Dreams of being on the cover of a major magazine often dance through the thoughts of executives. Covers symbolize arrival and success. The visibility is heady. "A *Time* cover," comments Shelby Foote, "creates its own ethos."[58] The executive, driven by blind ego, sees only the great benefit, never the disaster. Reaching the pinnacle of being a cover subject defeated both Michael Deaver, image *Meister* of the Reagan White House, and H. Ross Johnson, once RJR Nabisco CEO. Neither man realized that such visibility would fatally exaggerate their vulnerabilities.

Curiously, Deaver slipped on exactly what he managed best for the former President—visual image. Deaver understood for others exactly which photo-ops would sell and appeal best: flag waving, patriotic, simple themes. He was at the very pinnacle of public relations power when he left the White House in 1985 to form his own company, Michael K. Deaver and Associates.

With unexpected myopia, Deaver explains in his book *Behind the Scenes*,[59] he never conceived or described his firm as a "high-powered lobbying outfit"; nor did he consider that clients hired him for access or for being Reagan's friend. (Oh what fools these image-makers can be.) "With a small staff . . . who knew how the federal system worked, we hoped to offer management strategies to clients who needed a Washington presence."[60]

Rather than as a power broker or a "Daddy Warbucks," Deaver perceived his company as modest, interceding with the federal government as lawyers in the criminal justice system. "One needs a road map to get through the maze"[61]—the standard rationale of Washington lobbyists.

Media and political powers assessed it more realistically. In February 1986 a *Time* cover pictured Deaver "sitting in the back of a chauffeur-driven Lincoln town car, talking on a cellular phone." Bad enough, but the caption, which identified Deaver as a lobbyist, made it worse, "Who's this man calling?" "Influence peddling in Washington."[62]

Deaver writes that he knew immediately he'd been had, not by the magazine or "enemies unseen," but by himself. He had forgotten the counsel he'd given so successfully so often to others—think out every angle and detail; shield yourself from as much embarrassment and criticism as possible. Mrs. Reagan told Deaver, "You made a big mistake"; that he "would regret posing for that photograph." He had violated a cardinal Washington rule: "try not to have too much success too soon." If you do, be discreet. Even when you've got it, don't flaunt it. Remember your enemies. Although the article itself was "not really unflattering or damaging, . . . the picture, the car, the phone, the caption . . . were like bleeding in front of a shark."[63]

Deaver slipped by forgetting that the appearance of wrongdoing, in our image-driven age, damages more than reality.[64] The cover brought a fast, relentless, and very public descent for Deaver—loss of power and his firm, alcoholism, and charges of perjury.

Unlike Deaver, who willingly posed for the *Time* cover, H. Ross Johnson and his public relations handlers did see dangers. They attempted to control the media by granting the long–sought-after exclusive interview. It didn't work, of course. Johnson was too hot and too controversial.

RJR Nabisco was alerted that *Time* planned a "Greed on Wall Street" cover featuring Johnson. The bargaining chip was an exclusive interview, hotly sought by the media, but previously denied. Contacts were made with *Time*'s Atlanta bureau, but cover decisions were made in New York. Could the cover be a gallery of pictures, not just Johnson? The timing couldn't be worse—in the midst of a contentious and mega-buck, delicate MBO (Management Buy-Out) meeting. Johnson reluctantly agreed to the interview, reasoning, "How much worse could it be?" Lots. To minimize the usual banana peels, Johnson was prepped about his penchant for flip remarks, encouraged to stress shareholder value, not his gain, and to expect very tough questions about the lucrative management compensation.

All for naught. The cover, just as terminally damaging as Deaver's, was entitled "A Game of Greed." The accompanying blurb read "This man could pocket $100 million from the largest corporate take-over in history. Has the buy-out craze gone too far?" Johnson self-inflicted even more injuries. Asked about the "outside management agreement," he rationalized that it was the "best deal I can [negotiate] for my people." Damn few benefited. Queried about a CEO deserving such a rich reward, he kissed it off as "a kind of Monopoly money." Sure, people would lose jobs, "but the Atlanta people have very portable skills." He was not "putting them on the breadline" and the company "had excellent severance agreements."[65]

The board of directors, which Johnson had perked and pampered, were "incensed," horrified by public reaction. Had they forgotten Johnson's penchant for saying anything? The cover not only hobbled stock price negotiations, but made Johnson a national symbol of greed exactly when the general public was questioning the social costs of buy-outs and mergers. "No director wanted to hand the company to him."[66] The epitome of media visibility led to Johnson's departure in executive obscurity.

Deaver knew courting such arrogant visibility attracted like a powerful magnet, but threw PR caution to the winds. Johnson saw that the cover was just one step too far, but took it anyway.

The P&L of CEO Visibility

The risks and advantages of high visibility and personal involvement bedevil any CEO and his counselors. Crises only raise the stakes.

If one considers media relations a type of chess game, playing the king immediately leaves no wiggle room. It involves the most senior executive prematurely. Time-effectiveness may dictate a divisional or communications officer as the spokesperson. A local problem can be handled more to the company's benefit by the local manager. Conversely, reporters always want to talk to the top. Employees want to see the senior executives involved. Political leaders and royal families understand an ounce of visible compassion turns away lots of wrath—and lawsuits.

What decides go, no go? Veteran counselor John Scanlon sees a direct relationship between a company's or its CEO's response and its character or soul. "If a company has a corporate soul. If it knows who it is. If it is constantly involved in the process of self-determination or redefinition. Then it tends to communicate" well and appropriately. It's a perplexing problem with no cookie-cutter answer.

Most initially applauded the concern and caring that Warren Anderson, CEO of Union Carbide, demonstrated by flying to the scene of the Bhopal tragedy; others questioned whether it was in the best interest of anyone. Anderson was arrested by Indian authorities; Carbide tied its corporate presence directly to the disaster rather than localizing responsibility in its subsidiary. The chairman may have confused his humane reactions with his corporate responsibilities. He was key to Carbide's operational and financial turnaround.

One aspect of visibility is crystal clear. Vacationing during a crisis or flaunting perks while pleading tough economic times are symbolic disasters that court trouble—always. The chairmen of Lilco, Amax, and other companies learned this painful lesson. Hurricane Gloria hit Long Island hard on September 27, 1985, knocking out power for thousands of Lilco customers. Even as late as October 7, 1,000 customers still lacked electricity. Where was the utility's chairman, William J. Catacosinos? Vacationing in Europe, where he lingered until October 3. He attempted to save face at a press conference upon his return. He admitted that the hurricane damage was the "worst catastrophe" the community had experienced, but he praised Lilco's preparation and response as "outstanding." He contended that company officials handled the crisis smoothly in his absence and explained that he maintained close contact with them by telephone. "I came back at the appropriate time to assess the situation." But not to salvage his image as an executive sensitive to symbol as well as substance. Responding to a reporter's question later, he conceded that he had erred in not returning sooner to direct efforts to restore power.[67]

Catacosinos's delayed return allowed company-threatening problems—financial weakness, political criticism, and the licensing of the Shoreham nuclear power plant—to escalate. The company, near bankruptcy in 1984, omitted its dividend for five consecutive quarters. Long Island politicians praised the dedicated efforts of workers to restore power, but roundly blamed management for delays. One local leader spearheaded a costly campaign to transform Lilco from a privately held utility into a public power authority.

When the hurricane hit, some legislators already were opposing the federally supervised emergency preparedness test required by the Federal Nuclear Regulatory Commission before the Shoreham plant could be licensed to operate. Relatively patient summer visitors clog Long Island roads. Just how could panicked, frightened residents evacuate a nuclear incident? Management of Shoreham's construction had also been criticized. Maladroit handling of public concerns quickened the criticism.

Public takeover discussions emerged again early in 1986, when then-Governor Mario Cuomo and New York State Republicans and Democrats, in both Senate and Assembly, supported a state takeover of Lilco. Another group with 8,000 members proposed to accomplish the same aims by creating a new power authority to acquire Lilco's stock. Some criticized the company as one of the worst managed in the country, with rates among the highest in the United States—and predicted to go still higher. Others sought alternative sources of power and called for mothballing Shoreham or preventing its opening.[68] All illustrate a colossal lack of community support. Perhaps all these problems and critiques would have surfaced eventually, but knowledge that a chairman was vacationing while many of his customers on Long Island coped with darkness and cold dinners gave anger a focus and a thrust.

Absence or concentration on the trivial to the neglect of the important indicate executive malaise or incompetence. Both are often excused or covered up. Many executives immerse themselves in do-gooder activities or long quasi-business trips to retreat from intractable problems in the office. Or, like Captain Queeg of the USS *Caine*, they worry extensively about who ate the strawberries rather than why their ship cut its tow rope. They hide out, letting subordinates cope. When such actions have hardened into patterns and intransigence, no solution short of departure is feasible.

Other CEO visibilities can damage his performance. Obvious flaunting of senior-level perks, while others are losing jobs or having their careers blighted, discourages the sacrifice necessary for corporate survival. Golden parachutes and bonuses in spite of poor financial results are easy targets for media and stockholder criticism. One large corporation simultaneously announced the closing of several mines and the purchase of an expensive jet to ease executive travel to company facilities. The bearer of the bad news flew to the downsizing meeting in a helicopter. Another insensitive manager rented a stretch limo to reach a factory to announce its closing. Still another in a rather confined business community tooled about in his chauffeured Mercedes while red ink flooded the company's financial statements. He was wooing bankers for a stretch-out of loans. Quite different was Lee Iacocca's exhortation to share the suffering at Chrysler.

Absence, controversial decisions, and high-handed actions imperiled another CEO—Pierre Gousseland of Amax. He was vacationing in Corsica when Amax announced a lay-off of 12 percent of its workforce, including a large part of the headquarters staff—those most aware of Gousseland's whereabouts. A director bluntly told Gousseland to spend less time out of the country.

Gousseland also "galled insiders and outsiders alike." Despite longstanding financial problems, Amax belatedly sold its Newfoundland fishing camp, available to executives. Amax policy prohibits executives from flying first-class, even on Atlantic crossings, but a corporate favorite was publicly rewarded for being the most frequent user of the Concorde, whose fares are usually double first-class.[69]

Corporate air forces quicken the anger of travelers delayed by security checks and operational problems, or squeezed into seats designed for cost-effectiveness, not comfort. Visions of pampered executives—without recognition of pressures and schedules—are extremely negative visibility. Something in the psyche of young nations and imperial corporations needs a symbolic airplane.

Senior managers normally lead very private lives, avoiding or having little contact with the press and other publics until elevated to leadership. Their introduction must be carefully coached and planned. Too early a debut may reveal a natural (but possibly a hobbling) incomplete grasp of all operations and the new role. Too late may diminish the appointment's news value. Too much publicity risks overexposure and prompts questions of why all the touting, or who's minding the store. Too little raises questions of hiding. It squanders people's natural identification with individual managers rather than structures, and keeps financial analysts and others from studying the new executive. Managers often vacillate—hesitate to go public. Some eventually get too hooked on visibility. To be effective, the communications officer must plan, orchestrate, and balance conflicting needs and demands, then ration appearances to best serve both the executive and his company.

WHEN THE BOSS WON'T GO

Few corporate creators are as astute as the late Roy Little, who retired from Textron, severing all formal ties, including his board seat. Although Little conceived the conglomerate idea, made it work profitably, and chose his successors, he explained it was not fair to look over their shoulders, to second-guess. An imaginative entrepreneur, Little developed new and profitable interests in venture capital and start-up companies.

Such graceful, planned exits from power are relatively rare. It is very difficult to leave a company; it is psychologically akin to leaving a child in someone else's hands. If the former CEO remains on the board, unusual sensitivity and trust are required to make the relationship work. Often a person with the entrepreneurial, inventive skills essential to creating a company cannot refine operations and plan long-range, as in the case of Apple. The entrepreneur usually follows a single, even solitary trajectory. Lyle M. Spencer calls him the wild man in an organization who doesn't want to be bossed around.

Some CEOs, like Harold Geneen of ITT, harpoon a successor with hidden agendas, informal power, and criticism until he is pushed aside completely, but only after battles are fought in newspapers. Others, such as Harry Gray of United Technologies, are accused of attempting to harass selected heirs, again causing embarrassment for the individuals involved and the company (in UT's case, for the directors as well). Inventive fathers Steven Jobs and Steven Wozniak of Apple were pushed out in highly publicized battles. All these antics leave the public, stockholders, and employees concerned about management churn and messy public reports. Both winners and losers lose publicly.

Each struggle over succession has important communications components. Given the colorful, dominant personalities involved—

good copy for the media—it is difficult to control public damage, short of muzzling everyone involved. Golden gags—bonuses for shutting up—don't always work. H. Ross Perot's departure from the General Motors board is but one example.

Harold Geneen unwillingly surrendered his CEO title in February 1977—forced to step down after bitterly fighting the board's decision, according to his biographer, Robert J. Schoenberg.[70] The action was surprising on two counts: the early dispatching of Geneen, and Lyman Hamilton's selection as CEO. Geneen agreed to continue as chairman for a year to give Hamilton the benefit of his experience.

Publicly, Hamilton was hailed as a favorable development, a big plus for ITT. The press was sympathetic, writing that Hamilton was apparently taking hold and tidying up the structure. Actually, he had three strikes against him almost before he came to bat.

Geneen did not want him—or anyone. Publicly, he was self-effacing; privately, he barely tolerated what was happening. Also, ITT's structure and operations, its mixture of businesses and their management, were designed in Geneen's image. Some felt that only he could run the hodgepodge of unmanageable ventures he had concocted. And the former CEO retained enormous unofficial power among some staff, directors, and media.

As Hamilton assumed more control, differences deepened. Where his predecessor was growth-oriented, Hamilton aimed for profitability. He began selling off what he considered to be business dogs, many of which had been Geneen's pets. The Street and financial analysts had long experienced difficulty understanding the incomprehensible agglutination of 250 disparate businesses. Hamilton decided to conform operations to the five groups used in public explanations. As the sniping and meddling continued—much of it public—Hamilton began suspecting Geneen loyalists everywhere.

And then, in July 1979, Hamilton was fired. Most observers agree that the board would never have acted without Geneen, aging, shorn of power, devastated, even humiliated by the ITT board, but still able to wield power. Hamilton's apparent acceptance belied power dynamics.

Rand Araskog, Hamilton's successor, was freed of Geneen's presence, only to face many of the same business and public problems as Hamilton did—plus a new one. He, too, struggled to transform a museum of investments and management ideas from the 1960s into a more nimble, modern, technology-centered company. The profit machine, run to produce ever-increasing quarterly profits with scant regard for the long-term, was slowing down.

Araskog faced two important communications problems. First, he penalized the messenger who bore news he did not like to hear. Executives interested in survival soon conformed their presentations. Ned Gerrity, then powerful public relations practitioner and a confidant of Geneen's, was suspended. He subsequently left amid reports of an internal investigation into leaks to press and shareholders, particularly on the question of divestiture.

With a floundering giant and a relatively new CEO, another problem arose: possible takeover. Myron Magnet of *Fortune* explained the dilemma:

> Antagonists in takeover battles don't always look like armies marching into an open field in glorious formation, drums beating and flags flying. Often they act more like dogs circling their prey in the woods at night, driving it back and forth between them, while the alarmed target, with teeth and claws of its own, can't be sure if the dark shapes it sees are shadows or substance.[71]

Was Geneen still in one of the shadows? Possibilities of takeover, divestiture, softening results, problem subsidiaries, and public disagreement all left ITT with the chore of rekindling a positive image with the press, who once wooed the company as its darling. But ultimately Araskog succeeded.

Similarly, the very qualities that helped Harry Gray build United Technologies—forceful, flamboyant, dominant, great acquisitor and finisher—stymied his relinquishing of power. Edward Hennessey was heir apparent until he left for Allied Corporation. Then, Robert Carlson acquired the mantle, only to resign suddenly after publicly acrimonious displays. He charged that Gray had wiretapped his home and office. A board investigation, extensively reported in the media, uncovered no evidence of improper actions. When Robert F. Daniell became president and CEO, Gray continued as chairman, with no announced retirement date. There were public and embarrassing boardroom fights; the selling off of one of Gray's prized acquisitions, Mostek. The new CEO may spell greater caution and prudence for both business and communications.[72]

Without a doubt, the most public and most widely reported power struggle between founder and successor was the shoot-out in Silicon Valley between Steven Jobs and Steven Wozniak—who began Apple Computer in a garage—and John Sculley, brought in by Jobs to run the highly successful business. In turn, Sculley too was forced out with attendant public acrimony. Few executives can be the men for all the seasons of a company's evolution. But "saviors" sometimes do return. In January 1997, Jobs came back to a very different Apple from the company he had left—troubled in profits, products, and public image, and vulnerable to a takeover.

Jobs, who had built Apple into a *Fortune 500* company, felt forced out by his hand-picked CEO, and said so in many interviews. Executive personality was not the sole reason. The youth of the computer industry, Silicon Valley's boom-and-bust nature, and the intensity with which entrepreneurs develop and market new technology breed nasty disputes, sudden departures, and fights over trade secrets, inventions, and market advantages. But Apple's internal battle was particularly nasty and very public.

Charges flew from both sides. Sculley claimed that Jobs valued technological elegance over customer sales; that his intense involvement with the Macintosh project had demoralized other Apple divisions; that he ruffled feathers on staid Wall Street with his brashness and overbearing self-confidence. But Jobs's troubles also illustrate a generic problem. His vision, drive, charisma, and relentless championing of the personal computer had made Apple a success. However, these skills seldom transfer into the more mature stage: a structured company, a competitive environment, and long-range planning. Even his early collaborator, Wozniak, questions whether Jobs could put anyone's interests ahead of his own. Communicating such attitudes, no matter how obliquely, creates a morale problem.

Sudden, dramatic market changes dictated that Apple must become more structured to survive. It caused the crucial rift between Jobs and Sculley. Management style had to change also, but was the shift more apparent than real?

To be successful, any public relations person and management must change as the times do. Apple, once so avant-garde, seemed slow to sense these shifts. When Apple was riding high, "event marketing"—extravagant corporate announcements that reaped lavish press attention—was standard operating procedure. With a less successful business story to tell—rushed reorganization, 20 per cent of the workforce laid off, the first-ever quarterly loss, and a stock low—Apple sought less publicity. Unfortunately, turning off the publicity hype once so arduously sought is difficult. When business goes sour and the company prefers not to talk, the press starts digging.[73]

Only in very unique situations and through unusual press relations is such silence possible. For example, in 1982 at RCA, top management was absolutely chaotic. There had been four CEOs in ten years, politics was rampant, and morale was at rock bottom. The company was overdiversified and overextended.

However, the CEO, who understood the press, took the spokesman into his confidence. No news ironically translated into good news. Almost everything bad about RCA had already been written—many times. But, what is perhaps crucial, the communications officer, once a journalist himself, knew and was respected by many in the press and broadcasting. Even so, persuasion carried more weight than contacts. More stories about RCA would only bore readers, be terribly repetitious. The PR person appealed for a breather, promising to open doors wide when the company became newsworthy again. All unusual for a novice to try. After getting the corporate house in order and conducting research that indicated RCA had a neutral image, the company resumed its public presence, first with corporate advertising. The theme: "RCA: one of a kind."[74]

Although many other companies, such as Apple, might wish to emulate this success, RCA's position was unique. Nor did RCA's problems invite the high drama of the chips warriors. Initially, Jobs and Sculley looked like an unbeatable combination—a deliberate visionary and a driven corporate type, but good friends. Soon they differed on almost everything from authority to board instructions. What signaled to one a phase, the other saw as a reprieve.

Eventually, when Jobs left the company, it had been damaged by public squabbling and threats of resignations. Rumors filled information gaps. Little was explained publicly. With Sculley firmly in control, it was hoped the company could present one face to dealers, customers, and others. Many business prospects had been put off by the turmoil and conflicting messages from rival leaders and product divisions. Although Sculley imposed new controls, pared Apple's bloated operations, and said he wanted to build the company in his image—cool, disciplined, orderly, and driven—ego reared its head again. When Sculley presented Apple's 1986 plans in San Francisco, they featured a multimedia slide show, 22-city teleconferencing, and a specially written rock theme song, all presented in front of a huge blow-up of John Sculley.[75]

Sculley muted Jobs's public image, his enterprising and inventive drive. Even the settlement with Jobs was a joust of public relations people speaking for the silent principals. Jobs's representative explained that Jobs was happy to put it all behind him. Apple's public relations firm, Regis McKenna, in a prepared statement, said that the settlement protected the shareholders.

All this high drama and amusement in Silicon Valley and the computer industry made good copy. But more conservative investors, financial analysts, customers, and shareholders are attracted to a less turbulent image, and an orderly transfer of power. For Apple the management churn continued: too much was told publicly by angry principals. But the major communications challenge is to explain that this, as well as wide swings in earnings and product success or failure, are the nature of start-up enterprises in a volatile, young industry.

THE CHAIRMAN GOES TO WASHINGTON

Managing amid corporate turmoil can begin with a single announcement, a single news item. With instantaneous, global transmission by many highly competitive news wires and networks, companies are encountering great difficulty managing their news. For neophytes thrust into the public arena risks are high.

When President Jimmy Carter nominated Textron's chairman, G. William Miller, in 1977, to head the Federal Reserve Board, the company's relative normalcy was transformed into a maelstrom of events, tensions, and investigations. The microscopic, almost engulfing volume of attention from national media, government agencies, and financial analysts thrust the corporation, its management, and its operations under a magnifying glass.[76]

Such sudden, extensive media attention produces surprising ramifications—magnification of flaws, flaunting of well-stated policies, and exposure of weak individuals—that even the most seasoned managers can scarcely begin to imagine.

Even before the official announcement, Textron's telephone

switchboards lit up like Christmas trees. Media attention was extensive and constant. More like tough reporters than a corporate staff, Textron's communicators did a great deal of legwork: checking out rumors and constantly attempting to release as much information as was necessary and possible. Media people were in the company's offices, on the telephones, seemingly ever-present with more questions. Who was Bill Miller? Did his speeches give any clues to his possible positions at the Fed? Later, questions got tougher. Who paid what to whom for helicopter sales? Who knew about it, when? In all their responses, communicators stressed Miller's well-known and frequently announced policy of absolute honesty in company dealings.

A few less-than-professional journalists snooped around the offices, rifling through papers on secretaries' desks and creating a need for tighter security. Few executives had experienced such high-intensity press attention; they questioned why the media always seemed adversarial. Information revealed during confirmation hearings before the Senate Banking Committee and in the media resulted in four independent investigations by the Internal Revenue Service, the Justice Department, the Securities and Exchange Commission, and a special committee of Textron's board.

Headlines recreate the tension and eruptiveness—more like a newspaper city room than a corporate department. It started gently. *The Wall Street Journal* asked, "Bill who?" then waxed euphoric in a combined corporate-personal profile headlined:

> Golf Carts, Buses and Operas
> G. William Miller
> The Amalgam of Superman,
> Solomon and Sir Galahad

Other early headlines were equally complimentary: "Known for skill and public service"; "A decisive corporate humanist." But the early bloom soon faded. "The Senate digs deeper on Textron's payment in Iran, slowing Miller's track to the Federal job." Each morning, managers were happy not to see Textron's name emblazoned in headlines—the reverse of the usual PR practitioner's dream of visibility.

Textron's executives—already stretched by responding to investigations and allegations, a new management team, and adjustments to great visibility—were confronted in December 1978, by an international crisis: Iran. Bell Helicopter-Textron, then the largest U.S. employer in Iran, stayed on the longest with the most people. In addition to its concern about getting 6,000 to 7,000 Textron people out safely, the company had contractual obligations. Investors and analysts worried whether the loss of Iranian business would affect Bell's earnings. Because of the chaos, the press was getting very little information from any source, and much of that eventually proved to be false.

One morning, shootings were reported at the Hilton Hotel, the embarkation point and sanctuary for Bell employees. Some senior executives allegedly had been captured. Fortunately, both stories proved erroneous, but the truth didn't reach Textron for many anxious hours.

Dominating Miller's nomination process and the Iranian crisis was the pound, pound, pound of vast numbers of telephone calls, the sheer volume of complicated, delicate questions to be answered, and the constant surprises. Those two years of battle-like pressure honed a cardinal principle about crisis coping. Most of the major events that hit Textron in 1978—Iran, Miller's two presidential nominations, and the subsequent investigations—were external and largely unpredictable. Textron is not alone with that problem. Time pressures and demands on senior management force them to focus on internal operations. To balance this, corporate communicators must act like corporate radar, spotting specks on the horizon—almost imperceptible today, but potentially of serious concern to the company. The conventional wisdom is usually wrong, but difficult to confront. Iran, just before the Shah's fall, was touted everywhere—the state department, media, and pundits—as the Middle East's rock of stability. But some decidedly non-corporate publications, *The New York Review of Books* for one, were reporting trace-lines of trouble with imprisoned, silenced, and exiled critics. The best communications officers monitor the periphery, question the accepted. Then, what is most difficult of all, they must convince peers in senior management of their seriousness, and anticipate consequences.

POLITICAL IMAGE-MAKERS GONE AWRY

Image blunders are too well known, numerous, and frequent—Hair Force One, high level appointments announced prematurely without due diligence to details or liabilities—deflect attention from important issues. A *Guardian* cartoon shows all the banana peels President Bill Clinton and his staff slipped and slid on before the arrival of David Gergen. But even political image-makers can self-destruct easily.

Details, details, details, reality imagined, can make the difference between an event well run and a disaster. "Lincoln knew the dangers that lurk in iotas."[77] The outcry about President Reagan's visit to Bitburg Cemetery in Germany demonstrates that reality doesn't come from assuming but from careful observation.

Deaver, visions of photo-ops dancing before his eyes, tacked on Bitburg as an afterthought to the May 1985 economic summit in West Germany. Hailed as "Magic Mike" and "The Vicar of Visuals," he sought to capitalize on the fortieth anniversary of the end of World War II and mute Reagan's reluctance to visit a former concentration camp. "He is at his best when he touches nostalgia," Deaver explained. "Put him near a flag, around uniforms, or in sight of a parade, and he lifts anyone's spirit."[78] If anyone spotted the pitfalls, they kept quiet. In post-mortems, these same folks quickly asked, "How could you not see?" Deaver literally couldn't see the pitfalls— the graves were covered with snow and photo-ops would be great. Brush away the snow to check? Ask questions? Of course not. The only priorities were making sure the President was not over-scheduled.

But mistakes and controversy make news, not smoothly run operations. As soon as German newspapers reported that 49 Waffen SS men were buried at Bitburg, veterans marched, Jewish groups demonstrated, Holocaust survivors and others "begged the president to back off."

When caught between a rock and a hard place, image-makers turn to spin. The President wouldn't and couldn't cancel the trip, for domestic and international reasons. It seemed so stupid, but "escalated into the worst crisis of the Reagan presidency." How could anyone support or understand the decision?

The great damage of such uproars is that they push important issues into the shade. The average American may not understand the intricacies of the budget, but he understands $200 hair cuts and Congressmen bouncing checks. He may not know or care about Nicaragua, but the Waffen SS were his enemy. If he was not a participant himself, there are lots of old movies on late-night television to remind him.

Ah, never overlook the power of spin to sweep away the banana peels. Deaver admitted his mistake, but was trying to fix it. Rather cynically, he added a side trip to Bergen-Belsen after all. The Bitburg ceremony would be brief, clean, almost sterile. No speeches. Then luck intervened. General Matthew B. Ridgeway, who commanded the 82nd Airborne in Europe, offered to lay a wreath. The Germans countered with General Johannes Steinhoff, a Luftwaffe ace, who had served on Ridgeway's NATO staff. Deaver was impolitely cautious: "You better snake-check [him] . . . for everything he's worth."[79]

Deaver's spin, his staging worked. He wrote: the visit will be remembered for a gesture "well meant," and, against deep-rooted resistance, well timed. "For all the grim images and the raw, sobering, emotional scars, most of us left Germany lighter in mood than when we came. The president had endured . . . overcome barriers that some feared, or hoped, would endanger his authority."[80]

A bad situation was transformed into one with potential success. Reality, difficult as it is for image-makers to acknowledge, doesn't come out of wistful thoughts, but through the constant diligence of details, details, details.

How to Succeed Without Slipping

Just as banana peels can be avoided by watching where you step, or never scattering them in the first place, a few simple precautions can avoid a public slip. Here are some:

- Scope the environment internal to the company, but especially external, widely, pragmatically, never wishfully or optimistically. Analyze it as others would, not as you want to see it. Look and listen carefully. Don't take too much of yourself, or your hopes and fears, into the analysis.
- Seek out trace-lines of change. Look to the fringes, the outlying offices, not just the core, where trouble usually appears last. Change starts in surprising places. In retrospect, trace-lines are obvious. The challenge is to spot them early, before others do or before the crisis

hits. Early signals of trouble, ignored or played down, allow the problem to escalate and widen.

- Listen to the Cassandras, the doom-sayers. Sometimes they might just be right.
- Don't think, like a cocksure teenager, that disasters always hit someone else.
- Don't try to quantify every situation. That may be too narrow an analysis, or reality may lurk behind the numbers.
- Manage so that subordinates are applauded, not punished, when they flag a small problem rather than letting it erupt into a full-blown crisis. Encourage channels to let bad news and debates reach you. Don't fire the whistle-blower, especially when he's right.
- When a crisis hits, don't allow vested internal interests to minimize the risks or relegate it to a passing blip on the corporate radar. Conversely, don't exaggerate a crisis out of all importance.
- Never, never assume; never, never lie.
- Appoint a corporate devil's advocate, a gadfly. You are never smart enough to be your own. Cultivate a loyal opposition, people willing to question your assumptions without fear of retaliation. Remember, a blind spot is the one you can't see, but someone else, given a chance, might.
- Never think you can keep a secret.
- Imagine the strains; imagine the public hounding; imagine that good news is no news before you act. A private life or problem gone public has a dynamic, a propulsion all its own.
- Move quickly on rumors, toxic information, and data bank mistakes. Left uncorrected, they'll only metastasize.
- Look for the specks on the horizon before they become full-blown problems. Granted: trying to catch a trend accurately is like attempting to contain quicksilver in your palm, but it's worth a try. Be sure operations are squeaky clean, particularly after one incident or if you're in a hot-topic industry. Another incident, an encore echoes through the media. and multiplies the volume of coverage.
- Survey your situation for potential problems before you speak out. Keep your foot out of your mouth.
- Speak candidly—no weasel or mugwump words. This is particularly important with today's new work force—highly suspicious of authority, seeking lots of opportunity, knowledge, and freedom. Their bull-shit radar is very sensitive. Don't promise too much, or say too little. Show your concern for employees, not just for yourself and your clones.
- Attempt to see your situation as others do, particularly your enemies

or the press. When the author was running a corporate communications department, she often asked the newspaper people on her staff to sit on the other side of their desk to read the release they had written as an editor. Many, many of those releases went into the wastepaper basket. Almost all were rewritten.

- Think how others perceive a situation. President Clinton may have thought it easier to stay aboard Air Force One for the now infamous haircut, but the reality was Hair Force One jabs and damaging of the carefully cultivated populist image.
- Depoison your in-box. Remember that bad news gets strained, becomes more and more positive as it goes up the corporate command. Compensate by having channels for getting critical information and encouraging truth-sayers. That's what back channels are all about.
- Run your operation as if the whole world were watching or will be again soon.
- Image is never all. When reality and image diverge too far, reality always wins.
- Think with vision, but watch the nitty-gritty.
- Be modest. Don't believe all the hype you've paid for. Arrogance, bragging, and too much (or unwarranted) visibility court trouble.
- Remember that living too well courts a downfall, particularly if the job isn't being done well, compassionately, or profitably.
- Use a good story, market it aggressively, but be sure it's absolutely correct.
- Telling employees and the public anything doesn't work anymore. They've heard that story and suffered with the corrections too often. Employees are more prone to be cynical than automatically loyal today.
- Don't emulate dinosaurs; they may be popular, but only on the movie screens, with marketers and children. Otherwise they're in danger of being run over by survival-driven change.
- Don't kill your dreams of personal or corporate glory by doing anything necessary to reach it, by being romantic rather than realistic.
- Watch out for banana peels: they may be your own.

NOTES

1. *Guardian Weekly*, May 9, 1993, p. 10.
2. Marcia Vickers, "After Tripping on Its Laces, Reebok is Focused Again," *The New York Times*, March 2, 1997, Section 3, p. 3.

3. Ibid.

4. Sam Howe Verhouek, "A Store Manager Interrupts a Theft, and His Career," ibid., December 18, 1996, p. A16.

5. Jack O'Dwyer, *Jack O'Dwyer's Newsletter*, March 12, 1997, p. 2.

6. Richard C. Morias, "The Banana Skin Factor: Standard Charter Is a Cheap Bank Stock," *Forbes*, July 19, 1993, pp. 73–75.

7. General comments on the Salomon culture were gathered widely from business publications; Tom Wolfe's *Bonfire of the Vanities*; particularly John Gutfreund's conspicuous consumption; and Barbara Rush's "Playing in the Middle of the Court: The Salomon Treasury Scandal," written as a partial requirement for an MBA, Graduate School of Business, Fordham University, December 1992.

8. Michael Lewis, *Liar's Poker: Rising Through the Wreckage on Wall Street*, (New York: W. W. Norton, 1989), p. 41.

9. Ibid., p. 48.

10. Rush, "Playing in the Middle of the Court," p. 2.

11. Richard D. Hylton, "Salomon's Remaining Challenges," *The New York Times*, August 19, 1991, p. 41.

12. Robert Spector and Patrick D. McCarthy, *The Nordstrom Way: The Inside Story of America's #1 Customer Service Company* (New York: John Wiley, 1995), p. 16.

13. Ibid.

14. Ibid., p. 21.

15. Ibid., p. 29.

16. Ibid., p. 146, quoted from J. Glenn Evans's "A Place to Rest."

17. Fred I. Greenstein, in *The Hidden Hand Presidency: Eisenhower as Leader* (New York: Basic Books, 1982), details not only Eisenhower's easily misjudged management style, but also his "instrumental use of language." See pp. 66–72.

18. Ibid., p. 66.

19. Ibid., pp. 67–68.

20. Molly Ivins, *Molly Ivins Can't Say That, Can She?* (New York: Random House, 1991), p. 278.

21. Ibid., pp. 278–284.

22. Ibid., p. 280.

23. Ibid., pp. 283–284.

24. Celia Morris, *Storming the State House: Running for Governor with Ann Richards and Diane Feinstein* (New York: Charles Scribner's Sons, 1992), p. 101.

25. Ivins, *Molly Ivins Can't Say That*, p. 283.

26. Morris, *Storming the State House*, pp. 158–159.

27. Ibid., p. 165.

28. Kevin Phillips, *The Politics of Rich and Poor: Wealth and the American Electorate in the Reagan Aftermath* (New York: Random House, 1990).

29. Ivins, *Molly Ivins Can't Say That*, p. 283.

30. Ibid., p. 284.

31. Morris, *Storming the State House*, pp. 51, 83.

32. Richard Ben Cramer, *What It Takes: The Way to the White House* (New York: Random House, 1992), pp. 387–389, 442.

33. Thomas Hayes, "Taking on Big Oil," *The New York Times*, April 12, 1992, Section 3, p. 14. and the unsigned "Texas Official Resigns Over Falsified Résumé," ibid., September 26, 1992, p. A5.

34. Warren Hoge, "Prince Philip Angers Britons on Gun Control," ibid, December 20, 1996, p. A12.

35. Ibid.

36. Readers are encouraged to draw valuable corporate lessons from Gary Aldrich's book *Unlimited Access: An FBI Agent Inside the Clinton White House* (Washington, D.C.: Regnery, 1996), and from his "The 'Character Issue' and the FBI," *The Wall Street Journal*, October 11, 1996, p. A12.

37. Deborah Shapley, *Promise and Power: The Life and Times of Robert McNamara* (Boston: Little, Brown, 1993), pp. 65, 67.

38. H. Norman Schwarzkopf, with Peter Petre, *It Doesn't Take a Hero* (New York: Bantam Books, 1992), p. 119.

39. Ibid., p. 178.

40. Ibid., p. 253.

41. Shapley, *Promise and Power*, p. ix.

42. Ibid., p. 102.

43. Ibid., pp. 332–333.

44. Ibid., pp. 548–550.

45. Ibid, p. 562.

46. Ibid., p. 607.

47. Quoted in Lawrence K. Altman M.D., "Faith in Multiple-Drug AIDS Trail Shaken by Report of Error in Lab," *The New York Times*, July 27, 1993, p. C3.

48. Ibid.

49. Ibid.

50. Ibid.

51. Ibid.

52. Jody Powell, President Jimmy Carter's press secretary, put it more colorfully. Speaking to the Public Relations Society of America meetings in Detroit, in November 1985, he said, "If one is willing to grovel before one's inferiors, it is possible to have a positive impact."

53. Ron Nessen, *It Sure Looks Different from the Inside* (New York: Playboy Press, 1978). pp. 209–210.

54. Material for the Bendix phase of the Mary Cunningham–William Agee discussion was drawn from Mary Cunningham, with Fran Schumer, *Powerplay: What Really Happened at Bendix* (New York: Linden Press/Simon & Schuster, 1984), and from interviews with women corporate executives, those attending the Commonwealth Club speech, and the author's listening to the WQXR broadcast.

54. The Martin Marietta phase is based on Peter F. Hartz, *Merger: The Exclusive Story of the Bendix–Martin Marietta Takeover War* (New York: William Morrow, 1985), conversations with aerospace executives in other companies, and various newspaper accounts.

56. Edward Jay Epstein, *Dossier: The Secret History of Armand Hammer* (New York: Random House, 1996), p. iv.

57. This discussion was culled from George Reedy's *The Twilight of the Presidency* (New York: Mentor/New American Library, 1970). It is based not only on Reedy's long friendship with Johnson but also on his acute observations of personality changes when a friend becomes the President.

58. William C. Carter, *Conversations with Shelby Foote* (Jackson: University of Mississippi Press, 1990), p. 528.

59. Michael K. Deaver, with Mickey Herskowitz, *Behind the Scenes, in Which the Author Talks About Ronald and Nancy Reagan and Himself* (New York: William Morrow, 1987), pp. 179–180. For those interested in pursuing the use of image, spin control, and the use of public relations power, the Deaver book is a relative how-to-do-it and how-not-do-it.

60. Ibid., p. 216.

61. Ibid., p. 217.

62. Ibid., p. 215.

63. Ibid., p. 216.

64. Ibid., p. 217.

65. Bryan Burrough and John Helyar, *Barbarians at the Gate* (New York: Harper & Row, 1990), p. 528.

66. Ibid., pp. 452, 475.

67. "Lilco Is Praised by Its Chairman for Storm Effort," *The New York Times*, October 8, 1985, p. B4.

68. Clifford D. May, "Shoreham Plant Opponents Pressing for State Takeover of Lilco," ibid., December 28, 1985, p. B5.

69. Marilyn Harris and Judith H. Dobrzynski, "Judgement Day May Be at Hand for Pierre Gousseland: Amax's Financial Crisis and His Controversial Decisions Could Cost Him His Job," *Business Week*, September 30, 1985, p. B5.

70. Robert J. Schoenberg, *Geneen* (New York: Warner Books, 1985), and Harold Geneen, with Alvin Moscow, *Managing* (New York: Avon, 1984) are interesting, contrasting accounts of the once-powerful CEO's departure.

71. Myron Magnet, "Is ITT Fighting Shadows—or Raiders?" *Fortune*, November 11, 1985, pp. 25–28.

72. Thomas J. Lueck, "Chief's Post Given Up by Gray, Technologies Names Daniell," *The New York Times*, September 24, 1985, p. D1.

73. Deborah C. Wise, "Can John Sculley Clean Up the Mess at Apple?" *Business Week*, July 29, 1985, pp. 70–72; "Slowdown in Silicon Valley," *Newsweek*, September 30, 1985, pp. 46–57; Bro Uttal, "Behind the Fall," *Fortune*, August 5, 1985, pp. 20–24; "Apple, Part 2: The No-Nonsense Era of John Sculley," *Business Week*, January 27, 1986, pp. 96–97.

74. Thomas Ross, "RCA's Comeback, Communicating the Story," *Crosscurrents in Corporate Communications*, No. 14 (New York: Fortune, 1985), pp. 28–31.

75. John Eckhouse, "Apple Parties, Unveils Strategy," *San Francisco Examiner*, February 4, 1986, p. 4; and John Eckhouse and Vlae Kershner, "Apple Settles Case Against Steven Jobs," *San Francisco Chronicle*, February 4, 1986, p. 7.

76. The sources here are the author's experience as Textron's vice president for corporate relations; her speech "The Corporate City Room," given to the New England Section of Public Relations Society of America, Providence, Rhode Island, April 1980; *The Wall Street Journal*, *The New York Times*, *The Washington Post*, and *Providence Journal* accounts; and conversation with Textron executives and communicators in CEO visibility.

77. Carter, *Conversations with Shelby Foote*, p. 258.

78. Deaver, *Behind the Scenes*, pp. 179–180.

79. Ibid., p. 185.

80. Ibid., p. 188.

5

A Beguiling Conundrum

Communicating Executive Illness Across Cultures

"The event turned on his personality as the massive door of a vault turns on a small jewel bearing"

—HERMAN WOUK, *The Caine Mutiny*

"Is the fate of the world in the hands of sick men?"

—ARNOLD ROGOW[1]

"The secret malady of a statesmen can be as disastrous as his secret diplomacy"

—ARNOLD ROGOW[2]

DIMENSIONS OF THE DILEMMA

Is that rigorous, dynamic leader really as healthy as he looks, or merely a cleverly, even deceptively crafted image being manipulated to achieve an illusion, complete a mission? Communicating executive health problems seems so beguilingly easy. But even under the best, most candid circumstance, the issue poses a public relations conundrum.

- How open can communications be when the executive himself or his family seeks privacy? Must a CEO relinquish some privacy as a U.S. President does?
- Will telling all help or hurt the company? Its objectives and profitability? Its continuity, even existence?
- Does candor sustain employee morale? Or quicken fears for their own lives and careers?

- Should serious illness or impairment, physical or psychological, always be revealed? Ever concealed? Used to achieve personal or organizational goals?
- Will cultures, corporate or national, react differently? Will telling all console some but deeply offend others?

Few guidelines in law or policy are explicit. The answers, neither easy or uniform, are sometimes surprising.

Executive health is often scanted, downplayed, or rationalized away by succession planning, depth of the executive bench, even questions of how important any one executive is. However, several recent serious illnesses among corporate leaders are raising important new questions about candor, image, and the complexity in managing expensive consequences.[3] Just several examples:

- The late Dr. Theodore Cooper, Upjohn's chairman and chief executive officer, disclosed his bone-marrow cancer shortly after it was discovered. As Upjohn periodically reported on Dr. Cooper's illness, it won kudos from industry analysts, consultants, and shareholder rights advocates.
- In like manner, the late Michael F. Walsh, Tenneco chairman and CEO, announced his brain cancer just two days after a definite diagnosis. He won high media praise, particularly in a highly complementary *Business Week* cover feature.
- When Brinker Chairman and Founder Norman Brinker suffered brain-stem damage in a polo accident, he was replaced two days later. During the 3½ weeks he was unconscious, periodic reports speculated on the date of his return, who was running the company in his absence, and his attendance once at a board meeting.
- Less forthright and less successful was the hiding of TLC Beatrice CEO Reginald F. Lewis's brain cancer until he slid into a coma just one day before his death. Lewis's rationale: succession planning. Ironically, the surprise triggered rumors that Beatrice was about to be taken over or sold. Because Beatrice is privately held, Lewis and his family enjoyed a latitude denied a publicly held company.
- Even greater difficulty was created when MCI founder Bill McGowan kept news of his heart attack under wraps for two weeks. McGowan so personified MCI, was so key to its success that when the attack was revealed, MCI's stock plummeted almost $6 a share. Four months later, McGowan underwent heart transplant surgery, again not revealed for several weeks. Seething analysts took MCI to task. There is nothing Wall Street likes less than an unpleasant surprise.

- How embarrassing when a CEO's illness sends the stock up. Contel CEO Charles Wohlstetter's heart attack, reported four days later, sent the companys stock up 1⅞.
- It is equally embarrassing when death affects neither stock nor management. James Olson, AT&T CEO, died after a month-long struggle with colon cancer discovered during a surgical procedure. AT&T delayed any public announcement for two weeks and then made it only after persistent questions from reporters, tracking down rumors about Olson's health. When his successor James Allen had elective heart surgery to repair a congenital problem, little comment was made.
- Waffling and brief announcements concerning Time Warner's Chairman and Co-Chief Executive Steven J. Ross's prostrate cancer created questions of credibility and undue optimism. It had little apparent impact on the company, however. Six months after announcing he had begun therapy, Ross took a temporary leave. He died instead of ever returning to Time-Warner, as many expected.
- Even a hint of illness can unseat a troubled executive. Besieged General Motors Chairman Bob Stempel was admitted to a hospital after taking ill during a business meeting. Although GM attributed it to just high blood pressure, Stempel soon resigned under board pressure. A few days later, he reportedly had a coronary bypass.
- Illness and death, even Evita Perón's embalmed body, were manipulated for greater political power for herself and her husband—more power than most healthy leaders can ever think of aspiring to.

Questions must be raised about the political impact of former President George Bush's highly visible illness in Tokyo or the frequent rumors of ill health and heavy drinking of Russian President Boris N. Yeltsin. The cat-and-mouse game with the world press prompted questions whether his illness was eroding his political power and judgment. Even after successful heart surgery, questions remain. The Kremlin's long tradition of secrecy calls into suspicion even "apparent" health.

Disclosure of former Pennsylvania Governor William Casey's health problems, followed by a double transplant, doomed his political ambitions. As in the case of baseball great Mickey Mantle's transplant, questions of favoritism were voiced. Even the mixed approach of former President Ronald Reagan—applauded for announcing his Alzheimer's, but only after rumors had spread—contrasted with other aliments obscured by cleverly crafted images. An "apparent" quick recovery after an assassination attempt downplayed its serious-ness.[4]

OVERLOOKING THE OBVIOUS

Despite costly operational disruption, serious business considera-tions, and publicity conundrums, health has been generally over-looked as a performance criterion or an analytical tool. William H. McNeil's 1976 *Plagues and People* startled historians and others into wondering how they could have overlooked the great pain of Napo-leon at Waterloo or Lee at Gettysburg. McNeil considers diseases the background music against which human life has always been lived.[5]

Writing almost a decade later, Arno Karlen extended McNeil's concept to study the "odd allure" of a leader's health. Karlen wrote:

> It is fascinating to see medicine, biology, history, and other specialized knowledge dovetail, reflecting the complex interweavings of life. There is a delight in following intellectual detective work—especially when it seems to hand us a hidden, decisive way to decipher the mys-teries of health, behavior, and history. . . . The body helps shape per-sonality and behavior. We have long sought the roots of character and action in the flesh. . . . It seems logical that aches or itches which distract ordinary citizens . . . may become, in chiefs of state, forces of history. An adrenal tumor can cause psychosis; lead poisoning can in-duce hallucinations; tuberculosis brings extraordinary changes on mood and personality. Certainly, Franklin D. Roosevelt's life was deeply influenced by polio, Edison's by deafness, Dostoevski's by epi-lepsy. Hitler's performance during the Battle of Stalingrad was driven by stubborn rage caused by constipation.[6]

Analyzing leadership is never simple. Did Napoleon soar to great-ness on a churning pituitary, burn himself out, and collapse into a slump of obesity, impotence, crankiness, and lazy dullness? Or was he driven to his achievements as a compensation by physical defi-ciency? Or did man and opportunity uniquely coalesce?[7] Karlen com-ments: "Hereditary conditions have afflicted and shaped families, villages, nations. . . . Diet, climate, and a variety of biological clocks may strongly affect behavior. . . . Viruses can act like floating bits of genetic material."[8]

Between treating disease "like a big, ugly stone sporadically dropped into the stream of human events,"[9] and reducing leadership to a mere walking clinic lies the opportunity for understanding and communicating.

ATTENTION IS BEING PAID

Attention to disclosing or concealing CEO health was prodded by the chronological coincidence of Lee Atwater's death from a brain tumor, followed by announcements in three days of Lewis's, then Walsh's tumors, then Lewis's death. Pity a communicator dealing with such totally unrelated events linked publicly. Or with unfounded rumors such as heavy cellular phone use as a cause of brain tumors. Coincidence made the scientifically false seem true. When Intel CEO Andy Grove was treated for prostate cancer, *Fortune* ran a cover story about and by Grove, detailing how his strategy, borrowed from how he runs his business, helped him choose the treatment and handle other aspect of the illness. *Fortune*'s managing editor devoted his "Editor's Desk" column to complementing Grove's "compelling candor," "meticulous search for the medical protocol with the best odds" and life-altering experiences as a result.[10]

Given this random cluster of illness, cancers and rumors, headlines began to appear—"Corporate Conundrum: Disclosing Illness in the Corner Office"; "CEO's Illness May Endanger Company's Health as Well"; "How Healthy Are CEO's? Illness Often Treated as a Private Issue"; "CEO's Who Fell To Illness"—accompanied by the caveat that executives may be mortally ill and no one, not even directors, be aware: "When Fatal Illness Is a Public Affair—The Executive's Duty When Serious Illness Strikes."[11] These dilemmas and issues frame current discussions.

After analyzing a number of executive illnesses, Robert Seitz, writing in *The New York Times*, drew several conclusions. Applauding Walsh for "Putting it right out on the table," Seitz adds the longer a company delays disclosure "the more it runs the risk of misleading statements about its operations and corporate decisions."[12] In the absence of both news and the executive's presence, usually rumors, worse than facts, fill the void, fueling and exaggerating fears. Speculation in the absence of news, for instance, raised hopes that Steven

Ross would recover, that he was still actively making decisions until just before his death. All work against the organization and its media credibility.

Absent corporate, even SEC policy, and sensitive to privacy, reticent companies may not intentionally mislead the public. The issue, more emotional than financial, poses downside liability.

Serious illness defies prediction, creates that greatest of bugaboos for corporate control freaks—uncertainty. Diagnoses may be unnecessarily indefinite. Illness changes how the individual executive thinks, performs, and plans. That very uncertainty perplexes corporations most, writes Amanda Bennett in *The Wall Street Journal*:

> For shareholders, suppliers and customers, sickness raises questions of continuity. What would the succession be? What happens to the company's strategic direction? For employees and fellow executives, the concerns are more personal. They must grapple with worries about their boss and the illness's effect on their own lives and careers.[13]

Perhaps simplistically, she quotes experts who advise the standard Boy Scout PR tactic: be forthcoming, completely honest, as straightforward as possible. Difficult, for many reasons, not the least the milieu and culture in which a CEO operates. Control. Overcome odds. Just one more challenge. Deny any vulnerability. That's just not machismo. Face reality and overcome it.

Sometimes an illness—substance addiction may be the best example—inspires others to practice good health. A life-threatening illness, even with a "terrific prognosis," conversely moves employees to protect the sufferer by quietly assuming his or her duties, by hiding troublesome corporate news, or, under the guise of solicitude, to use illness to accomplish their goals at variance with the ill leader.

Colleagues and subordinates are likely to experience feelings of abandonment, and anger, as well as pity or concern.[14] Or, as everyone else has been all along, they may see the ill leader finally at risk. "Their response is an index of what sort of leader he has been. Resentment for past ill treatment from the boss may be given a chance to flower now that he is losing his grasp on power."[15]

Rules Fuzzy; Practices Fuzzier

In all other areas, U.S. corporations face some of the world's most extensive reporting requirements. But when deciding when and how much to disclose incapacitation of a senior officer, companies are on their own, adrift with only confusing counsel. Securities laws, very specific about reporting bankruptcies, acquiring or disposing assets, give broad latitude to "other events." Once termed "material,, the description was changed to encourage companies to provide more information. The New York Stock Exchange notes such a situation regarding illness may arise. Even when companies don't disclose, liabilities don't always follow. Most observers, public relations leaders, and corporate lawyers saw no problems, would not fault AT&T's handling of CEO Olson's cancer. However, the corporation's bench strength of executives, a clearly identified successor, and no dip in stock price are unusual. A difficult call, the right one here, but not always. Quite different would be a genius inventor, also a skilled administrator who led his company largely single-handedly. Most authorities agree such an individual's illness should be reported.

Company watchers, particularly arbitragers, frequently keep their antennas tuned to hints of executive illness, especially if he controls a large block of stock or is the "driving force" upon whom the company's fortune depends.[16]

One law—the Americans with Disabilities Act—designed in part to provide great confidentiality in disclosures of illness leaves the question largely to the individual. Walsh immediately disclosed his cancer, hoping to establish a model of responsibility and to prevent rumors and speculation that might impact Tenneco's stock price. Ironically, stockholders considered Walsh so key that Tenneco's stock lost $2 the day of his announcement.[17]

Is the Boss Really Healthy?

Just how healthy are CEOs? The truth is nobody knows. Often not even the board. Here too, no law, federal, state or corporate, mandates routine checkups. Instead, illness is treated basically as a private matter. "Whether a CEO runs three miles a day or smokes three packs a day, having a physical is pretty much up to the executive."[18]

Some shareholder activists and others are questioning this practice considering the risks—leaving a corporation rudderless, torpedoing stock prices, or becoming a takeover target. Is their blood pressure so high it might precipitate a stroke? Are there early signs of cancer? Dangerous stress levels? Worrisome behavior? Activists say CEOs should be required to present clean bills of health. They note the U.S. President has an annual checkup to demonstrate he's up to the rigors of his office, why not senior corporate executives? Ah, but do the President's medical reports always tell all?

Some executives take the initiative and volunteer information to their boards. Both CEO Charles Leighton and President Bob Tod of the publicly traded exercise equipment maker CML take annual physicals. Leighton explains, "if there's a physical ailment that prevents us from running the company, we have the responsibility to tell the board." That's quite simply a prudent business decision. Just imagine the fallout if a health-oriented company concealed illness. Most commentators agree that the board, not individuals, should decide on appropriate action.[19] Exactly this mechanism in the Twenty-Fifth Amendment for assumption or passing of presidential power is being debated and refined by a presidential committee. Denial is the first stage of serious illness. Nobody's immune, including CEOs.

That's the bad news. The good news is that CEOs today on the average are healthier than their predecessors, some even in better shape than when younger. Being proactive and assertive encourages many to exercise ambitiously. Contrary to conventional wisdom that all successful executives are hard-driving, stress-laden leaders, very prone to heart attacks and gastric ulcers, most CEOs are less disease-prone than the average. Studies suggest they may be more relaxed than their subordinates, more likely to be carriers or causes than sufferers of stress. Highest stress comes in very demanding jobs with little autonomy or gratification.

Researchers told the European Society of Cardiology to forget the notion that hard-pressed business executives are most likely to keel over with heart attacks. Most at risk are bus and truck drivers and unskilled shift workers. High-status executives can avoid stress by staying in control of their working lives, an option unavailable to blue-collar workers. "The stereotype of stress is the businessman with a suitcase and mobile phone facing many meetings, demands and little time. Actually, job stress and heart disease impact mostly the lower social strata." Working shifts rather than normal hours coupled with poor work conditions, job insecurity, or unemployment caused immense distress often revealed in physical symptoms. One researcher noted, "if you have a demanding job with little control and low rewards, particularly a blue-collar job, your risk of a heart attack is two to four times as high as a person in a job with lower demands and high rewards and security."[20]

CEOs can delegate widely, have broad powers, lots of gratification, and enjoy corporately smiled-upon perks. The Greenbriar isn't hard to take, even if the discussions are tough. There's always golf or jogging. Also, fewer impatient, hostile Type A's are making it to the top now than consensus-building and motivational leaders. Although age may naturally work against CEO health, many other factors and lifestyles tip the balance in their favor.[21]

A Quintet for Coping

Handling the crisis of executive illness allows no pat recipe or pattern. Rather, like a master chef, the crisis manager must constantly adapt the stew by adding or deleting tactics, as new questions, events, and pressures arise. However, most illnesses follow five generic approaches:

- TELLING: facing a serious illness immediately, addressing its corporate realities, internally with employees and externally, with openness and candor, courage and competence.

- CONCEALING: basically saying absolutely nothing until the obituary runs. The resulting shock and surprise create serious problems organizationally and, in publicly held companies, among shareholders and financial analysts.

- WAFFLING: telling basically good news laced with absolutely the barest of contrary details. Despite long absences from the office and obvious physical signs of a worsening condition, the optimistic stories continue to flow. Waffling puts media and management alike in the bind of complicity—sensing the reality, but being unable to act on it.

- BUNGLING: handling psychological illnesses is the most elusive and sensitive. Is the boss just stressed out or going crazy? Particularly in machismo corporate or military cultures, unsure associates blindside

	themselves at great risk of damage to institution and individual.
• IMAGING:	creating the illusion of robust health and great activity despite depression, clandestine surgery, drug therapy, and low energy. Imaging is endemic, but not exclusive, to political leaders. Photo-ops are the most used prop.

Very cynically, ill health may be used to achieve goals. In the movie *Bob Roberts*, the senatorial candidate, "paralyzed" in a campaign "shooting," "walks" to celebrate his victory. Such fiction is also fact. Historical health scams hold lessons for communicators today.

TELLING ALL

Total candor, quickened by confidence in beating the odds, typifies both the first brush with death and treatment for substance abuse. Positive outcomes can even inspire others to seek treatment.

The benchmark of telling all, of tying it to corporate strategies is Michael Walsh. Three other, shorter examples set the tone. When Richard W. Darrow, chairman of Hill and Knowlton in the 1970s, was first diagnosed with colon cancer, he turned over power temporarily and faced surgery with typical Midwestern optimism. Later, just the night before the painful onset of the terminal phase, he related how much the cancer had taught him to appreciate and enjoy.[22] When the pain resurged, signaling more serious surgery, his tone was somber, less was communicated, and power retained. A typical pattern, albeit disconcerting to employees.

A case of total telling, with a happy ending is that of Malcolm Borg, owner of MacMedia headquartered in Hackensack, New Jersey. In his fifties, Borg seemed to have it all. He was a powerful public figure who headed the family-held MacMedia—two daily newspapers and four television stations in New Jersey. He was routinely listed on *New Jersey Magazine*'s and *Forbes*'s richest people lists, his wealth estimated at $325 million.[23] Borg was very prominent, led public institutions, and once was even touted for governor. For three generations the Borgs owned *The Record*, the only daily in Bergen County, a wealthy New York suburb. All were outstanding and awesome. "My father was a genius. His learning intimidating."[24] But the very family that gave him prominence also gave him a problem, unacknowledged by Borg until May 13, 1991. Grandfather John and father Donald shared not only his journalistic prominence, but problems with alcohol as well. His aunt, mother, and brother suffered also.

Unlike many executives', Borg's drinking was episodal and no secret. When he was charged with DWI in 1986, the story ran in *The Record*. To hide a very public act by a very public figure, he reasoned, would undermine his personal and the *Record*'s credibility. Borg acknowledges now that "alcohol was getting to me." Typically, the decision to seek rehabilitation was forced by a May 1991 confrontation with the then-corporate secretary, Herbert Nelson, and Borg's attorney.

After telling his two direct reports—the presidents of newspapers and television—Borg himself "drafted with some precision" a bulletin board announcement saying: "I have concluded I can no longer tolerate alcohol. Although I have stopped drinking on my own, I have decided to enter alcohol rehabilitation, to let the pros do their thing." No other announcements or news stories followed. Borg would be "out-of-pocket" for 30 days. No business talk. No telephone calls except from his secretary and his wife, Sandy. As the family anchor and presence, she came to the office at least two days each week. According to Borg, her very presence was a reassuring and stabilizing element.

Some reactions were totally predictable. Some not. Long-time associates, witnesses to the progress of Borg's drinking and resulting business problems, applauded the move. "Thank God. He'll be different when he returns." He was. Many business changes were and are being made. By being open and up front, Borg hoped others would seek treatment. "I could have said I was just taking a long vacation, but I am too public for that to be credible. That would just prolong the evasion." Borg was well aware that newspapering invites drinking. "At *The Record* alone, ten employees sought rehabilitation"; others took out-patient treatment following the owner's announcement. Even when the *New York Post* ran a page 6 item on Borg, he treated it philosophically.

Among associates some sought help themselves, or attended support meetings to better understand and support Borg when he returned. Meanwhile, he "was concentrating on the ghosts, goblins and dragons, the depression and mood swings which increased a desire to consume more and more alcohol. It would make the pain go away. But it didn't."

Borg considers his problem, personally and organizationally, easier than most. "I had made the decision and was sober for three weeks before entering rehabilitation," he explains. Also, the two presidents were "accustomed to running their operations, so a 30-day absence wasn't critical." That MacMedia is privately held obviated the need for extensive public announcements. Most important for employees, the illness was finite—30 days of treatment, more predictable and less threatening than, for example, treatment for cancer.

Borg's return to work in July 1991 was gradual, low-key, and *sans* communication. In the late afternoon of July 2, dressed casually, he walked into his office. At first Borg assumed a low-profile, letting people come to him. Some were genuinely awkward, but most were enthusiastically supportive. He let people perceive he was different, no longer "my own worst enemy." After three months, Borg and MacMedia were back to normal—but sober. Still, Borg's illness was actually inspirational—a typical pattern. A former CEO of Kemper Insurance inspired a television advertising campaign on substance abuse. Lewis Bantle, CEO of UST, after completing his own treatment, devoted hours to encouraging others to do likewise. Michael Deaver, image guru to former President Ronald Reagan, lectures frequently on overcoming alcohol addiction. When a senior AMR executive, a lifelong smoker, lost half of one lung to cancer, his plight encouraged others, including AMRs chain-smoking chairman, Robert L. Crandall, to stop smoking—but only temporarily.[25] Explaining his "affection for nicotine", Crandall told a reporter: "Nobody lives forever—we're all just ants on a marble."[26]

Although Union Pacific CEO Drew Lewis shared Borg's problem and treatment, the corporate circumstances differed substantially. Reports conflict, but it appears the board of directors asked Lewis to take a short medical leave to enter an alcohol treatment program. Given a takeover battle for the Sante Fe Railroad, Lewis's condition was deemed material information. This required a public announcement, but it was delayed until Lewis was under treatment. Three senior executives shared the CEO's duties, with the senior vice president of finance overseeing the proposed merger.

Some newspaper accounts detailed Lewis's earlier stressful career. As high-profile transportation secretary in the Reagan Administration, he spent two hectic years marked primarily by an August 1981 strike by the nation's air traffic controllers. He fired 11,400 of them, but still managed to keep airplanes flying, albeit at a reduced level. In 1983, he became a chairman of Warner Amex Cable Communications, Inc. and in 1986, president of Union Pacific Corporation, the nation's largest railroad.[27] Lewis returned to work after six weeks of treatment.

The Classic Candor of Michael Walsh

Communicators looking for models of immediate candor and disclosure will long turn to the late CEO Michael H. Walsh of Tenneco. *The New York Times* report catches the business contradictions and medical problem: "A chief executive's life story is usually told in lifeless numbers—widgets sold, dollars made or lost. But sometimes all-too-human news intrudes."[28]

Just as soon as Walsh's diagnosis of an inoperable brain cancer was confirmed, he announced it publicly, setting an expectation of openness very much in tone with the corporation's business strategy. Walsh insisted he would stay on the job, that his judgement was unaffected. He definitely challenged the odds for recovery, waving aside "statistical probability." Although experts said his inoperable tumor could be cured, "the odds for recovery are not good." Timing heightened coverage. Walsh's announcement was sandwiched between the announcement of Reginald Lewis's tumor and of Lewis's death two days later. Also, Walsh's visibly acclaimed turnaround of Tenneco necessitated news to quell rumors. As a publicly held company, the U.S.'s thirty-fifth largest industrial, Tenneco had regulatory obligations to announce.[29] Walsh went far beyond.

His public relations strategy tracked the company's credo: face reality, be open and candid, demonstrate courage and competence. Walsh personally informed directors and six operations presidents, the latter by a conference call. According to Arthur House, Tenneco's vice president for corporate affairs, Walsh read the presidents the press release, then suggested how to tell employees.[30] The three-page release gave a prognosis—average survival rate for this type of brain tumor is five to six years. Directors immediately were given full details and access to Walsh's medical records. A two-page letter from

Tenneco's corporate physician, Kenneth D. Wells, assured directors Walsh could work during 11 months of aggressive treatment.[31]

The CEO also made an unscripted video tape explaining his illness in very personal, but rambling tones. It drew mixed reactions. Shorter would have been more effective. The camera angle showed the shaved spot of his hair. Although U.S. employees appreciated the candor, European and Japanese operations were particularly reluctant or did not show the video, deeming it too personal.[32] MBA students' reactions were equally mixed. One said that had he been a Tenneco employee, he would have greatly appreciated it. Another thought it made too much of business strategies. But, the most telling comment came from a cancer hospital supervisor—he's in complete denial. The tape was a generous gesture, but a script, cross-cultural editing, and other factors would have enhanced its effectiveness.

The announcement was driven by reality, too. Walsh was walking around corporate headquarters with a large patch of his head shaved. "My barber slipped" jokes last just so long. Corporately, as well as personally, it was a delicate time. Walsh, who had joined Tenneco in September 1991, was still turning around its financial and operating weaknesses. Walsh assured all that his mental processes and judgement would be unaffected, that he had no intention of resigning. This squelched not only internal rumors but also speculation that he planned to join the Clinton Administration. Walsh explained: "No News would have prompted rumor and speculation damaging to Tenneco investors." Little deceptions become big deceptions. Soon all your energies are going into managing the problem, not the business.

Numerous U.S. lawyers and management consultants applauded his exemplary full, frank, and immediate disclosure.[33] Others were candid, too. Dana Mead, eventually Walsh's successor, acknowledged to a leading business journalist, it is a "very, very tough battle," but he believed in "Mike's tremendous heart" and the "superb medical care." Asked if Walsh's condition had improved, Mead said, "No, it hasn't."[34] But the unpredictable course of any serious disease, as in Walsh's case, plus employee concerns, unspoken, unconscious, even denied, cloud even the greatest forthrightness and best of intentions.

Employees and subordinates naturally attempt to protect or help the sufferer, to treat him with undue tenderness, despite his an-

nounced wishes. Some experts note colleagues may experience abandonment, anger, or personal insecurity, which words, meetings, and
repeated assurance cannot completely assuage.[35] Walsh had been
stunned himself, despite the death of both parents to cancer.

In September 1993, Walsh made Business Week's cover, headlined
"The Fight of His Life, Michael Walsh's Battle Against Cancer."
Such positive press muted some practical concerns. Although personally, Walsh's "confidence and candor remained startlingly intact,", associates encountered difficulty following his admonition
not to worry about it. He was clearly battered physically—hair loss,
unsteady gait, and pronounced limp of the left leg. Walsh eschewed
the cosmetic. At first he wore a hairpiece. In March 1993, just weeks
after exhausting radiation treatments, he "orchestrated a $1.1 billion
equity offering to help pay for the makeover of Tenneco's troubled
Case, a farm-machinery maker. He attended critical meetings. Injected humor to put others at ease. He shifted more duties to
Mead."[36]

Throughout, Walsh put his fix-it strategy to work, instituted "no
excuses management"—make your figures despite outside forces—
and generally exuded a business-as-usual approach. Again, experts
applauded his ruthlessly rational approach, but some wondered if
denial wasn't causing problems.[37] Once again, timing proved ironic.
Just days before Walsh's cancer forced his resignation as CEO, a
major Fortune article, "Mike Walsh Takes on Brain Cancer," appeared. Unlike the Business Week article that painfully photographed
Walsh's current condition, Fortune's showed him in 1992 lifting
weights, the picture of health. Uncritically upbeat, it reported his
medical and business routines and quoted Walsh: "To a point, you
have to concede to medical realism and admit there are elements
you cannot control. . . . The personal dimension—the will to live,
support systems, and hope. They are under your control."[38]

The journalist John Huey noted Walsh was bringing all he had to
the fight, including his sense of humor. He was shuttling from the
hotel to radiation treatments, trying in between to prepare for an
upcoming meeting with New York security analysts. Using a regimen
common in cancer treatment, he organized his mental imagery into
a "red team" (his natural antibodies), which he visualized as building up his immune system, and a "white team" (his radiation treatments), which he visualized as huge snowplows from the Union

Pacific Railroad (Walsh was CEO there before coming to Tenneco) clearing the snow (his tumor cells) from the tracks. "Except for the partially shaven head and the chemotherapy pump slung over his shoulder, Walsh at 6-foot-2 and 200 pounds still presents the picture of health." He assured the *Fortune* reporter, he's "utterly symptomless," but for a slight limp on his left leg.[39] In the world according to Mike, nothing is impossible.

But, tragically wrong. On February 24, he stunned even close associates by resigning as CEO, but continuing on indefinite medical leave as Chairman. He had already told Tenneco's directors and officers his treatment "was impairing his ability to run the company." Tenneco's chief physician mentioned new symptoms *sans* elaboration or estimate for length of treatment. Mead, who had frequently functioned as the chief executive officer, was formally named to the position.[40] In January, Walsh had undergone surgery to remove remaining dead tissue remaining from the tumor, but the cancer wasn't back. However, Walsh told directors: "the cumulative effects of surgery, chemotherapy, other treatments have been more demanding than expected." Mead explained that Walsh, whom he hadn't seen since late January, sounded "fatigued" in recent telephone conversations, and described continuing weakness on his left side.[41]

Despite the surprise after mostly good or no news, Mead took over easily. He presented year-end 1993 financial results to analysts and promised no major immediate changes. "We have Tenneco on a terrific trajectory. Our cost structure is improved, our business positions are better and we have cleaned up our balance sheet. We have financial flexibility that we didn't have before. We're ready to enter a new phase—sustained growth."[42]

And then, tragically, Walsh died at 51 on May 6, 1994. His battles, corporate and personal, were enlarged upon as:

> epitomizing the relentless quest for efficiencies and economies that has transformed countless companies. . . . He took control of one company after another, slimming them down and shaping them up as if to remake them in his own lean, athletic image. But now, there arose a poignant difference: no regimen, no amount of determination could overcome the effects of the cancer that struck him just as he was emerging as one of the nation's most prominent younger executives. . . .

While other executives slowed by disease have tried to hide or play down their conditions, Walsh was so intent on remaining the visible leader of his company that the turns in his condition became immediately evident. His hair loss reminded those around him of the rigors of his radiation treatment and chemotherapy. He often discussed his disease with his aides or the press. Human beings manage their way through these things, he said. . . . "It's about 90 percent discipline and sweat."

Walsh continued working out with weights and a stationary bicycle even during his treatment. He claimed victory over the cancer last November. But when the cancer returned, candor diminished. When Walsh suddenly resigned as CEO, his doctor cited the weakening effects of his treatment, but in truth, the now fatal cancer had recurred.[43]

What difference does one man's leadership and illness mean? Two days following announcement of Walsh's new health problems, the stock fell $3.375 to $56.625—still nearly twice the price before he took charge.

A successful succession illustrates major difference between Tenneco and TLC Beatrice. Mead became Tenneco's CEO with "no apparent tremors," explaining: "Mike and I devised the strategy. We picked the team together. Called ourselves co-pilots." "Basically, we'll continue the transformation of Tenneco."[44] Investors, initially concerned about Walsh's illness, came to respect Mead. The West Pointer had already turned around the bloated, troubled J. J. Case division and worked closely with Walsh on corporate cost-cutting and restructuring. Was it unwitting prescience or irony that his MIT doctoral dissertation dealt with making battle-plans in uncertain times? Most analysts were optimistic: "Tenneco's rescue is nearly complete, Mead is at least as well equipped as Walsh to guide it from here." Walsh was a turn-around specialist, blunt and impatient."

Many employees, directors, and investors were just glad Mead was there. Tenneco didn't miss a beat in its restructuring efforts.

CONCEALING TO KEEP POWER: SUPERSTARS OF SPORTS, BUSINESS, AND POLITICS ALL DO IT

Concealing is an anathema to communicators. But telling all, their almost knee-jerk coda, can distance them from the intricacies of the problem and, lamentably, from the very executives they serve. This reveal/conceal conflict runs smack into the balancing of the individual's denial, the money or image to be gained or lost, with the simple wish to preserve a shed of privacy either to die out of the spotlight or to accomplish that single last task.

Stockbrokers and politicians conceal. Superstars of sports and business do it. Before condemning it out-of-hand, it is prudent to listen to the rationale of the two Lewises—Reggie, late of the Boston Celtics, and Reginald, late CEO of TLC Beatrice and widely recognized as the most successful black entrepreneur.

First, several short illustrations of concealing. Fund manager Kenneth Oberman, called by *Fortune* "the gifted steward" of Oppenheimer's Global and Bio-Tech Funds, was diagnosed with cancer before the funds were formed in 1987. Even as Oberman's health worsened, Oppenheimer decided not to tell investors. "It had no material impact on his ability to run the funds," a spokesman explained, then pushed too far, noting that Oberman's illness actually made him a better investor—it mattered to him more. He stopped coming to the office in October 1992 and died in February. How did fund investors find out? In the newspaper obituary.[45] Even if you were making money, wouldn't you like to know your fund manager is fatally ill?

Although politicians are prone to image-away ill health, several just concealed. Former Pennsylvania Governor Robert R. Casey and Russian President Boris N. Yeltsin, as well as fictional pol Bob Roberts, all concealed to accomplish their practical objectives.

When Governor Casey underwent dual transplant surgery—heart and liver—he issued the usual canard: cannot wait to return to work. He also faced totally predictable questions about his candor and ability to govern. Although Casey attempted to quell them by detailing his progress and determination to resume the governorship, his words fell on skeptical soil. One nonpartisan political watcher commented: "We're reduced to Kremlinology here. . . . He has no credibility in matters of his health."[46] The reasons are apparent. Questions about Casey's health persisted since 1987, the year he took office, when he had open heart surgery and a quadruple bypass. After that, he had a medical examination every six months, except during his 1990 reelection campaign. His cardiologist belatedly acknowledged the exam was postponed because "he feared the results could affect the race."[47]

For good reason. One month later, the delayed medical tests showed Casey had a rare and fatal liver disease, familial amyloidosis, which damages other organs. The public was unaware until July 1991. In 1993, the governor appeared increasingly pale and thin. Aides explained he worked his usual 10 to 12 a day until two weeks before he was evaluated on June 12 for a transplant at the University of Pittsburgh Medical Center. But, when he was admitted, doctors said he was unable to walk more than 100 feet and that his heart was barely functioning. Doctors saw a good long-term prognosis but "there isn't a lot of experience to fall back on."

The transplants themselves raised more problems for Casey. How did he get them so quickly? Favoritism? Could he return to office? Why would he want to? A poll taken in heavily Republican central Pennsylvania—Casey's a Democrat—created more concern and spin. Thirty-eight percent of respondents believed Casey would resign, thirty-nine percent that he would not. The rest had no opinion. Also, forty-eight percent said he should resign and thirty-five percent that he should not. Asked if doctors were being truthful about his recovery, forty-seven percent said they were, but thirty-two percent did not.

Vincent J Carocci, the governor's press secretary, spun into action. He denied Casey had ever tried to hide his health problems—"he has been completely forthcoming." Carocci dismissed the poll as defective in follow-up questions and in distinguishing whether concern was over the governor's well-being or fear about his ability to govern. The press secretary left no doubt. He put more credence in another public opinion measurement—10,000 get-well wishes.[48] But the ultimate test is votes. Constitutionally barred from another term, Casey briefly dipped his toe into the presidential primaries, but soon retreated to healthy obscurity.

Questions of favoritism similar to Casey's were raised when baseball legend Mickey Mantle received a liver transplant in 1995 at Baylor University Medical Center in Dallas. Jennifer Coleman, vice president for public relations at the Baylor Health Care Center, and Merrie Spaeth, president of a Dallas based communications firm, detailed the dilemmas for family and hospital in "Transplanting the Mick's Liver."[49] "It provides valuable lessons to any executive faced with a difficult decision that can't be 'wished away' which must be dealt with candidly, forcefully, and at all times, publicly." Given the current intensified public scrutiny of hospitals and health care, all involved must be increasingly concerned about the public image of their institutions. Few have faced a more difficult dilemma than Baylor's, when Mantle received a transplanted liver. "Almost immediately, the hospital was besieged by angry protests of favoritism and duplicity."

Celebrity patients are both boon and bane to a large urban hospital. "They bring visibility and increased scrutiny." Baylor, a large, not-for-profit system, a decade ago instituted public relations training programs for its more than 300 physicians, nurses, technical specialists, administrators, fund raisers, and volunteers. Despite dealing with sports and other stars previously, Mantle's treatment and eventual death presented unique strategic challenges. He entered the hospital in May 1995, complaining of stomach pains. He was placed on the transplant list because of damage to his liver caused by Hepatitis C infection, liver cancer, and cirrhosis. The Mantle family and their attorney made themselves available to the media. That could not stop the firestorm over preferential treatment. Mantle waited only two days for a transplant. Many wait months, even years.

Simply explaining criteria wouldn't be enough. Despite being generally misunderstood, they are controversial. Rather then one long, national waiting list, there are many shorter, regional ones where the sickest patients move to the top. Although Mantle was very sick, convincing a cynical public would be difficult. Coleman and Spaeth explain the strategy, orchestrated by the communicators, delivered by the medical team, and targeted to the media. First, documents were obtained from the national organ allocation system, verifying that Mantle had been treated like everyone else. Public comments such as "Fame is a factor, and favors were being played!" were countered by Baylor transplant recipients, saying, "I was transplanted in four days, and I was just 'Jane Doe.'" The Dallas Morning News wrote two supportive editorials. A large media event means putting out many fires. As the preference issue waned, giving a "drunk" a donated liver rose. Hospital guidelines allow liver transplants for alcoholics dry for at least 18 months. Mantle had been.

Next came the cancer controversy. Baylor, one of only six major U.S. centers that use transplants and chemotherapy to treat liver cancer, found a 60 percent chance of survival three years after transplant for the initial group of patients with cancer like Mantle's.

Knowing how closely the case would be scrutinized, as well as its possible impact on confidence in the program and willingness to donate organs, "Baylor physicians put Mantle through more pre-operative tests than usual to be certain his body, except for the liver, was clear of cancer." During the seven-hour operation, a pathology report showed microscopic cancer cells. "This was not a fatal sign to the physicians because cancer is *presumed* to be present. Chemotherapy is administered during surgery." However, communicators learned of this months later, after Mantle's death. Physicians told the press, however, "We feel very optimistic . . . the liver is functioning fine." When asked about the cancer, they said, "We hope we got it all."

Even the strategy/crisis team did not anticipate the media frenzy. Why? Mantle was a "cherished link to a perceived happier time. His candid confessions of past misbehavior—'I wasn't a good father'—and his acceptance of his position as a role model—'Don't be like me'—endeared him to the public." Nearly all 18,000 U.S. newspapers carried the story. T.V. coverage was extensive and global. About 20,000 pieces of mail, dozens of floral arrangements, and visits from friends and former teammates attracted more attention. Mantle, his family, and Baylor developed a plan for "Mickey's Team," and organ-donation cards resembling baseball cards. "I want to give something back," he said.

Reporters sought every tidbit of information. One got a surprising scoop. A *Dallas Morning News* reporter questioned a surgeon-in-training. Thinking he had the patient's permission, he said "They didn't get all the cancer." Another storm erupted. The standard PR principle of just one spokesperson and checking, not assuming, before making a public statement might have avoided this. Of course, reporters try to get information from any possible source.

Most of Mantle's doctors respected the wishes of their media-savvy patient, who had not yet decided to tell his wife and sons about the cancer. Not only the public-media situation, but Mantle's medical condition changed dramatically. The cancer spread aggressively. Options were narrowing. "Several checkbook 'journalism' TV shows were prowling around. It was only a matter of time before the news leaked out." Mantle changed his mind and agreed to make a video-taped comment on the spread of his cancer. Looking weak. but upbeat, he read a statement revealing he had cancer spots on his lungs.

"If you really want to be a hero, be an organ donor." He even decided which television anchorperson should have the tape first. ABC's *Good Morning, America,* and Joan Lunden aired the segment August 1, 1995, with the full press briefing at 11 A.M.

All very upbeat, but the media and family were at odds over specific predictions. Doctors responded with general comments how patients in the overall study responded. But more surprises came. According to Coleman and Spaeth, "a publicity hungry oncologist from out-of-state . . . told the press that Mickey's only problem was being in the hands of 'timid' Dallas doctors." Now the crisis team had to deal with 'offers'—a faith healer from Jamaica, special potions derived from a patient's own urine, miracle coffee enemas, and mysterious "mechanical" remedies.

On August 13, when Mantle died, the press briefing seemed to go well. A week later, *The Dallas Morning News* announced on the front page that the doctors had "lied" to the press. An accompanying editorial, "Mantle Episode Chips Away at Public Trust," "took Baylor to task for not immediately disclosing the cancer's spread and for not corroborating the physician-in-training's comment." Coleman and Spaeth conclude: "We're still not sure where the word 'lies' came from—apparently in one-on-one interviews after the news conference. Perhaps it was offered by a reporter. Our physicians know never to repeat negative words, even to deny them. But they were exhausted and upset after the loss of a patient. . . ." To repair Baylor's relationship with the local paper, communicators "reassured the paper that 'lying' was anathema to us, and thanked them for their coverage support of the donations issue." More positively, requests for organ-donation cards skyrocketed across the nation—confirming the initial strategy.

HIDING FOR POWER

Leaders caught in the vortex of highly public crises fear they may diminish their political clout if any illness shows. They go to dangerous extremes to hide even fatal illnesses. The Shah of Iran concealed his cancer, unnecessarily imperiling his life in the vain hope of reclaiming his Peacock Throne. Absent fact, rumor spreads. Each event becomes a sign of illness. The Oscar for concealing illness must go to the late President François Mitterand, who even in death remains one of France's most potent politicians. Not only did he successfully mask his prostate cancer for 15 years, but had the sang-froid to hide "an entire family at a second official residence."

In 1981, after 40 years of "mostly miserable political struggles" Mitterand won the presidency, only to soon learn of his cancer. The diagnosis was dire—it had already spread to the bone. Both his father and his younger brother had died of the same disease. The masquerade of survival, politically and physically, began. Not only did Mitterand keep it a secret, but it was "actively lied about in the President's health bulletins." "Had he been more honest, he would have been less effective." To Adam Gopnik, he "would have unnecessarily consigned his own fate to the shaky predictions of his doctors. . . . What Mitterand supposedly did wrong looks a lot more like a forgotten kind of rightness."[50]

"In a popular sense," Gopnik writes, "the French want a leader who is a double man—possessed of a secret life and private passions and dark secrets. Mitterand, with his stage-managed revelations and hard-headed betrayals, was that. . . . Not a single one of his Socialist Prime Ministers was taken into his confidence."[51]

Perhaps other cultures demand different disclosure from their leaders. Obviously, Mitterand knew his electorate—still? Despite the well-established Russian absence of any news about leaders' illnesses—death announcements are the first indication—glasnost and rapidly changing conditions defeated Boris Yeltsin's best attempts.

He is the cynosure of a high-stakes concealing game. How ill was he? Was it impairing his ability to govern? Alarm bells rang and questions were raised with each Yeltsin sighting. The CIA reported worsening problems with alcohol. Video footage showed him walking unevenly, grabbing an aide for support, speaking with difficulty. The Russian Government typically and officially rebuffed all inquiries. Besides, other issues—Chechnya and convincing lenders that economic and political stability will soon return—were far more important. Officials tried anything to deflect attention. But serious secrets must out.

Senior diplomatic watchers reported signs of illness, bouts of depression, and heavy drinking. Yeltsin became uncommunicative. "He appears swollen and puffy, his hands thick with edema, his gait ponderous. When he smiles, but rarely, in public, his eyes seem to disappear." Spin masters explained he drank no more than an average Russian man of his age and experience—a delicate way of saying "too much"—or attributed these appearances as a testament to the struggle to guide Russians away from a bankrupt totalitarian past.

Explanations and guesses, absent information, raise more questions. Does a back-pain condition require medication? Is he on Cortisone, hence the facial puffiness? Are there heart, kidney, and liver problems? Arteriosclerosis? Until thee heart surgery was scheduled, Russian newspapers ran only excerpts from the foreign press. Opponents called for Yeltsin to quit. Take an annual checkup. Say something.

Eventually, the illness became too big to hide. In mid-July 1995, the Russian president was taken to the hospital suffering acute heart pains, later described as ischemia, a shortage of blood to the heart. Spinning started again. Unfortunately, it fell on very suspicious ears. The pains have subsided. He continues to work. Nothing serious has happened to him. He is active. Gets up from his bed.[52] The ultimate spin was political. Yeltsin's stay in a secluded hospital underscored that the nation's fate no longer "hangs on a single leader." The 19-month-old constitution spells out not only succession, but provides for presidential elections. Power is decentralized.[53]

All this raised more suspicions that it dampened. Too much information contrasting with traditional silence about even life-threatening illness of former Soviet leaders. Was this one more politically convenient medical isolation? As war began in Chechnya, Yeltsin was hospitalized for an undisclosed nose problem, perhaps a deviated septum. He stayed in the hospital for more than a week, and in seclusion for another. News about his schedule conflicted; he was or wasn't going to Norway; would be released soon or later; doctors didn't want him to fly just yet; the treatment shouldn't be hurried. The Kremlin was reticent; his wife, Naina, wasn't. She criticized press speculation as "verbal sadism." He is working and his health is just fine.[54]

As if Russians already weren't skeptical enough about official information, Yeltsin and his inept handlers feverishly attempted damage control. They released a photograph of him working, which appeared identical to one filmed during an April vacation in southern Russia. The "episode was eerily reminiscent of days when Communist bureaucrats often airbrushed out their enemies, staged fake events or recycled old snapshots as new."[55] Such deception by tampered-with photographs and art is strikingly documented in David Key's recent *The Commissar Vanishes*. Even at Chernobyl, smoke plumes were removed from news photographs. Little wonder Russians don't believe icons they see. Yeltsin's unannounced appearance on television only created more rumors of worse health. The apparent relapse into Soviet-style public relations, and the president's critical role in reforms and power, all fed the frenzy of disbelief and questions. A case study in how not to handle questions of the boss's health. Yeltsin returned to seclusion once again, waving, looking good in staged television appearances.

As Yeltsin continued absent without explanation, worries widened. Some Russian legislators sought to remove him from office. Frequently, he sought to quell any discontent or concerns by vigorous appearances—dancing strenuously (how long was never mentioned) during the campaign, attempting to give a vigorous inaugural speech in March. But a tired Yeltsin was soon absent again. By May new speculations surfaced. Who would succeed him? The July 20, 1996 *Toronto Globe and Mail* czargazed, and asked, "What happens if Boris dies?" Then Yeltsin stood up Vice President Gore to take a vacation. Just tired, not sick, his spin doctors purred. On a television photo-op, Yeltsin's talk was so wooden, it only fueled fears of his illness. By August *The New York Times* was editorializing about disorder in the Kremlin.

Was it a preemptive strike or knowing that surgery was imminent that prompted the Kremlin to begin admitting issues of Yeltsin's health were bungled? His chief of staff promised a new information policy within a few days, adding the PR canard: "The less official information there is, the more rumors, conjectures and speculations there are."[56]

But the ducking continued. Not lots of news, except assurances of the president's good health. Damage control featured a few seconds of conversation on television. Yeltsin looked relaxed and smiled, but "the camera angles were distant and tightly controlled." Russians accustomed to little or misleading information just waited. "So did political opponents, who held back knowing that soon enough he would either be completely incapacitated or die."[57]

Just a few days later the story changed—to heart surgery. Will he have it? Can he? Have other lifestyles made surgery too dangerous?

Will it be in Russia? Or in Switzerland or Germany? Russian surgeons were grim until famed American heart surgeon Dr. Michael DeBakey declared, "his general condition is not all that bad." Surgery was planned. Somehow, Russia muddled through, kept some momentum. Yeltsin's heart won him victories. Now it was giving everyone jitters.

A new public relations strategy aimed to convince a deeply skeptical nation its stricken but resilient president was up to the job. With tactics reminiscent of the last years of President Franklin D. Roosevelt, press secretaries announced a "litany of new presidential decrees. He receives 20 to 70 documents daily and studies them from 20 minutes to 2½ hours." Some crowed about the new openness— getting the president to admit publicly he needed surgery. In reality it was openness forced by a deteriorating medical condition which couldn't be hidden.

Keeping the press at bay and distant from the Kremlin was explained by space restrictions, not allowing them to roam the Kremlin freely. That too sounds like a familiar rationale. Even the press that talked independence "mostly danced gingerly around the issue of whether the president was physically able to govern, apparently from fear of providing aid and comfort to the Communists." One correspondent concludes, "the Kremlin's brave talk about ushering in a new era of candor has been mostly a triumph of spin control over substance."[58] Surgery did not stay comments about medical, read national, rivalries threatening recovery. An American ran interference for Russian doctors treating a patient used to calling the shots.

Yeltsin, like any CEO/president anywhere, corporate or political, was restless to get back to work. Words and photographs sought to prove he needed no warm up time. But he still seemed frail and faced a host of problems. Even in January he remained largely out of the public view, then returned to work for two weeks, only to be hospitalized again with pneumonia. Aides worried publicly he would be unable to return soon. To counter this, Yeltsin made a cameo television appearance. In some ways he was lucky. Many were willing to settle for such stagnation rather than face the unpredictability of another course. On his sixtieth birthday, *The New York Times* ran before and after photographs—the first showing a puffy-faced president, the second a much healthier-looking and trimmer leader.[59] Ironies flummox and challenge public relations practitioners constantly.

President Bill Clinton, unexpectedly on crutches and in a leg brace, met Yeltsin in Helsinki where the summit conference had been moved because of the Russian president's medical condition.

In a larger sense, the press coverage and official covertness can be litmus tests for openness *vs.* traditional secrecy, the continuing importance of one leader, dictatorial or elected, the need to handle the issue in concert with the culture and its expectations. However, are Russians any less skeptical of official news? That would be a wonder of wonders.

"No one expects any more candor in the new Russia than in the old."[60] But outsiders always try to find out. *Time* tells this story: Like many Western governments, France was curious about the exact state of Leonid Brezhnev's health during his final years. A French intelligence agent was ingenious. While Brezhnev was staying at the Hotel d'Angleterre in Copenhagen during a state visit, "the French rented the suite under his and dismantled all the plumbing. They intercepted his toilet flushings and sent the samples to Paris for analysis." This unpleasant bit of spy craft revealed Brezhnev, a vodka lover, suffered severe liver damage. "The old boy didn't last long after that."[61]

Two Lewis Superstars Keep Secrets

The two Lewises, from very different worlds, shared health secrets: for basketball superstar Reggie with disastrous consequences: for entrepreneurial superstar Reginald, with succession and business problems still.

"Deadly Silence, How the Inner Circles of Medicine and Sports Failed a Stricken Star, After Reggie Lewis Collapse, Money and PR Worries Undermined His Care, NBA: Don't Ask, Don't Tell." That long *Wall Street Journal* headline introduced a major article—front-page column continued in a full page and two columns inside. It told the damning, tragic story of how attempts to hide health problems embroiled the star, his family, the Celtics, NBA, insurers, several physicians, and medical examiners.[62] The family and the Celtics immediately denied the *Journal* report, threatening to sue.[63] They filed a $100 million lawsuit.

According to the *Journal*, when the Celtic captain collapsed during a playoff game, his medical team seemed to agree that Lewis had a "severely damaged heart and that his career was probably over." The sticking point was getting Lewis and the Celtics to tackle the "issue of causation." "Reggie knew what we meant. We'd been pressing him about cocaine for days."[64] The *Journal* continues: "A few hours later . . . Lewis and his wife, Donna Harris-Lewis, fled the hospital, beginning a bizarre string of events that ended, three months later, with the 27-year-old black hero lying dead on a basketball court."[65] Part of the answer to how and why it happened lies in the willingness of many involved to sidestep the possible cause of Lewis's collapse.

What were the motives? Protecting the reputation of a hometown hero? Powerful financial interests—$15 million in insurance coverage paid to the Lewis family and the Celtics "only if no link to drugs was shown"? Potential damage to team and league from a drug scandal? Scuttling a crucial business deal the Celtics were negotiating? "Events would show that such considerations, abetted by the NBA's dismissive policies regarding drugs, may have affected human behavior and medical procedure in a fatal fashion."[66]

> Whether Lewis died from a heart damaged by cocaine—as many doctors suspected then and now—cannot be definitively shown. What is evident: The official cause of death, a heart damaged by a common cold virus, is a medically nonsensical finding by a coroner under intense pressure from the Lewis family to exclude any implication of drug use. What is undeniable: Cocaine was a central, explosive issue . . . that became untouchable because Lewis was a basketball superstar.

A cardiac pathologist familiar with the case commented that Lewis's superstar status "deprived him of proper treatment. . . . If he was just a guy off the street, he would probably be alive today."[67]

Just before his death, Lewis was put on "watchful waiting" or careful monitoring of his activity while testing continued. Then, on July 27, Lewis fell as he was lightly tossing basketballs into a hoop, a gentle exertion, albeit not cleared by his doctors. In a moment, paramedics were struggling futilely to raise a pulse.

Even death didn't stop the wrangling, the finger pointing, the hiding of cause. Other medical teams were consulted. His mother's cocaine problems surfaced. Friends, who denied Lewis's use of cocaine, introduced race as an issue. If it were a white player, the suspicions would not have arisen; the white doctors would not have been so insistent on testing. Paul E. Gaston, the Celtics' chairman of the board, contended racism was a motivating factor behind the *Journal*'s article. "When a black athlete dies, people do not believe it's not either guns or drugs." When reporters asked him if he were labeling as racist doctors who voiced concern about possible cocaine use, Gaston did not answer and walked out of the room.[68] The last of many stonewalls that ended a career and created a tragedy.

When one Boston sports reporter wrote that "an imminent drug-toxicology test by the medical examiner's office is the possible time bomb in the Reggie Lewis story" and another suggested "self-abuse" might have played a role in the tragedy, the *Boston Globe* was "flooded with angry calls and hate mail."[69]

Nearly four months later, cause of death was finally and quietly listed. It cited adenovirus 2-a, a common virus that causes the common cold, had led to an inflammation of Lewis's heart, widespread scarring of tissue and, ultimately, a fatal cardiac arrest. If the insurance company contested these findings, it would have to tackle not only Massachusetts's chief medical examiner, but a public backlash for withholding payments from the widow.[70]

The Celtics and family at a joint news conference, denied the *Journal* report that Lewis had refused to be tested for drugs or had used them. NBA officials denied any conceivable way the League's anti-drug program was involved in the testing issue: "When we should be elevating the legacy of Reggie Lewis along with his jersey to the rafters of the Boston Garden, we sit here and we have to try to dispel rumors about this young man . . . We're not going to let this taint Reggie Lewis's legacy."[71]

Controversies continued. Some sportswriters quoted medical sources that Lewis had used cocaine before every home game as a performance enhancer, even though doctors warned it could kill him. Others wondered how sports reporters could have missed the abuse or heard nothing about it in the two years following Lewis's death. Some were mute. As others attacked the story as wholly lacking in substantiation and unbelievably unfair, it lost its national legs. Defenders wrote, "the higher they soar, the more delight we seem to take in yanking them back to earth." Did Lewis do cocaine or not? One sportswriter, admitting he didn't know, added, he "was a pretty good player and a very good guy who did many good things for his community, which embraced him. That should be enough. Maybe not to get his number retired, but to rest in peace."[72]

Ignoring the swirling controversy, the Celtics retired their late captain's number and raised it to the Boston Garden's rafters. To give Lewis's widow the epitaph. After saying he cared too much about basketball to risk his life, she commented, "Always believe what your eyes see." In many instances, that's difficult today with computer enhancements, morphing, and other techniques.

SECRETS COMPLICATE SUCCESSION

Concealing health problems worked against the objectives of one of the nation's richest businessmen, Reginald F. Lewis. For about two months, he kept secret his brain cancer as "he worked feverishly to complete plans for a smooth succession" for his company, TLC Beatrice, and his family. Since Beatrice was a privately held company, Lewis had the option of concealing his cancer until a day before his death. Unfortunately, his rationale—a smooth transition—foundered. Once the country's largest company run by a black executive,[73] Beatrice is a leading wholesale distributor of dry groceries, beverages, and household products in Europe, of potato chips and snacks in Ireland, and a major manufacturer of ice cream in Europe. Even before Lewis's illness in 1992, Beatrice was restructuring operations and reducing its overall workforce by as much as 5,000 in 1992.[74]

Lewis's illness signaled itself gradually, cloaked by fatigue and innervation attributed to "incredible, international demands" professionally and socially. Denial is the first defense. Lewis blamed extra pounds. Dieting did not lessen his fatigue. He became allergic to his favored ice cream and champagne. Associates noted other signs: uncharacteristic reflection, particularly for not successfully taking Beatrice public; a desire "to pull back a bit"; weight loss; less intensity. After meeting with Lewis, Michael Milken observed subtle changes: "His voice didn't have the same ring to it." The twinkle in his eye was there, but the twinkle in his voice was gone.[75] By mid-1992, the almost 50-year-old Lewis was exhibiting more troubling signs. No longer able to attend long meetings without lapses in his "impressive concentration," breaks, or interruption. Now he needed to rest.

By Thanksgiving, Lewis was experiencing vision problems in his left eye. A battery of tests, including a CAT scan, "revealed an ominous looking growth inside Lewis's brain." A subsequent biopsy confirmed inoperable brain cancer. Even with radiation, the only option, "the odds of eradicating the cancer were nominal."[76] Although they handled their announcements diametrically differently, Walsh and Lewis both applied their business analysis to their health.

Faced with potential negative side effects from radiation—impaired memory and power of reasoning and possible loss of bodily function—Lewis made a risk/benefit analysis. The chances of successful radiation were practically nil. Without it, his faculties would remain intact. He had no viable chance. On December 8, Lewis made his last public appearance.[77] The disease was humbling for the once determined, hard driving entrepreneur. He could not cut meat on his plate. Still, he told only family, "I know I'll beat this thing." As the shock and disbelief gradually wore off, Lewis resolved not to let his illness derail his life. An associate said, "He was tired, but he'd talk about future plans, about buying things." "His mind was always going on a business cycle."[78]

By telephone, he presided over Beatrice. Just two weeks before his death, he initiated a profitable currency swap. Still only two TLC Beatrice executives knew Lewis was seriously ill. Another sensitized by his own spinal tumor just guessed. Basically, "Lewis was too private to discuss his illness."[79] In just two weeks, the malignancy obviously "was starting to overtake him." Still, no public announcement.

He lost vision in his left eye, control of the left side of his body. As late as New Year's Day, he assured a long-time colleague he would beat the illness, but never mentioned cancer. When conventional treatments didn't work, he turned, unsuccessfully, to a Philippine faith healer. Another hope—an experimental drug—materialized in Canada. The day before he flew there for treatment, he dictated a "remarkably focused, lucid" memo to shareholders. It alerted them to a forthcoming press release announcing Lewis's retirement from day-to-day operations and formation of an office of the chairman to assume many of his former duties. Lewis assured shareholders he was staying involved to some extent, but relinquishing operational management to "young, but highly seasonal executives in whom I have great confidence."[80]

He then briefly analyzed operations, profitability, and the new management team headed by Jean S. Fugett, Jr. Lewis predicted stability and continuity for Beatrice, greater activity with his family and philanthropy for himself. Later, he dictated a public statement outlining his planned involvement in the cause of social justice. Neither statement mentioned why Lewis was retiring abruptly.[81]

On the flight to Toronto in his company jet, the unaware crew were stunned by Lewis's weakness. When Lewis realized the medication was not working, "he pondered the irony [that] of all the places to be afflicted, it had to be his mind. . . . I used my brain as a weapon to go forward and to disprove a lie about people of color."[82]

On January 17, Lewis suffered a massive cerebral hemorrhage. Its irreversible brain damage left no hope for recovery. Hooked to portable life-support machines, Lewis was carried aboard his private jet for a flight to New York. Obviously Lewis's cancer could no longer be hidden. His relatives and the press were told that Lewis had brain cancer, was in a coma, and the prior week had created an office of the chairman headed by Fugett. On Tuesday, January 19th, Lewis was dead at 50.[83] But one last stunt was pulled on the press. Associates acted as decoys so his body could be secreted out of the hospital.[84] Why bother?

Fugett, Lewis's half-brother, would run TLC Beatrice. But not for long. Succession troubles soon soared. Phrases such as "turbulent year," "hastily drawn succession plan," "grand colossus floundering; in need of a CEO," "search for CEO still going on" replaced the highly positive press Lewis had enjoyed.

The spin control started too. Changes were downplayed—part of a long-planned succession. Shake-ups raised questions about how well Beatrice was coping without Lewis. When revenues slide 1.4 percent to $1.2 billion, the slide was attributed to recession and increasing competition in Europe. Spin controllers explained that despite unexpected poor financial results, Fugett was doing a good job. This wasn't all his fault.[85] The problem was Fugett was no Lewis, and Lewis had been the company. A seasoned, proven manager was needed. Lewis had hoped his successors would have fun. They weren't.

After a year, shareholders welcomed Mrs. Lewis's selection as

CEO. As her husband's informal adviser and confidante, she had gained sound knowledge of Beatrice. Within months, she sold off subpar subsidiaries, slashed staff, and calmed shareholders shaken by her husband's death. But rocky financial results aroused skepticism not only over general European economic conditions but over her background—immigration law, not business.

Secrecy still plagues Beatrice. Surprised by Lewis's cancer. Surprised by Fugett's actions. Surprised by belatedly learning of Lewis's bonuses of $22 million during the five years before his death despite TLC's sizable losses and cash-flow problems. Dismayed by Mrs. Lewis initial stonewalling of press requests for interviews.[86]

Keeping secrets cannot be justified by Beatrice as family business. Once one secret surfaces observers expect more secrets and more unpleasant surprises. Succession with Tenneco's openness worked smoothly. Secrecy led to more trouble for Beatrice.

WHEN THE PATIENT'S A CELEBRITY

In the novel *The Lost Honor of Katharina Blum* Heinrich Böll relates the woe that befalls a very private young woman thrust into the cynosure of press attention. Unprepared, she, all her friends and family are stalked by the press. Her mother, recovering from surgery, is tackled by reporters entering the hospital under false guises. Protecting a patient's privacy is an acute public relations problem when the individual is newsworthy, well-known or as controversial as the late Shah of Iran, Mohammad Reza Pahlavi. Consequences can be extensive.[87] President Jimmy Carter's 1979 decision to admit the Shah into the United States for medical treatment contributed to Carter's 1980 defeat and stressed American-Iranian relations for years. Two weeks after the Shah entered New York Hospital, a student-led mob of 3,000 demonstrators stormed the American Embassy in Teheran, imprisoning 50 U.S. employees. This connection is clear—medical-political events murky.

Secrecy driven by politics resulted in flawed medical treatment. In 1974, the Shah found a painless lump diagnosed as an enlarged spleen and lymphoma. For political reasons—emboldening his enemies—the Shah kept his cancer a secret from his wife, twin sister, the United States and any other country with vital interests in the

Middle East, even doctors treating him for other ailments. It prolonged his suffering by incomplete or faulty diagnoses. "The Shah's
cancer was, without question, one of the best-kept state secrets of
all time," states Gary Sick, a Carter expert on Iran. Not until the
Shah became gravely ill in Mexico in October 1979 did his long-held
secret come out.

President Carter's choice was a cruel one. As doors of diplomacy
and friendship relentlessly closed to the Shah, his cancer resurged.
Admitting the Shah could endanger the Americans still in Iran. The
Shah simply had waited too long diplomatically and medically. Still
he avoided local Mexican doctors, seeking evaluation from specialists
who originally diagnosed his cancer.

As the Shah now began suffering complications and severe side
effects from anti-cancer, he told his staunchest advocates, David
Rockefeller and Henry Kissinger. Still obsessed with secrecy, he
sought treatment from local physicians only for his most immediate
health problem—gallstones. Robert Armao, a public relations consultant, and Joseph Reed, both close to the Rockefeller family, arranged for a specialist in tropical diseases to treat malaria, the
presumed illness. Essential blood tests were ruled out. Such covertness created conflicting medical and political options. The lymphoma was not responding to chemotherapy, his spleen was
enlarging at an alarming rate, and gallstones were causing obstructive
jaundice. While the spleen could be treated easily in Mexico, little
could be done anywhere for the other ailments.

President Carter, pressured to admit the Shah, clearly distinguished between a humanitarian, purely medical visit and any other.
Public maneuvering began. The Shah still feared public exposure;
realistically, his stunningly worsening condition was difficult to hide.
He was emaciated, suffering from hard tumor nodes in the neck and
a swollen spleen. Political considerations narrowed choices for hospitalization. Not France. He was politically unwelcome. He could be
treated in Mexico, but not easily or quickly. That left the preferred
New York Hospital.

Webs of Rockefeller relationships now surfaced. In analysis of any
public relations problem, unseen ties are determinate, but difficult
to detect and evaluate, even in retrospect. Rockefeller interests publicly argued and pressured for entry into the U.S. The life-threatening condition could not be treated elsewhere. The argument

produced an immediate political turnaround, even by the last Carter adviser opposing the Shah's entry.

Alone, Carter held out, concerned that Americans in Iran would be seized or killed. Publicity stakes were upped. The health humanitarian hot button changed his mind. Tragically, his opposition had been the wisest course. Conditions of the Shah's entry were: only temporarily for medical treatment. Political activity was barred. These did nothing to slake the growing fury of Teheran mobs. Within 24 hours of his arrival in the U.S., the Shah's gall bladder and gallstones were removed. His cancer was still a public secret.[88] Six weeks later, he ignominiously became a man without a home. Four months later he died in Cairo where his odyssey for health care and his dangerous secrecy had begun more than a year earlier. Even after death, more secrets and manipulations surfaced. Flawed medical information, but even facts available at the time, indicated no imperative reason for U.S. treatment.

Were medical facts distorted to win refuge? The only American physician to examine the Shah in Mexico terms ridiculous "any statement that the Shah was at 'the point of death' and 'could be treated only in New York City.' " Were these facts distorted as they passed through many hands, or manipulated as power play? Did President Carter seek guidance from more objective sources such as White House physician, William Lukash, ironically a gastroenterologist. Apparently not. Sick concludes the Shah should have been diagnosed and treated in Mexico. But, believing him near death, what public official would risk disputing unanimous medical opinion? More seriously, politicians and others slighted accurate warnings of Iran's probable violent reaction—the hostage crisis. Had the Shah been more realistic, understanding that, whether healthy or ill, his chances of returning to Iran were slim, could he have avoided the mortification of a peripatetic exile? Would the U.S. Embassy in Teheran have been stormed? Difficult to answer, but secrecy dammed up sound decision-making. And many suffered.

CONCEALING CONTINUES

To paraphrase the historical canard about repeating the past: refusing to see the trouble others cause themselves by concealing court exactly the same problems, repeatedly.

Saul Steinberg, Reliance Group Holdings chairman and chief executive, suffered a mild stroke in June 1995. When was it announced? By whom? Not until mid-August by CNBC. Only then did
corporate spin artists begin painting a positive picture. The stroke
was mild, requiring only six days hospitalization. Minor motor problems on one side required physical therapy, but Steinberg's intellectual powers are unimpaired. He's running the company from home
until he returns to the office. Why no public announcement? The
spin masters explain: both inside and outside counsel agreed it
wasn't necessary. He's not seriously incapacitated. An SEC spokesman concurred, explaining no specific rules govern disclosure of executive health problems. Although industry leaders were surprised,
all doubted any serious impact on Reliance. Steinberg's brother Robert was already running day-to-day operations. Saul was "managing
some assets."[89]

The right way? Wrong way to handle news of a stroke? Time will
tell.

WAFFLING: GOOD NEWS, BAD NEWS, NO NEWS

Waffling is mixed messages—basically good news balanced by only
the barest of contrary details or just silence. Waffling damages a
company, its employees, public image, and media relations. Sensitive
questions such as succession cannot be debated. Employees and
media may sense, even know the truth, unofficially, but are in a
quandary about acting on it.

More than any other technique, waffling demonstrates the complexity of balancing privacy and family wishes with material need to
announce. Denial, hopes, and assumptions of overcoming the illness
are the first responses. Disease often does take surprising turns. Demanding total candor may be against the very nature of a health
crisis. Concealing and waffling are close, but different.

The most dramatic instance of waffling is the late Steven Ross,
co-CEO of Time-Warner, but other less complicated cases illustrate
the technique. It may be a matter of timing, getting business and
succession ducks in a row, or sheer oversight of a minor matter that
becomes major. Five waffling-by-waiting examples come from business; three waffling-by-imaging, from politics.

WAFFLING BY WAITING

Privacy is the first casualty of any executive illness. Newspaper chain executives enjoy none of the privacy afforded ordinary citizens. Delayed announcement, perhaps, but enduring privacy, no. Physicians may fight an ultimately losing battle.

Imagine this roller-coaster of personal and corporate emotions of Knight-Ridder, one of the country's largest newspaper companies and its once-chief executive, James K. Batten. One incident was relatively straight forward; the second, more complex. In October 1993, Batten, apparently in good health, blacked out while driving. The accident left him in a deep coma, near death. Associates struggled to balance personal feelings with "seamless management." Outside, analysts praised them for acting so coolly. The disruption had little noticeable effect.

Batten, who recovered slowly, eventually returned to his full schedule. In July 1994, he was experiencing severe headaches. Doctors quickly discovered a tumor, too small to detect earlier, that probably caused the blackout. After surgery to remove the plum-sized malignant brain tumor, Mr. Batten again tried to maintain a normal work schedule. Slowly, though, effects of his therapy began to appear. He appeared unstable on his feet, exhausted, winded when he spoke, and not focused on business issues. Repeatedly, doctors and treatments interrupted his schedule. P. Anthony Ridder, eventually Batten's successor, carefully made clear that he was leaving leadership questions to Batten, who saw dangers and pressures of leaders "slow to hang it up," vowing not to make that mistake himself.[90]

Batten asked close advisers to tell him if they detected any disability. By March, he stepped down from operational responsibilities but retained the chairmanship. He decided, not the board. Sometimes the board is forced to push aside an ill executive. A neurosurgeon interviewed for this book suggested: don't leave a brain tumor patient in charge. Gracefully maintain his dignity and presence, but leave decision-making to others. Knight-Ridder did this. Batten's health remained a factor. He missed a board meeting when hospitalized. Three months after resigning as chief executive, Batten died. Leadership had been transferred after some anguish but, in the main, well.

Culture, corporate or national, may delay the news or mute its tone. The reaction of non-U.S. operations to Michael Walsh's tape is one example. Sony founder Akio Morita's cerebral hemorrhage is another. Though Morita was more a highly visible symbol than an active operational executive, his illness nonetheless was important news. Feeling ill on a Tuesday morning after playing tennis, the 72-year old Morita was rushed to immediate surgery to remove blood from his brain.

At a hastily called press conference, a Sony senior executive said the surgery went well, but termed "premature" questions of when or if Morita would resume his activities. They included not only Sony but his prominent role as a soother of trade relations between the U.S. and Japan. Left unsaid was Morita's probable four-month absence. Rumors spread quickly that illness would force him to retire. The good news/bad news tone dominated. No, there is no indication that Morita would step down. Yes, he cannot speak, but he can respond to questions by squeezing someone's hand. No, there would be little impact on Sony, operations or stock. Yes, he is the psychological backbone of a company facing the toughest time in its history.

Why did the company wait two days to announce the surgery, and then only after leaks started appearing in the press? Early reports said Morita merely suffered a cold. Why wait? The family wanted to get a better sense of Morita's condition and inform associates at Sony and Keidanren. Understandable. The Japanese are normally reticent about health problems of prominent leaders.[91]

Another case of waffling by waiting is the late Dr. Theodore Cooper, the physician and scientist who headed the Upjohn Company. Only in early February, ten days after bone-marrow cancer was diagnosed, did the company announce that Dr. Cooper complained of back pain a month earlier. Upjohn reasoned there was "no immediate pressure to give out incomplete information" while Dr. Cooper's condition and treatment was being determined. Also, they issued the standard statement. Illness wasn't interfering with his normal activities. He was in contact with company headquarters several times daily. He expected to return to a normal schedule within a few days.[92]

Belated disclosure carried two unusual considerations: Dr. Cooper's own medical background and Upjohn as a diversified health-care company. Ironically, the news caught more media attention because in the same two-week period Walsh's, Lewis's, and Brinker's illnesses were announced. A rash of cancers and accidents among CEOs will get more play than one illness. The echo effect amplifies.

Business timing could not have been worse when Dr. Cooper was hospitalized again, suffering from severe respiratory problems. Upjohn was problem-plagued by four leading products losing patent protection in 1994, government attempts to control health-care costs, and a frail chief executive visibly losing his battle—which he did. Would transition to Ley Smith as chief executive been easier with an earlier announcement? Doubtful.[93]

Delayed announcements do not uniformly cause corporate or public relations difficulties. Within a month of a colon-cancer diagnosis, James Olson, CEO of AT&T, was dead. On March 18, 1988, he was felled by flu. On March 25, colon surgery was performed, but announcement was delayed until April 12. Why? AT&T explained it was too early to say when Olson could return to work. (He never did.) Hardly the point. AT&T enjoyed a depth of management talent and an office of the chairman. President Robert Allen ran the company while Olson underwent outpatient chemotherapy, and then for a decade more. Analysts doubted a smooth transition. It was.

The day after Olson died, and one day before the annual meeting on April 19, 1988, Allen was elected chairman and chief executive. He faced serious business problems such as losing share in the all-important long-distance market. Most wrenching was Olson's death. Psychologists say the death of a friend or close business associate can drive an individual to profound reassessment. Allen, personally and professionally, paused for a few months to rethink aspects of the business and where he should lead AT&T.[94]

AT&T delayed its announcement, and then only in response to reporters' questions—not what most communicators would counsel—but few criticized. A New York Stock Exchange executive saw no problem with the way it was handled. Others, terming it a difficult call, noted illness changes rapidly, as did Olson's. The initial announcement frequently becomes outdated. Has he ever heard of updates or a running story?

AT&T may be an unusual case. A successor, the key, was in place. Olson's death was very sudden. And one could argue that he and his family needed time and privacy to adjust to the cancer. The acid test: the company's stock showed no reaction to either the illness or death.[95]

Creating a Golden Coffin

Steven Ross, late co-CEO of Time-Warner, probably is the most interesting and important case of waffling. Not only did his cancer illustrate the delicate balance of privacy and shareholder need to know, but it magnified personality traits long evident. He ran a major public corporation as a private fiefdom. Ross was both a master of denial and of creating his own best public persona. Some liken him to F. Scott Fitzgerald's great self-created character—Jay Gatsby. Finally, Ross's illness stripped away the veils and optimism from business problems, succession struggles, and merger messes.

Ross strode onto the business deal-maker scene with daring and success. *The New York Times* described him in early 1992 as "an intuitive, gut-driven executive who says his favorite occupation is dreaming, imagining futuristic ways to bring more media to more people. A good deal maker, Ross possesses a great gift for numbers. He chooses talented people to lead businesses and lets them run— with generally good but occasionally disastrous results."[96] He had parlayed power from modest beginnings and the Kinney Parking System.[97] But by March 1992, the once darling of Wall Street, "the legendary deal maker," was struggling to beat cancer and public vilification. The *Time* merger was like a discordant, unfinished symphony.

Communicating his cancer tracked his 1980 heart attack. Ross ordered it kept secret. Public announcement would hurt the company. Oh, such narcissism: And his self-image? A "bad back" was the cover story for three weeks, until Ross was released from the hospital. Then the truth was told.

The heart attack was a wake up call. "He had lived as if exempt from basic physiological principles. He smoked several packs of Parliaments a day, exercised only sporadically, gorged on steak and eggs for breakfast". Now, however, he seemed to have recognized his mortality, if only in a glancing way. To the surprise of some family members, he heeded and believed his doctor's choice: keep smoking or live.[98] Ross changed his lifestyle, but not his communicating.

Five years later, he underwent surgery for prostate cancer. In 1991, a periodic blood test revealed a suspicious elevation. Further tests were delayed because of an "arduous schedule," currently closing the Toshiba-Itochu deal. Ross feared competitors wanted to "knock the statue off the pedestal." Kill Steve Ross; Worse, be Steve Ross.[99]

A reporter unaware of the cause described Ross as troubled by back pain: "He looks like a humbled man. Slumped in a leather chair, the co-chief executive officer of the world's largest media and entertainment company winces as he reaches for a glass of water. His smile is wan, his jowls sag, his once athletic frame appears bloated." Ross is quoted, "It's been a rough couple of years." "I've been hurt tremendously." The physical pain Ross feels is "concentrated, excruciatingly, in his back. Every movement is cumbersome; rising to his feet an intricate maneuver. Despite a life of sumptuous ease, Ross's appearance amounts to eloquent testimony that money is not everything."[100]

By October 1991, one struggle, the Toshiba deal, was over, but the final one, against cancer, just beginning. Ross was forced to take to bed. The cancer was back. Little could be done. Ross is said to have declared: "What a time for this to happen." Such a dominant figure in a public company should have disclosed his illness. Instead, Ross attacked it as he had other sticky business problems—preserve deniability. Even if treatment was successful, a very dubious if, doctors gave him six months, maybe a year to live. Typically, Ross is said to never have asked his doctors a direct question. Like the very ill FDR, he coped by denying or ignoring.

Only on November 26 did Ross announce his illness with a two-sentence press release. Following the formula of good news/bad news, he said physicians were optimistic and he was maintaining a normal work schedule. The bad news: he wasn't seen in the office. Sparse, consistently positive messages continued. Most ducked the truth. Were more personal then policy. He issued a short letter to employees. That was it.

How did Ross's family justify all this? Well, he isn't President of the United States. Why should he change now? He'd always behaved as if accountable to no one, rather than an employee of a publicly held company with stakeholders at risk. Even such relativism could not quell qualms about disclosure as months passed and suspicions grew.

Top aides knew the cancer had recurred. Given that fact and Ross's age, they doubted his full recovery; so did his doctors. However, long-time friend Arthur Liman, to whom the doctors' reports were encouraging, "persisted in giving upbeat reports."[101] Another friend, public relations guru Gershon Kekst, said: "The cancer and chemotherapy are nothing compared to the way he feels about the public and business abuse he's suffering"[102] Really!

Health problems ripped away the veils Ross held over problems of succession and over the *Time* merger—two uncongenial cultures trying to become a harmonious one—and over Ross's much challenged $78.2 million 1990 salary—more than any other executive of a public company. The myth of Ross's invincibility took a pummeling with the Time-Warner merger. The overriding question and worry—can he bounce back again? The '80's disease of "money, money, money is all that counts" seemed to be making him mildly passé.

Appearances were not reassuring. One reporter described him as seeming uneasy. "The tall, unfailingly ebullient, painstakingly coifed chieftain is a different man. The eyes are plaintive. They were skeptical, warned of the 'poor-Steve ploy.' But as Ross awkwardly pulls his chair closer to the table in front of him, he seems sincere when he says, 'When you're constantly attacked, you wanna go out and shoot yourself.' "[103]

He excused his staying home, saying, "I'm a family man." "I hate parties." Associates, when they spoke at all, said the therapy was going well. The first session halved the tumor's size. There was no indication the cancer had spread. Even though Ross sometimes felt terrible and his hair had fallen out, his wife assured, "He is very motivated to get well."[104]

The liabilities mounted. He meandered in disturbing ways. The obviously sick man fighting for his life soon would be forced by the merger agreement to vacate the chief executive office. The frenetic pace of the deal-making years was unthinkable now. "Ever mistrustful of journalists," Ross now had a house full of them.[105] Directors were making corporate strategic plans and choosing a successor. Connie Bruck opines, "Had they known the truth about Ross's prognosis, it is altogether possible they would still have chosen Levin, but certainly the choice would have been harder and more debated. In any event, they ought not to have made so momentous a decision on a false assumption."[106]

Uncertainties of Ross's health also prodded other action. He was flown to Los Angeles for surgery—it was futile. Although he had been unable to eat or drink in months, the charade continued. After a radical 10½-hour operation, a doctor proclaimed it a success. The family believed its own optimistic public reports.[107]

Instead, Ross died on December 20, 1992. The closely stage-managed funeral, "bent on creating a specific image,[108] revealed more weakness and storms. Just before Ross's death, Gerald Levin, co-CEO, restructured the board of directors, forcing off several strong Ross loyalists. Although Levin had not known Ross was dying, he knew Ross was weakened and incommunicado and he had seized the moment."[109] Business and succession problems linger. Some say even Ross couldn't have pulled off the Time-Warner merger. More than eight years later, Levin is "still mopping up debris." With yet another merger—with Ted Turner—questions of control and succession arise anew. Did the waffling about Ross's illness or the highly public contretemps discernibly impact the stock? Probably not.[110]

Steve Ross persists too—from his grave. *The New York Times* ran a full page advertisement paid for by Time-Warner. It began: "We are all better people for having known him. What greater legacy could any man leave? All he achieved in life—the institution he built and the frontiers he pioneered—was driven by the way he reached out and drew everyone he touched into the warm and vibrant circle of his being. Arthur Ashe? Jesus Christ? No, Steven J. Ross . . . by any measure, a towering success."[111]

Business writer Michael Lewis had more cynical responses. "While he lived, Ross had a knack for separating his shareholders from their money, which he spent on corporate jets, Italian villas and the good opinion of the people who mattered to him. He paid himself $69 million in a year in which the company's stock languished. So it is deliciously fitting that the beleaguered shareholders now find themselves stuck with the tab for a posthumous PR campaign."[112]

The unique burden Ross bequeathed the company, the "ultimate self-aggrandizement" is "a golden coffin"—agreements that the dead Ross will be paid his salary for the next five years. Even more delightfully strange: in any popularity contest, Ross will win handily over the cynic who dances on his grave.[113] Plagued, even driven, by image problems all his life, Ross has others creating and using his mystic style, even after death.

WAFFLING DRAWS ATTENTION

Succession planning is job one for CEOs and boards of directors. Sudden illness, such as that of GE's John F. Welch, reveals the weakness of the executive bench. GE's less than complete and quick announcement of Welch's heart problems created a churn of rivalries, rumors, and jockeying for promotion.[114] The important chronology, events, and announcements are:

> The 59-year-old Welch, suffering chest pains, entered a Bridgeport Hospital on Sunday, April 30. On Tuesday, he had a single Angioplasty, termed a success by GE in its May 4 announcement. It quoted a doctor saying Welch would be home within a week and back to work on May 15. Attempting to dampen any concern, GE spokespeople noted the CEO had no previous history of heart trouble; nor had he suffered any major illness. However, earlier in the year, he had picked up a severe parasitic infection that persisted for months draining him of energy according to friends, not GE.[115]

To add to the optimism, the routine nature of the non-surgical Angioplasty, Welch's conducting business from his hospital bed, the promised return to work on May 15 and the doctors' assurance of a full, complete recovery were stressed. But Welch headed instead for Massachusetts General Hospital and five grafts to bypass obstructions in three of his heart's main arteries. He was released on May 22. Once again, the PR mills ground out nothing but good news. On May 14, investors and analysts were told and assured that Welch would be back at work by mid-June. His own quotes were used. Retire? Retire? A lot of guys are just getting this job at my age.[116] At 59? Maybe. Succession? Not necessary, responded GE.

Not so simple. The leader often determines outcomes. A once-neighboring company, Singer in Stamford, was realigning its business mix to high technology and aerospace, fighting off a hostile takeover bid, when its CEO, Joseph Flavin, dropped dead one morning—just after a complete physical and clean bill of health. The leader gone, Singer was taken over, then dismembered to bring down the takeover-created leverage.

The GE assumption—revealed now in error—was that a well-managed $60.1 billion company has not only a succession plan, but players in place. Not so. GE turned away any questions of succession, assuring all that Welch would run GE, as he had planned, until 2000. Of course, the board of directors of any well-managed company has a plan, but now's not time to discuss it. Welch will be back.

Meanwhile, the corporation, according to The *Wall Street Journal*[117] is "burning with rumors and rivalries as speculation rises as to who will eventually succeed Welch." That won't be easy: "Welch is acknowledged as a superb, hands-on manager, who often helps personally to close major deals." Observers liken GE to a "bumblebee that flies—aerodynamically. It isn't supposed to but it does." Others questioned how serious illness may change Welch's management style. Quit? Work on, not picking a successor immediately. Forced out by poor health before a successor is chosen or in place? The mills of optimism continue. The CEO is recovering faster than the average patient. Employees are exhorted to work hard to ensure that Jack's imminent return home is made an even happier event by the flawless performance of the business.[118]

As with Walsh, announcements were linked to business strategy, to beating the odds. Denial abounded. Even successful surgery may impact the individual. Will there be a dramatic change in attitudes, aggression? Will heirs apparent keep the bumblebee flying profitably and amicably? Others bet on outside directors, scarred by the chaos created by the sudden loss of a CEO elsewhere, not to let that happen to GE. For a time at least, the worries proved unnecessary. Welch returned, continued his leadership, retained admiration of the business community, even published his wisdoms.

WAFFLING BY IMAGING

Escalating attention by overlooking the obvious is dumb, but a trap fallen into repeatedly. When every inch or color tone of a President's hair is noticed or commented upon, why on earth would the White House only belatedly mention removal of skin lesions from President Clinton's face and behind his ear? Everyone, including doctors and Clinton, considered removal of actinic keratoses as a precaution, so ordinary it didn't deserve mention. Not media smart. For ten years, at most check-ups, such lesions had been removed. The 1995 annual physical was touted as a clean bill of health; lesions were not mentioned. When the press spotted red blotches, they started asking questions. Had the President bumped into something? Finally, several days later the announcement was made.

Not only the minute scrutiny, but the baggage Clinton carried personally and as President dictated announcement. Presidents and candidates have become more open about health problems since revelations about how White House doctors and aides hid and lied about medical problems of Franklin D. Roosevelt, John F. Kennedy, and other Presidents. But not always. Lyndon B. Johnson had a skin cancer removed secretly as President, it was acknowledged only after his death. Mr. Clinton declined, for reasons of privacy, to fully disclose details of his health or allow reporters to talk with his doctors. Despite repeated promises to open medical records details were dribbled out and incorrect rumors filled the void until the 1996 campaign.

During Jacqueline Kennedy Onassis's last illness, the good-news-only cover story prompted a health worker to speak out. She feared the public would gain a false impression of the medical treatment Mrs. Onassis received. Nancy Tuckerman, her spokeswoman, said: "She's fine. She goes in for routine visits, routine treatment." Later, Ms. Tuckerman acknowledged she understated the severity of Mrs. Onassis's condition. "We were trying to low-key this whole thing. . . . Her medical situation is private. . . . We didn't have to reveal everything to reporters." Ms. Tuckerman explained she was not being deceptive, merely trying to protect the children so they could visit with ease. This waffle demonstrates that many audiences must be considered—a prominent hospital worried about a perception of mistreating a celebrity patient, children, and privacy.[119]

As political needs change, so do imaging techniques. President Ronald Reagan's sophisticated communicators downplayed the near fatalness of the assassination attempt and the length of recovery.[120] Imaging changed to laudable candor when it was announced in November 1994 that the former President was entering the early stages of Alzheimer's. Even before becoming President, Reagan said publicly he wanted to be watched for senility. His mother had been senile several years before her death at 80.[121]

The announcement quelled rumors and protected Reagan, but questions persisted. How long had he been suffering from Alzheimer's? In 1990, lapses of memory about Iran-Contra and his inability to remember the name of the chairman of the Joints Chiefs of Staff were discussed widely. Rumors spread, spurred by friends struck "by deterioration of his thought process" or his forgetting the punch line of a favorite story. Some of his doctors considered the diagnosis a year earlier. Others reported definite memory problems two years before. Associates said he changed markedly in the months immediately before the diagnosis.[122] Although one must applaud the courage of the Alzheimer's announcement, it also explains and protects the image while removing Reagan from hostile public scrutiny. Candor was used to political benefit, but as imaging, also.

BUNGLING: IS THE BOSS JUST STRESSED OR GOING CRAZY?

Bungling is endemic to any handling of executive health issues—telling too much or too little, too early or too late, building a false image that crumbles when reality intrudes, or sending out confusing, mixed messages. But the risk is greatest in psychological illness. The untrained might willingly rush into questions of alcoholism or lifestyle, but judging aberrant behavior poses much greater difficulties for lay persons. They prudently question, hesitate, and watch, but such inertia escalates the risks.

Are people really following the boss? Has he just been working too hard? Is he paranoid? Has the loneliness and stress of wartime command warped a once good commander into self-preservation at all costs? How differently do judgments made during the maelstrom of crises look when most answers are known, no danger is involved, and the critic risks nothing personally?

Bungling is exemplified in two examples from the machismo world of the military, one a real executive, the other fictional. James Forrestal, the first secretary of defense, tackled the insurmountable task of harmoniously unifying savagely competitive branches of the armed forces;[123] the character of Captain Queeg of the USS *Caine*, in *The Caine Mutiny*, derives from novelist Herman Wouk's service in the World War II Navy. They illustrate the dangers in seeing too little in Forrestal's case and too much in Queeg's.

Forrestal was a fascinatingly complex person, driven to strive. Dedicated as a politician and public servant, he created an image more akin to the Horatio Alger myth than to the reality of his Hudson River Irish Catholic background.[124] A driven workaholic, he left little time for personal reflection, restocking, or assimilation of events. His stability, according to his biographers, Townsend Hoopes and Douglas Brinkley, came to depend on his work. That was threatened by vicious, irresponsible and personally painful poundings by columnist Drew Pearson, an active opponent of his policies. Also, Forrestal was left in limbo for months by President Harry S. Truman—would he or would he not continue as secretary of defense. Apparently not, but nothing was announced. Forrestal was left twisting in the wind of uncertainty for almost five months, excluded from the meetings of the Joint Chiefs of Staff—notations on the official calendar read, "You are not expected"—walked around gingerly by associates.[125] Was he seriously ill? Imagining? Were the job and relationship with the President exacerbating problems? Forrestal's case ended tragically with his suicide—the highest-ranking official ever to do so, despite the recent tragedies of Admiral Jeremy Borda, U.S.N., and Deputy White House Counsel Vincent Foster.

A THRICETOLD TALE

One of Forrestal's successors, Robert McNamara, despite experiencing very similar problems and questions, rose to other positions of power and wrote a *mea culpa* book. Reviewing *In Retrospect: The Tragedy and Lessons of Vietnam*, Sidney Blumenthal notes President Lyndon Johnson believed McNamara was going mad. "That man could have a mental breakdown. . . . I'm afraid we could even have another Forrestal on our hands." Johnson "diagnosed" incipient suicidal psychosis by observing the Defense Secretary's anguish over the futility of the war and his attempts to get Johnson to enter negotiations. Later Johnson attributed McNamara's "ungluing and betrayal" to the pressure of his own nemesis, Robert F. Kennedy. Kennedy was pushing McNamara ever harder, calling daily, saying the war was terrible and immoral. He had to leave. Just before McNamara did, Johnson said, "he felt he was a murderer and didn't know how to extricate himself. . . . I was afraid he might have a nervous breakdown."[126]

Johnson was not alone in noting the secretary's "aching conscience." However, the press was not as vicious as Pearson had been to Forrestal. David Halberstam wrote that McNamara was "a man so contorted and so deep in his own unique self-delusion and self-division that he still doesn't know who he is and what he did at that time."[127]

Both secretaries were steel-trap-minded bureaucrats in the grip of a Cold War myth. But when the "hero technocrat" heard Johnson comparing him to Forrestal, McNamara countered that he was not getting answers to his questions, making him as "tense as hell." He had told the President point-blank achieving objectives in Vietnam was impossible.[128]

Forrestal absorbed more, countered and defended himself less. He simply plunged into work even harder, longer. Two biographies of Forrestal, written 30 years apart, reflect little change in perceiving and handling psychological illness in a senior official. Although the fault lines of Forrestal's early life and career flash warning signals of future trouble, the focus is limited to the communications handling of the final fatal incident.

The earlier work, Arnold A. Rogow's 1963 *James Forrestal: A Study of Personality, Politics, and Policy*, reflects the temper of those times—inflamed Cold War fears, a press even more vindictive than today. The clinical psychobiography focuses on the concept of neurosis at the highest level and its impact on image- and decision-making.

Rogow's study of the mythology that a VIP does not become mentally ill, at least not in office, startles today. The leader may be called exhausted, overworked in the cause of the country. Only years later, if even then, can it be "discovered" that "exhaustion" actually was "incapacitating psychosis."[129] Even posthumously, families and organizations attempt to protect images. Most books and films don't explore the existence of "psychotic" military leaders, much less the possibility that sick men are deciding national fates.[130] Ironically, during the Cold War, keeping secrets from the Russians was the rationale. But they knew; they had good spies. Only Americans were kept in the dark.

Driven Patriot, published in 1993 by Townsend Hoopes and Douglas Brinkley, is a wider study benefitting from the greater breadth that 30 years of memoirs and other documentation produce. Surprisingly, their analysis differs little from Rogow's in substance, much more in tone and depth of detail. They track three strains of difficulties—personal background, ferocious battles over military unification, and Washington's destructive infighting by politicians and media. (Shadows of Vincent Foster's tragic suicide cluster about that much earlier assessment.)

They view Forrestal "as a man being eroded by cumulative fatigue and a mounting sense of personal failure" to bring order and harmony to military unification, to persuade the President to support an adequate military budget, "to arouse the American people or even his governmental colleagues to what he saw as a mortal threat to the survival of the nation and of human freedom. Exhaustion bred anxiety, and anxiety distorted his sense of proportion."[131]

SIGNALS MANY; RESPONSES FEW

Few crises, health or otherwise, spring from a single source. Forrestal also was "cruelly disillusioned by the attitude, behavior, and tactics of many senior military officers." He was worn down not just by "villains" deliberately intent upon his defeat and destruction, but also by an impersonal clash of forces represented by men serving specific interests they had been taught to equate with the national interest.

"By late summer of 1948, Forrestal was slipping into a deep sense of disillusionment, impelled by some penchant for dark tragedy in his Irish soul. Yet he rejected the idea of resigning. An obsessive sense of urgency about the world and national crises made it impossible for him even to consider a vacation. Given the milieu, even members of his staff failed to recognize the signals." In retrospect, they attribute their failure to Forrestal's formidable self-control, his brusque, impersonal method of dealing with staff, and the simple fact they saw him too frequently to note much change in his condition or demeanor. Certain friends caught revealing glimpses of his inner state, but only in the privacy of small dinners at home. "Work became his armor against the world . . . and illness."[132]

Once known socially and professionally for his "great charm and wit," now he appeared tense and nervous, gray with fatigue, and obsessed with Russian intentions. Remarkably, he maintained outward self-control. As perceived threats increased, he developed the nervous habit of dipping his fingers into his water glass and compulsively wetting his lips as he talked. Forrestal picked or scratched a portion of his scalp so continually, it became irritated. He made mistakes of identity and memory slips. By late summer, he seemed calm again. His armor against the world, long and assiduously developed, concealed a vulnerable and wounded man.

Inwardly, uncertainties of his standing with the White House "filled him with anxiety."[133] He was "slipping ever deeper into anxiety and depression from which he never recovered." Associates were noticing now. He grew listless, indecisive. His unspoken unhappiness "permeated the office." He refused to be rushed. "He became loath to leave his desk, clinging to it as though it were a life raft." When asked about going home, he responded, "Home to what?" He "dropped the silent guardrail" he had erected around the failure of his family life. Outsiders, even the press, began to comment that he never seemed at peace, was nervous, shifting from subject to subject."[134] As one reads the sad accounts of Forrestal's decline, one must ponder how little others saw and did. Perhaps they expected too much, so saw too little. He had withstood a year of "ceaseless rivalry" and "relentless cannonading" with little perceptible impact on the man or his reputation. He gave off discordant vibes, "a detachable intellect" at odds, with a wariness of eye.[135] When finally forced to resign, he seemed unable to admit even to himself that his long, distinguished public service was over. His diaries are quiet on key issues. His letter of resignation was "more elaborately casual that seemed necessary."[136]

Complexity and lack of closure haunted Forrestal. Little save his executive decisions were clean-cut or fast—and later nor were they. Cumulative reports of unstable and eccentric behavior finally forced Truman to conclude Forrestal had to go. In retrospect, that very delay and uncertainty was blamed for the loss of physical stamina, uneven capacity to concentrate, and nervous uncertainty. One associate remarked: "This was a man who a year before had been keen, quick and decisive, who had given me twelve answers in as many minutes or less. Now in twenty minutes he couldn't answer one question."[137]

OTHER EARLY WARNINGS DISCOUNTED

A parallel of presidential indecision harming a cabinet official is Ronald Reagan's relationship with National Security Adviser Bud McFarlane. As his mental state raised concerns during Iran-Contra, Reagan's "pernicious indecision," like Truman's, left McFarlane feeling helpless, not up to his job. Like Forrestal, he dragged scarring childhood experiences into maturity. Resignation, in December 1985, did not improve McFarlane's mental destabilization. He was distressed sitting on the sidelines, out of the action, a has-been, another K Street kibitzer.

What triggered his suicide attempt? Robert Timberg in *The Nightingale's Song* seems to echo accounts of Forrestal's suicide. McFarlane "had surrendered too much of himself, cut too many corners, played too many Washington games, mortgaged his integrity to feed his ambition. And, when the loan was finally called, he was damn near bankrupt."[138]

Unlike Forrestal, McFarlane, despite "unremitting desolation," talked about Iran-Contra. Rather than attacking him, the media merely showed his increasingly erratic behavior on major television programs such as *Nightline*. As his depression deepened and the Iran-Contra shrapnel was "flying furiously," he wrote night and day, furiously to compose a national security policy package that might salvage his reputation and brighten his mood. Not a word in response to any of it from anyone. He too worried about his good name, about tarnishing his long, distinguished public career. The organization was selecting out, isolating the troubled one. But, unlike with Forrestal, associates and family acknowledged what was happening. But, they delayed acting.

As he recovered from the failed suicide attempt, McFarlane said that "he felt as if he were lying in a giant pit and people were standing around the rim pelting him with garbage."[139] One can imagine feeling that way about the media. Actually, the press treated McFarlane gingerly, but he resented being treated "like a rather fragile flower."

Denial and myth were still alive and active in Washington of the mid-eighties. The suicide was a sham, designed to fail; others dismissed it as a transparent plea for sympathy and clemency. Still others saw it as a cry for help by a man who had "depleted his emotional resources."

Forrestal's "cries" went unnoticed, except by Mrs. Arthur Krock, wife of a *New York Times* journalist, who cautioned her husband, "Jim is cracking up". Krock dismissed it as silly. Their friend was too strong and durable to lose command of himself. He'd be all right once he left government and rested. But work was his indispensable life-support system. Every day deepened his obsessive need to stay. Departure was emotionally unbearable.[140]

One who took seriously Forrestal's belief that he was being followed and his phone tapped was Secret Service Chief U. E. Baughman. Much later it was determined several groups opposing his policies were. Forrestal became so overly suspicious he peered out to see who was ringing his bell. He wandered around his home wearing a hat. Baughman's "final discovery" was that Forrestal had drawn up a will and acquired a large number of sleeping tablets. Baughman was virtually convinced Forrestal was suffering "a total psychotic breakdown . . . characterized by suicidal features" and told the President.[141] Still, most colleagues assumed Forrestal was just exhausted.

Often ignored in any executive illness, but especially psychological, is the impact on the organization and its image. In Forrestal's case, he was increasingly excluded, an invisible leader until the final exclusion—Truman's request for his resignation. Rogow describes the process:

> The Defense Secretary . . . was consulted less; involved less in decisions. Intentions conflicted. One hoped that reducing strains of office would facilitate his recovery; others were simply expediting decisions Forrestal was having difficulty making. Still others sought to protect the military establishment from having to change bad policy made by someone seriously ill.

That sounds like a good reason for the real reason—slowing Forrestal's prime project, unification. Bureaucracies, whether governmental, corporate, or academic, do not welcome in their ranks the odd, deviant, or excessively nonconformist in behavior. Exclusion may effectively isolate the individual, but also endanger a nation's security or even world peace. Tragically, for Forrestal, exclusion only increased his anxiety and sense of failure.[142]

A Vicious Media Frenzy

With Forrestal's departure, the sniping in government and destructive media attacks by Drew Pearson intensified. Pearson makes feeding frenzies in Washington today look positively benign. Demagogic themes were played and replayed in prescheduled weekly assaults. At first, "endless repetition of stale falsehoods" were calculated, like Chinese water torture, to drive the victim to distraction, to destroy a high reputation and to hound him from office. Friends watched "the dismal spectacle of a man they cherished and admired—at bay alone, persecuted and on the defensive." Although the Navy psychiatrist retracted it later, in a post-mortem interview with a *Time* reporter, the Navy doctor said "Drew Pearson and Walter Winchell killed Forrestal."[143]

Immediately after the presidential retirement ceremony, Forrestal's behavior left no doubt of serious illness. Arriving for lunch at his home, he took a seat away from the windows to "avoid giving a sniper a good target." He talked of "they"—Communists, Zionists, persons in the White House—all conspiring to get him. He cautioned visitors to speak softly for "they" had wired his home.

As the disorder and insomnia increased, mentions of suicide appeared. Friends urged he seek seclusion, treatment, and rest in Florida. Escalating risks of suicide began. He flew unaccompanied. The country's most eminent psychiatrist, Dr. William Menninger, based on sessions with Forrestal, reported no traces of combat fatigue or any other mental or emotional abnormality.[144] Later, Menninger reversed himself, concluding "severe reactive depression."[145]

Now considerations far beyond his recovery came into play. The White House wanted all the facts to influence how "the matter" would be presented publicly. Early spin control. The stakes were high. Allegations a "crazy" made national security decisions could seriously damage the administration domestically and might even affect questions of peace or war.

The Navy psychiatrist's concern for a man admired and regarded as one of their own framed information flow and tone, and choice of a hospital—Bethesda, a general Navy hospital, not the Menninger clinic. A high-stakes conundrum. Should the prime consideration be recovery, protecting Forrestal's reputation, or avoiding embarrassing the administration?

Aspects of Forrestal's return trip to D.C., his hospitalization on Bethesda's sixteenth floor, not in a building specifically organized and staffed to handle mentally disturbed patients (probably on

White House orders) and stonewalling the press only fueled the rumor mill. They also goaded Drew Pearson to further attacks.

If ever an unethical journalist was able to inflict great pain, some even say death on his opponent, it was columnist Pearson. Early on, he and Walter Winchell began an "ugly, unrelenting attack" on the Secretary as a "sinister agent of Wall Street and major oil companies." "The heated emotional debate" over the partition of Palestine and the creation of a Jewish state"[146] inflamed the attack.

Leaks of damaging information have driven Washington leaders of sounder mind and body to great anger and revenge. It became clear, according to Hoopes and Brinkley, that Forrestal's enemies within the government, who either disagreed with his policies or stood to lose power from their implementation, were leaking information to Pearson. Great grist for his malicious mill.[147] In Pearson's eyes, Forrestal was a primary cause of the Cold War, the Cabinet member most responsible for pushing Truman into a tough anti-Russian stance. Pearson was not scrupulous about facts. He turned and twisted them to reinforce his attacks. He would personalize abstract symbols and identify a particular person with particular iniquities defined by himself. Pearson then pounded these themes relentlessly until the "great rancid mass of the American people" could think of the person only as the symbol of the iniquities. One senator commented: "he gathers slime, mud, and slander from all parts of the earth and lets them ooze out through his radio broadcasts." Driven by his self-righteousness, Pearson had an almost inexhaustible zest for the ugly, protracted vendetta.[148]

Dubbing Forrestal "Trojan Horse of the Right," Pearson used bitter interservice competition to gather "slanted disclosures of antagonisms and administrative fiascoes inside the Pentagon." With doubly cruel timing, Pearson dug up an old story of jewel thieves in New York to impugn Forrestal's personal courage. "Always emotionally affected by attacks on his personal integrity, Forrestal was now profoundly vulnerable."[149]

In the absence of information about Forrestal, rumors filtering through official and social circles eventually drove even mainstream, responsible journalists to write stories. Absent any official announcement, they had not published what they knew. To avoid giving Russians any embarrassing propaganda opportunity? To protect the reputation of a man they generally admired? Their reasons are still not clear. Would this restraint be possible today? Doubtful.

Just as supermarket tabloids inject maliciousness into the mainstream today, Pearson did then. Pearson conceived it his "moral duty" to expose the former Secretary as a "madman" who had access to atomic bombs. How long had he been impaired? How gravely had this jeopardized the U.S. national security? Fueled the cold war? Forrestal's "sudden" incapacity was catnip to questioning policies and decisions.[150] A more adroit spin master might have diffused Pearson or used the mainline press as an antidote. But, as in most health crises, the handlers were causing their own media troubles. Despite urging from friends, even Dr. Menninger, the White House stonewalled. Not until April 11 did it announce the Secretary was suffering from "occupational fatigue" but was "progressing satisfactorily" and expected to leave the hospital shortly. Behind the scenes, media, psychiatric and procedural risks were being taken that endangered Forrestal himself as well as accurate public presentation of his case.[151]

To counter Pearson, both before and after the suicide, some journalists attempted to mitigate and explain Forrestal. Syndicated columnist Marquis Childs commented critically on "sensational deceptions" of Forrestal's illness, particularly the charge that he was "out of his mind" and had walked onto the street screaming "The Russians are attacking." Childs wrote: "The charge that Forrestal had been mentally unbalanced before he resigned . . . became the basis of a wide-spread Communist propaganda campaign . . . "Millions are being led to believe that Forrestal's insanity is the explanation for the Marshall Plan and the Atlantic Pact."[152] Childs noted that withholding news "the public should legitimately have opens the way for sensationalism and exaggeration." Despite appeals such as Childs's, the facts of Forrestal's illness were not disclosed until after his death.

Walter Lippman, one of the most respected journalists then, attempted both to position the man's accomplishments and the "public factor in this tragedy." Had Forrestal known he was wanted elsewhere, would be valued elsewhere when he left the Pentagon, the "fatigue would not have overcome his will to live."[153]

The communications post-mortem scored Pearson's sensationalism, which few others believed or would publish. They accepted the official line that Forrestal was suffering from no more than fatigue. Even government officials and newspapermen familiar with the details were unable or unwilling to make an accurate public report. Throughout Forrestal's seven weeks in Bethesda, unauthorized gossip and speculation swirled about his condition. Despite his severe psychosis, the public was repeatedly assured by government spokesmen and the news media that Forrestal was not seriously ill. That his complete recovery was probable, even certain.[154]

And then a troubled life ended on May 22. Forrestal had been copying two lines from "the Chorus from Ajax" by Sophocles. "Worn by the waste of time / Comfortless, nameless, hopeless." Now the kind words and explanations poured out among the many mistakes analyzed. Hoopes and Brinkley list three:

- the political decision to hospitalize Forrestal at Bethesda rather than the Menninger Clinic
- an equally political decision to put him on the sixteenth floor of the general quarters rather than in the one-story psychiatric building
- the culminating error—to relax restrictions, stemming, perhaps, from the penchant to see more rapid recovery than was real.

POST-MORTEM STONEWALLING BY FRIENDS AND FOES

Newspapers, predictably, criticized the stonewalling. A *Washington Post* editor wrote: "There was something wicked about the disingenuous way in which the illness was handled. The medical men certainly owe an explanation for their false reporting or for their carelessness in looking after their distinguished patient."

The American Psychiatric Association weighed in against the Navy: "The Brass Hats not only told the public that Forrestal had no psychosis, but they really believed what they said. It is no secret that Navy medicine is hostile to psychiatry, believes mental illness is a disgrace," that it is unpatriotic to admit the possibility, especially in any case involving a Very Important Person. The Navy's frequent references to battle fatigue and nervous exhaustion and its placing of the patient in the VIP suite underline the Navy's adherence to these pernicious myths.[155]

But even death and the release of information did not stay questions of murder, not suicide. Nor did it stay Pearson's attacks, now augmented by attempts to ooze away from the blame. Once he grew frustrated to the point of explosion by reticence of leaders to expose what Pearson called the "Forrestal Cabal." He tried to shift the blame to friends and newspapermen who had urged Forrestal to say in office long after he was "not a well man." Pearson later attributed the death to "no spiritual reserves and no calluses. . . . He had traveled not on the hard political path of the politician, but on the protected, cloistered avenue of the Wall Street bankers. . . . He did not know what the lash of criticism meant." Such demagoguery proved an unconvincing defense. Several years later, Pearson's right-hand man, Jack Anderson, indicted Pearson's behavior as "deliberate, carefully calibrated character assassination." Anderson acknowledged, "our hand was surely in this tragedy." Pearson's methods flagrantly exceeded the norms of legitimate reporting, even the further limits of advocacy.[156]

While not letting Pearson off the hook, it must be noted that continued White House silence and Navy mythology prevented even Forrestal's well placed friends and responsible media from making a counter attack of truth. The "cur-pack yelped at Forrestal's heels." Hyped by personal innuendo and vilification, it created a sea of calumny.

How can handling of his death be assayed? Hoopes and Brinkley think only a novel "could encompass the subtle shadings and contradiction, the central characteristic of elusiveness". It's "the stuff of ancient legend."[157]

FICTION MORE TELLING THAN FACT

To Vietnam War writer Robert Stone, "fiction refines reality, refracts it into something like a dream." It is a deliberate effort to render more truly events that did happen to people who really exist. Fiction performs for history or for life what dreaming does for the mind.[158] One novel illustrates this. *The Caine Mutiny* by Herman Wouk[159] is one of the best studies of flawed command, of reality *vs.* expectations, of judgments made in the maw of crisis later analyzed by those who know all, risk nothing, and have never shared the dangers of command. Lt. Commander Philip F. Queeg appears crazy to his psychologically untutored junior officers, most of whom left prestigious colleges for combat. Wouk's book cautions whistle-blowers that there are penalties ahead for saying the boss is paranoid.

The author's analysis of a flawed, threatened command viewed from the hothouse of a wardroom by civilian sailors functions as a more compelling, complete study than a factual account of an individual superior. The wardroom was a "tangle of subtle complex evaluations of officers, knitting centrally on the captain's person and attitudes. It forced and magnified personality quirks."

As the school boy officers assay their regular Navy commander, they grapple with the regular Navy and its structure. They see and later record Queeg's "irrational discipline and priorities." Exhaust your time and power of command on trivialities not the vital—shirt tails hanging out, cigarette butts and a search for who ate the gift of strawberries ranks above severing a tow rope, typhoons, and commands from headquarters. Alternate between rashness and exaggerated caution. Be absent at key moments and too present to rail against trivial breaches of orders. Prop up your weak and needy personality, demanding loyalty up but giving little or none down. Inflict martial austerity. Dismiss mistakes as "unfortunate incidents." Build a pattern of perfection after the fact. In all moments of stress, publicly palm and roll steel balls.

Queeg's officers, innocent of command or combat, but, unfortunately, not pop psychology, start watching closely and documenting flaws. The officers fall into three traps of dealing with executive illness: true psychological difficulties may seem benign, almost normal, to the untrained—as they all were. A psychiatrist at the hearing warned, "the distinguishing mark of this neurosis is extreme plausibility." Second, judgments made by those never stressed by command magnified flaws into symptoms. And, finally whistle-blowers anytime, but never more than in the murky area of psychological illness and the military, are setting themselves up for real trouble. The *Caine* officers kept their logs, watched, then mutinied during a typhoon.

Crisis managers counsel: look for signals of trouble and act on them. Making judgments on the captain's mental health, however, was telegraphing trouble.

LOOKS DIFFERENT ASHORE

A board of investigation is convened. The "mutineers" expected absolute justification of their takeover, imagined themselves as stars in a grand drama. Instead, hearings are bureaucratic and legalistic. Everything looks very different when the crisis is past and the captain is in control of himself—at least temporarily. Had there been distortion in scale? Had irrefutable facts softened, been objectified into anecdotes that discredited the crew, not Queeg? The meticulously kept log was dismissed as whining, used only to document disloyalty. The defense lawyer, a pilot recovering from severe combat burns, appears in contrast to psychological experts and some officers on the panel who lacked combat experience. Shore-based *vs.* combat reservists; college boys *vs.* academy veterans; commanders *vs.* whistle-blowers. Queeg is found disturbed, but not disabled.[160] When not under pressure, Queeg became a poster picture of a Navy commander.

The mutineers get off the hook, but their lawyer gives them a lesson in leadership essential for corporate executives also. You can't understand command 'til you've had it, the lawyer says. It's the loneliest, most oppressive job in the whole world. It's a nightmare, unless you're an ox. You're forever teetering along a tiny path of correct decisions and good luck that meanders through an infinite gloom of possible mistakes. Queeg had no brains, but he had nerves and ambition. It's no wonder he went ga-ga. "Exec is nothing. It's command, command."[161]

As the mutineers start their *mea culpas*, they see a newspaper announcement of a new command. "Battle-Scarred Pacific Veteran, New Exec of Local Navy Depot." Accompanying a picture of Queeg is copy touting his exploits on the *Caine*, but omitting the mutiny or court-martial. The mutineers scattered, black marks on their records, dreams of a Navy career dashed. One is now stressed by command himself. As Wouk writes:

> He experienced the strange sensations of the first days of a new captain: a shrinking of his personal identity, and a stretching out of his nerve ends to all the spaces and machinery of his ship. He was less free than before. He developed the apprehensive listening; he never quite slept. He had the sense of having been reduced from an individual to a sort of brain of a composite animal, the crew and ship combined. Power seemed to flow out of the plates into his body. It was a loneliness such as he had never known, but it wasn't a "frigid loneliness." The men seemed to like and believe in him.[162]

Just you wait, new captain.

The corporate executive health lessons are readily evident, but three deserve comment. Don't see too little or too much in eccentric behavior. Don't play psychiatrist. Realize events look very different when all risks are past, all answers known; experience and objectivity rule over fear and proselytizing.

IMAGING: SEEING ISN'T BELIEVING ANYMORE

Media relations are used, more often abused, in creating images of companies, countries, and their leaders. Personas created for Presidents and other political leaders, highly visible and much better documented than the quiet work of corporate communicators, illustrate principles, techniques and lessons.

One President, Grover Cleveland, was secreted aboard a yacht for delicate oral cancer surgery rather than upset conflicting Democratic factions during the 1893 economic crisis. The cases of Woodrow Wilson, paralyzed by a stroke but still functioning of sorts as President, or the vigorous, youthful President John F. Kennedy, his pain and Addison's disease screened from the press by adroit public relations, are too well-known to be intriguing.

Imaging was seriously more involved in presidencies of Dwight Eisenhower, Ronald Reagan, and Franklin D. Roosevelt, which Robert Gilbert analyzes, among others, in *The Mortal Presidency*. In *The Splendid Deception*, Hugh Gregory Gallagher explains how the press, secret service, staff, and family all cooperated in presenting Roosevelt as vigorous and physically fit—a carefully constructed and artfully maintained image. Throughout his presidency, photographs of FDR being carried, crawling, or fallen were banned. Someone, usually a family member, always bore his weight or helped him rise, then locked his heavy leg braces, which were blackened so they would not be obvious.

Just before his death, the President's few public appearances were carefully orchestrated, widely publicized, and heavily photographed. His skillful press secretary, Steven Early, made full use of releases, statements, short press conferences, and radio talks. Roosevelt continued to dominate the war news, but far from the public eye and the press, who saw only what he wished them to.

Decades after his death, FDR's image is still disputed. To Garry

Wills, FDR "perfected a deceptive case, a casual aplomb, in the midst of acute distress. He became a consummate actor." Wills describes the technique of "walking on your tongue"—telling jokes, teasing others, locking their eyes on his, making them think of their own vulnerability, not his. Everything was stage-managed to seem informal, even intimate. He sat at his desk and let the world come to him. "The man who seemed so immobilized had ghosted himself into their front rooms."[163]

Imaging is not all things for all times. The jaunty cigarette in its holder, so effective a symbol of the President's confidence and insouciance, attacked now by anti-smoking zeal, may be banished on signs at his home in Hyde Park. Should his wheelchair, so absent during his lifetime, be prominent at the planned Washington D.C. memorial? "He lived his life [some of his adulthood] in a wheelchair; history should record it," proposed the National Organization on Disability. Others, including a grandson, argued that "any portrayal of his disability would be historically inaccurate, . . . an affront to his memory."[164] Oh what tangled webs imagers weave when first they decide to deceive.

SECRETS HURT POLITICALLY, MEDICALLY, AND PERSONALLY

President Grover Cleveland's risky surgery, kept secret to maintain his political leverage, as well as his careless physical habits, seem old-fashioned. Yet the Shah of Iran concealing his cancer in hopes of returning to the Peacock Throne is little different. Cleveland's cat-and-mouse game with the press, leaks, rumors, and eventual political pitfalls are instructive still.

Edward B. MacMahan, M.D., and Leonard Curry, authors of *Medical Cover-Ups in the White House*,[165] describe President Cleveland as an overweight cigar-smoker who savored beer and heavy foods. When he awoke one May morning in 1893, he felt a swelling on the roof of his mouth. Fears of cancer had haunted Cleveland ever since Ulysses S. Grant, also a heavy drinker and cigar smoker, suffered a painful death from oral cancer. Despite these fears, Cleveland did not summon the White House doctor until June 18. The dangerous ineptitude began. Though he was hampered by poor light, the doctor's superficial examination concerned him sufficiently to ask a dentist to examine the President. He determined not teeth, but "an ulcerative surface nearly as large as a quarter with cauliflower granulations and crater edges" was creating the irritation. The painless but frightening ulcer suggested either syphilis or cancer.

Now secrecy began escalating the risks. Even without a definite diagnosis, doctors had good reason, based on Cleveland's previous lifestyle, to suspect syphilis. Imagine the political damage. Without knowing the patient's identity, pathologists initially found no positive proof of malignancy, but when pressed, conceded neighboring areas could be cancerous. Some of Cleveland's doctors were convinced, even before this report, that the ulcer was malignant.

The timing could not have been worse for Cleveland. Convinced public disclosure would irreparably damage his ability to force his tough, conservative economic policies[166] on a recalcitrant Congress, Cleveland conspired with his doctors to deceive the public, Congress, even the vice president. Like many executives since, he deemed his illness—even though life-threatening—a private matter. Cleveland succeeded long enough to prevail politically, but at a very heavy price.

Despite the "ambiguous," "insufficient" pathology report, it was decided that "treatment must be quick and secret." The President's friend and prestigious surgeon, Joseph Decatur Bryant, would remove the growth, an epithelioma (today, a carcinoma). To ensure secrecy, surgery and treatment were planned aboard a yacht, with recovery at the President's summer home on Cape Cod, rather than in Washington.

Dr. Bryant recommended major surgery to remove the upper jaw on one side.[167] President Cleveland was adamant the surgery be performed in secret. One non-medical person shared the secret—Cleveland's trusted friend, Secretary of War Daniel S. Lamont, who arranged for use of his yacht, *Oneida*. Under sail, it would provide security and anonymity. Cleveland was a frequent guest aboard the vessel. The cover story? The President's infected teeth had to be extracted in the fresh sea air. Details and incidental players often leak secrets. The yacht's crew, although accustomed to having the President aboard, wondered at such extra precautions such as completely disinfecting the yacht.

Escalating Risks

Rush escalated risks. The lesions appeared to be responding well to treatment; if cancerous, they would not. Still no questions were raised. The early, secret diagnosis not only was severely limited, but precluded consideration of contradictory symptoms. The panicky Cleveland, not content with a simple complicity, devised a more elaborate deception. He would divert press attention long enough to undergo surgery and recover—easier then than now, when the presidency is constant cynosure of press attention. Next, Cleveland decided to push his economic program through Congress before any disability would be visible. Under cover of a dramatic reconvening of Congress in August, very rare before air-conditioning, he would slip away for surgery.

The President was already en route to New Jersey by train before reporters were told. They could only wait and speculate about the abruptness. In a chance encounter with a *New York Times* reporter Cleveland commented only that he was going to Buzzard's Bay to rest. Behind the carefree façade, five doctors and a dentist with no idea of their patient's identity boarded the *Oneida*. This escalated the risk. So did Dr. Bryant himself, who had published a history of 250 cases of excision of the upper jaw, but had performed only two such operations. One of every seven patients died from this procedure, usually from a hemorrhage or subsequent infection. The plan was for the dentist, a specialist in the use of nitrous oxide, or laughing gas, to remove two healthy teeth to aid surgeons during the extensive surgery. Ether would be administered. The doctors, strangers to each other, had to operate as a team. A nationally renowned neurosurgeon lent only his prestige and a guarantee that the surgical "team" could perform the most modern techniques under very adverse conditions.

The President's generally poor physical condition presaged additional risks. "Just the build and age for a stroke." Although his pulse was good for a 56-year-old, grossly overweight, 250-pound man, doctors found early signs of chronic kidney disease. Despite being worn out mentally and physically by four months of political exertion, the President was, the doctors declared, fit for surgery. The diagnosis of a rapidly growing malignancy was accepted without question, even though he had reported no oral roughness four months earlier and the doctors found no enlarged lymph nodes in his neck.

As the yacht steamed at half-speed, doctors converted its salon into a crude operating room. About midday, they washed Cleveland's mouth with disinfectants as he sat in a chair lashed to the interior mast. With the ship's steward serving as the surgical nurse, the dentist easily extracted two healthy teeth. As surgeons began their procedure, Cleveland's restless movements indicated that more than nitrous oxide was needed. They injected cocaine into his mouth. As surgeons made their incisions, the President began to bleed profusely and struggle in a half-alert state. Surgery could continue only by administering ether, a risk given Cleveland's age and physical condition. The primitive electrical equipment created the danger of explosion.

Nor was the surgery going easily. After 45 minutes, a significant amount of the larger-than-expected lesion remained. Doctors discussed more radical surgery—removing the entire left upper jaw, sinus and floor of the bony eye socket, resulting in a sagging eye and possible double vision. Incomplete removal of the tumor might threaten Cleveland's life, but a less drastic procedure with fewer visible problems was followed. The recuperation seemed encouraging. By Sunday evening Cleveland was out of bed. On Monday he walked about the yacht.

Secrecy and surgery seemed successful, but not for long. To escape press attention, the medical team left the yacht separately. The patient, believing himself cured, greeted a small crowd gathered at his summer home. No external wound or dressing was visible. Speaking or normal activity, however, would have given away the secret, so the presidential party stayed secluded.

Soon a thoroughly modern media saga began to unfold. On July 5, United Press reported surgery of a "malignant growth." Briefing White House reporters, two doctors resorted to a medical disinformation ploy: they deflected inquiries by supplying irrelevant, unimportant health details on rheumatism and teeth, while denying any existence of major illness. They stonewalled any questions about the surgery and a malignant growth. The spin control seemed to be working. Dispatches from Buzzard's Bay began to dispel the UP report of a malignancy. *The New York Times* swallowed the White House line, reporting checker games and the beautiful weather. But Dr. Bryant took the hype too far saying, "the President is absolutely free from any cancer or malignant growths." The only operation was extraction of a bad tooth. Meanwhile, medical sloppiness was breeding other problems. Normally, pathologists examined specimens taken during surgery, but standard record-keeping procedures were not followed. Were records destroyed? That's uncertain, but none have ever been found.

Suspicious reporters began probing. Why was Cleveland kept from public view or at a considerable distance? To squash such speculation, Cleveland went fishing. As if tempting the fates, by mid-July Bryant decided that a second operation was necessary. "He reassembled his team aboard the *Oneida*, as secretly as before. On July 17, the President came aboard, ostensibly for a pleasure cruise. What was done? Participants later wrote that "all the suspicious tissue was removed." Once again, the President appeared to suffer no complications.

Secrets Broke the Secrecy

The dentist had planned to return immediately to New York, but surgeons, fearing post-operative complications, refused to let him leave the yacht or communicate with land. When the dentist finally returned to New York, several irate colleagues demanded an explanation. He told them the truth. They spread the tale. In contrast, the surgeons kept silent even when the President's inability to talk—officially attributed to dental work—aroused new press suspicion. Speculation ran rampant in Washington. Even cabinet members were rebuffed. Finally, Attorney General Richard Olney visited the President. He came away gravely and rightly concerned about a President pale and haggard from pain. His mouth was still packed with gauze, making eating difficult. He was beginning to lose weight. "My God, Olney," the President mumbled, "they nearly killed me."

The cosmetics continued. A dental specialist fashioned a rubber prosthesis to fill in the hole in Cleveland's mouth and improve his speech. Apparatus in place, he returned to Washington in early August, looking and sounding his usual self. He rounded up enough votes for the House to approve his economic reform legislation by a 2-to-1 vote.

But in Washington, then as now, perception counts far more than accomplishment. The dentist's unwitting 6-week-old leak to associates made the front page of *The Philadelphia Press*. The surgery, doctors' names, all details were unimpeachably accurate. The deception was compromised. Cleveland and his advisers turned on the media. He counted on a public willing to discount one negative story with all the obvious positives. No scar showed. Accustomed to the prosthesis, he was speaking normally and gaining weight. Gone was the haggard look of someone afflicted with cancer.

Sympathetic newspapers rallied to his side, attributing the President's problem to no more than a toothache. The outpouring of public support for the President and a round of appearances helped defuse the issue. Eventually the press stopped pursuing the story. Ironically, the President's first major appearance was at the Pan American Medical Conference in early September. Later, he delivered a commemorative address and mingled with the crowd. His speech, so unclear in July, was now strong and resonant.

But all his victories were pyrrhic. His hard-won economic program could not withstand falling prices and wages and the resulting labor unrest. An unpopular ex-President, he retired to Princeton, New Jersey, where he died at 70 in 1908, without any recurrence of the "cancerous tumor." Even death did not stop the speculation.

Dr. Bryant died in 1914, still silent regarding the surgery. Another participant published an account, not in a prestigious medical journal, but in the *Saturday Evening Post*. Understandably, doctors may have hesitated to publish during the nervous 1893 economic conditions or Cleveland's presidency. But they never shared with the medical community an apparently new technique and the virtual breakthrough in the "successful" removal of mouth cancer.

Did reluctance to take credit for medically historic surgery, performed on a U.S. President, suggest another secret? Were there second thoughts about the surgery? Medical opinion later deemed it highly unlikely that Cleveland suffered from a fast-growing malignant tumor. Even today, successful, total removal of such a large cancer is extremely rare. After 15 years, with their supposedly mortally threatened patient still alive, questions persisted. Had the doctors performed a brilliantly successful operation? Or was their diagnosis wrong, exposing Cleveland to extensive surgery unnecessarily?

At the Mutter Medical Museum in Philadelphia, a relatively neglected case holds the two healthy teeth and eight pieces of the upper jaw removed during the *Oneida* operation. No physician was allowed to examine the specimen or read the scrapbook until 1967. They disclosed that doctors and pathologists in 1893 actually held a wide range of opinions about the illness and the growth's malignancy. In 1975, a panel of experts, after examining tissue, found no evidence the lesion was carcinosarcoma, mixed tumor or cancer, or myxosarcoma. Rather, they were convinced the lesion was a "verrucous carcinoma, a low-grade tumor that looks like a cancer (carcinoma) but does not spread. It behaves like a wart. Common among tobacco chewers, it could be excised by simple removal of the lesion and surrounding tissue.

Had Cleveland's doctors' diagnosis been accurate, no radical surgery would have been needed. Given the technology and knowledge of the time, the doctors probably did as well as could be expected. But doubts were fueled by secrets atop secrets—the surgery, the media cover-up, the doctors' silence and the nonexistence of any pathology reports. In the absence of facts, rumor persisted in both medical and non-medical circles. They ranged from harmless inflammations to syphilis. Relatively good health for 15 years virtually disproved syphilis and "made it improbable" that the oral lesion was the source of his terminal gastrointestinal symptoms. Will we ever know? Probably not. No tissues obtained at Cleveland's autopsy or an autopsy report was found. Keeping a presidential illness secret entails great risk to health and image. Surgery, considering the patient's physical condition, in a makeshift, floating operating room, subordinated medical standards to political ends.

Today, a President's health arouses concern about its impact on leadership and foreign affairs. Yeltsin is but the most recent example. Less often is the risk to the individual considered. Cleveland ran grave risks when he conspired to cover-up a major illness. Was it all for naught? His economic reform passed, but accomplished little. Was the diagnosis made in secret so wrong he suffered unnecessarily? Did it make the press more questioning the next time? Obviously not, for the most massive cover-up of presidential disability, Woodrow Wilson's stroke in 1919, was mostly hidden until he left the White House. One must not be too sanguine as to assume it can't happen now.

IMAGE ALTERING, ILLNESS, AND PERIPATETIC BONES

Fatal illness in a powerful spouse can be hidden to sustain political position. Eva Perón's cancer, death, even her mummy were major factors in Argentine politics and Juan Perón's presidencies. Her physical health directly influenced her husband's political health.[168]

Despite staged appearances to display good health, everyone was lying and hiding the cancer. Autobiographer Alicia Dujovne Ortiz quotes Evita herself as saying: "I know the enemy with whom I must fight. The doctors are lying and I am lying back. We are all lying. But we all know the truth."[169] But the charade continued. Evita attempted to delude the doctors by eating before blood samples were drawn and taking her temperature by putting the thermometer in backwards. Scales were hidden so the weight loss was unknown, even to Evita. "Denial killed her body, but anything else would have killed her heart and soul."[170] When she was near death, newspaper and radio broadcasts reaching her were purged of news of her condition. Instead, associates encouraged her to plan new trips and wardrobes. It had the taste of a soap opera.[171]

By 1950 she wielded enormous, decisive political power, particularly among the poor, labor, and women. Words can be "grimly prophetic" if heeded. On June 14, 1950, she addressed a national conference of governors in Buenos Aires. To her usual expressions of fidelity she added a new note: "I think the best tribute I can give to General Perón is to burn my life on the altar of happiness for the lowly . . . until death if necessary." To audiences inured to her hyperbole, these morbid phrases meant nothing special. But they were grimly prophetic. Months earlier in the middle of a ceremony, a stabbing inguinal pain convulsed her. She masked her discomfort and weathered the ceremony. Others say she fainted. Like much about Evita, ambiguity rules. Her health, always delicate, make exact dating of the illness difficult, but January 9, 1950 is accepted by one biographer.[172] Several days later, when the pain worsened, her condition was diagnosed as acute appendicitis and surgery performed.

Official bulletins assured the operation had been successful. However, behind the scenes a stark drama was unfolding. Only many years later it was learned, tests revealed she was suffering from uterine cancer. She angrily refused a proposed hysterectomy, maintaining that there was nothing wrong, that the diagnosis was the work of her enemies, who sought to eliminate her from politics. Evita's mother had had similar cancer. After a hysterectomy she lived to 77. According to Juan Perón's biographer, Joseph Page, verifiable information about the deterioration of Evita's health does not exist. Peronist mythology holds that Eva-the-martyr's love for the poor caused her to sacrifice her energy, health, and eventually her life.

Health problems had haunted Eva Perón throughout her adult life. But that frailty "served only to inflame her determination to reach as quickly as possible the goals she had set for herself." Physical difficulties beset her seriously during the 1947 Rainbow Tour of Europe. An acute bronchitis made her cough often.

In August 1949 she admitted to shedding 22 pounds. Vanity or illness? She did not say. Had Evita known for some time she was suffering from a chronic ailment, but hidden it? Visiting dignitaries noted her skin color had become "suspicious"—amber, emitting an insalubrious though attractive glow. Was she anemic? Receiving blood transfusions? Suffering from leukemia? No one was talking. Even observant physicians were puzzled. One watched her carefully during a 30-minute speech in late 1948 for the signs of fatigue or the heavy breathing an anemic person would display under great emotional and physical stress. Eva displayed none. Was it "a case of inexplicable biological and physical resistance, or a colossal victory of willpower over bodily weakness"?

For Evita to escape the consequences of serious illness, her condition would have had to be diagnosed and treated in time. Was the malignancy found? Was she told? Perón? How did he react? Little is known even now. Possibly she could not bring herself to permit the removal of her womb for psychological and even cultural reasons. The "Spiritual Mother of All Argentine Children" perhaps could not cope with the symbolism inherent in a hysterectomy. Rather than reacting rationally, "she may have seized upon the paranoid suspicion that the diagnosis was somehow the work of enemies who wanted not merely to force her into a prolonged convalescence, but also to destroy her last link to motherhood. Did she not understand how sick she was? Did doctors inadequately explain to her? Was her uterine cancer not really diagnosed in January 1950?

Murkiness of health data may even have effected Eva's possible run as vice president with Perón. While historians find no evidence to suggest her nomination was withheld because of the cancer, they do question whether the gravity of her condition was understood. Joseph Page explains either Perón hadn't accepted that Eva was "beyond cure," or, not certain how much longer she had to live, had decided to avoid even the short-term political problems the nomination might cause.

But Peronistas, noting her absence at a large rally, said, "we can't go on without her." She came, but looked far different than the First Lady in 1946 or on the Rainbow Tour. The blond hair and gaudy attire had been replaced by a "streamlined, eternally classic style." Her hair was pulled back severely, accentuating the growing gauntness of her features, a shapeless robe hid both her thinness and burns from radiation treatments. Her speech was classic, also. "The ravages of illness may have taken their toll upon her body, but they also hoarsened her voice to a lower, more dramatic pitch." She said nothing new, but she never said it better.

Rumors began to plague Argentina like locusts. A coup attempt was kept from Evita, but simultaneously, for maximum political impact, the presidential press office released the first announcement of her serious illness. Her condition was "an anemia of regular intensity that is being treated with transfusions, absolute rest and general medication." To heighten the drama and impact, Evita spoke that evening on radio "in the name of the humble and the *descamisados*, for whom I have gladly left behind me the shreds of my health." The following day, an official medical bulletin announced her great weakness, intensified by "the profound emotions she had to endure" after another blood transfusion. A relatively prolonged period of treatment and total rest was required.

She continued to confer with union leaders and others from her bed, and be an icon of support for her husband. He decided to dedicate Loyalty Day, October 17, to "his stricken wife". Masses were offered for her speedy recovery. Pilgrims made the long trek on foot to ask the Mother of God to cure the "Mother of All Argentine Children."

An unusually large crowd gathered for what might be the first lady's last appearance. Evita, heavily medicated, on her feet for the first time since September, feebly acknowledged the cheers. "Pale, emaciated, a wisp of her former self, she needed physical support from Perón." The swiftness of her decline startled even those who had seen her the most recently.

"Perón placed the emerald-studded pendant around his wife's neck and embraced her"—"a moment frozen in eternity for those who witnessed it." Not to be completely cynical, but the staging was impeccable for political purposes. "When Evita took the microphone, she was speechless for the first time in her life."

In a barely audible voice she gave an unmistakable last will and testament, saying a vote other than for Perón would betray the fatherland. The faithful responded with ear-shattering zeal. Behind the façade of anti-Yankee rhetoric during the presidential campaign and Evita's well known animus, she was secretly examined in Buenos Aires by a New York specialist. He concurred with Argentine doctors that surgical intervention was necessary, and performed the surgery. "His involvement was not announced," even to the patient. Politics, image, privacy, or all three?

While Evita's physical image was being managed for political ends, a hagiography, "My Mission in Life," was hailed with great fanfare as a masterpiece. Perón's propaganda machine extolled its greatness, circulated it among the masses and made it required reading in the nation's schools. Actually, it trivialized its subject, downplayed the role of women in politics, and became a digression from the concerns of her health and its impact on possible coups. Public preoccupation diverted attention from a very dark economic picture. Her recuperation did not go well. Anemia was accompanied by a persistent low fever. Her weight had fallen from 128 pounds to 112 and she was experiencing kidney problems. Her constitution had little resistance to illness. One visitor described her as bone-thin and "as green as spinach."

May Day was her farewell performance, save one. She looked like a doll supported by Perón. Nonetheless, she made "a short speech laden with violent images" and aimed toward solidifying support behind the president.

She insisted on attending his inauguration on June 4, which necessitated pain killers and a brace under her long fur coat so she could stand. Ortiz notes she could "barely stand up straight," but for her finale did not want to be seen seated next to the standing Perón. Her pain killed with morphine, she was encased in plaster so she could stand; her large fur coat hid the belt that held her to a window behind the driver. Some speculated that even her right arm was encased in plaster. Despite her weakness, she waved to crowds, never resting her arm.[173] Whether she was encased in a brace or in plaster, it was truly an actress's Oscar winning performance. Was Perón "heartlessly exploiting her," trying to squeeze "the last gram of profit from her pathetic presence"? Page thinks this underestimates Evita. "Although a cancer was destroying her, . . . her willpower had not been broken. The fierce determination that had carried her to the summit would not permit her to die quietly and out of view."

"Tributes to her work and courage" dominated the proceedings. Propped up next to her uniformed husband in the Packard convertible . . . she endured the afternoon chill and saluted the crowd. Her skeletal frame seemed barely able to support the glistening emeralds of the Grand Peronist Medal that hung from her neck." Her "youth, glamour, adoration, agony and early death fed Argentina's lust for sentimentality. . . . As the end approached, a mass psychosis seemed to grip the country," and Evita participated. An original plan for a tomb of an unknown *descamisado* became an Argentine Taj Mahal for Evita, with her likeness dominating.

Even before her death, plans were made for elaborate embalming. Although use of Evita's body for political purposes—its international "travel," hiding, stealing and homecoming, became a politically potent "bacchanal of necrophilia"—is tangential to the beguiling conundrum of communications, it is truly a fascinating, intriguing tale in itself.

Her end imminent, a giant altar was set up and a Mass offered for the dying Evita and broadcast to the nation. Among the lower classes, followers of orthodox Catholicism, the death throws touched off an outpouring of gifts believed to have curative powers. "Charms, holy water, scared bones and objects of every description arrived daily at the residence and were carefully stored. . . . hundreds of people gathered in round-the-clock prayer vigils. On Saturday, July 26, Eva Perón lapsed into the final coma. Deception and disagreement plagued even the time of her death. The only certainty was it was not at 8:25 P.M., but that was the time she chose—the hour of her marriage to Perón.[174]

Immediately after her death, new imagineers—embalmers, doctors, hairdressers, and manicurists—went to work, "to give her a beauty that would last 100 years. An attendant following Evita's instructions replaced her natural color with a red fingernail polish. The "Bacchanal of Necrophilia" went into high gear. Genuine expressions of unrestrained grief, huge crowds, newspaper headlines such as "Even Heaven Weeps," closing down of all commercial activity for two days, were not just Perónista manipulation. Evita's death shook Perón personally and politically, created a power vacuum at the very top. Evita's importance, the imaging of her image, illness, and death, can best be demonstrated two ways. Perón never enjoyed again such power and popular support. But Evita's body was feared by subsequent Argentine governments and leaders.[175] She continued to annoy. She had been a living scandal; now she was a dead scandal—and power. Even her cadaver must be excluded from the political scene.[176]

"BOB ROBERTS" WASN'T FIRST

Attempting to hide or image illness for political gain is more common then using illness to gain power. One world leader ran his government-in-exile from a tuberculosis sanitorium, maintaining his clout although he never again set foot in his homeland.

Manuel Luis Quezon Antonia y Molina was voted Philippine president by a landslide in November 1935, then re-elected as interim leader until the islands achieved full independence from the U.S. in 1946. General Douglas MacArthur, fearing Quezon's capture by the Japanese, convinced President Franklin D. Roosevelt that it was in U.S. interests for Quezon to establish a government-in-exile. And so he was evacuated to Saranac Lake in New York State. Behind the obvious escape drama lay an even more intriguing one. The flights posed great physical and public relations risks to the then desperately ill Quezon, tubercular for 15 years. Despite a premium on space, the flight had to be equipped with oxygen and include a valet. An unwarranted luxury? No, the valet was as essential to Quezon's public image. In his vigorous youth, the President had been dapper and gregarious. Even in his mid-60s, ill and wan, he retained a peacock's strut of pride. His mien had its reasons—charming, cajoling, trading or bullying his way to victory. His charismatic personality combined Spanish courtesy and American dynamism. Trappings, considered empty pomp by Westerners, attested to and enhanced Quezon's authority in the Philippines. Behind such pomp and power, lay the family's secret history of tuberculosis.

During his rise to power, Quezon seemed free of the disease. But late in 1927, he was bothered by a wracking cough. New York specialists told him stresses of the past six years had undermined his constitution; both lungs were infected. He must rest for at least a year. If pulmonary tuberculosis put Quezon in a Monrovia, California, sanitarium, it also served his political ends. He stayed there rather than accompany an outspoken U.S. opponent of independence to Manila in 1931. When he did return home, Quezon submitted his resignation as Senate president, explaining that at such a decisive moment "a man of greater physical energies than I should direct it." Three doctors, including a tuberculosis specialist, affirmed Quezon's fragility. He was granted an eight-month leave of absence by the Senate; his maneuvering "was a resourceful effort to avoid losing ground." In 1943, with complete independence promised for 1946, not only was Quezon's leadership assured, but he defeated his old foe, Emilio Aguinaldo, leader of the Philippine insurrection.

Quezon's poor health helped him secure his position and deflect criticism of leaving his country. During the siege of Corregidor, Quezon lay helpless in a field hospital inside a damp tunnel, torn by spasmodic coughing. Efforts to relieve his condition proved futile. Amid smoke and confusion, he was transferred to a tent near MacArthur's quarters. After leaving the Philippines for Washington, Quezon quickly sought to stem criticism, explaining the trip "was not planned or contemplated by me."[177] Determined to return, Quezon could only bide his time and observe the phantom protocols of an exiled head of state, mostly at Saranac Lake in New York State. Quezon spent most of his time in bed, following the Pacific campaign. In November 1943, when it appeared he would lose the presidency, his ill health became useful. Wheezing, his face twisted in paroxysms of pain, Quezon thrashed about on his mattress alarmingly. "If you want the government you can have it!" he blurted out to Vice President Sergio Osmena. Osmena hesitated. What political baggage if the question were raised: "Did disappointment kill Quezon?" Quezon left the decision totally up to Osmena; of course, Quezon remained president. The next morning his physician was surprised to find Quezon looking hale and cheerful. Had yesterday been a *palabas*, a show? A decade later, the doctor mused, "What a great dramatic actor the Philippines lost when Quezon took up the law instead of the stage!"

Although his will was strengthened by war news, his husky voice forced Quezon to scribble responses. By June 1944, the president's condition deteriorated so rapidly that uniformed Filipino doctors alternated shifts at his bedside. "He wrote testy directives—illness had made him petulant—but for the most part he sat silent, occasionally mustering strength" to reminisce.

Quezon died in Saranac, making General MacArthur the "sole idol" for Filipinos, the sole representative of the United States.[178]

PRESCRIPTIONS FOR HEALTHY IMAGES

Communicators are world-class deplorers and Monday morning quarterbacks. Nothing they like more than a juicy museum of mistakes to analyze. To function more efficiently they must anticipate and honestly accent the positive.

First, a short, positive story of advertising executive John Zimmerman introduces prescriptions of how to handle executive health well. Zimmerman was thrust into the presidency of an advertising firm, Steiner/Bressler by an accidental death, then the suicide of his senior partner. Rather than let the Birmingham, Alabama, firm slide into financial ruin, he mobilized his colleagues to redefine the agency's culture. Methods were "unorthodox, even eccentric," in part tracking Zimmerman's own recovery from substance abuse. He engendered teamwork, mutual support, and common goals. "Even when bad things happen, I can see good in them." First, Zimmerman tackled the money mess. The metamorphosis was dramatized by a wake for the firm that was. Old stationery was symbolically (and literally) tossed into a fire. Employee teams were organized to devise the ideal agency and heighten participation. Zimmerman brought in motivational speakers to rally and encourage employees.

The result? Zimmerman became a hero. No client walked away. New business doubled. Seven employees added. Comments Zimmerman: "Change has become so natural to us that it isn't disruptive anymore. . . . Trauma can be productive."[179]

Here are some of the generic ways to handle executive illness successfully:

1. *No Template Exists* • Analyze how others have handled their boss's illness. Know the principles and pitfalls, but treat each illness

as a unique communications problem. Balance individual privacy *vs.* media and shareholder need to know, family wishes *vs.* corporate spacing responsibility. Decide the best way to tell or not to tell in sync with corporate and off-shore cultures. But, sorry, the wisdom of communicator and unique needs of the situation are the only real guides.

2. *Secrecy Magnifies* • Keeping illness secret is a double-edged sword. It grants great power, albeit usually short-term, to the ones who know. At Beatrice it was a cover to accomplish objectives. It may protect the emotions of the individuals involved. But secrecy also can precipitate problems, questions, and continuing distrust. Wall Street likes nothing less than surprises, nasty ones least of all. Keep one secret, and analysts are sure more and worst are to come. Absent candor and information, rumor fills the vacuum. And rumor is always grossly more extravagant than fact.

3. *Secrets Will Out Even if It Takes a Long Time* • Telling all immediately may be very painful, destructive to political power or corporate strategy. It may prematurely force the issue of denial, endemic to early stages of serious illness. But, eventually, someone talks, documents and body tissue are found and examined, or public images revealed. Russians tried, but Boris Yeltsin's health problems were too obvious to be hidden.

4. *Images Are Designed to Fool* • The old canard—seeing is believing—didn't anticipate sophisticated public imaging. Pictures are staged. Airbrushing, now computer morphing, move people, scars, surgical tubes in and out of photographs, radically change tone and shape. Disabilities are disguised à la FDR and created à la Bob Roberts for political gain. Famed photographer Walker Evans, when asked if the camera can lie, said: "Certainly. It almost always does."

5. *The Guy Wearing the T-Shirt Saying "It's Me, It's Me" Is the Guy*[180] • Corporate executives overlook the purloined letter of illness out of embarrassment, genuine concern for themselves and the corporation. Despite clues, despite obvious, inevitable signs they continue to conduct business as usual. Government addiction to such oversight magnified a "wretch like Aldrich Ames into a threat to the nation."

6. *You're Just Tired, Just Stressed Out, Jim* • When James Forrestal complained people were following him, rather than listen or, heaven forbid, investigate, associates attributed it facilely to overwork.

Armed people really were stalking him. Listen to the cries for help; heed the signals of impeding illness. Interception at their incipient stage will help the individual and surely stay major media and corporate damage.

7. *Accent the Positive* • Substance addiction and poor lifestyle habits attacked specially at the top can inspire others to do likewise. But two caveats: Preaching and look-how-I-converted stories only irritate; quietly demonstrating the changes and benefits inspire far more. Second, when a senior executive returns from rehabilitation, he may be very changed, make very different judgements and see more clearly organization strengths and weaknesses.

8. *Leaving the Seriously Ill in Charge—Don't* • Granted, a very sticky, delicate issue. Temporary transfer of power during surgery for a serious illness or during substance abuse treatment is usually manageable. But what happens when the brain tumor patient wants to keep running things? "Dangerous," said many consulted for this book. As harsh as it may seem for individual and organization, gently moving the ill executive aside to a ceremonial role is advisable. Soften the reality, perhaps, by announcing it as temporary, but keep him/her away from making vital decisions. When power is great, as with the U.S. presidency, the question becomes infinitely more acute. Even with the Twenty-Fifth Amendment and private agreements between President and Vice President, issues are murky and subject to possible power play abuse.

9. *What Should I Do?* • Admit the boss is ill? Yes, no, sometimes, maybe, not at all.

Truly a communicator's conundrum.

NOTES

1. Arnold A. Rogow, *James Forrestal: A Study of Personality, Politics, and Policy* (New York: Macmillian, 1963), p. 319.

2. Ibid.

3. Material has been drawn from Robert Seitz's "Corporate Conundrum: Disclosing Illness in the Corner Office," *The New York Times,* May 2, 1993, p. 9; and Blair Walker's "CEOs Who Fell To Illness," *USA TODAY,* January 25, 1993, p. 2B, among other sources. The author values greatly examples of executive illnesses suggested by public relations colleagues, friends, and MBA students at Fordham University's Graduate School of

Business. Specifically, she appreciates the generous, thoughtful conversation with Dr. Paul Bernstein, a neurosurgeon, on issues of impairment and patient privacy balanced against outsiders' need to know. Mr. Eamon Brennan, vice president for public information at New York Hospital during the hospitalization of the Shah of Iran there, taught me many non-medical considerations—not the least being privacy when the patient is a celebrity—elaborate security precautions, and remarkable measures to cloak cancer treatments. Professor Robert Gilbert, through his book *The Mortal Presidency* and frequent conversations, intrigued me with leaders' illnesses. William McNeill's *Plagues and People* surprised me with how often health is ignored in analyses of leadership, its successes or failures. Last, but surely not least, was my graduate assistant, Mr. Scott Morcaldi, who stayed with an ever expanding tome through a long hot summer of research.

4. Lawrence K. Altman, "Reagan and Alzheimer's: Following Path His Mother Traveled," *The New York Times*, November 4, 1994, p. C3. For an analysis of how Reagan's health image was managed, see Robert E. Gilbert's *The Mortal Presidency, Illness, and Anguish in the White House*, 2nd ed. (New York: Fordham University Press, 1998), pp. 221–265.

5. William H. McNeil, *Plagues and People* (Garden City, N.Y.: Anchor Books/Doubleday, 1976), p. 13.

6. Arno Karlen, *Napoleon's Glands and Other Ventures in Biohistory* (New York: Warner Books, 1984), p. 4.

7. Ibid., p. 22.

8. Ibid., p. 5.

9. Karlen is quoting Hans Zinsser, ibid., p. 151.

10. John W. Huey, Jr., "Our Reluctant Author Comes Forward," *Fortune*, May 13, 1996, p. 8.

11. Seitz, "Corporate Conundrum," p. 9; Amanda Bennett, "CEO's Illness May Endanger Company's Health as Well," *The Wall Street Journal*, January 21, 1993, p. B1; Blair Walker, "How Healthy Are CEOs? Illness Often Treated as Private Issue," *USA TODAY*, January 25, 1993, p. 1B; Walker, "CEOs Who Fell to Illness," p. 2B; Martin Dickson,"When a Fatal Illness Is a Public Affair—The Executive's Duty When Serious Illness Strikes," *Financial Times*, January 25, 1995, p. 8.

12. Seitz, "Corporate Conundrum," p. 9.

13. Bennett, "CEO's Illness May Endanger Company's Health as Well," p. B1.

14. Ibid., p. B2.

15. Private correspondence with Professor Katherine Gambellick following her reading of the manuscript.

16. Cal Mankowski,"US Rules on Reporting Executive Illness," *Reuters*, April 26, 1988.

17. Walker, "CEOs Who Fell to Illness," p. 2B.

18. Walker, "How Healthy Are CEOs?" p. 1B.

19. Ibid.

20. Chris Milhill, "Low-Paid Most at Risk from Heart Attacks," *Manchester Guardian Weekly*, September 3, 1995, p. 1.

21. Ibid.

22. Personal conversation with author in Georgetown, Washington, D.C., May 1994.

23. This 1987 figure is from *Forbes*, October 26, 1987, p. 70. UPI estimated Borg's 1988 wealth at $400 million or fourth in New Jersey. "Borg Family Member Is Richest New Jerseyan," UPI, December 11, 1988.

24. The Borg section reflects a lengthy telephone interview with Malcolm Borg on March 25, 1994, and discussions with long-time *Record* executives such as Peter Hearne, formerly night city editor and vice president of marketing, augmented by the author's own 10 years at *The Record*, as a political reporter and department editor.

25. Bennett, "CEO's Illness May Endanger Company's as Well," p. B1.

26. Holman W. Jenkins, Jr., "Hope vs. Experience: The Rematch," *The Wall Street Journal*, January 14, 1997, p. A23.

27. Tony Monroe, "Union Pacific's Lewis at Alcohol Abuse Unit," *The Washington Times*, January 24, 1994, p. A19.

28. *The New York Times*, January 24, 1993, p. B2.

29. Material information means any news about a company's highest officers that materially affects the stock price. Obviously, the turnaround CEO's health meets these requirements.

30. Bennett, "CEO's Illness May Endanger Company's Health as Well," p. B1.

31. Ibid.

32. Telephone discussion with Arthur House, vice president, corporate communications, Tenneco.

33. Dickson, "When a Fatal Illness Is a Public Affair," p. 9.

34. Lou Dobbs, *Moneyline*, CNN, 26 April 1994.

35. Bennett, "CEO's Illness May Endanger Company's Health as Well," p. B6.

36. Wendy Zellner, "The Fight of His Life: Michael Walsh's Battle Against Cancer," *Business Week*, September 20, 1993, pp. 55–57.

37. Ibid., p. 62.

38. John W. Huey, Jr., "Mike Walsh Takes on Brain Cancer," *Fortune*, February 1993, pp. 76–77.

39. Ibid.

40. Caleb Solomon and Robert Johnson, "Tenneco's Walsh Gives Up CEO's Post, Remains Chairman; Mead Is Successor," *The Wall Street Jour-*

nal, February 25, 1994, p. A3; and Allen R. Myerson, "Top Tenneco Official Quits to Fight Effects of Illness," *The New York Times*, September 25, 1994, p. D1.

41. Solomon and Johnson, "Tenneco's Walsh Gives Up CEO's Post," p. A3.

42. Ibid.

43. Allen R. Myerson, "Michael Walsh, Executive, Dead at 51," *The New York Times*, May 7, 1994, p. 30.

44. Dobbs, *Moneyline*, April 26, 1994.

45. William A. Sheeline, "The Quiet Passing of a Star," *Fortune*, February 8, 1993, p. 32.

46. Michael De Courcy Hinds, "Pennsylvania Governor Faces Health Questions," *The New York Times*, July 18, 1993, p. 24.

47. Ibid.

48. Ibid.

49. Jennifer Coleman and Merrie Spaeth, "Transplanting the Mick's Liver," *The Public Relations Strategist*, September 1996, pp. 51–55.

50. Adam Gopnik, "Elvis of the Elysée: How François Mitterand Orchestrated His Own Afterlife," *The New Yorker*, November 7, 1996, pp. 40–45.

51. Ibid., p. 45.

52. Michael Specter, "Yeltsin Taken to Hospital Suffering Heart Pain," *The New York Times*, July 12, 1995, p. A3.

53. Claudia Rosett and Steve Liesman, "Yeltsin Takes Sick, But Russia Stays Calm; Constitutional Septem Appears to Have Taken Hold," *The Wall Street Journal*, July 12, 1995, p. A11.

54. Steven Erlanger, "Speculation Rises About the State of Yeltsin's Health," *The New York Times*, July 15, 1995, p. 3.

55. Alessandra Stanley, "Yeltsin Displays His Health on TV," ibid., July 19, 1995, pp. A1, 4.

56. Alessandra Stanley, "Issue of Yeltsin's Health Bungled, Kremlin Admits," ibid., September 5, 1996, p. A8.

57. Ibid.

58. Gopnik, "Elvis of the Elysée," p. 45

59. Week in Review, *The New York Times*, February 2, 1997, Section 4, p. 2.

60. Erlanger, "Speculation Rises About the State of Yeltsin's Health," p. A12.

61. Thomas Sancton, "A Lunch With France's James Bond," *Time*, April 4, 1994. p. 16.

62. Ron Suskind, "Deadly Silence: How the Inner Circles of Medicine and Sports Failed a Stricken Star," *The Wall Street Journal*, March 9, 1995, p. 1.

63. Mike Wise, "Celtics Deny Reports About Lewis," *The New York Times*, March 10, 1995, p. B12.

64. Suskind, "Deadly Silence," p. 1.

65. Ibid.

66. Ibid., p. A12.

67. Ibid.

68. Ibid.

69. Ibid., p. A13.

70. Ibid.

71. Wise, "Celtics Deny Reports About Lewis," p. B12.

72. Dan McGrath, "As Two Mikes Return, Recall How They Left," *Sacramento Bee*, March 26, 1995, p. A2.

73. Jonathan P. Hicks, "Reginald F. Lewis, 50 Is Dead: Financier Led Beatrice Takeover," *The New York Times*, January 23, 1993, p. 4.

74. Rhonda Richards, "TLC Beatrice's No-Nonsense Boss: Lewis Ends Mourning, Takes Helm," *Money*, January 11, 1994, p. 58.

75. Reginald F. Lewis and Blair S. Walker, *"Why Should White Guys Have All The Fun?" How Reginald Lewis Created a Billion-Dollar Business Empire* (New York: John Wiley, 1995) p. 295.

76. Ibid., p. 296.

77. Ibid.

78. Ibid., p. 297.

79. Ibid., p. 298.

80. Ibid., pp. 300–301.

81. Ibid., p. 302.

82. Ibid., p. 303.

83. Ibid., p. 306.

84. Ibid.

85. Ron Stodghill, "TLC Beatrice Could Use More Than TLC," *Business Week*, January 24, 1994, p. 35.

86. Tony Chapelle, "Time to Take the Spotlight at TLC," *The New York Times*, November 27, 1994, Business Section, pp. 1, 6.

87. For a full discussion of not only the medical but also the political ramifications of the Shah's cancer and treatment in the U.S. see list in Edward B. MacMahan and Leonard Curry, *Medical Cover-Ups in the White House* (Washington, D.C.: Farragut, 1987), pp. 138–153.

88. Eamon Brennan, vice president for public information at New York Hospital during the Shah's treatment, relates not only elaborate security precautions, but also the remarkable measures that were taken to cloak cancer treatments. Although registered at New York Hospital, the Shah was also treated for cancer at Sloan Kettering. At night, he would be wheeled through a tunnel connecting New York Hospital and Sloan Kettering. From private conversations between Brennan and the author.

89. *The Wall Street Journal*, August 10, 1995, p. B10.

90. William Glabuson, "At Knight-Ridder, a Struggle of Illness, Not Power . . . and a Protector of Profits Takes the Helm," *The New York Times*, April 3, 1995, p. D8.

91. Andrew Pollack, "Morita, Sony Founder, Hospitalized," ibid., December 3, 1993, p. D2.

92. Milt Freudenheim, "Upjohn's Chief Getting Treatments for Cancer," ibid., February 2, 1994, p. D2.

93. Stodghill, "TLC Beatrice Could Use More Than TLC," p. 36.

94. Andrew Kupfer and Kate Ballen, "Bob Allen Rattles the Cages at AT&T," *Time*, June 19, 1989, pp. 58–72.

95. Mankowski, "U.S. Rules on Reporting Executive Illness."

96. Roger Cohen, "A Divorce in the Executive Suite," *The New York Times*, February 24, 1992, p. D1.

97. Readers interested in Ross's career should read Connie Bruck, *Master of the Game: Steven Ross and the Creation of Time Warner* (New York: Simon & Schuster, 1994. For his last great deal—acquisition of Time Inc., Richard M. Clurman's *To the End of Time: The Seduction and Conquest of a Media Empire* (New York: Simon & Schuster, 1992) is recommended. Neither is hagiography.

98. Bruck, *Master of the Game*, p. 190.

99. Ibid., p. 317.

100. Roger Cohen, "Steven Ross Defends His Paycheck," *The New York Times*, March 27, 1992, p. 28.

101. Bruck, *Master of the Game*, p. 318.

102. Cohen, "Steven Ross Defends His Paycheck," p. 28.

103. Ibid., p. 30.

104. Ibid., p. 66.

105. Ibid.

106. Bruck, *Master of the Game*, p. 319.

107. Ibid., p. 334.

108. Ibid., p. 12.

109. Ibid., p. 10.

110. Paul Farhi, "Is Time Finally on Time-Warner's Side?" *The Washington Post National Weekly Edition*, July 3–9, 1995, p. 20.

111. Lewis and Walker, "*Why Should White Guys Have All the Fun?*" p. 14.

112. Ibid.

113. Ibid.

114. Discussion of Welch's health and GE's dilemma is taken from William M. Carey, "CEO's Heart Surgery Is Giving GE a Case of Succession Jitters," *The Wall Street Journal*, May 24, 1995, p. A5; and from Tim Smart,

"Who Could Replace Jack Welch?" *Business Week*, May 29, 1995, p. 32, and the unsigned "GE's Chief Undergoes Angioplasty," *USA Today*, May 4, 1995, p. 18.

115. Carey, "CEO's Heart Surgery Is Giving GE a Case of Succession Jitters," p. A5.

116. Ibid., p. A1.

117. Ibid.

118. Ibid., p. A5.

119. Lawrence K. Altman, M.D., "No More Could Be Done, Mrs. Onassis Was Told," *The New York Times*, March 28, 1995, p. B10.

120. Readers interested in the detail of the imaging of Reagan's presidency should consult Robert E. Gilbert's *The Mortal Presidency: Illness and Anguish in the White House*, 2nd ed. (New York: Fordham University Press, 1998), pp. 221–265.

121. "Reagan and Alzheimer's: Following Path His Mother Traveled." *The New York Times*, November 4, 1994, p. C3.

122. This author would disagree somewhat with Altman's uncritical comment on Reagan's candor of health. Yes, he openly discussed prostate enlargement and colon cancer, but allowed imaging to take over when the issue was his ability to perform as President after the assassination attempt. Candor must be analyzed about the issue and power.

123. Just how difficult and continuing Forrestal's task was is commented upon in a recent book on Desert Storm. The authors, a defense correspondent and a retired Marine general, state flatly that military reforms to encourage joint warfare service are still incomplete. "Jointness" became the military mantra, they write particularly following 1986 passage of the Goldwater-Michaels Act. Its aim was "not to erase the differences in service philosophies and culture." Rather each service's unique characteristics and strength" would be molded to complement the other—making the whole more than the sum of its parts. But that's not the way it worked in the Gulf. In his ground-strategy planning, General H. Norman Schwarzkopf violated the spirit of jointness by excluding the Marines—not as a deliberate slight but as "an unconscious reflection of service culture." The war was "riddled with interservice tensions"; at sea, Marines and Navy were at odds. Hence, the authors concluded doctrinal differences still exist, even though "frequently papered over." See Michael Gordon and General Bernard E. Trainor, *The Generals' War—The Inside Story of Conflict In the Gulf* (Boston: Little, Brown, 1995), pp. 471–472.

124. Space restrictions preclude a full discussion of Forrestal's image creation. Readers are directed to Townsend Hoopes and Douglas Brinkley's *Driven Patriot, The Life and Times of James Forrestal* (New York: Vintage/Random House, 1993), p. 589.

125. Rogow, *James Forrestal*, p. 319.
126. Sidney Blumenthal, "In Retrospect: The Tragedy and Lesson of Vietnam," *The New York Review of Books*, March 1995, p. 66.
127. Ibid.
128. Ibid., p. 69.
129. Rogow, *James Forrestal*, p. 11.
130. Ibid.
131. Hoopes and Brinkley, *Driven Patriot*, p. 426.
132. Ibid.
133. Ibid., p. 427.
134. Ibid., p. 432.
135. Ibid., p. 435.
136. Ibid., p. 439.
137. Ibid., p. 444.
138. Robert Timberg, *The Nightingale's Song* (New York: Simon & Schuster, 1995), pp. 425–426.
139. Ibid., pp. 426–429.
140. Ibid., p. 444.
141. Rogow, *James Forrestal*, p. 307.
142. Ibid., p. 352.
143. Hoopes and Brinkley, *Driven Patriot*, p. 461.
144. Ibid., pp. 449–450.
145. "Reactive depression"—essentially the condition of battle fatigue—results from an accumulation of intense external pressures that overwhelm the mind and nervous system. In Forrestal's case, according to Dr. Menninger, the principal symptoms were anxiety, paranoia, and a sense of total failure that produced impulses to suicide.
146. Hoopes and Brinkley, *Driven Patriot*, p. 452.
147. Ibid.
148. Ibid., p. 434.
149. Ibid., p. 439.
150. Ibid., p. 455.
151. The press relations, Navy judgements made about the location of Forrestal's room, privileges, medical progress, and surveillance feed this analysis but would lengthen it greatly. Interested readers are referred to the heavily psychological analysis of Rogow (*James Forrestal*), and the wider, later analysis by Hoopes and Brinkley (*Driven Patriot*).
152. Rogow, *James Forrestal*, p. 13.
153. Ibid., p. 39.
154. Ibid., p. 14.
155. Hoopes and Brinkley, *Driven Patriot*, pp. 467–468.
156. Ibid., p. 455, 471.

157. Ibid., p. 472.

158. Eric James Schroeder, ed., *Vietnam, We've All Been There: Interviews with American Writers*. (Westport, Conn: Praeger, 1992), pp. 111–112.

159. Herman Wouk, *The Caine Mutiny* (Garden City, N.Y.: Doubleday, 1951).

160. Ibid., p. 415.

161. Ibid., p. 463.

162. Ibid., pp. 475, 482.

163. Garry Wills, "What Makes A Good Leader," *The Atlantic Monthly*, April 1994, pp. 71–76.

164. Megan Mutchler, "Roosevelt's Disability at Issue at Memorial," *The New York Times*, April 10, 1995, p. A10.

165. Discussion of President Cleveland's oral cancer and secret surgery is distilled from MacMahan and Curry, *Medical Cover-ups in the White House*, pp 38–55. Readers interested in additional presidential coverage and mistreatment by White House and other physicians will find full discussions in their book of Presidents Garfield, Wilson, Harding, Eisenhower, and Kennedy, plus Carter's admittance of the Shah of Iran to the U.S. for medical treatment. A more recent study of deception is Gilbert's *Mortal Presidency*, which features six case studies—Presidents Coolidge, Roosevelt, Eisenhower, Kennedy, Johnson, and Reagan.

166. "The panic of 1893 began 10 days before Cleveland took office, when one of the nation's biggest railroads went bankrupt and the New York Stock Exchange was rocked by a record-breaking selling spree. Two months later, the market collapsed. Banks were failing daily. Prices and wages were dropping and mobs of unemployed people roamed the streets of the big cities. As the economy worsened, despair of a magnitude not seen again until the Great Depression of the 1930's spread across the country." MacMahan and Curry, *Medical Cover-Ups in the White House*, p. 504.

167. The elaborate detailed report, received two days before the surgery, has disappeared, hence it is unknown whether the diagnosis confirmed or repudiated Bryant's "presumptive diagnosis." Ibid., p. 42.

168. The author is indebted to MBA student Jacqueline Molin for first seeing the Evita links.

169. Alicia Dujovne Ortiz, *Eva Perón*, trans. Sharon Fields (New York: St. Martin's, 1996), p. 323.

170. Ibid., p. 260.

171. Ibid., p. 275.

172. Ibid., p. 260.

173. Ibid., p. 272.

174. Ibid., p. 277.

175. Joseph Page, *Perón* (New York: Random House, 1983), particularly

pp. 235–236, 243–244, 249–254, 257–259, 261; and Thomas Eloy Martinez, *Santa Evita*, trans. Helen Lane (New York: Alfred A. Knopf, 1996).

176. Ortiz, *Eva Perón*, p. 282.

177. This comment reflects the criticism when General Douglas MacArthur was ordered by Franklin Roosevelt to leave Corregidor for Darwin. Although from the point of view of military leadership and strategy, the decision withstands criticism, many charge elitism, venerating General Johnson Wainwright, second in command, who stayed.

178. William Manchester, *American Caesar: Douglas MacArthur, 1880–1964* (Boston: Little, Brown, 1978), p. 376.

179. Patricia Sellers, "When Tragedy Faces Change," *Fortune*, January 10, 1994, p. 114.

180. Thomas Power, "No Laughing Matter," *The New York Review of Books*, August 10, 1995, pp. 4–6. In this review of recent books on Aldrich Ames, Powers gives many insights, particularly about detection and secrecy useful to the question of executive health. Secrets act the same in any bureaucracy—just are more dramatic and more costly in the CIA.

6

Assets Don't Talk to Assets
Merging People and Cultures

The optimist brings his lunch on Friday.
—Corporate folk wisdom

Mergers are the corporate equivalent of war. The jargon and zeal are martial: raiders and white knights, poison pills and war rooms. Greenmailers and buccaneers strap on their six-shooters to prey on flabby, unsuspecting managements.

Joseph A. Schumpeter, an Austrian economist best known for his studies of business cycles, views such creative destruction as natural, even essential. Capitalism can never be stationary. In Schumpeter's terms, the realistic capitalist, rather than seeking to administer existing structures, studies how to create and destroy them. Others see tender-merger spurts as part of a business cycle—from entrepreneurs and founders to professional managers to institutional investors and savers. T. Boone Pickens notes that by the early 1980s American industry was no longer a money-making machine. Many companies were too large and too inefficient. Managements had lost their edge or were doing too little work. Turbulence and globalization have unseated many a manager who once thought he was entrenched for life. Younger executives expect to have four or five employers, even several distinct careers.

Business unrest has also expunged many once-venerated corporate names: Conoco, Kennecott, CIT Financial, Standard Brands, Seven-Up, INA, Connecticut General, Salomon Brothers, and Anaconda, among others. The dying is often very obvious and painful. One morning I noticed workmen removing the large bronze Girard Bank nameplate from the patrician headquarters in Philadelphia. The Girard name, long venerated for the man Steven Girard, and the school and bank he founded, was erased by the purchasers, Mellon Bank, from all offices and a major plaza in Center City.

As long as resources, plants, products, and companies are cheaper and more exciting to buy than create, as long as markets, operations, and executives move with ease about the world, variants of corporate raiding will dominate managers' lives and communications. High visibility, megabucks, and great ego trips accorded to the winners only encourage the great corporate wars to continue. After a lull following the merger mania of the '80s, the late '90s are again seeing a billion-dollar wave of mergers and acquisitions. Many question how productive these company couplings are, but not why they founder: underestimating the human factor and conflicting corporate cultures. One senior executive involved, not entirely happily, in an acquisition said, "They forget assets don't talk to assets." Even a merger that looks good on paper will fail if people don't trust each other, or if they feel the other side is winning more battles and getting most of the best positions. A consultant working on a merger, an ideal fit on paper, sensed the cultures would never mesh. He encouraged the two chairmen and their spouses to spend a weekend together. It was an instant, mutual deal breaker.

Cultures in conflict can be deadly serious, but also humorous. General Motors, Hughes Aircraft, and EDS are an odd threesome. The footwear of choice and the chairs tell the story. At General Motors, scientists and engineers wear traditional black brogues; at Hughes, sneakers; at EDS, even shoes with buckles or tassels are outlawed. At GM's Allison Gas Turbine gun-metal-gray desks and chairs are crammed against each other and institutional green walls; at Hughes's modern, almost plush facilities, engineers sit at computer terminals in ergonomically designed chairs. Another stumbling block arises from regional stereotypes: the views outsiders hold of natives of the Midwest, California, or Texas, for example. Conflicting attitudes also can be a problem, as when people with a no-can-do attitude come up against free spirits willing to tackle anything.

Jones and Laughlin and Republic Steel literally were on opposite sides of the river—and much else. Their computers didn't talk to each other. Different terminology and business systems created other inefficiencies. In truth, both the former entities are dead, except in the mind-lags of employees.

Gulf's merger into Chevron, touted as the perfect match on paper, in reality was very difficult. The relatively posh Gulf offices in Pittsburgh, with personal secretaries and considerable managerial autonomy, contrasted with Chevron's austere quarters in San Francisco, with crowded secretarial pools and complicated systems even for something as simple as requisitioning material. Many in Gulf's management were outsiders in contrast to a majority of home-grown executives at Chevron.[1] In another company, even the process of press releases created problems: one communications department popped them out without fanfare; the other wrote clearance procedures often longer than the release itself.

TENDERS, MERGERS, AND ACQUISITIONS

Communications plays a major role in helping or handicapping a tender offer. Richard Cheney, former chairman of Hill and Knowlton, has been in the thick of many battles—with T. Boone Pickens, Marathon *vs*. Mobil, and the Carrier case.

In discussing Marathon, long a Hill and Knowlton client, Cheney cites reports in the media that compared Marathon to a Jujitsu wrestler, using Mobil's weight against it. Marathon energetically emphasized Mobil's size, its well-known desire to obtain oil cheaply, its high public profile, and its perceived to-hell-with-them-all attitude. Marathon's executives and 2,000 employees at its headquarters in Findlay, Ohio, worked hard to stir up the greatest public outcry ever against Mobil's takeover bid.

Marathon's eventual success may seem a bit surprising. Mobil's legions of experts appeared splendidly equipped to fight a public relations battle, but Marathon's guerrilla campaign was highly effective. In fact, it may have even strongly influenced the court proceedings.

The Carrier case, to Cheney, illustrates another rule of takeovers: fight to win with every argument and action at your command. If you have hometown strength and support, as Carrier did in its ultimately unsuccessful struggle with United Technologies, you can attract public attention, stiffen management backbone, and boost morale.[2] Raymond D'Argenio, Cheney's opponent, agrees that communications played a central part in UT's tactics. The not entirely amicable acquisition, he explains, was fought out in the streets of Syracuse. Opposition was spearheaded by the Chamber of Commerce, quickly joined by the local Catholic bishop, a group of ministers, the city council, the small business council, the local congressman, the Sheet Metal Workers Union, The United Way, state legislators, county officials, the media, the Junior League, and just about everyone else with clout in the community. Cheney, D'Argenio recalls, was always somewhere in the background of the fracas.

To counter this, UT's chairman made himself available for questions and answers from the local press. Had we hunkered down and avoided the media, D'Argenio explained, we could not have gotten our side across. UT also combated dark rumors swirling about Syracuse that they were a bunch of corporate rascals in Connecticut. Television people asked to visit UT. They toured plants, flew in a UT Sikorsky helicopter, talked with employees, and lunched with, then interviewed Chairman Harry Gray on camera. In Syracuse, UT's chief financial officer spoke to analysts; press people talked straight to the media. According to D'Argenio, reporting changed gradually from hostile to balanced and even friendly to UT's point of view. Legal and communications departments coordinated efforts, so that the company could stay on the offensive with well-timed salvos. In sum, communicators were part of the company's top strategy team, working closely with financial people and lawyers, writing their own press releases (instead of farming them out to a counseling firm), and being accessible to the press. And "we were plain lucky."[3]

More companies are better prepared to put up a good fight than they might think, Cheney comments. Once you decide a takeover attempt is not in the stockholders' best interest, you cannot neglect any weapon. Each attack requires its own strategy. There are no set rules. If you resort to dirty tricks, Cheney points out, the odds are overwhelming that you will soon be discovered and lose the day. Cheney himself uses only materials in the public domain—often his adversaries' own statements and failings—which he assembles very carefully as background to interest reporters in a story.[4] In addition to the easily recognized, insidious costs of a public battle, there is the risk that aggrieved employees or members of the former management will badmouth the company.

Cheney, a pioneer in merger and acquisition PR, is now practicing psychotherapy, replaced largely by boutique firms of specialists. The long-term leader, Kekst and Company, is "the high priest of financial

PR and crisis consulting." The fast-growing Abernathy MacGregor Group is number two, followed by Sard Verbinnen and Company, involved in four of the biggest deals in 1997, with a combined value of $30 billion.[5] Still in the game are Burson-Marsteller, Fleishman-Hillard, and Robinson, Lerer & Montgomery. Not even mentioned is Cheney's former association, Hill and Knowlton.

While finance remains the driving force, more executives believe communications may be determinant. In a *New York Times* business section feature, "Goodbye Takeover Pain: The Spin Doctor Is In, Merger Messengers Have Plenty to Do," Charles Bagli details their new importance. Like all savvy PR counsels, communicators are less seen than heard. As Bagli explains, "Depending on the transaction, financial publicists do everything from writing press releases and co-ordinating conference calls for analysis to advising on strategy and the proper spin for layoffs and corporate raids. They also ply reporters with information that they hope will strengthen their client's case and undermine the company on the other side."[6]

Although retainers are less common in the PR business generally than a decade or two ago, monthly retainers of $10,000 to $50,000 are frequent in M&A PR. Some retainers are defensive—hiring the best just in case. Problem? The opponent may have done the same with the same firm. Billing rates for a crisis or one-shot event can rival those of white-shoe lawyers, $400 an hour plus expenses. Most clients are corporations, but corporate raider Bennet S. LeBow, Joseph Jett, and former Disney President Michael Ovitz have Sard Verbinnen's help. Jett, the bond trader accused of creating $339 million in phony trades at Kidder, Peabody & Company, has been positioned as a scapegoat. Ovitz sought to escape being pilloried in the press for leaving Disney by mutual agreement with Michael Eisner.

Business is generated by firm reputation, as well as personal contacts and association with the large M&A law firms. Bagli explains what communicators add. They must "understand the sore points of various constituencies in the deal." As investors, mutual fund managers, employees, and politicians increasingly scrutinize "mergers, corporations seek communicators who know how [to] make sure the story is conveyed clearly, consistently and frequently [to] various constituencies: investors, employees, customers."[7]

Massaging the message may be even more crucial in friendly than in hostile deals, simply because companies are likely to combine.

Employees and customers need to understand their fates. That takes a great deal of orchestration. PR firms help smooth the process.

Ironically, employees too often are treated like mushrooms—kept in the dark. They are the last to know, or hear the news first outside, often from a media report. From the author's own experience and that of colleagues and students, it is clear that employees at all levels are forgotten, overpromised. A few true war stories. One company forgot to tell an officer for two weeks he'd been declared redundant, that is, fired. Two others prepared releases explaining layoffs, or did the termination personnel work, only to be fired at the end. Work completed. Promises welshed on. Many employees, bewildered, even angry, at mergers, understood only later when they objectively analyzed all the information, not just scanty news from the employer, aimed more to convince than to inform.

When the merger is unfriendly, economics may dominate, but press connections and accurate telling of the story publicly grow in importance. What better gauge of how important crisis spin-doctors are becoming than insurance? In 1996 American Insurance Group announced it would reimburse companies under their corporate liability policies if they had to hire authorized crisis consultants.[8] Looks like a PR growth-area—at least for now.

Not only communicators but some lawyers consider talking the key in takeovers. Martin Lipton, a senior partner at Wachtell, Lipton, Rosen and Katz, explains that lawyers have their reasons and bankers theirs for not talking, but any deal "has a life structure of its own." That involves how two companies communicate with each other. How do they cut a deal if one doesn't want it? Most counselors advise that, if a company wants to remain independent, it should say so, loud and clear, unequivocally. Otherwise, rumor alone can spark interest, where in fact there is none.

Bendix failed to consider communications and psychology in their unsuccessful attempt to take over Martin Marietta. Instead of the CEOs talking, a letter was sent to each director saying, in essence: I control your corporation. Instead of sensible communication covering the essence of the situation, the Bendix management decided they had a legal edge. They tried for a purely legal victory—and lost. (Many corporations scant the court of public opinion for the court of law alone.) Lipton concluded that "people in charge of communications should run corporations."[9] Little chance of that.

And Then There Was
One Floundering Giant

Although trace-lines of change can be detected in slower-moving, less-secretive situations, mergers like that between the insurance giants INA and Connecticut General, now CIGNA, usually burst upon all but informed insiders. Mergers may dominate the corporate milieu and be much bruited about in the press, but your own merger always shocks and surprises.

In 1980, INA represented solidity, tradition, and more than a century of successful operations. The elegant colonial and Georgian headquarters buildings dominated one of Philadelphia's beautiful main squares and European-style boulevards. The hushed, lush ambience of the executive floor, the original art, symbolic silver ink-wells, old fire engines, and other Philadelphia memorabilia—the sense of class spelled continuity. But one fateful decision to merge with Connecticut General turned the structure into the shell.

The rationale was faultless. It was a merger of equals. The companies were mirror images of each other: INA was essentially entrepreneurial, property/casualty, and international; Connecticut General was more process-oriented, known for life and health insurance, and strong domestically. In theory, the volatility of the property/casualty cycle would be softened by the more predictable, actuarially driven health and life insurance operations. Together, the two companies' almost $12 billion in sales would be safe from other raiders.

Given the current business climate, most managers are likely, at some point in their careers, to be immersed in mergers, takeovers, downsizings, and other bewildering, formless, unpredictable situations. A merger usually looms secretly and comes swiftly. Secrecy is essential for legal, productivity, morale, financial, and many other good reasons. But when only a few in the inner circle know of the merger, it gives them great power. They can plan the company's and their personal futures much more profitably than someone lower in the organization, even vice presidents, who become pawns of shock.

The individual officer is left to prepare for the unpreparable with little solid information. He must identify his audiences, friends, and possible enemies; develop strategies of when to fight and how; and seek a few experienced guides, who will prove invaluable. The situation he faces is amorphous and unique, requiring very specific yet flexible strategies. Tactics may change daily, as givens constantly shift. Even senior executives are plunged into a heady, frenetic, and exhilarating situation, a crucible where careers and companies are at jeopardy. Their lives will be in the eye of the hurricane for months. Relationships begin to assume the nature of plots for power and alliances to win or, more often, just to survive. The penetrating glare of high visibility and media attention sharpens these problems and relationships.

Secrecy is a great burden. Before each comment, before each assignment, an executive must ask himself if an individual knows or can be told. Because the communications department deals primarily with external audiences, a mere whiff of hesitation or fear can be easily detected by trained company watchers. It can be hyped to the detriment of the individual, the company, or its shareholders. The communications staff must be told what is essential to know soon enough to prepare themselves psychologically and to develop the necessary press releases, but not so early as to breach confidentiality.

The day of the INA-CG announcement, emotion and future concerns were submerged by the immediacy of activity. Joint announcements to the press, local community, and employees were followed immediately by a New York City press conference. Spokespersons were prepared privately for the tough, searching questions that reporters would ask them publicly. Such a briefing is probably the most delicate, perilous role for a communications officer. In the euphoria of the moment, most executives are fervently convinced their decisions are right and sound. They cut off advice. Any negative thinking is dismissed as disloyalty, not being a team player.

When the media hone in on weaknesses or confusion in public statements by executives, it's too late. Thinking on one's feet is not always wise when every word is weighed and reported on. Many heaped scorn on President Eisenhower for his tangled syntax at press conferences. They were confounded to learn that early in his career he wrote speeches for General Douglas MacArthur, known for his grace with words. In interviews after his presidency, Eisenhower was "surprisingly" articulate. The answer is quite simple: Eisenhower learned to carefully weigh his public utterances.[10]

Initial reaction to the insurance merger was euphoric. The press called it a merger made in heaven with enormous potential, a shrewd effort to squeeze out rising costs. Financial analysts applauded also.

Not a discouraging word was heard on Wall Street. In the hubris of the moment, guarantees were given to the headquarter cities, Bloomfield, Connecticut, and Philadelphia, and to the employees that would return to haunt the leaders when cost avoidance emerged as the dominating goal.

I Guarantee You . . . Cost Avoidance

The guarantees given to employees illustrate the danger of saying too much, too soon. Initially, INA's CEO, Ralph Saul, said, "Not only will it [the merger] not have any adverse effect on jobs in the Philadelphia area, but over the long run it will have a positive effect." Later, Saul said, "Ninety-nine percent of the people will stay right where they are." The story soon soured. Newspaper headlines began to read: "Layoffs begin of a magnitude almost unheard of in the insurance industry, but were called 'absolutely necessary' to cut expenses and save $40 million in 1983." And next: "Company gives generous payment; hopes to retire some additional employees as layoffs continue." And a final quote from Saul, "If we could get it through people's heads that one of the reasons for the merger was cost avoidance . . . After all, we are running a business."

There are many pitfalls in attempting to strike a balance between promising employees too much too soon and saying enough honestly to quell fears and premature, costly departures. In such situations, some managers retreat into silence. They create communications vacuums for fears to fill; others give hydra-headed, confusing messages or stress legal, financial, and structural aspects at the expense of people. Also in CIGNA's case, drastically different corporate cultures were generally ignored, except by employees, who circulated a cartoon showing two armies falling on each other—INA, a howling horde of Huns, and Connecticut General, a mechanized, orderly mass.

One of the undiscussed, sometimes disconcerting challenges of mergers is to manage essentially three structures simultaneously: that which was, that which is, and that which will be. Announcement of a merger—even an unsubstantiated rumor—changes the existing organization, irreversibly. The charts may stay the same, but the dynamics and the power are very different. Everyone is scrambling for new, expanded turf or fighting fears of job loss or demotion.

Between announcement and consummation, the structure is subtle, perhaps not even consciously acknowledged. No one really knows where he or she fits in or what the outcome could be. It's difficult to keep equilibrium or perspective. This period can be productive, even creative, but it can also detour, dismay, and defeat some managers. Meanwhile, a third organization is evolving to meet new demands, power realities, and personalities. Even a senior manager may have very little influence on what happens to him or to his department. He may not even know what is being planned or being driven by the process itself. Rumors fill information voids. Shifting people to different jobs, relocations, demotions, and layoffs create morale problems that internal communications and assurances from supervisors can only partially mitigate. Decisions often appear whimsical, unjust, and unnecessary.

The melding and crunching of the two insurance giants demonstrates many communication opportunities, some overlooked at great cost by CIGNA. First was a name search. The aim was to incorporate the initials of both, first as North American General, until the acronym NAG was recognized as pejorative. Finally, CIGNA was selected. The headquarters seemed to be on a helicopter halfway between Connecticut General in Bloomfield and INA in Philadelphia. New York was halfway-house until Philadelphia eventually was chosen.

Senior staffing was like ordering from a Chinese menu: one from column INA and one from column CG. The dual CEO seemed to work at first: Ralph Saul of INA was Mr. Outside, handling government affairs and public presence; Robert Kilpatrick of Connecticut General was Mr. Inside, running operations. Their apparently complementary skills seemed necessary to accomplish the myriad tasks of merging. Early on, little friction was evident between the two men. They were always interviewed together and pictured side-by-side in pink chairs. Later, difficulties between them would surface dramatically.

Eventually, the press began to criticize what they had once touted. "They're trying to control a ship in a storm with two captains and two crews who don't know each other." Also, the first management shuffles began in preparation for the merger. It became a Darwinian struggle for survival and clients. Employees became victims of the much-heralded synergism. Ten percent redundancy was declared, and 4,000 jobs were purged by the end of 1982. A nation-wide, five-day, 46-city road show attempted to sell the shakeups and quiet fears.

To bolster employee morale, there were more pep rallies and merger newspapers. Employees reflected the reality more accurately through clandestine cartoons and "please fire me" letters to local newspapers. Shuffle, shuffle, and change continued. Employees worried about the veracity and dependability of what they were being told. Outsiders were plainly bewildered. The vitality and life were draining out of what only eighteen months before seemed like a cornerstone of Philadelphia. Listening to executives' war stories, a senior public sector officer confessed, "I believe you, but I don't believe it."

Merger euphoria evaporated quickly. On April 18, 1982, a financial analyst meeting put the "stocks on skids." From a post-merger high of 55 3/8, the stock slid to the 40s after the analyst meeting, then continued down during 1983 to the high 20s. Wall Street judged events harshly. "After premature analyst meeting, maladroit pitch and poor first quarter results, stock price slides." Others critiqued the CIGNA presentation as: "Vague, unfocused, less than straightforward, no solid information;" "no speaker mentioned current results;" "didn't have their act together, have a credibility problem." Merger costs—$14 million to $15 million more than anticipated—surprised management.

Even so, CIGNA ran merger-announcement advertising that quoted the once-ecstatic comments of financial analysts, Wall Street, and the press. New corporate advertising mutated the once cerebral, problem-solving tone into huge photographs showing apparent guerrillas with bandoleers slung over their shoulders, entitled: "Not all corporate takeovers are the result of winning a proxy fight."

Aftershocks continued, mucking up the merger made in heaven. Key executives, mostly from INA, began to depart, led by John Cox, the very visible head of INA's property/casualty company. Eventually, Ralph Saul went, leaving Robert Kilpatrick in full charge. Their bitterness surfaced publicly. "This isn't a fallout of the merger, but a very orderly transition that will give Mr. Saul the chance to put his feet up and take it easy for a few months," the new, sole CEO said.

"Mr. Saul stepped out of management really a year ago. The Chairman's role has been a very part-time job for us."

Saul explained, "After forty years as a working stiff at various kinds of institutions and then ten years here, I'm really going to pause and think about what I'm going to do."

Other problems continued. Employee firings and voluntary departures. Loss of market momentum. Personal futures suddenly loomed far more important than corporate activities. Few new products were developed. Earnings declined 18 percent the first year and more steeply later. The press and Wall Street soured: "Wall Street mistook future potential for present profit." "It's a case of corporate indigestion." "There was entirely too much optimism." "No experienced executives are left to solve the massive property casualty problems." "The struggling giant seems to be floundering." Huge underwriting losses reached a record $1 billion in 1984. Two sales told the story poignantly. Early on, Saul saw the potential in insurance companies widening their financial services. INA bought a position in Paine Webber. After the merger, CIGNA's 24 percent position was sold. Also, INA's headquarters and tower were sold for $135 million, with a 35-year lease-back agreement. There would be two more moves before the headquarters settled in.

How was the public assessing the merger? A *Fortune* article, "Help, My Company Has Just Been Taken Over," by Myron Magnet, noted the Darwinian struggles and how paranoia reigned supreme. Connecticut General discovered that its new partner wasn't all that it was cracked up to be. Many said that they got less than they had bought. Another former officer said "the multitudinous and whimsical" management changes did not produce the management wattage needed.

CIGNA purged 4,200 people, the majority from INA. Morale scraped bottom. The quality of work suffered, as did CIGNA's financial performance. As the miracle marriage became an odd couple, the press began to ask: "Who's in charge?" Prosperity turned into scrimping. The emotional integration will take years.

For several years, CIGNA faced a mixed communication challenge. On the positive side, it positioned itself as a strong firm, innovatively marketing insurance as a constellation of employee benefits. However, it had to overcome publicly the decanonization and disruption of the equity, credibility, and operational history that INA enjoyed. Return to profitability was another must.

Managing communications during a merger teaches many things, indelibly.[11] First that, by their very nature, mergers burst swiftly and unexpectedly into one's life. Secrecy becomes power. Layers and loyalties that once seemed so solid and so clear become rooted in quicksand. Everything will be magnified, inflamed, and often appear amorphous. A manager will experience conflicting loyalties between being up-front and honest with subordinates and adhering to procedures and messages agreed upon by superiors. Lying may produce a short-term advantage, but it destroys credibility in the long run. Employees will sacrifice if they feel they are being treated as adults equitably and honestly, or, as Lee Iacocca says in his autobiography, feel they are "sharing the suffering." A manager forgets at his peril that strong, volatile, even destructive emotions are involved when someone's employment future is at stake.

Executives, tempered by corporate change, know the dangers of initial euphoria among colleagues, the media, and the financial community. Everyone is excited by the idea of a new or larger company. There's a great deal of macho thrill in acquisitions and tender fights. But if the financial and other promised results are not produced in the long-run, those wonderful kudos will turn to very sour criticism. Some messy recent mergers are creating even initial skepticism. Veterans of corporate turmoil agree that an executive can never be completely prepared, but if he ignores the communications aspects, or handles them maladroitly, the results are guaranteed to be expensive.

NOTES

1. Readers interested in the important subject of mergers—particularly the crucial issues of culture and people—might consult some of the newspaper articles on which this discussion was based: Ken Wells and Carol Hymowitz, "Takeover Trauma: Gulf's Managers Find Merger into Chevron Forces Many Changes," *The Wall Street Journal*, December. 5, 1984, pp. 1, 24; Thomas F. O'Brien and Mark Russel, "Troubled Marriage: Steel Giants' Merger Brings Big Headaches, J&L and Republic Find," ibid., November 30, 1984, pp. 1, 20; Roy J. Harris, Jr., and Damon Darlin, "GM, Hughes Face Culture Clash: Mixing Opposite Corporate Styles," ibid., June 6, 1985, p.

14; Damon Darlin and Melinda Grenier Guiles, "Whose Takeover? Some GM People Feel Auto Firm, Not EDS Was the One Acquired," ibid., December 19, 1984, pp. 1, 20; and the *Fortune* report on its 1983 Corporate Communications Seminar.

2. Richard E. Cheney, "What to Do When the Plant Blows Up and the CEO Steals Company Money and Runs Off with His or Her Secretary," a speech given before the Negative News Seminar, sponsored by the practicing Law Institute on October 16, 1984, in New York City.

3. Raymond D'Argenio, "How to Conduct a Takeover," *Crosscurrents in Corporate Communications*, No. 12 (New York: Fortune, 1983), pp. 17–23.

4. Cheney, "Playing Defense," ibid.

5. Charles V. Bagli, "Goodbye, Takeover Pain: The Spin Doctor Is In, Merger Messengers Have Plenty to Do," *The New York Times*, March 2, 1997, Section 3, pp. 1, 12–13.

6. Ibid., p. 1.

7. Ibid., p. 12.

8. Ibid., p. 13.

9. Martin Lipton, "Takeovers and Communication," *Crosscurrents in Corporate Communications*, No. 12 (New York: Fortune, 1983).

10. The CIGNA merger section is based on the author's observations as vice president of corporate communications, discussions with other communications and operating executives who have experienced a merger or takeover, and research in the volumes of media reports, including *The New York Times, The Wall Street Journal, Fortune, The Philadelphia Inquirer* and the now-defunct *Bulletin*. All quotes are from these publications, between November 1981 and June 1983.

11. Employee reactions and suggestions for communicating internally during a merger are based on insider discussions, cartoons, and merger newspapers circulated within INA and Connecticut General; and on interviews with Mr. Daniel Picard, president of Picard International, Mrs. Faye Olivieri, president of Agenda, and Dr. Jan Shubert, at the time an adjunct professor of communications at the University of Michigan.

7

Eruptive Disasters
Of Accidents, Leaks, Fires, and Deaths

"Emotion will always triumph over reason,
Yet reason will always persist"

—ALAN K. SIMPSON[1]

A telephone call reporting a chemical leak, an industrial accident, an airplane crash, a skywalk collapse, or a nuclear meltdown can entangle a corporation in a maelstrom of public exposure. Even handled well, such crises are expensive in management time, reputation, and dollars; mishandled, they court disaster, even corporate death.

Some eruptive disasters can be sensed, but not always, even by intelligent, intuitive managers. In hindsight, trace-lines of trouble can be seen. To see the chain of causality as it is developing and interrupt it takes constant vigilance and skill. Senior executives must hope each individual within their organizations will be resilient and intelligent enough to slog through wearying, discouraging, tense days. Such days always last longer than anyone ever thinks. There will be moments of anger and frustration when the media, even colleagues not in the trenches, protected by all the wisdom and knowledge of Monday morning quarterbacks, will carp, criticize, and second-guess. Colleagues may attempt to use the inevitable mistakes, even essential personal visibility, against individuals involved particularly in media relations. A plant manager taught not to discuss company policy publicly or to refrain from press statements is in a cruel bind when his plant blows up. Even if he handles the media well, he may be criticized; should he louse up through inexperience with reporters, or be accused of grandstanding, he may find himself a sacrificial scapegoat.

Bureaucrats do not like surprises. In times of quiet they can act smoothly and effectively, can control. But when conflict breaks out, managers must give way to leaders, a painful, but thoroughly necessary sorting out. Sometimes skills are needed in a different configuration or reporting relationship. The formal organization chart may or may not change, but power and respect shift.

The greatest trap is the eternally optimistic can-do attitude on which Americans pride themselves. Young men recruited by spit-and-polish Marine sergeants raised on John Wayne–type heroes, who always won rather painlessly, were stunned by battlefield realities in Vietnam. Wayne's heroics had taught them to expect easier victories. Corporate battles are little different, although the pain may be more psychological than physical.

Each case to be discussed illustrates important communications points. Bhopal raises questions of CEO visibility, cross-cultural communications and management, the absence of a communications representative, liabilities of hobbling media relations by stonewalling important reporters.

Most airlines accept the inevitability of a crash, and therefore have carefully developed crisis plans readily available. Airline accidents usually are rather narrowly focused in terms of time, location, and procedures. Still, managers in other industries can benefit from the airlines' communications planning.

Many executives are stunned when their company's good reputation becomes a powerful magnet for adverse attention. Alfred Geduldig, veteran PR counselor, sees the press, cans of spray paint in hand, eagerly waiting to cover the cleanest corporate wall with graffiti. Good relations with the press or various other constituencies offer scant protection when scandal hits. GE and E. F. Hutton have learned that even white hats get hurt; General Dynamics found that doing what everyone else did in the defense industry was little defense when the rules changed.

LOVE (CANAL) ISN'T WHAT IT SEEMS

In literature we are taught to wince at George Orwell's cynical use of a word to express the opposite of its normal meaning. In history, the late Fernand Braudel, luminary of the French *Annales* School, analyzed events on two levels: the surface—easily seen and understood, dramatic and fast-moving—contrasted with the almost hidden and difficult to comprehend—the mundane and slow-moving. The first level is quickly obvious, but the second is far more important and decisive.

Love Canal illustrates these ideas, as well as the way the media can exaggerate and inflame, particularly when the company involved plays pussycat or stonewalls initially. Fads and hot causes, whether whipped up or real, must be dealt with. It really does not matter in such instances if something is true or people merely believe it to be so; the result is the same.

Ironically, the site of the future chemical dump was named for an ambitious entrepreneur, William Love, who envisioned building a huge hydroelectrical project in the Niagara Falls area. In the 1890s he began digging a canal between the upper and lower Niagara River to generate inexpensive power. Technological advances and lack of funds caused him to abandon the canal at 3,000 feet long, 80 to 100 feet wide, and 15 to 40 feet deep. Nearby residents used it as a swimming pool until Hooker Chemical Corporation purchased it in 1941 and for the next 11 years dumped almost 22,000 tons of toxic waste, chemical by-products. The number of chemical-waste compounds may exceed the 200 identified.[2] Love produced an environment dramatically split between the spectacular natural beauty of the Falls and the "tired industrial workhorse," "a festering blister of the Industrial Age."[3] Complicating the community's adverse reaction to industrial blight was its dependence on industry, particularly Hooker, for jobs. Tourism could not take up the slack.

Love Canal became widely known as a chemical dump whose seepage created panic among nearby residents and wide controversy about culprits, causes, and controls. On the surface, Hooker, once owner of the site, was the great public villain. Less recognized as responsible were the U.S. Army's dumping, the local school board's role, panic inciters, the self-serving actions of some government agencies, and a symbiosis between environmental-extremist scientists and scoop-seeking journalists.

Although the conflict is supposedly well known, its roots are not. Hooker chose the site because of its soil's characteristics—impermeable clay—and its sparse population. That was good planning at the time, but yesterday's rural chemical dump or airport often becomes tomorrow's suburb, as growth creeps outward. The customary practice in the 1940s was either to pile up wastes in un-

248   COMMUNICATING WHEN YOUR COMPANY IS UNDER SIEGE

lined surface impoundments in secure lagoons or pits, usually on the premises of a chemical factory, or to burn or dump wastes into rivers or lakes. Donald L. Baeder, then Hooker's president and chief operating officer, told financial representatives in July 1980 that Love Canal was an appropriate waste disposal site, which had been used responsibly as landfill from 1942 until 1952. Even with all the advantages of hindsight, he pointed out, an American Institute of Chemical Engineers task force concluded that the original site design would essentially conform to most of federal regulations pending in the early 1980s.[4]

In 1952, when the land was no longer needed for disposal, Hooker deeded it to the Niagara Falls Board of Education for $1, warning that chemical wastes made the area unsuitable for construction. The agreement included a clause that absolved Hooker from any damages caused by the industrial waste. By accepting this deed, school district counsel Ralph A. Boniello warned, the board was assuming liability for any possible damage.

The board proceeded. In 1954, it approved removal of up to 9,000 cubic yards of fill from the canal site, and more the next year. Despite Hooker's advice against subdivision, storm sewers were constructed across the landfill, cutting both the clay covering and the walls of the disposal area. Removals of soil continued; construction of homes began. An elementary school was built on the land. Two concerns dominated the board minutes of the 1950s: construction of the new building to accommodate the recent influx of residents and overcoming a monetary shortage. The long-term consequences of their actions did not appear to be considered. While developing the land, architect and contractor alike had to discover the chemical dump for themselves.

Baeder reacted to media and Board of Education accusations that Hooker had acted irresponsibly in its use and disposition of the canal. He pointed out that Hooker had not "foisted" the site upon an unsuspecting local school board. It had warned about previous use and the problems related to disturbing the protective cover. The Hooker executive cited correspondence with the school board, its minutes, articles from the local newspaper, and the deed. Before the transfer, Hooker made tests and inspections to determine that the clay walls had not permitted leaching of chemicals and that no drums containing chemicals were within four feet of the natural surface. A park would not have disturbed the site. Ironically, after all the passion and pain, that's what it became. New York State proposed a park after completion of remedial work.

What went wrong? Lots, according to Baeder. Chemicals migrated from the canal largely because the property was not maintained during the twenty-seven years after Hooker relinquished control. Intrusions—storm drains, sewer lines, and removal of fill—allowed surface waters to seep into the site. Construction of the Lasalle Expressway in the 1960s blocked the natural run-off into the Niagara River, leaving waste no outlet except into adjoining property. In 1976, after record precipitation, the canal overflowed like a bathtub, permitting chemicals to migrate onto adjoining properties. Residents already suspected something was wrong. Sludge appeared in their basements. The remedial program to prevent further migration cost $2 million.

Those are the technical and legal aspects of a story that became a media event in August 1978, when a health emergency was declared. About twenty families with pregnant women and children younger than two were relocated from the first two rings of homes around the site. The evacuation was prompted by the suspected presence of chemicals in the basements of the homes, and fears of higher-than-expected levels of spontaneous abortions, miscarriages, and congenital malformations. The fear and anxiety that pervaded the population following this emergency declaration were the prime reason for the subsequent purchasing of the homes of 236 families and paying for their permanent relocation. This "botched" management of human emotions, contentious at the time, returned to haunt rehabilitation in 1988.[5]

Media coverage created strong perceptions, many considered excessive today. First, concentrations of chemicals, measured by New York State and the EPA contractor, were lower than permitted under comparable government workplace standards, Hooker explains. Some of the chemicals singled out, chloroform, trichloroethylene, and tetrachloroethylene, either were not manufactured by Hooker while it used the canal for disposal or are considered ubiquitous.

Presence of chemicals was one concern; health was an important other. Here, too, Baeder notes, analysis of data available from the New York Department of Health indicated that problems at Love Canal did not exceed those expected in the general population; also, no link was demonstrated between chemicals and health problems. Residents believed chemicals were present in dangerously high concentrations, and health problems were rampant in their neighborhood. They responded very naturally and predictably with ever-increasing demands for permanent relocation. The government and the media frightened them, according to Hooker.

Love Canal may or may not have been polluted beyond repair by chemicals. Some media and cause-pushers decided it was. Eric Zuesse, in the February 1981 issue of *Reason*, blames the U.S. Justice Department; the EPA; various New York State agencies; Michael Brown, author of *Laying Waste*; and Lois Gibbs, president of the Love Canal Homeowners' Association.[6] Why were they successful and Hooker's counter-fight ineffective? According to Zuesse, Hooker wasn't helped by its parent, Occidental Petroleum Corporation, which met initial public relations challenges with a "practically unbroken string of catastrophically bad decisions." First, they tried stonewalling. Predictably, cracks appeared. Change was forced, but slowly. In 1980, Hooker publicly defended itself for the first time in a booklet, *Love Canal: The Facts*. Until then, the company had not boldly stated: "We did not do it." Instead, as Zuesse puts it, it had given only "a meek squeak." The consequences burned off $.5 billion of Occidental's stock value.

Nor did the company sue Brown or his publishers, Random House, for what Zuesse calls a libelous book. *Laying Waste* discusses toxic waste problems, not just in Niagara Falls, but throughout the country. A reporter, Brown talked with many residents, reporting the story emotionally and mostly from their point of view. At first, Hooker met Brown's request for an interview with "prolonged silence," then agreed to some questions with Brown's publisher present. The journalist viewed this as an attempt to soften his reporting. Drums dumped in the canal, he writes, "contained a veritable witches' brew of chemistry, compounds of a truly remarkable toxicity. There were solvents that attacked the heart and liver." He explains the dilemma of individuals and community: Hooker was vitally important as a provider of 3,000 blue-collar jobs and substantial tax revenues. Many feared distressing Hooker.

At first, Brown writes, ignorance and uncontrollable circumstances seemed responsible for the illnesses, not corporate insensitivity and ruthlessness. But it became apparent that the site was in fact "part of a general Hooker pattern." It dumped in other parts of town, too.[7]

In the public mind, even today, the company appears guilty. Yet anyone who objectively analyzes Love Canal must assess the temper and causes of the time, as expressed by government agencies, media, and issue-directed scientists. Zuesse points out that Hooker may well have been the only participant that behaved responsibly. It chose an exceptionally fine chemical dump site; later, it ceded it to the school board under some threat of condemnation, but with warnings. Private winners may still become public punching bags.

In 1981, *The New York Times* editorialized: "When all the returns are in . . . it may well turn out that the public suffered less from the chemicals there than from the hysteria generated by flimsy research, irresponsibly handled."[8] Former New York Governor Hugh Carey commented: "The costly relocation of more than 700 homeowners . . . is medically unnecessary, but has to be carried out to assuage the panic caused by the Environmental Protection Agency."[9] An article in *Science* concluded that the EPA may have hurt its suit against Hooker Chemical by causing panic at Love Canal, and damaged its standing with the scientific community.[10]

At first, clean-up consisted of short-term containment of leakage, followed in 1984 by a permanent cap over the entire canal site. The courts ruled Occidental Chemical was liable for maintenance of the containment area. Wiser now, the company built confidence among residents that it was committed to environmental safety and the minimizing of pollution. Local advisory panels and less formal resident participation in Oxy's operating policy helped. But skepticism remained. With visual reminders of the trouble, the past was difficult to forget.

A remarkable but understandable aspect of Love Canal is the number of longtime residents who chose to stay in their homes even after the majority accepted the state buy-out plan and moved away. Leaving one's home after a crisis calls into question issues of protection, personal and cultural beliefs. They hold even in a danger zone. Some residents were fatalistic about pollution, "commenting that the causes of their ailments are not necessarily tied to the Love Canal spill."[11] Others saw the area as "peaceful and quiet." One author noted residents "talked about a mysterious section of Love Canal buried under a golf course in another part of town." Why has it never been dug up? "They rubbed the thumb over the first two fingers in a lucrative motion. The conversation became a workshop in worldly wisdom, a lesson in lumptaking. They talked of people who lived inside the fence and outside the fence as if living inside the fence conferred a special authority where suffering was concerned." "Environmental activists were in it for themselves, the government was a patsy, the chemical industry had been good for the city, life was full of risks, you took your chances," residents concluded.[12] Newcomers to Love Canal similarly accepted the risks—a trade for the financial incentives. Homes are offered at 15–30 percent below market price. Others waxed nostalgic for life before the evacuation and a return to happier times.

What resulted? In September 1985, *The New York Times* ran a headline: "Despite Toxic Waste, 350 Seek Love Canal Homes." "These days," the article read, "Love Canal, once home to 1,000 families, has the air of a suburban ghost town. No children play, no dogs bark in the silent streets. In some less traveled sections, tufts of grass have started to sprout through cracks in the pavement. In front yards, overgrown shrubs have obscured the steps. Boards placed over broken windows have yellowed." Then Mayor Michael C. O'Laughlin, chair of the revitalization agency, was quoted. "Hysteria caused much of the problem. I don't feel the houses are in jeopardy at all." In 1990 the mayor told protesting homeowners: "You're hurting Niagara Falls with your publicity. There's no problem here."[13] In August, lawsuits were filed by a property owner and a businessman seeking a total of $15 million in damages from Occidental and Olin, the current owner.[14]

When an issue becomes inflamed and emotional, any company will take public lumps fair or unfair. Attempting to calm the hysteria, speaking to genuine human concerns, showing a humane as well as business face, and telling the facts, loud and clear, frequently help. While Hooker may have neglected this initially, the media and government agencies bear the brunt of the blame for "inherent dramatic hyperbole"; television reporters would say: "This is Love Canal. Here, below my feet, is what has been described as one of the worst . . ." In his review of Elizabeth Whelan's *Toxic Terror*, Daniel Henninger, assistant editorial page editor of *The Wall Street Journal*, wrote that the opinions of toxic terrorists lent credence to the most extreme interpretations of the health dangers posed by various chemicals and technologies whose value came under sustained attack. Journalists too often sought out horror-story scientists, while giving less or no space to authorities who would offer a more modest, qualified interpretation of events. This affiliation between environmentally extreme scientists and sensation-seeking media may be weakening. Henninger thinks toxic terrorists cried wolf too often. Journalists don't like getting burned by their sources—in this case, glib, all-purpose scientists.[15]

The state began selling rehabilitated houses deemed safe in 1995. Verlyn Klinkenborg in "Back to Love Canal: Recycled Homes, Rebuilt Dreams" describes potential home-buyers as seeing what its first residents saw—a suburban innocence of a generation or more ago, "a neighborhood where every day creates a sense of protective closure." They are eager to believe the past can be recaptured.[16]

The government sales office doesn't assure buyers of a safe environment; nor is there any allusion to the "emotions that erupted" at Love Canal a decade ago. However, concerns about potential hazards are addressed. Who seeks the bargain? Like the original residents, whether young or middle-aged, "they are blue-collar workers, squeezed by housing costs."[17] A bargain is a bargain. They seem to trust the clean-up, acknowledging "there are chemicals all over the town." Some dismiss the brouhaha and condemnation "as a lot of hooey."

Curiously, those who live with the problem are more sanguine than outsiders often whipped up by media coverage. It wasn't the chemical factory—they knew it "didn't produce chocolates"—that bothered residents as much as "the attempt to shift liability for chemicals."[18] One government salesperson noted: "It was a sad story, full of good intentions gone awry but with a great evil remedied in the end."[19] To the surprise of this author, the same sentiments were voiced by Alaskans about the *Exxon Valdez* spill. "We live in an extractive economy. These things happen. Prince William Sound is beautiful again."[20]

The sales are not without opposition. Some members of the original homeowners' association see the revitalization as an "unfair ploy to get less wealthy people to assume an unacceptable risk."[21] Lois Gibbs, the original organizer of the fight to have the community moved, tried unsuccessfully to block the selling of homes in 1990. Other residents continue to fight for environmental studies and tests to determine the effects of contamination. Rather than reinhabiting the area, some want it used as a research facility.

Responsibility for Love Canal and the criticism remain ambiguous, except for Hooker Chemical. This is not entirely fair: the state acted only after publicity and protest. The state, slow to act and disseminate even minimal information, aggravated already high tensions. The struggle culminated in two EPA officials' being taken hostage by the homeowners' association. The state government compounded its problems by slow and incomplete disclosure of the results of health studies. Did it conclude that strong negative results of long-term testing of inhabitants would negatively impact plans to sell the Love Canal homes? No way to maintain a positive public image or foster trust with constituents.

A *New York Times* article, "Home to Some Is Still Love Canal to Others," echoed this ambivalence. It still feels and looks like a ghost town, a ghost suburb. "Dislocation Boulevard," which runs along the canal, "could be an anthem to the toxic waste movement." The dump is a crested, closely cropped pasture, isolated by miles of gleaming cyclone fence emblazoned with Day-Glo–yellow diamond-shaped warnings signs : "Dangerous—Hazardous Waste Area—Keep Out."[22] Homeowners trust "Mother Nature as the best indicator." The ducks, possums, and turtles multiply every year. They consider "the danger overrated in the first place." "They just got scared." Others want to believe "the government won't lie."[23] But did it, activists, reporters, and many others?

Love Canal, once a poignant example of Orwellian use of language, now illustrates how the apparent and the real are merging into a cautionary tale for any company caught in the vise of an inflamed and not always accurately informed public. It also illustrates that companies don't always learn from the mistakes of others. The best-selling *A Civil Action* by Jonathan Harr cites the health problems and deaths allegedly caused in Woburn, Massachusetts, by effluent from a tannery owned by Beatrice Foods, a W. R Grace and Unifirst Corporation operation. The Woburn case was a depressing dose of reality. Children died, but their defenders lost the case.

EVEN WHITE HATS GET HURT

Scandal haunts even companies long-known and respected for ethical operations and as good employers. GE, E. F. Hutton, Union Carbide, and Exxon in Prince William Sound are obvious examples. Scandal surprises other companies, such as General Dynamics, who thought they were just doing what everyone else in the defense industry was, or what the government expected, only to find themselves singled out for censure.

During scandals, communications functions like medical triage on a battlefield: sorting out priorities under extreme pressure and shortages of time and resources. If communications and senior management ignore root causes, abuses metastasize, spreading the exposure. If managers permit too much public, unconvincing hype, credibility is lost. But, if used effectively, internally and externally, communications can help explain and mitigate damage. It cannot function as a mere blow-out patch creating false security and unconvincing images, and leaving managers to think that their job is done. Abuses must be cleaned up promptly; indictments, answered. A public sense that nothing has changed or a second round of revelations courts even greater disaster.

Trouble usually brews internally before it breaks into public awareness. Curative procedures, logically, should start with analyzing operations and contact with employees. But communications must also address financial aspects: how to shore up the business and the stock price; explain the extent of financial liability; keep banks, vendors, and customers from unrealistic worry or desertion; forestall a lynch-mob mentality, which encourages lawyers, legislators, and media from attacking the wounded corporation.

Employees, dedicated for years, may be traumatized by wrongdoings exposed in headlines; embarrassed when friends question them about the scandal or when strangers ask where they work. Some years ago, when *Life* pictured a GE vice president in jail, employees were stunned. Some wondered if they still wanted to work for GE. Many, fearing for their futures, may focus on personal concerns: writing and circulating résumés, networking rather than selling products. Even when Johnson & Johnson employees knew that their company was blameless and had been praised for its handling of the Tylenol recall, they still worried about their job security. Companies are brittle structures even in the best of times. When a company is guilty, it's worse. However, handled effectively, candidly, and promptly, the right messages can boost employees' morale mauled by a public scandal and redirect their thinking toward productivity and the future.[24]

Some employees may be angered and frustrated to see their company's once-good name besmirched or singled out for legal action over practices accepted industry-wide. General Dynamics was accused of procedures that most defense contractors privately admit they normally followed. But conventions change. General Dynamics overstepped the bounds of the new propriety, and was made the example. How do companies react? Very differently, but usually poorly and seldom in their own best self-interests. Reacting quickly and candidly is the best damage control.

Repeatedly, however, companies initially attempt to stonewall, to fluff and puff internal messages. Some just plain lie. Others flirt with overexposure. Alan R. Bromberg, professor of law at Southern Methodist University, advised Texaco to tone down its public relations, fearing it could boomerang in Texaco's court proceedings against Pennzoil. Shouting disaster or threatening Chapter 11 could make Texaco creditors and suppliers very, very nervous, he explained.

Too much unconvincing *mea culpa* make the public wonder what manner of wimp is running things. Suddenly a chairman whom employees have seldom seen, much less heard, begins issuing soothing comments from every loudspeaker, appealing to workers from strategically placed video terminals. (Even here, insensitivity holds. Often screens are placed in lunch areas, so workers feel that they cannot even eat without a message.) Letters, some sent home to families, memos, and advertisements attempt to convince employees and others over and over again that the company is decent and ethical, is being made a scapegoat, or is wrongfully accused.

Overkill is rampant. Previously unquestioned procedures are scrutinized minutely. Corporate cannons are rolled out to kill public gnats. The scapegoat search begins. Soapbox sermonizing sprouts. More letters, written like moralistic homilies, seek to dissuade the corporate flock from future sins. More systems, more rigid checks and balances, are instituted. But the fallacy is relying on systems alone to do the job. Without a sense of individual ethical responsibility, employees bent on wrongdoing can still circumvent procedures in spirit and purpose. Review boards are created, and an ombudsman is appointed. Outside review by a court or government agency is accepted, although reluctantly. Words like ethics, integrity, reputation, and honesty are sprinkled throughout speeches, annual reports, shareholder letters, and interviews like raisins in a good cof-feecake.

Adversity, however, can produce positive results. A thorough audit may reveal additional abuses that can be corrected before they damage publicly. Communicators like to say that such an exercise strengthens their hand for the next crisis. Maybe. After the initial shock and denial, employees may rally in defense of their employers; those previously tempted to wrongdoing may be dissuaded by seeing the penalties, formal and informal, meted out to wrongdoers. Every manager in one major company remembered vividly the psychological and corporate decline of a once-respected senior executive who was marched out of his suburban home at midnight in handcuffs in full view of his neighbors and family. He became a company ghost, present but neither seen nor acknowledged.

Does the public care about wrongdoing? Are they morally outraged, or forgiving? Or do they know or care only about the immediately relevant? Cynically, a company can profit from short memories. Ask a young executive about the 1950s GE conviction for price fixing and he'll likely react with surprise.

Those intimately involved in companies under intense scrutiny tend to think everyone else is just as agonizingly aware, forever. Wrong. The author, immersed day by painful day in the details of accusations against Textron during the U.S. Senate confirmation hearings for its chairman, G. William Miller, to head the Federal Reserve System, shrank from talking to anyone. She wore obscuring fur hats and sunglasses in midwinter to keep from discussing details in the small Providence community. Chagrined, she realized few people knew much, fewer cared; relieved, she discovered that some supported the company, which had been a good neighbor to Providence for years.

E. F. Hutton's struggles illustrate the folly of rushing to resolve surface symptoms, in this case check kiting, while hoping to leave systemic causes intact. For more than a year then-Chairman Robert Fomon tried, unsuccessfully, to remove Hutton "from the uncomfortable glare of public scrutiny and scandal."[25]

Executives in a fix similar to Fomon's can sympathize with his astonishment: "I never dreamed there would be an indictment." He explains that Hutton was caught in a political crossfire between

Democrats out to embarrass the Republican-led Justice Department. A private, orderly man, "he is still groping to understand why he has been unable to contain the scandal," a profile in *The New York Times* concluded.[26]

Why did Hutton's chairman fail? First, he did not sufficiently take into account how unruly and uncontrollable the public turf is. Second, he thought one guilty plea alone would blunt public awareness of abuses. When that failed, he tried a single high-level investigation into practices by former Attorney General Griffith B. Bell. That failed to quell public outcries, too. Many people still think the executives involved escaped unscathed; many remain unconvinced they've seen the last of the abuses. Hutton was an industry leader. Who better to make an example of?

Third, white collar crimes are hot news. Legislators and courts sense that the public is tired of seeing the mighty apparently getting off easily. Perhaps executives don't have the dodging and eeling-around skills that politicians have developed to an art form. Paul Thayer, former business and Pentagon official, must have been shocked first to be convicted and jailed, then to be denied quick parole. Reading the temper of the times and news angles is vital. Fourth, and perhaps most important, internal actions lag behind demonstrated need. It took some time before Hutton's generally reported operational looseness was tightened; a smaller, more powerful board of mainly outside directors was organized; and different executives were put in charge. Robert Rittereiser, the new president, came from the outside, from a competitor, Merrill Lynch. Pleading guilty was the past; thorough housecleaning was still the future.

Cynical communicators think that the cleaner the company and the more respected it is for corporate responsibility and fine products, the greater the desire either to mete out harsh judgments or dramatize every infraction. How much more satisfying to knock off the white hat than to throw one more mudball at a black hat. General Electric is a case in point.

Wall Street Journal reporter Douglas R. Sease wrote that the company has long been regarded as one of the nation's exemplary corporations. But, along the way, it has also acquired a less enviable record. Three times in twenty-five years, GE was convicted of price fixing, bribery, and fraud. In April 1986, the company pleaded guilty to charges concerning missile warhead contracts.[27]

Although GE was not singled out, its "carefully burnished public persona made GE's crimes particularly jarring." Management's reaction suggested to Sease "how easily ethical standards can become blurred within big organizations." The incidents also showed how pressures can force otherwise honest people to violate their own principles and break the law. It becomes difficult for managers to enforce ethical standards and to make sure the incidents are isolated, not encouraged by the system. Younger executives, sensitive to ethical issues in their training, complain they are the sandwich generation, caught between the push for ethical behavior and a superior's push to make the numbers.

Lester Crown, then longtime director of embattled General Dynamics, blames the imperfect procurement system for General Dynamic's troubles. He could have cited another: a senior management either unaware of or unconcerned about overbillings on defense contracts, then unable to staunch the criticism and publicity. Every executive should have a sign on his desk today: "There are no secrets."

A strong argument against wrongdoing, heeded more in hindsight than beforehand, is to imagine an action or memo in front-page headlines or on the network news. Crown reflected, after the fact, on millions of dollars of improper overhead expenses—country club memberships, dog-kennel fees, and personal use of corporate jets—all made to seem worse because a House committee discovered and announced that they had been charged against Pentagon contracts.[28]

Public risks escalate dramatically when the abuse or perks either are easily understood by Joe Six-Pack or incite envy. Understanding all the intricacies of the federal budget challenges even the experts, but bouncing checks—everyone knows the penalty for that. Congressional bouncing of checks didn't cost the taxpayers a cent. Careless accounting, rather than more venal motives, caught Representatives in the headlines. It became a major brouhaha. The average traveler, forced into long queues for ticketing, security, and food, romanticizes the ease of corporate jets. The perks and comforts are great, but so are the unseen tensions and pressures. They make surroundings infinitely less noticeable. When President Clinton had a $200 haircut aboard "Hair" Force One at Los Angeles airport, criticisms spawned many damaging remarks.

The greatest trap is rationalizing actions and finding false safety in the assurance that peers in other companies share the same practices and perks. Given public sentiment, which thinks that corporate officers are too powerful and overpaid (although rock and sports stars who earn millions more escape the same censure), abuses, even when isolated, bait a skeptical public to call for harshly punishing the offenders. Any communicator worth his salt knows this, but he is pushing against the stream into personally perilous waters if he tries to bring this message to management. Often, he has little opportunity to prevent the abuse. Once it's in headlines, he may become the fall guy.

Executives suddenly find themselves embattled on unfamiliar terrain. To succeed, they must transform their mindset to understand how the "enemy" views the revelations. When then-General Dynamics Chairman and CEO David S. Lewis faced a "barrage of bare-knuckled questions from outraged legislators," all his study of military strategy, all his company's missiles, fighter planes, tanks, and submarines were useless.[29]

Few can control a troubled genie out of the bottle. But the predictable consequences usually surprise participants. The price is high. GD's troubles produced damaging publicity, greater government restrictions, Lewis's retirement, casualties within management ranks and financial accounts, loss of security clearances, damage to the defense industry, and diminished popular, even congressional, support for the defense budget. Investigations may become an Achilles' heel, damaging the industry and the nation's defense. "Being a defense contractor could be looked upon as having a license to steal."[30] A *Business Week*/Harris poll confirmed that the public distrusts the defense establishment and thinks the game between contractors and government is rigged.[31]

These scandals and indictments have produced at least two long-range consequences crucial to communications. When legislators and activists are anxious to attack, in this case an incestuous military-industrial-congressional complex—academic could be added—it is stupid to think they will not find ammunition. Second, giving them a loaded gun is even dumber. Conversely, previous transgressions of defense contractors have been forgiven and forgotten, once they disappear from the front page. That should militate against overreaction. However, even short-term damage, as Hutton and General Dynamics have experienced, can extensively hurt individuals, projects, and essential relations of trust. The challenge for the communicator is to convince the unscarred executive of those realities before the battle begins—and to keep his job.

FLYING TROUBLED SKIES

Recent years, tragically, have produced many fatal air crashes. The pictures are indelibly etched in many people's minds, not only for their drama but by constant repetition on T.V. Five USAir crashes. TWA Flight 800's destruction off Long Island. American Airlines's crashing into the Andes near Cali, Columbia. Searchers trawling the Florida Everglades for bodies and wreckage. It's a continuing saga.

More people died in air disasters during 1985 than ever before: victims of bombs, hijackings, wind shear, faulty design or maintenance, pilot misjudgment, or incomplete instructions from the ground. Cause, circumstance, location, and cultural response varied widely, but managing air disaster communications did not.

More diffuse and protracted crises—Tylenol, Bhopal, extensive scandals, and takeovers—require daily flexibility and long-term coping. While grace and intelligence under tension and media fire are just as important for airline crashes, the focus is more clearly defined: on people and just a few locations—the crash site and departure and arrival points. Thus, routine planning, lists of contacts, and procedures are more important in airline disasters than in most other emergencies. This information should be on every manager's desk, not stashed away.[32]

Airline crashes happen without warning and are very visible: survivors and the media begin clamoring immediately for information. To cope, those experienced in handling crash communications offer these suggestions:

- Make available to the duty officer the names, phone numbers, and locations of all key airline officers, those who need to know in case of a crash, and members of federal and state agencies, such as the Federal Aviation Administration and the National Transportation Safety Board. Since accidents seem to happen at the most inconvenient times—weekends, nights, and vacation times—standby phone numbers and alternates should be included.
- Establish functional priorities: who should be called in what order.

It feeds any ego to call the CEO first, but lower-ranking managers may have a much greater need to know.

- Have statistics available on the type of plane, cruising speeds, number of seats, safety record, revenue, passenger miles flown without fatalities, names of the crew, and other details that help position the airline positively despite the accident. Such background furnishes balancing information to accompany pictures of burning wreckage and grieving survivors. (NASA officials were criticized for not having such statistics—the amount of liquid fuel in *Challenger*'s external tank—available for reporters after the explosion. The spokesman's lapse was compounded by turning the question away as inappropriate.)

- Release crash information as soon as the facts and names can be verified and the next of kin notified. Here the interests of airlines and press coincide: to get as much information out as quickly as possible. Quick release expedites coverage, minimizes drawn-out follow-ups, and quells rumors, which are usually more horrible than the truth. Slow release angers families and friends of those aboard the downed flight, as the continuing anger engendered by Pan Am 103 indicates.

After one crash, for example, wild stories started circulating that a hospital had asked patients to sign release forms in return for money—victims were supposedly paid to sign away future claims. Actually, the airline had given patients small sums to tide them over; the forms merely acknowledged receipt of the money. Often stories circulate about spectral images walking away from burning wreckage, even after everyone has been accounted for.

The *Challenger* disaster also illustrates the problem of news lag. The agency ignored its own crisis plan, which calls for announcement of the crew's status within twenty minutes. It was made after five hours. Even after observers had witnessed the tragedy, reports came from a disembodied voice, not a flesh-and-blood NASA official. When an official did appear, the cosmetics were all wrong: outdoors in poor lighting, which left faces totally in the dark or in deep shadows. Transmission was impaired by faulty sound connections. Nor did the representative say much that could not have been reported right after the explosion.

The success and apparent milk-run safety of space shuttles had gulled everyone, even NASA, into treating the launches as routine. *Challenger 10*'s explosion blasted a carefully created image of invincibility and of superhuman technical and managerial proficiency. It also caught the space agency leadership in disarray and public information people ill-prepared. William Safire noted in a column in *The New York Times*, "Handling Bad News," that the space agency's leadership was in flux: the director, indicted for fraud, had been forced into a leave of absence; his successor had been in place just one week when the accident happened. The former public information officer had just been replaced.

NASA missed the chance to put human feeling into their announcements. Although President Reagan spoke sensitively to school children, who had been attracted by all the pre-launch hoopla and the media's almost exclusive focus on the presence of an all-American school teacher, NASA ignored the students. They misused their own public relations theme. Safire concludes that NASA showed a shadowy and ill-prepared face to the world. Its reputation for sophisticated and effective public relations had taught everyone to expect better.

A no-no from every point of view—legal, insurance, and other liabilities—is speculating on the causes of a crash. One communicator bridled when the legal department, worried about disclosure, advised the company to say nothing, do nothing, admit nothing. Some middle ground must be brokered. Causes are appropriately announced by the National Transportation Safety Board only after thorough investigation. The first apparent cause seldom proves to be the actual one. Usually, there are several interlocking causes; the truth may be hidden by the immediately apparent. The Japanese wisely distinguish between *honne*, truth, and *tatemae*, appearance.

Hijacking or attempted extortion is more complicated to handle than a crash. In such cases, the airline's obligation is totally to the passengers and their security, not to the press. Terrorists listen to press reports and bask in the attention. One way of balancing the hype is by providing background on earlier hijackings—how they were handled, how passengers fared. For instance, Cuba, once the destination for many hijackers, usually returned most passengers quickly and safely.

Despite all their highly visible, emotional troubles, airlines are more fortunate than many other companies. The Food and Drug Administration requires pharmaceutical companies to run corrective ads for false claims and to announce widely and expensively any product dangers or withdrawals from the market. Newspapers routinely list restaurants that violate health and safety codes. Such punishments or shame ads are not required of other corporations whose employees also make life-and-death decisions. U.S. airlines with documented deficiencies do not have to express remorse or give a public apology. Increasingly, they do, however. Some officials are prone to speak of disappointment, not with their company's workers, but with the FAA for imposing fines: nuisance regulators at work again.

Questions of public shame illustrate cultural differences in air crashes.[33] When the Japanese airline, JAL, suffered its worst-ever crash in August 1985, with 524 dead, the airline followed an elaborate protocol to atone: personal apologies by the company's president, memorial services, and financial reparations. For weeks, more than 400 airline employees helped bereaved relatives with everything from arranging funeral services to filling out insurance forms. All advertising was suspended voluntarily. Had JAL not made these acts of conciliation, it would have courted charges of inhumanity and irresponsibility.

At the memorial service, JAL's president, Yasumoto Takagi, bowed low and long to relatives of the victims, bowed again to a wall covered with wooden tablets bearing the victims' names. He asked forgiveness and accepted responsibility. This uniquely Japanese sensibility did not, however, stem persistent criticism from politicians and the media; nor did it cushion the company from the realities of a business downturn. The crash also brought about dramatic changes. The president and several other senior managers resigned or retired; the maintenance chief committed suicide. And the future became much more competitive as domestic customer demand slumped and other airlines competed on international routes.

Airlines' crisis planning must center on people: a possible media advantage. With the press penchant for human-interest stories, crash communications can be somewhat easier and more straightforward than those involving other industrial emergencies. A major explosion at a chemical plant or mine is complicated: the scene might be dangerous, chemical formulas may not be easily understood, or their affect on the public may not be fully known. But woe to the profit-and-loss sheet of any airline that comes across as unfeeling, that lies, or that continues to be weakened publicly by other crashes or near-misses.

Looking Beyond the Bottom Line:
Expensive Product Disasters

When crucial questions of product quality and safety are stifled by internal politics, absence of corporate courage, or a focus purely on profits—what the product will reap in the market rather than what it may cost in the courts—expensive troubles are brewing. Too often ignored is what withdrawal of public trust will cost not just the product under fire, but all the products the company makes.

There's nothing new about the fact that whistle-blowers are few, usually pilloried, and almost universally ignored as nags or cause-pushers. In the last century, Henrik Ibsen in *Enemy of the People* dramatized the unworthiness of those who do not dare. He understood that truth is in the minority—the first casualty in corporate wars.

Examples of obtuseness abound, from basic quality control to disasters such as the Dalkon Shield. In one food company, pseudoscientific tasting designed to test product-merit alone was debased into questions of who was the brand manager. Rating tended to be based on his political stature and power. As a result, some ill-tasting flops went to market, some good products died in the testing stalls. Although this cost the company some product leadership and market share, it did not court the disaster that silence and cover-ups have brought upon some pharmaceutical companies.

To cite two current examples: Monsanto bought threats of hundreds of suits when it acquired G. D. Searle & Co., maker of the Copper 7, an intrauterine device. Eli Lilly and Company pleaded guilty to criminal charges that it failed to inform the federal government about four deaths and six illnesses related to its arthritis drug, Oraflex.

The most tragic illustration of a good company's making a greedy mistake and trying to smother effective communications is A. H. Robins, producer of the Dalkon Shield. The company enjoyed great respect and financial strength. These cherished attributes may have blinded it to the need for scrupulous self-examination and to an understanding of how quickly a good name can be tarnished. Also, for years they had manufactured cough medicines, not emotionally charged contraceptives.

In 1970, Robins bought rights to an allegedly superior IUD called the Dalkon Shield. This single decision, compounded by subsequent cover-ups, destruction of evidence, and tasteless inquiries into the personal hygiene and sexual practices of litigants, plunged Robins into a descending spiral. In August 1985, it filed for preemptive bankruptcy.

At first, the company ignored early warnings of serious health risks; later, it chose to conceal them. It suppressed or misinterpreted physician and employee complaints; it ignored independent medical studies that questioned the birth control device's safety and reliability. When lawsuits started, documents were either destroyed or withheld on improper claims of privilege. Little thought apparently was given to how the public would react.

As in most visible crises, lapse was laid upon lapse. Robins was not the sole irresponsible player. Few others spoke out initially, even though one health organization estimated that as many as 500,000 wearers might have been injured by the shield. Nor did the federal government take quick and effective remedial steps. The FDA waited four years after the first reports of trouble to investigate the shield and then, after the product was removed from the market, did little to ensure that the device was removed from women still wearing it. Lawyers, eager for a quick dollar, advertised for shield clients, gave them assembly line treatment, and settled as quickly as possible for whatever they could get. One book on the subject, *Nightmare*, views this as a story of corporate greed, blind consumer trust, government ineffectiveness, and medical apathy.[34]

Robins's actions set it on a path of public deceit from which its reputation probably will never recover. Some observers equate the legal and moral cover-up to Watergate. As of mid-1985, at least 21 women were dead, at least 13,000 were sterile or infertile, and probably hundreds more were mothers of damaged children. And 16,000 liability cases are logjammed in the courts.

Some critics say that the tragedy was created because Robins officials looked only at the bottom line, ignoring the long-term impacts. Gross revenues from sale of the shield were about $11 million, which pales beside the company's worth and the millions in claims it risked and lost. As of June 30, 1985, Robins had paid $375 million in damages, $25 million in punitive damages, and $107 million in legal expenses. And those figures do not include loss of the customer confidence vital to the pharmaceutical industry. Robins traded off visible potential profits and invisible liabilities. Losses from drugs not sold do not show on the balance sheet or make great copy.

The shield decisions also demonstrate the chasm between the flesh-and-blood person and the paper corporation executive. Face-to-face, an individual may be charitable, civic-minded, and caring. Behind the corporate veil the same individual—forgetting or lacking the imagination to understand the impact of his own actions or what he is asking others to do—can wound and kill. It's like the deskbound, bureaucratic military commander who does not fully understand the pain and death he is ordering the grunts into.

Judge Miles Lord, in his stern and unusual lecture from the bench to corporate executives, called the Robins case an accumulation of corporate wrongs that manifest individual sin. He admonished company executives to lift their eyes from that guiding beacon, the bottom line. Actually, if they had weighed all the components of the bottom line, not just profit from sales, they would have made much more profitable decisions. The consumer movement of the 1960s called it "above the bottom line."

After all the costly public disasters, many managers still neglect to factor possible public liabilities into their product and other planning. Even a wise business decision can turn financially sour if not handled well publicly. A poor decision, compounded by attempts to hide or stonewall once the press focuses in on product problems and consumer complaints, is a prescription for serious, long-term trouble.

THE GREATEST TRAGEDY: BHOPAL

Few industrial tragedies have been as grave or complicated, or covered as widely, as the December 4, 1984, leak of 40,000 kilos of methyl isocyanate gas into the atmosphere around a pesticide plant operated in Bhopal by the Indian subsidiary of Union Carbide Corporation. Horror resulted: in more than 3,000 dead, 200,000 major injuries, and many thousands more condemned to suffer aftereffects throughout their lives.[35]

The tragedy raised management questions that will fuel business school debates for years. Did careless supervision, faulty equipment, sabotage, or all of the above cause the initial water leak? How responsible was the American parent? The Indian subsidiary? Where were the major decisions on design, maintenance, and managers made or cleared? In India? At corporate headquarters? Where is the legal venue? How damaging to the United States and the legal profession was the spectacle of death-chasing lawyers rushing to Bhopal? Should squatters be permitted to live, or return, near plants purposely built in remote areas? What misunderstandings and faulty assumptions were bred by cultural differences? By nationalism vis-à-vis a multinational?

Carbide is paying very dearly in all ways. When the tragedy hit, the company was just beginning to shed its reputation as a polluter. Then-CEO Warren Anderson was widely respected as a good, decent, and caring executive. Long-range strategy focused on Carbide's strong and well-known consumer products. One leak changed everything.

The communications implications of Bhopal will haunt not just Carbide, but other companies and CEOs for a long, long time. The questions cut to the very core of executive visibility, media and community relations, absent press experts, and unforeseen disaster, life-threatening to people and corporation.

First, should Anderson have gone to India? Probably not. He made his decision immediately, explaining, "I sort of felt that if I were over there I could make judgments and decisions on the spot."[36] He was spurred by humanitarian concerns to speed aid to all who needed it. But this humane, responsible, even generous gesture accomplished little. Anderson was jailed briefly, denied access to the plant, and threatened with criminal proceedings. On the first anniversary, he was burned in effigy. Despite all his good intentions, human feeling seemed to be lacking in the company's responses. And his presence encouraged a focus on one individual as responsible.

In retrospect, Anderson should have sent his chief operating officer, more medical assistance, trained media people, and possibly even encouraged the trade press to go. They could have reported knowledgeably on complicated questions of chemical production and safeguards.

Like many of his peers, before Bhopal the chief executive was very private and kept a low profile. Suddenly he was thrust into the grueling public spotlight, forced to balance often-conflicting demands of stockholders, company attorneys, reporters, employees, congressmen, foreign governments, and other constituencies. If you listen to lawyers, he told a reporter from *The New York Times*, you would lock yourself up in a room somewhere; if you listen to your public relations people, you would answer everything and appear on every television program. These dilemmas are familiar to communicators caught between lawyers who want executives to say nothing and knowing that information vacuums are always filled, usually to the company's detriment. Experienced communicators use the CEO's presence very judiciously: only in the forum and at the time most appropriate and useful. Reporters naturally seek to talk as high up in a company as they can. Once Anderson's trip made him the Carbide symbol, it was more difficult for others to act as spokespeople. Practically, Bhopal meant that Anderson had to turn over to others responsibility for day-to-day operations.

Carbide has been criticized rather widely for its media relations during the Bhopal tragedy—somewhat unfairly, considering the distances, language barrier, magnitude of the crisis, and the general lack of information. Anderson himself relates his frustration at getting news first from television. Other contacts were difficult or slow. Some perceived the company as unresponsive, confused, inept, reluctant, or unable to provide information. At best, confusion reigned initially; at worst, media relations were botched. It is difficult to make a fair judgment, even now. Some communicators criticized the company's initially cautious, defensive stance; it neither admitted knowledge of the cause nor accepted blame. Some interpreted stonewalling of the press as concern about legal liability and suits.

"No comment," always a red flag to the bullpen of reporters, produced several negative articles. "No comment" may have been the only possible answer, but other words should have been used. Today, pleading the Fifth Amendment implies guilt. In like manner, "no comment" means that you have something to hide, not that information simply is not available or not yet verified.

Despite enormous public interest, no press relations specialist went to India, which is very typical, even in a communications crisis. Most communicators are treated as ancillary, called in after the major decisions are made, when it is too late to take simple corrective actions to prevent public damage to the company. Or they are shunted aside when something very visible or exciting is happening, even in the communications area. Every executive is his own PR man until he's in deep trouble, and sometimes even then. Nor was the press assisted well in the aftermath of the Bhopal tragedy. Stuart Diamond of *The New York Times* was denied official access to workers and ex-workers, officials and others, both in the United States and in India. Naturally, he found other sources.

Coverage, though extensive, omitted some Indian realities. The press quickly alleged gross negligence at the plant, primitive safety precautions, workers' not wearing required safety equipment, understaffing of the plant, and unavailability of critical spare parts. The press was not equally as hard on the lawyers who rushed in, or on India. Author Ved Mehta, an Indian, detailed how the health, living, and commuting conditions of local workers could have made the Bhopal plant more accident-prone. Another journalist criticized the "notorious Indian bureaucracy's" irregular and insensitive handling of unfortunate survivors. Hundreds of the dead were cremated without being taken to hospitals, which means no death certificate and possibly no financial aid to the surviving family. Bribes were sought. Victims became entangled in disputes over who was responsible for what and in red-tape–bound relief efforts.

Carbide, while concentrating on the Bhopal tragedy, made another classic communications management mistake. When an industry or company is under intense scrutiny, when it is hot, every operation must be squeaky clean. Assumptions and assurances are not enough; "Cussed, I'm-from-Missouri" checks must be made. Any sister plant, particularly in another developing nation, must be as safe as possible. After another leak from a Carbide plant, headlines read:

"West Virginia Officials Assailing Delay in Alert"
"250 Flee Toxic Cloud as Train Derails in Arizona"
"A Toxic Chemical Spill in Camden; 35 Injured and 200 Evacuated After Dye Plant Accident—3,000 Gallons Leak"
"Spill of Caustic Agent Routs Hundreds Near Washington."[37]

In August 1985, a leak of a toxic gas, aldicarboxime, from Carbide's plant in Institute, West Virginia—sister plant to Bhopal—sent 135 people to the hospital and the company's credibility plunging still further. A second story increases risk and criticisms geometrically. Avoiding this echo-effect dictates an immediate risk-assessment of operations. Once more the communications and management doors were closed. Prompt reporting of leaks was promised, again. Even after Bhopal, many West Virginians still regarded Carbide as a major employer and a good corporate citizen. They accepted its assurances that warnings would be given in sufficient time for safe evacuation. Now they wondered and worried. Back-to-back incidents eroded the long-standing confidence of employees and supporters of the chemical industry; many began to question the safety of chemical facilities in the Kanawha Valley.

Now the company could talk itself blue in the face and people would remain skeptical. Or, as Anderson put it, "If we have a release of Arpège [at the plant], 135 people would go to the hospital." The second accident, at Institute, weakened the negotiating position with India. Coming on the heels of Bhopal, Institute became a turning point in concern. It made the unthinkable thinkable, again.

Then came the watermelon scare. Temik, a highly effective but controversial insect killer manufactured by Carbide, is based on the same toxic chemical that escaped from Bhopal. Even though federal authorities had barred Temik from use on watermelon crops (unlike other fruits, watermelons retain the pesticide), it was misapplied by some farmers seeking to save money. Temik kills bugs with only one application, unlike other pesticides, which require several. The sickness caused by Temik has flu-like symptoms, but is not life-threatening. Nonetheless, Carbide was back in credibility-damaging headlines. Carbide's association made farmers and consumers fear and claim the worst.

As a result of Carbide's problems and those of other chemical companies, Americans are beginning to demand a right to know more about potential hazards. Although chemical companies have opposed greater disclosure in the past, arguing that trade secrets would be involved, they are accepting the necessity, given current suspicions. Monsanto Company distributed information about possible hazards and precautions to residents near its fifty plants. The Chemical Manufacturers Association prepared guidelines for its members. It also considered a national clearinghouse for information about toxic chemicals and explored ways to develop better emergency response plans in cooperation with local citizens.[38] Other companies are attempting to allay the fears of their neighbors by inviting them to open houses, to see the production and safety precautions that go on behind the fences. In India, Bhopal quite simply has changed everyone's consciousness about what companies must do to make operations safe.

Bhopal's impact on Carbide and its management is staggering. Aside from the direct tragedy-related problems of litigation and public relations, the depressed stock price and need to conserve cash to cover legal claims against the company halted its aggressive acquisitions policy. Write-offs and charges resulted in a $371 million loss for the first three quarters of 1985, compared with earnings of $310 million for the same nine months of 1984.

Weakened companies attract raiders as blood in the water does sharks. To fend off successfully a late-1985 tender offer by Samuel J. Heyman, CEO of GAF, Carbide decided to sell the consumer products line upon which it had planned to build its future. More than 4,000 employees were terminated. Acres of headquarters property in Connecticut were put up for sale. A comprehensive, some say long-overdue, restructuring was undertaken. A smaller Carbide, while still viable, but with consumer products gone, it is in exactly the position its long-range strategy was attempting to avoid: dependence on less stable, cyclical, mature businesses.

Anderson, long known for his sensitivity to employee concerns, for his chats with them over breakfast in the company cafeteria, made morale-boosting videotapes for employees worldwide. Some report employee morale was high after Bhopal. Many worked harder and contributed $150,000 to relief efforts. Restructuring and layoffs, however, have left many bitter. They thought, unwisely, that Carbide would take care of them for life. Few would assume that today.

How could the company have handled its communications differently?

- First, involve communicators when major decisions are being made, and treat their counsel not as nay-saying or do-goodism, but as wise cautionary advice.
- Second, imagine worst-possible scenarios, ultimate disasters, then prepare as much as any individual or company can for handling them.
- Third, initially be more candid with the press. Who understands better the difficulties of gathering accurate information on a fast-breaking major story at great distance, during an engulfing emergency?
- Fourth, with all the clarity of 20/20 hindsight, run operations to

minimize emergencies and to be sensitive to surrounding conditions and national practices. Ask how a safety lapse would look on the front page or the network news. Months after the accident, Anderson reported conditions were so poor, so unprofitable at the Bhopal plant in December, it should not have been operating.

Despite all, in a letter to shareholders, the chief executive pointed to clear signs of progress. But a news report may be closer to the mark. It noted Carbide had fallen deeper into a corporate quagmire: litigation, overburdened management, and public cynicism about safety. And the problems appeared to be growing worse. Carbide successfully fended off GAF, but was left highly leveraged, dependent on cyclical, limited growth businesses, and with a sullied public image.

Soon Carbide was back in damaging headlines. In April 1986, the Occupational Safety and Health Administration proposed a $1.4 million fine—the largest penalty in its history—for 221 alleged health and safety violations at Carbide's Institute plant. Then Labor Secretary William Brock lashed out at what he termed "complacency" and "willful disregard for health and safety." The company termed these charges "grossly distorted" and vowed to appeal the proposed fines.[39]

Two management professors, Falguni Sen and William G. Egelhoff at the Graduate School of Business, Fordham University, reprised the tragedy in "Six Years and Counting—Learning from Crisis Management at Bhopal." They assess the impact of actions taken to resolve the crisis and its immediate effect on management in such areas as short-term rescue-and-relief operations. Very long-term costs include an increase in the cost of regulatory compliance, a more unattractive business environment where non-management stakeholders (such as environmentalists) have greater bargaining power, and opportunity costs associated with the firm's inability to take risks it previously took with ease. Despite a favorable court-initiated settlement with the government of India, the final chapter on Union Carbide's liability with respect to the Bhopal incident is yet to be written.

Union Carbide today is still a *Fortune 500* company, but was forced to restructure, downsize considerably, and get out of its profitable consumer products businesses. At the time of the accident, Union Carbide had $10.5 billion in assets and approximately 98,000 employees.[40] By 1988 this figure was considerably reduced. The profitable division that made Eveready Batteries, Glad Bags, and Prestone Anti-Freeze was sold, decreasing annual revenues by $6.9 billion, one-third of its 1981 peak. The number of employees dropped to 43,000.[41] Sen and Egelhoff noted that firms changed how they evaluate risk. They now look at the "worst case scenario" to assay whether they can live with it if such a scenario becomes real, or even if the probability is very real.[42] Some firms are turning to computerization to provide advance warnings of potential releases of toxic gases.[43] Communities are more involved in planning response to industrial accidents or natural disasters.

Another public effect: if you don't keep your house in order, others will make sure you do. For instance, the "Coalition for a Responsible Carbide" was formed by environmentalists all over the U.S. At the April 1990 shareholders' meeting, the coalition presented research indicating that "toxic waste at several Union Carbide facilities has actually increased in the last year." An environmentalist group forced the Carbide plant in Henderson, Kentucky, to release information on chemical use and storage at the site—the first time the company was challenged for refusing to comply with community requests for information, according to Sen and Egelhoff.

Communicators often justify their programs with the high cost of public tragedies. Not always. Financially, Union Carbide came out of Bhopal virtually unscathed—1988 was a record year for earnings at $4.88 per share. Its stock price is back to the pre-accident level, and Union Carbide continues to operate in India.

In many wide exposures such as Bhopal, certainly the health problems connected with silicone breast implants, and possibly the Gulf War Syndrome, perception is more important publicly than scientific links. As Sen and Egelhoff point out, "numerous long-term effects of toxicity are being continuously discovered. . . . While there may be a scientific debate on establishing the causal link . . . victims seem more than convinced that they are linked. In India the perception is that a powerful foreign firm in collusion with a compliant local government has gotten away with murder." The financial settlement was perceived as being woefully inadequate, and the Indian government's role was suspect.

How well did Union Carbide manage the Bhopal crisis? Effectively in the short run and financially, conclude Sen and Egelhoff. "The investment community gave Carbide far more latitude than other companies in similar situations. . . . But the long run costs are difficult to measure and may prove expensive. . . . Many people [were] disappointed and angry. . . . Carbide felt the pressure of bad publicity, greater environmental review, and a loss of strategic flexibility. Employee morale was alleged to be very low at Carbide plants worldwide after the tragedy." All are bound to have long-term repercussions.

At the risk of redundancy, the communications lessons of Bhopal are clear: Once a company or industry is the cynosure of public attention, only scrupulous examination of every operation and action is sufficient. Every weakness potentially damaging or expensive must be cleaned up, corrected, or explained—convincingly. That, ultimately, is the only way to protect a company's public reputation and its bottom line.

NOTES

1. Alan K. Simpson, *Right on the Old Gazoo: A Lifetime of Scrapping with the Press* (New York: William Morrow, 1997), p. 267.

2. Jeffrey Lattime, "Love Canal Today," as partial requirement for an MBA at Fordham's Graduate School of Business, April 1996.

3. Background information on Love Canal, Hooker's role, and subsequent problems comes from *Love Canal: The Facts (1892–1982)*, Occidental Chemical Fact Line, No. 13 (September 1982), balanced by conversations with chemical industry communicators, newspaper reports, and Michael Brown's *Laying Waste: The Poisoning of America by Toxic Chemicals* (New York: Pantheon, 1979).

4. Occidental Petroleum executives, "The Other Side of Love Canal: A Presentation Before the Financial Community Representatives from New York, Philadelphia, Boston, and Hartford," in New York City, July 31, 1980.

5. Lattime, "Love Canal Today," p. 6.

6. Eric Zuesse, "Love Canal: The Truth Seeps Out," *Reason*, February 1981, pp. 17–33.

7. Brown, *Laying Waste*, pp. 9, 13, 25.

8. *The New York Times*, editorial, June 20, 1981.

9. Some charge a hidden agenda: the EPA's goal of creating massive public support for its proposed superfund.

10. *Science,* June 1981.

11. Andrew J. Hoffman, "An Uneasy Rebirth at Love Canal," *Environment,* March 1995, p. 27.

12. Verlyn Kilkenborg, "Back to Love Canal," *Harper's,* March 1991, p. 78.

13. Ibid., p. 74.

14. James Brooke, "Despite Toxic Waste, 350 Seek Love Canal Homes," *The New York Times,* September 22, 1985, p. 54.

15. Daniel Henninger, "Keeping Cool About Environmental Disaster," review of *Toxic Terror* by Elizabeth Whelan, *The Wall Street Journal,* November 1, 1985, p. 34.

16. Kilkenborg, "Back to Love Canal," p. 78.

17. Ibid., p. 75.

18. Ibid., p. 74.

19. Ibid., p. 72.

20. Conversations in Fairbanks, Alaska, July 1996.

21. Hoffman, "Uneasy Rebirth at Love Canal," p. 26.

22. Lindsay Grusen, "Home to Some Is Still Love Canal to Others," *The New York Times,* December 3, 1991, pp. B1, 6.

23. Ibid., p. B6.

24. N. R. Kleinfeld, "When Scandal Haunts the Corridors," *The New York Times,* June 16, 1985, Section 3, pp. 17, 26.

25. Hutton was accused of an illegal check-overdraft scheme, popularly known as kiting. Fomon tried to minimize the damage by pleading Hutton guilty of 2,000 felony counts in one fell swoop, owning up to the fraudulent over-drafting.

26. James Sterngold, "The Undoing of Robert Fomon," *The New York Times,* September 29, 1985, Section 3, pp. 1, 10, 11.

27. Douglas R. Sease, "GE's Image Makes Conviction More Jarring; Fraud Case Illustrates Difficulty of Enforcing Standards," *The Wall Street Journal,* July 5, 1985, p. 4.

28. Wayne Biddle, "Lester Crown Blames the System," *The New York Times,* June 16, 1985, Section 3, pp. 1, 26.

29. The photograph of Lewis testifying editorializes. He is shown tight-lipped and stern with anger. The cutline reads: GD is being "badly maligned by forces beyond our control." Another picture in the same *Business Week* cover story shows Lewis wrinkled and worried, his eyes staring as if at some awesome act. By contrast, P. Takis Veliotis, former GD executive vice president, is shown almost thoughtful and serene. *Business Week,* March 25, 1985, pp. 70–72.

30. William Proxmire, "Why Military Contracting Is Corrupt: Cleaning Up Procurement," *The New York Times,* December 15, 1985, Section 3, p. 3.

31. "General Dynamics Under Fire: As the Circle Widens, Indictment May Be Under Way," *Business Week*, March 25, 1985, pp. 70–76.

32. The detail for airline crisis planning was developed in conversation with Jerry Full, formerly a crisis manager with major airlines.

33. The most important sources for the section on differences in cultural reactions to airline crashes were: Susan Chera, "JAL's Post-Crash Troubles," *The New York Times*, November 8, 1985, p. D1; and John J. Nance, *Blind Trust: How Deregulation Has Jeopardized Airline Safety and What You Can Do About It* (New York: William Morrow, 1986).

34. This material was distilled from extensive coverage by *The Wall Street Journal* and *The New York Times*, and from Susan Perry and Dawson Perry's *Nightmare: Women and the Dalkon Shield* (New York: Macmillan, 1985).

35. Falguni Sen and William G. Egelhoff, "Six Years and Counting—Learning From Crisis Management at Bhopal," *PR Review*, Spring 1991, pp. 69–83.

36. Bhopal has been so extensively covered that only major sources will be noted. Also, this section reflects the understandably great attention the tragedy has attracted among communicators, who continue to discuss it from many angles. Insights into Warren Anderson come from those who know him and his reputation, and from Stuart Diamond, "Warren Anderson: A Public Crisis, a Personal Ordeal," *The New York Times*, May 19, 1985, Section 3, pp. 1, 8, 9.

37. Ibid., August 13, 1985, p. B9.

38. "Bhopal Has Americans Demanding the 'Right to Know,'" *Business Week*, February 18, 1985, pp. 36–37.

39. Cathy Trost, "OSHA Plans to Fine Carbide $1.4 Million: Alleges Violation at West Va. Plant," *The Wall Street Journal*, April 2, 1986, p. 2.

40. *Annual Reports*, Union Carbide Corporation.

41. Clayton R. Trotter, Susan G. Day, and Amy E. Love, "Bhopal, India and Union Carbide: The Second Tragedy," *Journal of Business Ethics*, 8 (1989), 439–454.

42. Edward Bowman and Howard Kunreuther, "Post-Bhopal Behavior at a Chemical Company," *Journal of Management Studies*, 25 (July 1988), 4.

43. Edward J. Joyce, "To Stop Another Bhopal," *Datamation*, 32 (March 1, 1986), 5.

8

Winning with Communications

Any corporate activity shares successes and failures with others, but communications, by its very nature, must be both more deeply and more widely involved in the organization. Few communicators enjoy the satisfaction of their lawyer peers, who can point to winning an important decision, or a product manager, who can dramatize the ascent of sales. And much that communications does is unglamourous or soon-forgotten damage control.

But sometimes communications can quell rumors potentially damaging to business, can demonstrate how dramatic graphic and verbal public presentations distinguish a company, or can plan long-range with marketing to create a craze for a product. Managements have been forced to reverse optimistic, expansive business plans. Rather than open new markets, they must close or shrink unprofitable ones; must terminate rather than recruit employees. When the community unit is small, the operation vested with emotion, and the workforce into its second or third generation of dedication, the challenges are particularly acute. In all the examples discussed in this chapter, communications were the catalyst for solving a corporate or marketing problem.

BANKING AGAINST RUMORS

Rumors damage any business, but few more than banking, which is grounded on the implicit trust of its customers. The mere whiff of trouble, even when denied cogently, convincingly, and quickly, can start a run on deposits. When savings are endangered, something in our shared psyches flashes danger, panic. Normally objective business ears open to hearsay. The media delight in showing long lines of people waiting overnight for banks to open—the worse the weather conditions, the deeper the scare, the better the story. Lines become infectious and impel many other patrons to get their money out fast. Millions of dollars can be lost on a single shred of misinformation.

What can be done, short of slamming shut bank doors until realism has replaced rumors? One answer, very simple in conception but seldom practiced, is to conduct business honestly, with an eye to public exposure. Unfortunately, after-the-fact denials and attempted cover-ups are more common. Bank of Boston's public relations horror show, the cozy naïve relations between Ohio regulators and bankers that contributed to the Home State Savings Association's going bust, Bank of America's highly visible actions, as well as the American Banking Association's preventive work, all document the range of financial communications problems.

Bank of Boston hid from the media until serious allegations surfaced. Then bank executives came out slugging like tough guys. Two wrongs made the situation worse. Then-Chairman William L. Brown held his first press conference in his thirty-six years with the bank to deny reported links between the bank and organized crime. The bank tried to characterize currency-reporting problems as a systems error. These efforts revealed just the tip of serious communications problems that had been building for years.[1]

The bank operated very privately and aloofly. It projected an elitist, uncaring attitude and suffered from a reputation for heavy-handedness. Consequently, it became a voodoo doll, easily stuck with pins by community organizers and Boston politicians eager to blame local economic woes on unfeeling bankers.

Instead of confessing to lapses promptly, Chairman Brown took on the media in a letter to shareholders. He complained of "inaccuracies and misunderstandings," but never mentioned ongoing investigations. Communications dinosaurs believe they can dish out anything when they are in trouble and the public will believe it. The public reads nothing else. Wrong, as Bank of Boston discovered when it tried to deny that its international dealings had come under scrutiny.[2]

The quagmire of public communications seems beguilingly easy beforehand. Its harshness and tenacity appear only when it is too late to recoup. Internal wishfulness dominates; ramifications are minimized or deemed easy to control. Executives assume secrets can be kept, the rowdy public controlled, and business conducted as usual. Bank of Boston fell into all these traps and reaped a harvest of ill will: closed accounts, federal investigations, and state hearings into its international activities. Doubtless, the management was stunned. But the worst mistakes lay in stonewalling or in acting only when under censure but in not factoring the public response into initial decisions, then trying to tough it out. The window of opportunity—the time a company has to convince the public of its story—narrows dramatically as the velocity and extent of news coverage and competition escalate with each technological advance.

Cincinnati-based Home State suffered from internal casualness and unfounded assumptions concerning regulators, which resulted in massive failure to regulate the savings and loan. A whistle-blower is never popular; in this case, superiors simply ignored him. He was not surprised when the association went bust early in 1985. It seemed as if the trivial had stymied the important. A pencil draft wouldn't do; his report had to be typed. When it was, some mentions of a cease-and-desist order were deleted. Regulators relied on assurances, grandly given, on productive ties between savings and loan superintendents and Home State's chairman, Marvin Warner. They wasted time and effort fighting over who was autonomous and who subordinate. The saga is over.[3] Its communications message is simple: abuses only fester when swept under carpets by influence, wishful thinking, assurances based on quicksand, or lack of institutional courage. Once abuses are public—and they are guaranteed to be—it's only worse.

When a company is big and visible in an industry under intense scrutiny, crisis becomes the everyday norm, no longer an isolated spike on a communications fever chart. The bigger the institution, the longer the needles and the more they're used. That's exactly the situation Ronald E. Rhody stepped into when he became senior vice president of Bank of America. We're too big to hide, too important to be ignored, Rhody told the San Francisco Public Relations Roundtable. Measured by deposits and depositors, B of A was the largest bank in California and the United States. In absolute terms, it was the biggest earner in the state and fifth in the country.[4]

"No other industry has been caught up in a maelstrom of such massive change," Rhody noted, "confronted with such stress and strain, cast in such a malevolent economic and political environment, or scrutinized so intensively and extensively by media and government in such a compressed time frame" as banking. National uneasiness about banks generally is heightened by well-publicized worries about repayment of loans to developing countries and failures of financial institutions.

Understandably, B of A became the litmus test for the industry. Its own actions attracted even more attention. In 1984, the bank closed more branches than most others had. As a result of this and other actions, Rhody reported that, between September 1984 and May 1985, the bank was "favored" with twenty-six major negative news breaks or situations with negative potential, all drawing extensive attention in almost every major publication and wire service. To cope, Rhody and his staff developed strategies and wisdoms of value not only to banking, but also to other industries under public pressure.

First, two schools of press relations exist, crisis or not. The take-charge school gives a corporation the best chance of getting the story told right. The company tells it first: defines the problem, sets the context, and, in some instances, preempts criticism. The other, the sit-on-it school, is arrogant and only delays the day of reckoning. It also flies in the face of reality: there are no secrets anymore.

Second, it is vital to level with the media, or they will just go elsewhere to seek information. They cannot go away from a major story empty-handed. Granted: the media can surprise with unanticipated questions, or all the facts may simply not be known yet. Legal, competitive, or negotiating positions could be damaged by premature or incomplete release of information. Internal clearances, although quickly criticized by an impatient press, are essential for the communications officer. He needs the cooperation of peers to get information. Surprise them with a press announcement, exclude them from the clearance loop, and he's in trouble. Conversely, the corporate spokesperson should not allow himself to be forced into releasing 'information' just because an editor says he is going to write the story anyway.

In dealing with specific situations, B of A's management aimed to:

- Limit liability
- Cushion the investors involved
- Determine whether similar exposure existed elsewhere in the bank and impose strict safeguards to prevent further incursions

- Protect the privacy of employees being investigated
- Maximize possibilities of recovery.

Communicators implemented this strategy by:

- Telling shareholders as quickly and accurately as possible the extent of the loss
- Maximizing opportunities for recovery by not exposing investors whom speculative publicity might damage
- Protecting the privacy of discussions so settlements with investors can be reached *sans* the glare of public attention.

What did Rhody and the Bank of America learn from these experiences? First and foremost, candor is the best policy. Admitting that you don't know or are not going to answer a particular question is not as damaging as attempting to cover up or lie. Journalists understand a developing story—the facts sometimes are not available immediately.

A negative story is not the end of the world. Others have been there and survived. Some people won't see it. Others will view it skeptically, as more a matter of media hype than substance. Still others will understand it for the blip it may in truth be. Thick skins and objectivity in media relations should be as required as MBAs are elsewhere in a corporation.

Planning has no substitute. He who wings it is a dummy. But a plan is merely a road map, not the journey. It will not succeed if treated as a rigid be-all-and-end-all.[5]

Rumors—"improvised news"—plague financial institutions generally. Frederick Koenig, professor of sociology at Tulane University, points out that the trader's jungle drums are among the most sensitive in the world.[6] Rumor has as strong an influence as fact on the prices of commodities and companies. Pennzoil Company stock soared in January 1986 on rumors that it had received an attractive tax-free takeover offer from its legal sparring partner, Texaco. Proclivity to rumor is endemic in a business where everyone operates with high-powered antennae. People under stress need order and a feeling of completion, need to assemble pieces so they make sense. Hard facts and verification cannot always keep pace with hearsay. Koenig illustrates his points with Continental Illinois, which was done-in by rumors, and Manufacturers Hanover, which survived.

Granted: Manny Hanny's situation was more easily and factually explained.

It was no secret that Continental was in trouble. It bought $2 billion in loans that became worthless when Penn Square Bank in Oklahoma went bust. Continental's $3 billion to $4 billion in loans to Third World countries might not be repaid. Within the bank and in the market people grew jittery. A great seedbed for hearsay.

Bits and pieces of rumor that Continental was on the verge of bankruptcy or filing for Chapter 11 (banks can do neither) began circulating among people with limited knowledge of banking and finance. The very outlandishness of the stories lulled bankers into a false sense of security. The bank's treasurer denied "the preposterous rumors." Instead of quelling the incorrect, he merely focused more attention on the bank's difficulties.

Panic followed rumor. A Japanese journalist gave substance to speculations by reporting that a New York bank had "disclosed" the possible purchase of Continental by a Japanese financial institution. Wide coverage of this "news" widened the panic. It stopped only when the federal government threw its full faith and credit behind Continental in an unprecedented attempt to halt an international run on the bank and prevent a wider crisis. Eventually, Continental disappeared as an independent entity when it was acquired by B of A.

Manufacturers Hanover was hit next. Word circulated in May 1984 that the bank could not fund itself because of a 3 3/8-point drop in its stock price, heavy exposure to Latin American borrowers, and liquidation of its portfolio of British government bonds.

Manny Hanny had an easier time than the Illinois Bank in stanching rumors. The bank had posted high earnings the previous year— the twelfth consecutive year. And the rumor, itself a sign of troubled, uncertain times, was very specific, hence easier to refute. The positive reaction was swift, partly because enough people with sufficient background could judge the realities of the situation.

To counter rumors, Professor Koenig first counsels credibility. Denials from a captain that his ship is not sinking will hardly be believed when water is obviously pouring into staterooms. Second, business could adopt to its benefit the practice of many cities, which have set up rumor-control centers to deal with natural disasters. But, Koenig concludes, rumors in the financial world will probably continue, perhaps become even more prevalent. As computers and electronic communications continue to speed information, bombarding people without giving them the time or the wisdom to understand and evaluate the material, stress and anxiety will grow. People will conjecture and talk. An old World War II poster warned a careless slip of the lip would sink a ship. Careless talk—the more amorphous, the more dangerous—can likewise damage banking.

Other experts offer ways of killing rumors before they inflict great damage. When word was spread—wrongly—in late 1990 that Equitable Life Assurance Society was going bankrupt, its executives immediately launched a major truth effort: memos to employees, letters to customers, and statements to the media. Executives enlisted the New York State Insurance Department to certify solvency.

When a major financial public relation's firm heard a large retailer/client was troubled financially, they took "a controversial step" in a trade publication to dispel rumors. What makes rumors so eminently believable and hard to refute is twofold: they may portend the truth—the retailer did eventually file for Chapter 11—or they may have just enough truth to seem credible.

What to do?

- Stop gossip about an event that hasn't happened—and may never.
- Understand the unique hazards in fighting rumors. Denial, perversely, may spread them. Because some rumors signal an early version of the unhappy truth, PR advisers occasionally counsel silence. Says James Fongeroth. a Kekst and Company principal, "Sometimes you have to withstand a battering until you have a cogent case to make." More often, the advice is to refute the chatter quickly.

Professor Irv Schenkler of New York University's Stern School of Business, has an entire program to zap rumors, starting from memos to employees and culminating in ads. His four steps are:

- To buoy employee morale and keep the rumor from leaking to the outside, distribute a memo quashing it in conversational, credible tones.
- Ask middle managers or direct superiors to talk with the staff. According to many employee communications surveys, known supervisors are more believable than remote corporate officers.
- Once the rumor goes external, start a press offensive. Don't wait. Issue a statement. Have PR staff start calling reporters.

- If the rumor still lives and circulates, run an advocacy ad, laying out the case with facts and figures. No rah-rah tone. It invites skepticism. Facts fully disclosed usually drive out distortions—but monitoring should be maintained.[7]

Avoid spin and talking before the facts are known. Imagine knocking down a bankruptcy story, then the airline goes belly-up.

The American Banking Association assists financial institutions in preparing before they get into public difficulties and in speaking out in their self-interest.[8] State associations are encouraged to participate in media training seminars to help them handle incidents such as bank robberies or a crisis in confidence. Scare stories are rare, but very damaging when they occur. The ABA suggests taking the sting out of situations by educating the public beforehand. The surprise can be taken out of non-performing loans, for example, by explaining the market discipline that regulators impose to ensure that these loans perform in a safe and sound manner. Specific techniques are suggested also. When a newspaper ran misinformation about a bank, the bank not only responded to that publication, but conducted a wide-ranging information campaign including all the media in coffee klatches with bank officials. This broke the web of fabrication.

One ABA focus is on three legislative areas: basic banking, rate disclosure, and uncollected funds. Banks are urged to participate through materials designed to brief members on the current consumerists' positions and perceptions, outlines of federal and state legislative activity, practical guidelines for implementation strategies, and samples of materials to spread the local banks' positive message.

Banking is more in the limelight and under more intense scrutiny than ever before. This calls for greater public relations expertise from banks and a significantly better-trained breed of journalists covering banking.

THE DEVIL AND P&G

Moving quickly to squash stories—even one as ridiculous as the rumor that Procter & Gamble's products were promoting the devil's work—is the only way to go. Otherwise, rumors evolve, emerge, and go underground, only to reemerge and recycle, each time with greater force, outlandishness, and potential damage. Quick, authoritative denial, substantiated by as many facts as possible—even if the most fervent rumor-mongers ignore them—limits the damage.

The dynamics of the devil story paralleled an earlier tale that McDonald's was putting worms into its hamburgers and that its executives had discussed the rumors on the Donahue television show. Neither story was true, but reality did not stay the rumors. The companies reacted differently. McDonald's refuted the stories immediately; P&G acted more slowly.

Rumors of the giant consumer products company's connection to the Church of the Devil had been circulating for about three years. Initially, the devil story and an associated tale that P&G's man-in-the-moon logo was the sign of the devil were more of an annoyance, even amusement, than a threat to sales. In P&G's early days as a soap and candle maker, its crates of Star candles were easily identified by the moon-and-stars symbol. This evoked the man-in-the-moon corporate trademark. Rather than sinister, the 13 stars simply represented the 13 colonies.[9]

But news coverage spread. Housewives began clearing their kitchens of the "devil's products" and demanding that supermarkets do the same. One Cleveland television commentator, Dick Feagier, wondered if he should throw out all his detergents and toothpaste or engage an exorcist to banish the devil. He complained that, "Instead of ignoring the yahoo, red-necked, hair-brained gaggle of self-raptured morons that started this drool, [P&G] has bowed to their sensitivities." Easily said, when you are not watching sales decline and reading damaging headlines.

Although P&G executives knew the stories were ridiculous, the stories became an "enormous distraction." The company spent probably several hundred thousand dollars on anti-rumor public relations, extra phone staff who fielded thousands of calls, detectives to track rumors to their source, and four lawsuits filed against people said to be rumor-mongers.

Eventually, P&G gave the devil his due, dropping the symbol from future package designs, while retaining it on company letterheads, the annual report, and the Cincinnati headquarters building. However, when the new twin headquarters towers were designed, use of the logo was nixed because of the rumors.[10] Executives explained that the 103-year-old man in the moon logo no longer had any real promotional value. It was easier to expunge it. These actions stopped further publicity and spread of rumors. Daily call counts about Satan dropped from as many as 500 to 50, and 15 percent of those supported P&G's actions.[11]

Alicia Sevasy, a *Wall Street Journal* reporter, who covered P&G for three years, puts a nastier, competitive spin on the rumors. In "Guerrilla Marketing," a chapter in her book *Soap Opera*, Sevasy details a series of competitive dirty tricks, the strangest of which was that P&G executives were "really closet Satanists."

Among the many rumor sources was a supposed link with the Unification Church. The 13 stars were "merely a clever disguise for three sixes, a satanic symbol." Even the curls in the moon's hair were seen as sixes. Specially irksome to P&G was a flier accusing executives of appearing on T.V. talk shows, pledging some corporate profits to the Church of Satan. But first, according to the flier, "Beelzebub must boost P&G sales." Although it was easily established that executives never appeared on the shows, much less pledged profits to Satan, the rumors persisted.

Initially, P&G reacted by removing its symbol from packaging, giving the moon a more contemporary look, and straightening his curly hair. The company sent "truth packets" to churches, schools, newspapers, and radio stations in areas where the rumors had appeared. They became more bothersome and concrete as some salesmen "had 666 written on their lawns and their tires slashed."

Reactions and rumors became more serious. "P&G filed and settled more than a dozen suits against those allegedly spreading rumors." This included a $75,000 judgment against competing Amway distributors. P&G dispatched ex-FBI security guards to track down rumors and Pendleton and Wackenhut detectives "to track down scofflaws." Still, the story flourished in small towns, even among people expected to be more objective and dismissive.[12]

A rumor, crazy and irrational as it is to executives, cannot be dismissed out of hand until its sources and seedbed are analyzed. If people want to believe the craziest untruth and act upon it, any company can be damaged.

FEDERAL EXPRESS: MARSUPIAL MARKETING

Rather than hand-wringing over diminished market opportunities, innovators look harder for the niche, the marsupial pouch, in which to grow a new business. It not only must supply a need—in the case of Federal Express, overnight delivery of small packages—but must communicate its services vividly, in refreshing, pungent language that speaks to today.

Although corporations spend millions on logos, colors, a design system, many PR practitioners and MBA students forget their importance—to identify or irritate. Federal Express is a success story; a small bagel chain, a disaster. When the chain opened a new branch in a very conservative small town, its choice of graphics not only annoyed residents, but threatened profitability. The store, despite town ordinance, wanted to stay open 24 hours. Then they adorned the windows with throbbing, bright-colored neon signs. But the pièce de résistance was the huge canopy—larger than any other on Main Street, garish, with a naked babe popping out of a bagel. Then owners pushed their luck too far. To distinguish their home delivery, you guessed it, they topped the truck with a three-dimensional naked babe and bagel. After howls and threats of legal action, the owners shortened hours of operation, changed the graphics, banished the delivery truck, and settled into being the coffee-klatch site of choice.

From the very beginning Fred Smith, founder of the highly successful Federal Express, was much wiser. He sought a niche of need. By adapting a wartime technique—hubbing flights—he created a company almost single-handedly. Despite astonishingly rapid changes in operating habits and marketing, American business clings, as if to a security blanket, to the antiquated medium of paper. Authority and veracity are vested in paper. The same piece is passed from hand to hand—even across country.

Using primarily his Vietnam experience, Smith determined that the speedy delivery of small packages was a potentially profitable niche. Existing services moved packages like passengers: comfortably, directly, but slowly. Smith realized that fast, on-time delivery was the key. Senders did not care about the route their package took to its destination, just when it arrived. What would be unacceptable inconvenience and routing to an air passenger was dispatch for a package. Smith's concept of hubbing—later adopted by passenger airlines, with less customer applause—and much of his initial planning demonstrate involved marketing savvy. Implementation was a tour-de-force in communicating in vivid, effective language and graphics.

The company's image was carefully planned and nurtured. Considerable time and money was spent to position Federal Express as a progressive, opportunistic, efficient company. Smith considered this the prototype of a new generation of ventures to be spawned in the future. Every detail was important. Highly successful advertising featured humor based on empathy. A dramatic color scheme and logo—brazen purple, orange, and white—identified the company visually on planes, trucks, and envelopes, and in print advertising. Among employees, Smith stressed politeness, personal grooming, and the Protestant work ethic.

However, as Robert A. Sigafoos, author of *Absolutely Positively Overnight: The Story of Federal Express*, points out, had the corporate headquarters been located in a large city, even Smith's highly skilled powers of persuasion and leadership might have been overwhelmed by the forces against him. Organized labor would have been much more persistent and gotten a more sympathetic ear from employees. Urban workers would have been more cynical, less idealistic, and preconditioned toward Smith's message than workers raised and educated in the cul-de-sac of Tennessee, Arkansas, and Mississippi.

Unshackled by business jargon, Smith's terms were colorful and clear. He likened stages of planning to the life cycle of a butterfly: caterpillar, into chrysalis, into butterfly. One memo Sigafoos cites was entitled "Holding on to the Tiger's Tale," a forceful appeal for change. Smith often emphasized his arguments for change with aphorisms:

> What once were attributes can and will become serious detriments in the future. "Che" was essential to Cuba until it was liberated. [Juan] Trippe built Pan Am and stayed long enough to sow the seeds of its destruction. Patton was marvelous in war, a disaster in peace. . . . The price of not curing the disease will be considerable. Emotion and ego satisfaction are a luxury that Federal Express cannot afford.[13]

Today, Federal Express, its name shortened to FedEx, is still a visible success, but competition is keen. Public relations supplies a competitive advantage. Early advertising touted FedEx as a larger company than Purolator Courier in terms of revenue. Less known is that in the 1980s Purolator carried 52 million overnight packages—as opposed to FedEx's 38 million—at drastically lower rates. Competition has increased with UPS and the U.S. Postal Service flying packages domestically and globally. FedEx also had to overcome its unproven business concept operating nationally from an unlikely geographic area, Memphis. (This assessment by Sigafoos may overlook the fact that innovative growth industries such as Holiday Inns share the Memphis location. Also, enterprise often comes from the rim land, not from the entrenched, conservative forces at the center.)

In a time of tangled, pallid corporate prose often laden with weasel words, mugwump reasoning, and hide-bound thinking, Smith's marketing and communications are bold, refreshing, and at times audacious—a competitive asset.

PROFITABLY PUBLICIZING HISTORY

Astute publicists look for every opportunity to create visibility and public interest in a product, client, or cause. Anne Klein, president of a Mount Laurel, New Jersey, public relations firm, reverses the dictum that those who cannot remember the past are condemned to repeat it. Anne not only remembers the past, but revels in repeating it—in modern terms and to the benefit of the client, or, as she says: "We've learned to use history to call attention to the present."

Over the last ten years her firm has used historical precedents to promote the groundbreaking and opening of the Hamilton Mall in South Jersey. Because the mall is adjacent to the Atlantic City Racecourse, the groundbreaking followed a racetrack theme. To capitalize on the history of the location, a starting gate was a backdrop. A racecourse bugler signaled the call to post—start the groundbreaking. Jockeys and their horses joined in. To launch the Piers at Penn's Landing apartment and condominium complex on the Delaware river, a nautical theme was developed. Once the site had been used to store cargoes unloaded from globe-circling ships.

Klein explains that such one-shots are easy to promote based on history. Ongoing projects such as the Arsenal Business Center are more of a challenge. The Center, an office and industrial complex, was developed on the site of the historic Frankford Arsenal, a munitions facility in northeast Pennsylvania. The Klein firm sought to capitalize on the owner's efforts to preserve and renovate the registered historic landmark. Each subsequent event highlighted the historical. The Second Pennsylvania Regiment with its fife and drum corps played at the opening of the complex's industrial center. Colonial troops fired muskets in salute to usher in a new era at the arsenal. Great T.V. visuals.

When the office district opened, soldiers wearing military uniforms from colonial times to the present paraded. "This walking museum catalog, showing how U.S. military uniforms have evolved," provided visuals for the guests and media. "Ben Franklin" helped open a bank branch whose tellers wore colonial costumes. The opening of a restaurant was linked to the site of the officers' mess hall.

To celebrate the Arsenal's 175th anniversary, Anne Klein & Associates proposed a museum dedicated to the arsenal's history. NASA astronaut Col. Guy Bluford, national honorary chairman, had roots at the arsenal. His father had worked at its laboratories. Displays included memorabilia donated by the former arsenal workers, military articles, and other artifacts.

The acid test of such efforts is publicity. A reunion party of former arsenal workers engendered five-minutes of local television coverage—business aspects, interviewing tenants, even giving costs per square foot. To Klein, "Where history goes to work," the arsenal's logo, sums up the harmony of combining past with present. But she cautions history to promote the present should be used only when and where appropriate.[14]

CREATING THE CRAZE FOR CABBAGE PATCH DOLLS

Profit-oriented executives have two stinging criticisms of communicators: they cannot quantify their contributions and they shoot from the hip. Both are too often true.

Unlike marketing or product publicity, which can demonstrate increased sales volume or heightened public attention, corporate communications seldom translate into dollars earned. Essentially damage control, communications successes are conveniently forgotten once a threat is past. Often demonstrable value is possible only in the long term. Communicators must possess the same patient faith as teachers waiting years for students to demonstrate their capabilities. When corporate communications can produce hard figures—a costly strike averted, potentially costly legislation mutated or killed—they milk that one shining achievement throughout their careers.

The charge of shooting from the hip is equally unfair and just as well grounded. It stems from the conflicting demands, deadline pressures, and even personal styles between operating executives, who strategize six months to five years out, and managers of corporate city rooms, who must respond immediately to media opportunities and questions. Hip-shooting may be the most efficient, perhaps only, way to handle volatile media relations.

The best public relations practitioners seek techniques and actions which strip away accepted wisdoms and masks to reveal sometimes unexpected basic interests and values. Beauty is valued over ugliness. Standardization over uniqueness. One craze—Cabbage Patch Kids—demonstrated that communicators can plan long range, and produce a profit, that a runt of the litter can be a superstar.

The campaign was "created" cooperatively by the manufacturers, Coleco Industries; their advertising agency, Richard & Edwards; and their outside public relations counsel, Richard Weiner, Inc. What began as a $100,000 public relations campaign to promote offbeat-looking dolls quickly became a masterstroke of marketing communications.

The doll was originally "found" amid Georgia legends in a cabbage patch, Xavier Roberts remembered from his own childhood. He invented the "oath of adoption" making kids promise to care for his creation. Individual names came from 1938 Georgia birth records. Later the doll was sold to, not adopted by, Coleco. The distinctively ugly—the more charitable may say homely—kids caricatured their owners: plump, with straight, stubby arms and legs; squashed, ovoid heads; small, close-together eyes; and uniformly blank expressions—eternally between a gurgle and a sob. Almost antiheroes, they represent real people, warts and all. And they require lots of care and loving. But how would they appeal to a society infatuated with beauty?

First, in-depth research explored the psychological and emotional aspects of looks and adoption. Richard Weiner, president of RWI, sought the counsel of child psychologists, pediatricians, early childhood educators, even a doll historian. Focus groups tested their suggestions.

The selling points emphasized the dolls' homely but huggable

likeness to real babies; appealed to nurturing instincts, parental responsibility, and loving qualities. We learned, Weiner explained,
that children do not consider themselves beautiful; that their parenting nature is aroused more by homely than by glamorous dolls.

In January 1983 the dolls were introduced in a "hospital nursery"
at the American Toy Fair. By summer, mass adoptions were staged
at press gatherings in several cities. Extensive trade press and general
media interest—the "Today" and "Tonight" shows, a six-page spread
and cover in *Newsweek,* and a *Wall Street Journal* editorial—fueled
the moppet mania. Weiner and his staff sought every publicity opportunity—dolls to the then-pregnant Jane Pauley, dolls to accompany Nancy Reagan's visit to Vietnamese children recovering from
surgery in New York City.

Promotions supported the media attention. A fourteen-page
"Cabbage Patch Kids Parenting Guide," featuring photos of children
with their adoptees, gave practical advice on how to tie shoelaces
and cross a street safely. Each owner became a member of the Cabbage Patch Kids Parents' Association. Accessories—fold-up carriers,
slumber bags, and extensive wardrobe choices—increased sales.

Coleco ran no print advertisements; television commercials were
shown only on Saturday mornings and in early evening, fringe hours.
Even so, *Ad Week* claimed the public relations coup, crediting advertising for pushing the demand for the dolls beyond the supply. The
hand-made Roberts version sold for $125; scalpers got the same price
and higher for the Coleco dolls priced around $25.

If the publicity worked exactly according to plan, exceeding even
Weiner's expectations, the shortages it produced caught everyone by
surprise. Christmas shoppers fought and clawed their way to the few
remaining dolls. A Kansas City postman flew to London to buy a Kid
for his daughter. A dozen or more Wisconsinites braved a cold dawn
to wave credit cards and catcher's mitts so they could be photographed from the air. As a spoof, a local radio announcer had said a
B-29 would make an airborne drop of 2,000 Kids. Harried parents
took the bait. A Texas shopper clung to her purchase despite another
shopper's purse strap wound around her throat. As many as 50 people jostled at each other to get at six dolls. An angry crowd threatened a store manager to unload a crate of dolls immediately, or else.

Many sought to explain the Kid's appeal and the craze. Bright
colors and soft textures. Sheer ugliness. Uniqueness contrasted

against standardized toys. Empty nesters seeking a second family. Allowing children to work through the typical fantasy that they are adopted. Children's need to identify with parents. A sense of belonging. Sheer possessiveness. Attachments external to the children themselves. Adopting adult roles.

All agreed both appeal and craze benefited from extraordinary media hype. Looking for reality behind the fairy tale, many noted that even the most careful planning and publicity cannot guarantee a blockbuster. Truly popular toys just seem to well up, take off, thanks to an unpredictable but right mix of circumstance and luck. The great consumer quest revealed a mix of motives—grand and ignoble. Even veteran toy makers wish they could predict such success. You hope it happens. You do your best to make it happen. When it comes, you capitalize on it. Where do crazes end? Usually, quickly and cheaply at next fall's garage sales or stashed away and totally ignored.

Faced with this unusual but potentially damaging problem—demand overwhelming supply—Weiner and Coleco suspended advertising, but continued the publicity program. Coleco speeded production and delivery; offered dolls as prizes at charitable and public interest events.

The entire campaign, Weiner explains, was researched, developed, and executed for less than $500,000. It produced profits estimated between $50 million and $60 million in 1983. Even so, Weiner notes, public relations is still viewed skeptically by media and some businesspeople; is still associated with chanciness. Many considered the craze a lucky fluke; others wanted the same excitement created for their products.[15]

Communicators planned, strategized, and produced continuing profits, benefits, and attention. New sizes, shapes, and costumes—twins, world travelers, ponies, dolls with a first tooth and glasses—were introduced. And the dolls still attract national publicity. When an orthodontist in Arlington, Texas, began gluing metal on the mouths of Cabbage Patch dolls as he put braces on the teeth of the dolls' owners, it was reported widely.

Cabbage Patch mania was born again during the 1985 Christmas shopping season on Fifth Avenue in New York. Babyland, the new store (birthing facility), is a clinical study in marketing motherhood and Orwellian abuse of language. The store was packaged with sales help (nurses and doctors) in full uniform, a special delivery stork, adoption cubicles where prospective customers (adoptive parents) pledged their care and paid adoption fees. Nostalgia was abundant—an old-fashioned country store and Dickens-like carolers in the windows. Men and women, old and young, stared at the windows, enraptured. Lines snaked around the store for blocks. But the pièce de résistance is the Cabbage Patch itself. A salesperson (doctor) scrubbed, put on fresh gloves, and felt the cabbage heads. When mother cabbage dilated to open four leaves, he announced that another Kid was about to be born.[16] An unusual coup for communicators.

For Coleco, the dénouement was not all happy. Shortages created criticism and doubts. When the company tried to introduce the Adam computer, it failed, bankrupting Coleco.

During the 1996 Christmas season, the Kids gave their new owner, Mattel, problems to chew on. Snacktime Kids, designed with mechanical jaws that allow the "little person" to "eat" plastic food, instead snagged hair and fingers and kept on chomping—some 35 children. While none needed medical attention, the "gift monsters" were ordered to carry warnings about their munching mouths.[17] Mattel pulled the chewing toy from shelves, offered refunds, and took an $8 million charge in the fourth quarter, or 3 cents per share.[18]

A TICKLING ENCORE

Luck, shrewd publicity, akin to Cabbage Patch, and Internet sales vaulted Tickle Me Elmo to the top of 1996's toy list. The furry 16-inch Sesame Street–based figure giggles and squeals "That tickles" when its belly is squeezed. Its manufacturer, Tyco Preschool, felt it had a winner when Elmo was introduced at the American International Toy Fair in New York City in February 1996. To ensure, needlessly it turned out, that the initial manufacturing order of 400,000 would sell out, Tyco and Freeman Public Relations orchestrated marketing, advertising, and publicity.

To enhance Elmo's lovable character and giggle, packaging invited consumers to "try me right on the shelf." Television personalities, as with Cabbage Patch, accelerated interest. Two hundred Elmos were supplied to the "Rosie O'Donnell Show" for her "secret word" contest. The show's core audience, stay-at-home mothers of preschool children, was exactly Tyco's target market. More publicity followed. On October 15, USA Today cited Elmo as one of the season's hottest toys. Other awards and Bryant Gumbel's fascination with the doll on the "Today Show" followed.

By Thanksgiving, Tyco knew it had a winner, but still hadn't realized how great. Production was doubled to 800,000. Even so, the day after Thanksgiving "Where's Elmo" calls poured into Tyco's Mount Laurel, New Jersey, headquarters flashing sell-outs and shortages. By Christmas one million units—not nearly enough—had been shipped.

As shortages grew, a Cabbage Patch déjà-vu blossomed. Somehow, any way, getting the toy seemed vital to one's existence, even for those not knowing what an Elmo is or does. Women ran alongside delivery trucks. Any possible source of the toy was explored, even by professionals who usually stood aloof and scoffed. Internet auctions and hard-luck stories upped the ante. Mob mentality and acute possessiveness took over—again.

Thousands of Elmo's were sold by E-mail at $200 or more for the $30 toy. One sold on an E-mail auction for $7,500. "The line between absurdity and reality became awfully fuzzy." A Green Bay, Wisconsin, man set up a Netsonic Elmo clearing house to match buyers and sellers. Within days he received more than 2,500 messages. A web-page offer resulted in four to six E-mail messages hourly. Others who offered Elmos for sale got pleas about cancer-struck kids and crazy mothers cursing the owner. Cyber abuse included suggestions to make donations to charity rather than ripping off children at Christmas, charges of swindling people because their children must have an Elmo, and "Your greed makes me seriously sick."[19]

Surprised, Tyco "pulled its Elmo T.V. commercials, fearing the sight of the bug-eyed muppet would only generate ill will among the have-nots." The company also had to deny "deliberate shorting of production."[20] Any further publicity only worsened the problem. Seekers were assured that lots would be available after the first of the year.[21] Too late.

Where is that next great supertoy? It's here. It's "Goodbye, Tickle Me Elmo: Hello Beanie Babies."[22] Not just children, but adults are once again going to extreme lengths to get the newest Baby to build their collections. The "colorful, plush-covered, fist-sized beanbags come in 77 animal shapes with such beguiling names as Wrinkles the Bulldog and Radar the Bat." They have swept across the country "in a word-of-mouth firestorm the likes of which many toy merchants say they have never seen." Enthusiasts dismiss Elmo as "an insignificant blip on the retail horizon" in comparison.[23]

The frenzy for dolls, priced at $5, has boosted "prices in the underground economy to $1000," sometimes even more. A national phenomenon without let-up. Toy merchants and child psychologists attribute the frenzy not just to the toy's "cuddly wholesomeness," but also to "marketing genius." First, the $5 cost "allows children to buy them with their allowance and softens up parents who might otherwise recoil at a child's impulse purchase." Many boys and girls accumulate the entire menagerie—77 characters and still collecting.

As with Cabbage Patch Kids, the lack of television advertising imparts a cachet and exclusiveness. Hi-tech spreads the messages, however. The Beanie Babies' Web site which has all available types appears on the toy's tag. Chat rooms, or bragging sites about numbers and types a child has, fuel the fad. Trades, baby-sitting for Beanie Babies, and just plain T.V. watching pals are part of the appeal. Adults and robbers collect, too. One owner's car was broken into for a retired Beanie Baby (no longer on the market) on the dashboard. The radio was untouched.[24] What a satirical *New Yorker* cartoon that would make!

ALOHA TO PUNA SUGAR

Sugar is an emotionally laden product, a way of life rather than merely a cash crop to the thousands who work all their lives in Hawaii's cane fields or mills—often as their fathers and grandfathers did before them. Sugar, with tourism and the military, dominates the state's economy. In its peak year, 1931, Hawaii's plantations employed more than 50,000 workers who produced more than a million tons. By 1995, production had plummeted to 495,000 tons. Neither Oahu or Kauai had a working plantation.[25]

The Americans of Hawaii are leavened by many unique influences—the Japanese, Chinese, Polynesians, Hawaiians, Haoles, and a mixture of just about every other people on earth—and by optimism bred in a seeming paradise of constantly warm weather and sunshine. Many came as contract laborers. By the heritage of great courage demonstrated by those who sailed enormous distances across the South Pacific in primitive outriggers. Hawaiian terms infuse business discussions in Honolulu as Yiddish does in New York. And decisions tend to be made more meditatively, with wider participation, than on the mainland.

Sugar's many and intractable problems severely impact the state and its companies, including the largest, Amfac—a $2 billion diversified corporation. The state's leading private-sector employer (10,000 employees), it produced almost one-third of Hawaii's crop. In the United States, sugar depends on government price supports, which cannot be counted on forever. Cane can be grown almost everywhere—from cold Scandinavian countries to southern Argentina and most places in between—usually more cheaply than in Hawaii.

Compounding these problems are changing tastes, a world sugar glut, nutritional activists, falling prices, cheaper sweeteners, and disappearing tariff barriers. The United States market is declining rapidly: from 101 pounds per capita in the early 1960s to 70 pounds in 1984, and still falling. Sugar no longer sweetens canned and bottled beverages—high-fructose corn sweeteners do it more cheaply. New global divisions of labor and rising Hawaiian costs of labor and shipping to the mainland further weakened King Sugar.

Faced with these realities and high production costs, Amfac decided it must close its least efficient plantation, the Puna Sugar Company on the Big Island (Hawaii). At one time it covered 32,000 acres and employed 3,000 people. In 1982, Puna was losing $10 million annually. Losses were projected to double over the next two years, although closing would not end the losses, merely cut them substantially.

Few Hawaiians were surprised, but economic reality stunned. Local legislators considered any shutdown to be catastrophic, a severe blow to the economic health of the Hilo area, where most of Puna's 500 employees lived. This first plantation closing since Kohala in 1972 seemed to portend other shutdowns. Even so, when Amfac made its case candidly and sympathetically, legislators, trade union officials, and the community supported the action.

Henry A. Walker, Jr., at the time Amfac's president and CEO, today its chairman emeritus, sought the cooperation of everyone involved to make a painful necessity understandable and to cushion its effects as much as possible. Included were the governor, United States congressional delegation, community councils, local legislators, affected employees, landowners, other companies, and officials from the Hawaii Department of Agriculture. Walker estimated that "hundreds of thousands of hours" had been devoted to Puna's problems when the closing was announced. Everyone sensed that what in 1982 was Amfac's problem tomorrow would be another grower's and Hawaii's.

At a news conference hosted by the governor in the state capitol, he noted: "The coming together today of labor, government and management demonstrates that sugar is everybody's business. We must work together to ease the pain." Walker detailed the exhaustive evaluation of Amfac's sugar operations, aimed at cutting current and anticipated sugar losses on all its plantations. The conclusion: Puna had to be closed, phased out over a two-year period ending in 1984 to allow for harvesting of the crops already in the ground and for an orderly economic transition.

Congressman Daniel Akaka commented that if the closing signaled a trend in Hawaii, "then no one's life in this state will remain unchanged." He urged a new partnership in sugar: federal, state, industry, and labor interests. Labor was involved in discussions from the beginning, as Amfac sought alternative opportunities for displaced workers—raising mangos, papaya, or other fruit, macadamia nuts, exotic flowers, biomass fuels, and feed grains or relocation to other plantations.

The greatest innovation and generosity, however, was the gift of five acres of Puna land to each eligible employee to work as he chose. Arable land is exceedingly precious and scarce in Hawaii. The company also donated $2 million, plus road work equipment, to a nonprofit corporation to be devoted to, owned, and operated by employees. The company sought no financial assistance from any government agency, only cooperation to ameliorate the impact of Puna's wind-down and to help the Hawaiian sugar industry, even more embattled today, to survive.

At the news conference, ILWU President Tommy Trask said, "If there is any hope in this situation, it lies in Amfac's program, in its openness and sense of corporate responsibility." Some attendees were understandably skeptical about workers converting from large-scale farming to cottage agriculture, but Trask explained that the majority were experienced farmers who could adapt quickly and well. Others questioned the land gift: No propaganda? No strings attached? Walker assured them that all the land would be contributed just as soon as the maze of zoning, legal, and other considerations was worked through.

Amfac's proposal ran a cropper of government restrictions and other conditions, principally county zoning and development costs. Eventually, the most workers had to pay was $20,000 for the one acre they could receive, still a bargain for scarce, valuable Hawaiian land. Another stumbling block was revealed by a University of Hawaii survey of Puna Sugar employees. Eighty-one percent said that they did not want to farm.

Even this unusual cooperation has not cured sugars ills. However, its plight became well understood through Amfac's extensive public relations program based on grassroots, community involvement. In 1981, Amfac, facing heavy losses ($30 million that year alone), used all means of formal and informal communications to dramatize the sugar industry's historic and contemporary importance to Hawaii. A day-long Save Our Sugar (SOS) rally was attended by almost 10,000 people in a Honolulu park.

Pau bana (the end) came for Puna on September 19, 1984. A somber, ceremonial caravan of fifteen cane trucks—the lead one piled high with the final load of cane, the other big rigs empty—wound their way down Volcano Highway to the mill. Drivers tooted their air horns; it sounded like a giant horde of bumble bees amplified many times. Employees, many with no solid job prospects, gathered to watch the final unloading. They had worked hard to the very end so the mill would be closed with dignity. As the unloading began, someone inside the factory dropped a few gallons of crude oil into the boiler. Suddenly a thick, black column arose from the smokestack. A death pall over the dying sugar mill and the only industry Puna had ever known. Just an hour later, Kilauea erupted, sending a thick column of lava almost 1,000 feet into the air. Its red fountaining could be seen throughout the Puna district.

The lessons of this Pacific Rim action? Many executives expect—and experience—only labor/management antagonism. Even in times of genuine economic hardship and drastically diminished markets, appeals to workers' sense of fairness and intelligence can produce beneficial results to everyone.[26] Sugar workers and the community, because of the extensive communications efforts, understood how threatened all their futures were by declining acreage, lower prices, and endangered supports. Puna demonstrates how cooperation of labor, government, and company, how open and candid communication, can make the best of a dim present and perhaps an even more difficult future.

Amfac's closing down with great reality and compassion could not stay Hawaii's problem. Closing of the McBryde Sugar Company, the last on Kauai, in late 1996 raised the same specters and questions. Instead of growing sugar, they grew hotels. Companies are still experimenting with replacement tropical products—forage grasses for cattle, exotic flowers, papayas, and coffee—and explaining to employees and others why there's such financial trouble in paradise.[27]

SAVING PRODUCTS FROM EXTINCTION

Because public relations is essentially incremental and integrated, examples of dramatic turnarounds are rare. However, saving a product through a public relations campaign is both dramatic and easily demonstrated. Hill and Knowlton's counselors saved two products threatened during pre-FDA approval testing. One was an anti-rabies vaccine for wildlife and livestock; the other, a new treatment for enlarged prostates.[28]

The turnaround of the Wistar Institute's rabies vaccine was complete. Before the public affairs program began, testing was viewed as unethical, possibly even illegal, by important publics—mostly in Argentina—such as the media, scientific community, industry, and government agencies. Ultimately, these same publics recognized all allegations as false. A number of scientific colleagues apologized. And the vaccine is on its way to approval.

Initially, the situation was inflamed and litigious. The Wistar Institute, a private not-for-profit research institution in Philadelphia, had developed a genetically engineered virus to be used as a vaccine against rabies in wildlife and livestock. The Wistar name was one of great influence and importance in Philadelphia during the nineteenth and early twentieth centuries. Founded by German immigrants, the business evolved from what is believed to be the first glass factory in the colonies. Caspar, a grandson of the original immigrant, received his medical degree from the University of Edinburgh. When Thomas Jefferson resigned as president of the American Philosophical Society in 1815, Wistar succeeded him. Well known for his work in biology and anatomy, Dr. Wistar founded what became the Wistar Institute of Anatomy and Biology in Philadelphia.[29]

The first test site chosen for the vaccine was Argentina. Sensitivities of Latin American countries to drug testing and use exacerbated the problem. In January 1988, newspapers in Argentina, Europe, and the United States reported Argentine government allegations that several farm workers had been infected with the virus during a field test. One article referred to the incident as a "genetic Chernobyl." A gross overstatement, but Chernobyl was a scare word guaranteed to get instant attention. In a less serious, but equally effective manner, French opposed to Euro-Disney called it a "cultural Chernobyl." Adverse publicity threatened the future of the rabies vaccine program, particularly planned tests on wild raccoons in Virginia or North Carolina.

Following the allegations, the Argentine government filed suits in the Argentine Supreme Court and the World Court. Argentine officials making the charges gave frequent interviews to reporters and presented the allegations at international scientific conferences. "They accused the Wistar Institute and its collaborator, The Pan American Health Organization (PAHO), of conspiring to use the Argentine workers as unwitting guinea pigs in an experiment forbidden in industrialized countries." Some involved thought PAHO, an affiliate of the World Health Organization, could prove the charges false, but PAHO would neither release this evidence nor comment. Argentine officials had publicly threatened to nationalize PAHO's research station in Argentina. According to Hill and Knowlton's assessment, this silence led some to assume guilt.

"Wistar was widely condemned by environmentalists, members of the scientific community, and even representatives of the biotechnology industry." "A public interest group opposed to the development of biotechnology exploited the Argentine situation to push for strict U.S. government regulation of overseas research by U.S. institutions."

The Wistar Institute hired Hill and Knowlton to develop and implement a public affairs program to restore its good name and foster a public policy environment conducive to continued development of the rabies vaccine. Hill and Knowlton responded with a detailed plan of target audiences and technologies. Major audiences included:

- Argentine government officials
- Officials of the U.S. Department of Agriculture, which regulates field tests of veterinary vaccines, and committees of the U.S. National Institutes of Health, which establishes guidelines for genetic engineering research
- Media in Argentina, Europe, and the U.S.
- Leading environmentalists and biologists
- Leaders of the biotechnology industry
- State wildlife, environmental, and public health officials in Virginia and South Carolina where the next tests were scheduled.

To shift attention to the vaccine's potential benefits, while countering Argentine allegations, a series of activities were suggested:

- Meetings with Argentine officials and ambassador to the U.S.
- Private briefings with potential allies and supporters as well as selected environmental groups
- A news conference in Washington, D.C., to announce the Institute's application to test the vaccine in the United States, to provide a progress report on previous research, and to answer questions about the Argentine allegations
- Preparation of Wistar spokespersons with media training and expected questions
- Distribution of a detailed press kit to reporters who cover biotechnology or who wrote articles about the Argentine allegations or the wildlife rabies epidemic in the eastern United States (this technique would not only update reporters, but also, as in Wistar's case, encourage a second look at the situation; it was a key element in the Wistar turnaround)
- Interviews with Argentina's leading daily newspaper, *La Nación* and top weekly magazine, *Somos*
- Circulation of a white paper, answering Argentine charges, to Argentine officials, leading biologists and environmentalists, and other interested scientists (white papers are used to address a long, somewhat complicated issue, to present a company's position or correct what it perceives as public misunderstanding)

The Wistar Institute announced its support of compromise regulations that were eventually adopted in place of the more stringent proposal.

Alert practitioners have very sensitive antennae for flukes and chance crossings that help or damage their cause. It's the great fun of PR. With Wistar, the next selected test site, South Carolina, was represented by Senator Ernest F. Hollings, chair of the subcommittee that approves appropriations to PAHO. Through this cluster of efforts, PAHO announced "The data indicated workers were *not* infected with vaccine."

A video briefed state and local officials in South Carolina. Personal meetings there and in Virginia further supported the effort. Such grassroots work is often crucial to a project's success. Wooing top officials and the media is not always enough, as Disney learned in its loss of a Manassas, Virginia, theme park.

Results of the Wistar program were unusually dramatic. It halted allegations from Argentina. Press coverage turned from unfavorable to positive. Major general and scientific press, here and in Argentina, ran positive articles. Most environmentalists who follow biotechnology came to regard the Wistar vaccine as safe and potentially beneficial to wildlife. Scientists and industry leaders who once condemned Wistar over the Argentine affair first apologized, then spoke out favorably about the vaccine.

Argentine officials quietly "backed away from their position," stopped public statements and legal action. U.S. regulators "appeared satisfied. . . . The vaccine was safe." Reasonable, rather than the proposed stringent controls were adopted as guidelines for overseas research. A PR campaign demonstrated it could save a threatened vaccine at much less cost than a nasty legal fight or adversarial advertising.

A second Hill and Knowlton save was for Dornier Medical Systems. The company was conducting clinical trials for FDA approval of a new treatment for enlarged prostates. Dornier had to treat 200 patients in six markets. Initially, Dornier ran advertisements in local market newspapers to interest patients in the experimental treatment. The ads produced hundreds of calls to Dornier's toll-free number, but insufficient numbers of volunteers. Hill and Knowlton/ Atlanta identified several problems:

- Wording in Dornier brochures explaining the procedure became more "patient friendly" and less clinical
- Press releases for local markets announced a new, free treatment

- Doctors and nurses explained the treatment in community seminars/events, as well as on local news and medical programming.

Although it was a male health problem, women, who might influence the decision for treatment, were included in the target audience. At one point during the trial studies, Dornier's parent company in Germany considered stopping clinical trails in the United States. They perceived lack of interest.

As the PR program was rolled out, patients began not only calling about the treatment, but undergoing it as well in all the required test markets. In October 1996, Dornier completed FDA clinical trials leading to approval of UROWAVE.

PR can indeed save important products, explain candidly and convincingly tough financial actions, quell rumors, even create crazes for toys. Despite critics who see only manipulation and self-serving intent, practiced intelligently and professionally PR can serve good causes, too.

NOTES

1. "Bank of Boston: A Public Relations Nightmare," *Business Week*, March 4, 1985, p. 78.

2. Ibid. The bank pleaded guilty to charges of failing to report $1.2 billion worth of international cash transactions.

3. The bank's closing sent tremors through world financial markets: the dollar dropped and gold soared. Seventy other Ohio thrift institutions closed temporarily. See James Ring Adams, "How Ohio's Home State Beat the Examiners," *The Wall Street Journal*, September 15, 1985, p. 5.

4. B of A is an important symbol in the Bay Area. Its phoenix-like rise to a banking giant symbolized San Francisco's recovery from the 1906 earthquake and fire. Its towering black stone headquarters, now sold, is an important part of the city's skyline.

5. Ronald E. Rhody, "Nobody Told Me It'd Be Like This," a Bank of America Speech, reprint of remarks made at the Public Relations Roundtable, San Francisco, May 28, 1985. For further analysis on the weakness of detailed plans under crisis, see the discussion of Tylenol in chapter 3.

6. Fredrick Koenig, "Rumors That Follow the Sun," *Across the Board*, February 1985, pp. 25–30.

7. Larry Light, with Mark Lander, "Killing a Rumor Before It Kills a Company," *Business Week*, December 24, 1990, p. 23.

306   COMMUNICATING WHEN YOUR COMPANY IS UNDER SIEGE

8. Information here has been gathered from conversations with American Banking Association representatives, bankers, and regulators. Instructions to individual banks are contained in a press kit, "Priority: The Voluntary Effort, Banker Commitment to Consumer Concerns."

9. Alicia Sevasy, *Soap Opera: The Inside Story of Procter & Gamble* (New York: Touchstone Books, 1993), p. 107.

10. Ibid., p. 166.

11. John Bussey, "Wise Guys—and Newspapers—Still Bedevil P&G About Its Infamous Corporate Logo," *The Wall Street Journal*, May 29, 1985, p. 21.

12. Sevasy, *Soap Opera*, pp. 166–68.

13. Robert A. Sigafoos, *Absolutely Positively Overnight: The Story of Federal Express* (New York: Mentor/New American Library, 1983), p. 223.

14. Anne Klein, "Historical Events: Metro Marketing," *Focus*, June 15, 1992, pp. 66–67.

15. In addition to a conversation with Richard Weiner, material was gathered from *Jack O'Dwyer's Newsletter*, December 14, 1983, p. 1; *PR News*, Case Study no. 1963; and *Burrelle's Clipping Analyst* (July 1984).

16. N. R. Kleinfield, "Coleco Moves out of the Cabbage Patch," *The New York Times*, July 21, 1985, p. F4.

17. "Some Cabbage Patch Dolls to Carry Warning Labels," *The Wall Street Journal*, January 2, 1997, p. 13.

18. "Mattel Profits Lowered By Hair-Chewing Doll," *The New York Times*, February 6, 1997, p. D4.

19. Hubert B. Herring, "Elmo Black Market Goes On-Line," ibid., December 23, 1996, p. D5.

20. Joseph Pereira, "Toy Story: How Shrewd Marketing Made Elmo a Hit," *The Wall Street Journal*, December 20, 1996, pp. B1, 7.

21. Material for this section, except where specifically noted, is from Pereira's "Toy Story," Herring's "Elmo Black Market" and Joe Sharkey's "Elmo: The Spirit of Christmas," *The New York Times*, New Jersey section, December 21, 1996, and "Answers to Most Frequently Asked Tickle Me Elmo Questions," and Susan Jelinek and others' release for Tyco Preschool by Freeman Public Relations, New York City, through telephone interview with Jelinek, January 29, 1997.

22. Joseph Berger, "Goodbye Tickle Me Elmo; Hello Beanie Babies," *The New York Times*, March 13, 1997, p. B1.

23. Ibid.

24. Ibid., p. B6.

25. Carey Geldberg, "As Sugar Fades, Hawaii Seeks a New Cash Crop," ibid., August 9, 1996, p. A16.

26. The Puna case reflects the author's own fifteen-year association with

Amfac, first as a consultant, now as a member of the board of directors; conversations with Henry A. Walker, Jr. (CEO during the Puna closing); Harry Matte (senior vice president for public affairs, based in Honolulu); the transcript of the press conference to announce the closing; various newspapers articles from the *Honolulu Bulletin* and *Star Advertiser*; and Silver Anvil Winner abstracts from 1982 and 1983.

27. Geldberg, "As Sugar Fades."

28. Both these cases were submitted for outstanding achievement awards at Hill and Knowlton, Inc.: "Rabies Vaccine Public Affairs Program for the Wistar Institute," submitted for John W. Hill Awards for Outstanding Communications Achievement, 1989; and "Dornier Medical Systems, Inc.," Submitted for Hill and Knowlton At Its Best, 1997. The author chaired both the 1989 and the 1997 panels. Material is used with permission of Hill and Knowlton.

29. James Crutchfield, "German-American Yesteryears, The Philadelphia Elite," *German Life*, February–March, 1997, p. 50.

9

Talking to Scared, Skeptical, Grasshopper Employees

> Management theory has always alternated between cold
> mathematics and warm humanism.[1]
> —JOHN MICKLETHWAIT AND ADRIAN WOOLDRIDGE

> "The modern ersatz for profundity is unintelligibility."

Mealy-mouthed obfuscations, woefully lacking veracity, abound in employee communications. They must be in deep trouble when employees seem to be listening more avidly to a corporate dropout and his dog than anyone else. About 60 million people follow Scott Adams's comic strip featuring "a sack-shaped, ever threatened corporate loser named Dilbert and Dogbert, his bespectacled canine companion."[2] Why? Because they're listening to complaints from the cubicles. Telling it as it really is. Gathering material from people's actual rather than wished-for experiences at the office.

Just a taste of comments to illustrate why Adams's books and columns are so hugely popular. Employees like to be treated like adults, recognized as valued. Instead, they get silence. Recognition breeds self-esteem, which leads to "unreasonable requests for money." Employees of the month at one company are given the Fuzzy Bunny Award by messengers in rabbit suits bearing balloons, a coffee mug, and a certificate of merit.[3]

Senior executives, alas even communicators, endlessly bore on about messages cascading down through the organization; how at the mere touch of a button messages spread like amoebas to every nook and cranny of every remote division. The zeal for hardware as a panacea is akin to little boys let loose in a toy store at Christmas, or grown men grazing through business supply depots during lunch break. But such techno-toys have downsides. While e-mail messages today get more priority attention than other means of communicating—except an irate, profane boss in the office doorway—they too may fade as fads as have hula hoops, Cabbage Patch Kids, even the primacy of fax machines.[4]

How do the messages, their veracity, begin to match sophisticated machines? Is anybody listening? Believing? Acting upon the information? Not many, as a recent Yankelovich report and Dilbert illustrate.

Jack O'Dwyer's Newsletter headlined the "alarming but understandable" steep decline in confidence accorded corporate statements. Only 55 respondents to Yankelovich's corporate survey have great confidence in such statements, down 23 per cent from just five years ago. Why? Some note it's no coincidence that this is the same level as confidence in advertising. The PR practitioners see advertising dominating their turf, quickened by going public and the many advertising/PR mergers of the last decade. Others blame control freaks "who promise management a single message orchestrated by a single source that will permeate the company and public." That's nothing new. Presidential press secretaries have honed and orchestrated the message of the day for administrations.

Other reasons include the dominance of bad corporate news—"rapacious, sometimes ruinous acquisitions, high CEO pay, scandals, and environmental abuses." Well, yes. *A Civil Action* by Jonathan Harr, recounting deaths from environmental controls and a legal system gone awry, has led the bestseller lists for months. Spin doctors further lower trust in corporate statements. Finally, O'Dwyer points to companies creating their own credibility problems by ignoring the obvious, what everybody knows.[5]

Adams makes essentially the same points, but more colorfully. The warm fuzzy "employees are our most valuable asset" cloaks the reality of treating such valuable assets "the same way a leaf blower treats leaves"—blown away. Adams also lists the great lies of management:

1. Employees are our most valuable asset.
2. I have an open-door policy.
3. You could earn more money under the new plan.
4. We're reorganizing to better serve our customers.
5. The future is bright.
6. We reward risk-takers.
7. Performance will be rewarded.

8. We don't shoot the messenger.
9. Training is a high priority.
10. I haven't heard any rumors.
11. We'll review your performance in six months.
12. Our people are the best.
13. Your input is important to us.[6]

WHY MANAGERS TURN A DEAF EAR

Skeptical young managers tune out. They resent being treated too long like children—kept in the dark until either they are needed or their heads are cut. They've been overpromised—and they remember the promises. Overcommunicated with through cloying messages from Oz-like executives, designed as a screen behind which reality is maneuvered.

Truly, here actions are speaking much louder and more convincingly than words. Large increases in senior executive compensation and bonuses, especially signing bonuses or those that reward the unprofitable performance, communicate very clearly to the just-downsized employee. Peter Drucker, in his late eighties still the most convincing critic of corporate life, says very directly that the great desire of employees to retire, to quit just as early as possible, not only flies in the face of rapidly increasing longevity, but is the greatest indictment of management.

The intentions and meanings of brash talkers like chainsaw Al Dunlap are eminently clear, but nettle just the same through their insensitivity and danger to job security. What a contrast to all this are the simple words of commitment and deeds of Aaron Feurstein, who kept most of his employees on full-pay while the burned-out Malden Mills was rebuilt. He could have walked away, but stayed. Not only were employees amazed and tearful, but the action proved to be sound marketing, too. How many stores and catalogs feature Malden Mills fabrics? How many people now seek out and buy products made with them?

Nor are academics much help in heightening the credibility or effectiveness of employee communications. They collude in cascading messages laden with jargon—normative context, human symbolic attitudes, interaction management strategies, patterning—and in qualitative research reaching such startling conclusions as that communication is a two-way process, that listening is vital. They endlessly analyze the obvious. Or develop a paradigm, a theory, then stuff it with ideas and examples, apt or not, until a simple idea bloats into a fat Strasbourg goose. Jargon-laden theories, free-floating of reality-honed experience, accomplish little.

The author cannot recount all the times she has been admonished to speak properly—more like an academic and communications professional. Others question whether she could possibly have the "terminal degree" and talk so directly. That the Ph.D. is in history, not communications, shows. The more that people invoke Harry Truman, the less they even attempt to emulate his plain speaking.

Other communicators tout the fad of the day—cross-cultural, for instance—but don't apply it. Instead of pondering whether a booklet should be translated into Spanish for Brazilian audiences (simple English, or even better, Portuguese, is a good idea), what color signifies what, where or if women executives will be accepted, they should attack the cultural dissonance right in front of them, generational and technological. Three distinct generations—pre-boomers, baby boomers, and the MTV group—compete uneasily, creating many misunderstandings in companies. As employees understandably become more mobile and less loyal, less trusting and more skeptical of messages and promises, internal communications presents a great opportunity to motivate, inform, and build that all-too-lacking but still vital trust.

Whatever the medium—newsletter, video, e-mail or face-to-face—it must be candid, believable, up-to-the moment. Of course, everyone mouths that, but too few do it. Or, to lapse into jargon: they don't walk or write the talk. Effectiveness means no more executive-ego publications, or news stale for months, or safe items of interest to no one. Properly used, employee communications can be the corporate solvent to raise realities to executive consciousness, the litmus test of how workers view management, the early radar warning of dangers and opportunities. What an important growth area for the mature public relations business!

Sound thinkers and progressive executives realize human capital drives and develops financial capital. *Focus*, the magazine of Zurich Insurance, devoted an entire issue to "The Individual and the Organization." The authors—management gurus, insurance executives, and consultants—offer many prods to conventional thinking and op-erations. Unfair and unsatisfactory as brief comments are, these at-tempt to illustrate their ideas. One suggests management by atmosphere, replacing intimidation and fear with an informality that motivates intelligent people to be productive. Others define knowl-edge management as "creating, capturing, sharing and using com-pany-wide knowledge." And trust as not only knowing there will be no retribution for intelligent mistakes, but also, more positively, as expecting ethical, predictable behavior that follows mutually under-stood protocol of work and performance. All that must begin at the top.

The danger of homogenization, not only domestically, but surely as economies globalize, is important as well. Why is intellectual mo-tivation important? Quite simply, no one jumps out of bed just to make some unknown financier seriously rich.[7]

What Your Young Managers Won't Tell You

Barbara Carmichael[8] tells an allegory of the sea that too often charac-terizes corporate communications—top down, deaf to audience, and no truthful feedback.

A captain entering a port sees a light on the horizon and fears a collision at sea. He instructs his signalman to flash the message "steer ten degrees north." Much to the captain's surprise the signal comes back, "No, you steer ten degrees south." Shocked, he responds "No, you don't understand. I'm a captain of a ship. You steer ten degrees north." And the signal comes back very quickly, "No, you turn ten degrees south. I'm a seaman." A third signal goes out, "I am a battleship. Turn ten degrees north." And the response comes, "I am a lighthouse. Turn ten degrees south."

Carmichael's point is both obvious and too often overlooked. Communicators understand very well how to use technology to send messages out, but fail to heed feedback, even from key constituen-cies. "If you think the only challenge is to get the right message out in the least amount of time with the most, best packaging, you'll fundamentally miss the point." You need information flowing back in real time to understand what you really need to say.

Too many senior executives, lamentably even communications officers, emulate the captain, arrogantly cascading messages down to the troops with scant thought of reality or what they want and need to hear. On the receiving end, young managers scared of their jobs and cynical of all those cloying messages from the chairman tune out, believe the opposite, and pick up unintended but accurate clues. They know better than to be candid, even when cajoled to be so. Whistle-blowers, truth-speakers, and even loyal devil's advocates suffer a high employment-mortality rate. So they turn off the lighthouse signals and don't stay around to watch the ship founder on the rocks of low employee morale.

Communicating with employees is scanted by too many executives, dismissed as mundane internal communications, stodgy house organ stuff, and willingly left to human resources departments. They have largely seized the opportunity, appreciate the power and needs, not always with all the expertise of professional communicators. Work forces are increasingly mobile, disaffected, pressured, or downgraded as a corporate priority. Motivating, explaining to, and retaining employees is critical. But, despite all the cooing rhetoric, the messages aren't getting through.

Technology is pushing many print media such as employee newsletters into obsolescence. Employees at one major company reported getting most company news from an internal T.V. network. Even during an important merger, e-mail, faxes, and T.V. monitors transmitted printed updates internally.[9]

Almost more than in any other field, generalities seldom hold for long in communications. Along comes *Stars and Stripes*, the newspaper burr under the saddles of military leaders. A front-page *Wall Street Journal* story, "The Pen Is Mightier," detailed its strengths and weaknesses. Reporters can ask tough questions of brass, dig up hard-hitting stories even about the Pentagon, as well as provide both a link to home and an introduction to areas of overseas deployment. But for many reasons—downsizing and some competition—readers are fewer.

Stories do not burnish military images. An exposé about financial irregularities in a military-sponsored school in Germany and "unblinking coverage of sexual harassment allegations" both make the paper controversial in military circles and gain it a begrudging respect. Freewheeling letters to the newspaper are monitored to gauge morale and to spot problems.

Why is this "house organ" still vital? *The Wall Street Journal* interviews revealed several reasons. First, reporters, knowing what soldiers will hear through command channels, go out and dig for "details that animate a colorful news story." Military deployed to trouble spots are cut off not only from families, but often from the unknown countries in which they serve. For example, a special 32-page section on the former Yugoslavia's history and disintegration enhanced understanding of the mission. The paper's independence, autonomy of its editors, and presence of an ombudsman, who can go over the publisher's head, add to credibility. Although some major U.S. newspapers have an ombudsman, the function usually is more adjudicating disputes over fairness of coverage.

To further enhance the role of *Stars and Stripes* as a community paper, carrying a mix of news and features on military topics as well as political, business, and sports news, an electronic edition will reach remote installations and cut circulation costs.

Although a study found weaknesses—bloated staff and weak financial management—it concluded that the paper's availability "remains a major quality-of-life issue for soldiers and their families"—with no viable substitutes in sight.[10]

Enhancing Effectiveness

Why aren't senior executives analyzing lack of effectiveness? Because chairman knows best. Like the old television show "Father Knows Best," such attitudes should be banished to nostalgia. Senior executives tend to view the world from their formative years and corporate perch. Former President George Bush used World War II words and symbols to explain the Gulf War to a half million young troops facing the first post–Cold War, fault-line, ethnic conflict. In contrast, the Army, cauterized in its communications during the Vietnam War, understood symbols, CNN as a strategic weapon, and visits to the front—or, in business jargon, supervision by shoe-leather. Corporate messages are often printed rather than visual. Messages from the executive offices are often suspect because they come only in time of trouble.

Gary Grates, the president of Boxenbaum Grates, New York, is convinced that "Employees, especially line employees, know and trust their first-level supervisors much more than any other level of management." Human Resources people must think of communications as a "process that includes human interaction," not just the passing along of information. "If front-line managers don't have access to top management and a steady flow of 'high-demand' information, their credibility as communicators will be worthless."[11]

Why are younger managers tuning out? A few war stories and humorous use of euphemisms illustrate:

- A very senior communications executive saw no threat to his job as his company split, laid off thousands, and lopped off even profitable divisions. He'd been in on all the strategy sessions. He'd written all the warm, fuzzy, inspirational releases, messages from the chairman, and talking points for divisional executives. He'd overlooked in his loyalty the vulnerability of his high salary and large department. The immediate assignment complete, he was called in, and, of course—you guessed it—fired.

- During a complex merger of two industry giants, a woman officer expected to be declared redundant, but as weeks wore on she was still employed. She thought. One day a human resources supervisor spotted her and asked why she was still around. They'd forgotten to tell her she'd been terminated two weeks earlier.

- Signs of the impending sale of a prestigious venture to an off-shore conglomerate were apparent for weeks. Strangers prowled offices. Doors were closed; conversations, furtive. Management was unseen and silent. Frightening rumors circulated among everyone else. A young financial analyst watched it all, but heard nothing until the evening news. There were all the usually invisible corporate leaders on television bragging about the sale, its wonderful global synergies.

  Nary a word then or ever about employee concerns. Two cardinal communications principles were broken. First, don't let employees hear news important to them first from the outside. Second, treat them like intelligent adults and address their pain and concern.

  The next morning efforts to recoup were equally ham-handed. Hastily written, incomplete memos greeted employees. Hard to believe, but communications went down hill. While leaders addressed the cosmic possibilities of the acquisition and obviously rushed about to secure their perks, apartments, and offices, employees got scant attention, save ambiguous assurances of greater opportunities in store for them. Like the communicator of the previous story, the analyst had made study after study, all fulsomely praised, as she was

316 COMMUNICATING WHEN YOUR COMPANY IS UNDER SIEGE

personally. When the carnage of redundancy began, she was assured repeatedly, until the very last day. Task done; analyst gone.

Lack of loyalty despite long, devoted service, letting the affected employee learn of his fate third- or fourth-hand, even worse from the media, is not endemic to corporations. It flourishes among pols, too. Once loyalty was the absolute coin of the realm in Washington, D.C. No more. This was brutally evident when President Clinton dropped Harold Ickes, a friend of 25 years and a tireless, highly partisan campaign aide. Although Ickes's fierce partisanship turned some influentials against him, he had hoped to succeed Leon Panetta as White House Chief of Staff.

Not only did Ickes lose out, he learned it from the public announcement of Erskine Bowles's selection. No prior notice. No conversation with the President. Even those accustomed to Mr. Clinton's demonstrated lack of loyalty were appalled. One aide said: "It was horrifying—just what you tell every corporation not to do. Did he deserve to be dumped like that? No. No one does."[12] Networking does not mean true friendship. Loyalty up is not always reciprocated by loyalty down. But, ultimately, the President breached an even more critical PR principle: Don't make those with lots of information angry with you.

Each reader could tell equally revealing tales, replete with the almost humorous euphemisms used to cloak the reality. What a contrast between how Truman fired General Douglas MacArthur during the Korean War and the mealy-mouthed explanations today. After many warnings and MacArthur's continuing military and political Caesarism, Truman said, "MacArthur left me no choice. I could no longer tolerate his insubordination." The issue was simple: civilian control of the military as constitutionally required.[13]

Once business was just as blunt. Firing was called "the axe, the boot, the chop, the elbow, the bum's rush."[14] Now, as John Ezard writes in a *Manchester Guardian Weekly* article, "Fifty Ways to Lose Your Work Force," they dress it up in polysyllables: "getting yourself out of a rut, re-rating your future, democratic streamlining, flattening organizational structure, shaping up for tomorrow." These are among the 50 euphemisms for the sack gathered by a British union in a new mini-thesaurus. Other new phrases for an age-old fate include: career realignment scheme, personal premature exit agreement, concentrating on core activities, equalization of the payroll to manpower requirements, production schedule rearrangement initiative, and re-configuring the business. Managements talk of "delayering, dehiring, deleveling, right-sizing, skill-mix readjustments, unassigning, core re-emphasis and 'volume reduction windows.' "[15]

Whatever the euphemism, it all means sacking without the employee's knowing what's going on. One union leader wondered in print if the gurus of downsizing are now beginning to question its lasting accomplishments and profitability. Isn't it time "managers of disinformation" jettison some of their favorite jargon? One could suspect that whatever is talked about most means the least. Any wonder nobody's listening?

A U.S. version, "You're Dehired," excerpted both brutal and banal euphemisms from "A Litany of Euphemisms for 'You're Fired,' " in the November 1990 issue of *Executive Recruiter News*, a newsletter for executive search consultants published in Fitzwilliam, New Hampshire.

Outplacement
Downsizing
Right-sizing
Force reduction
Work force adjustment
Indefinite idling
Redundancy elimination
Involuntary separation
Skill-mix adjustment
Work force imbalance correction
Chemistry change
Negotiated departure
Redeployment
Destaffing
Dehiring
Degrowing
Dismissal
Axed
Canned
Let go
Deselected
Decruited
Excessed

Transitioned
Vocational relocation
Release
Selective separation
Coerced transition
Executive culling
Personnel surplus reduction
Career assessment and reemployment
Fumigation.[16]

Even face-to-face firings duck candor and realities. Al Dunlap talks big and brash on television and in his book, but does he personally fire someone with the same tough gusto? Stanley Bing finds it ironic "how few of the Robespierre types" can do the job themselves. In fact, he sees "one route to salvation" for the few middle managers left (in plain speak, securing their own jobs) is being very good at firing others. No sensitive types need apply. Does fear of litigation, emotional encounters, and physical reaction turn even the toughest manager mealy-mouthed? Some cave in or compromise at the last minute, in fatter corporate times even finding another, sometimes better job for the about-to-be-terminated.

Bing's prescriptions (paraphrased and augmented by this author) seem to cloud the realities:

- "We're thinning out part of your job." Or, it's moving to a location where the employee is not located or never could/would be.
- The manager admits that he is having difficulties finding focus for the position, or that the only really suitable one is his—and he intends to keep it. The problem is that after years of wooing words, offices, salaries, perks, and prestige cultivating the now expendable one as a good staff manager, now only "worker bees" are needed and venerated. All that surely induces greater skepticism about corporate motivational messages.
- Any irrefutable cause will do, no matter how tangential—cold winters, unusually heavy rainy seasons, a rush away from the season's touted color fad, Nafta, GATT, sudden shifts in major corporate strategies—will do. Or, as Bing writes, various factors "have produced incremental need for additional margins, particularly in cost-based operations that produce no revenue, or some incomprehensible blather like that." Public relations people have taken heavy hits for years of corporate downsizing precisely because they are

viewed—not always fairly—as profit-draining rather than profit-pro-
ducing.

- "I'm only following orders."[17] After the Nuremburg trials of National Socialist leaders, isn't that totally and forever discounted as a
reason?

GENERATIONAL GAPS: XERS, BABY BOOMERS, AND WHITE HAIRS

Robert L. Dilenschneider, who heads the New York-based Dilenschneider Group, warned about "the MTV Wall" in a speech to the
International Association of Business Communicators.[18] He views
the Great Divide between youth and age not only as a de facto separation that no one planned, but also the most critical issue facing
communicators. In the workplace and socially, the clustering of
youth in one corner, age in another diminishes communications with
clients, colleagues, subordinates, and, in some cases, bosses. "Do you
read what young people read?" he asked his audience. Watch MTV?
Are your heroes those of the 25-year-olds in your office? Do you even
know whom they admire?

Names are many for this new generation: Generation X, Baby
Busters, Screen-Agers, the Cable Generation, Thirteeners, and Slack-
ers. But none satisfactorily describes the 65 million 20-to-36-year-
olds rapidly forming a critical mass. "By 1980, they outnumbered the
Baby Boomers. By the year 2000, they will number 80 million, the
largest generation ever in the United States." Langdon Jones dramatized this in *Great Expectations*, his book on the baby boomers. Attention fastens on demographic bulges—the mongoose in the belly
of the python. Why else are advertisements for hair coloring and
retirement savings becoming so prominent?

But power is shifting, according to 50-something Dilenschneider.
Ask not "how can Xers succeed in a Baby Boom work world? They
are!" "Boomers are being laid off. Look around next time you're on
a plane. You may be the oldest person." Also, Xers are flocking to
professions and jobs created by technology, global shifts, and other
factors.

Dilenschneider sees Xers molded by the convergence of several
forces: First is technology, "the DNA of business." "When I encounter voice mail, I 'feel' that I've 'missed' the person. . . . Xers 'feel'

that it's mission accomplished. And Xers like to surf the Net or Internet—a place in cyberspace" some senior executives haven't even
visited yet. Second is television, "their babysitter, best friend and
classroom." All that exposure created skepticism to consumerism
and "clunky attempts to manipulate opinions and assets." Rather
than criticize, they analyze what the medium was doing to them.
"That's how they got control over it." "This generation is media-
savvy, street-smart, skeptical and highly visual. . . . They think in
icons."

Third is social change. Many are children of divorced parents, with
no economic safety net. When mothers worked, they became latch-
key kids. The reaction? Later marriages and a sensitivity to money
akin to that of those who experienced the Great Depression.

Fourth is the end of post–World War II affluence and the rise of
global competition. When it's hard to find "a job that leads somewhere," hostilities rise between the generations.

Fifth is the emergence of romanticism, a scanting of science, and
a trusting of intuition. Young managers talk about "gut" feelings and
instincts. "Religion—or more accurately spirituality—has become
cool. Being creative is a must." Given such shifts, communicating
with Xers—motivating, marketing, even just competing with
them—poses new challenges. Among strategies Dilenschneider suggested is to think growth, not contraction. Considering work a zero-
sum game—a win for Baby-Boomers means a loss for Xers—naturally
breeds wariness or worse. "Baby Boomers have seen the enemy and
it wears plaid flannel. Xers in turn would say: I've seen the enemy
and it wears Brooks Brothers."

To counter a zero-sum game, think niches, Dilenschneider advised. Despite a glut of business communicators, there's a scarcity in
niches such as financial media, ghostwriting, damage control, and
the non-profit sector. Can't find a niche? Create one. He cited two
examples. When Ben & Jerry appeared, the world surely didn't need
another brand of ice cream. So they created a niche: Funky. "Eating
their ice cream was an 'experience.' " Jack O'Dwyer serves a public
relations niche. He packages information in a variety of forms from
newsletters to directories. Perhaps over-optimistically, Dilenschneider concluded, "the pie isn't shrinking. It's just changing."

He also suggested being visual. Xers grew up with images. To explain a reorganization, don't talk until their eyes glaze over. Illustrate the changes. *USA Today* caught the attraction of nugget stories and graphics early. It forced news snippets, color, charts, and illustrations on even staid, mainstream media. If you want to get an Xer's attention, hold the language, bring on the images.

Don't use hype. Xers have seen and heard it all many times already. Give them the cold facts and a demonstration of the product. A show, not tell. How does that translate into PR? If "you're recommending a financial services institution sponsor an ethnic festival to gain name recognition and customers," suggest the client attend an ethnic festival to a personal appraisal, or show video tapes of festivals you've coordinated. And don't forget the effective cost per new customer at the festival.

Xers seek warranties or money-back guarantees, accountability. "Should PR practitioners think about giving warranties?" Suppose when we're ghostwriting and promoting a book, we guarantee a client so many books will be sold by a certain date, and give a rebate if we don't deliver.

Dilenschneider urged addressing Xers' self-interest. "Baby Boomers could 'afford' to be idealistic . . . to demand the warm and fuzzies from their jobs." For Xers, going to work is about making money and paying bills, not making a difference or changing the system. They don't want work cutting in on family activities. Also, they believe deeply in themselves, despite having gone through the wringer. "All hell will break loose if you tamper with their confidence." They deify creativity. "If a job is boring, they'll probably quit or do it badly." Highlight the imagination involved in assignments. "Show that you too are creative."

How can older managers stay in touch with Xers? See their needs and interests, not yours. Read what they read. "Watch what they watch, listen to what they listen to." *Wired*, for instance. Be enthusiastic to new approaches. Listen. "Old fogeys are always talking."

Dilenschneider echoed the author's own MBA classroom assessments. Generation X has a lot going for it. "They love technology. They have no illusions about work. They're focused. And they have a spiritual underpinning which helps them get through work's ups and downs. But they still must acquire wisdom and that comes from the seasoned pros in the office."

QUIDDIES: QUESTING, UPWARDLY INTELLIGENT DOERS

Stereotypes, generational generalizations, even gross deploring fall before the fresh green shoots of change emerging among some MBA students. They are questioning such prevailing stereotypes and verities as addiction to money, career, and quantification regardless of the cost to long-range, analytical thinking or to the well-rounded lifestyle that produces survival, business and personal, over the long haul. The Quiddies (questing upwardly, intelligent doers) are contesting the decade-long Yuppie dominance. So are events.

As with any change, trace-lines are faint, detected in important interstices of time and talk: a moment in a professor's office, personal notes written on term papers and examinations, the flash point of excitement during discussions, or at-home visits by students bearing term papers, but in truth just wanting to talk off campus. Public relations, well taught and practiced, can be the early radar (and encouragement) for such change.

Quiddie values are most evident in issues of sheer quantification opposed to no single, easy answers; in hubris, ethics, and social entrepreneurialism; in such lifestyle values as friends, reading, and career decisions; and in the touchstone of most business debates today: Is the frenzy of mergers and acquisitions an unqualified good for the future of United States business and for the milieu?

Let's examine each of these issues in more detail. First, quantification—it is never enough. Although purely numerical analysis has been demonstrated repeatedly as incomplete, even dangerous to sound decision-making, quantifiers cling to their craft as threatened ideologues do. Such thinking in public situations can be disastrous.

Into the author's public relations classes march many quantifiers, soon baffled by the very idea that there is no easy answer, indeed if any at all, to many public issues. Public relations simply is not easily added up. As student quantifiers begin reading with an eye to how public events impact the bottom line, their analysis and spirit change. By the final examination—questioning how a CEO would handle a surprising, highly visible problem—numbers were absent from their answers. Rather, they spent two hours after class debating possible solutions.

Most Quiddies escape the overbearing hubris that has characterized too many Yuppies. A decade ago, a panel of Ivy League MBA students first lectured the senior management of an insurance company about how smart they were, how lucky any company would be to hire them, and how much it would cost (lots), then told industry veterans, who had produced profits before the panel members were born, how to run their business.

Another young woman, explaining her career trajectory straight to a vice presidency by 30, was stunned when a seasoned executive asked her what would happen if she were in the wrong place at the wrong time. She was polite and bland, but the meaning of her answer was very clear: I'm too smart to make that mistake.

At one elite business school seminar, students nestled comfortably as birdies in a nest, awaiting worms of wisdom, the food for success, to be delivered up automatically and painlessly. Have market share and other details of the product under discussion at their fingertips? Someone will supply them. Their shock of realism will be chilling. Former Brown President Vartan Gregorian warns: we teach our students to deal with success, but never failure.

The Quiddie approach is tinged with pragmatism, some fear and uncertainty, but a sure knowledge that the U.S. dominance such as that enjoyed by the Harvard Business School Class of '49 is gone, probably forever. (This class the dollars fell on walked into markets starving for U.S. goods, services, and expertise.) Quiddies know there will be no certainties in their careers. They work, many full-time, come to class prepared, and fully understand they must produce.

Ethics, too often kissed-off as a commodity lacking contribution to the bottom line, cannot be ignored by Quiddies. They respond skeptically and, in some cases, resentfully. Some feel they are suffering the sins of their bosses. Pressured for good numbers, caught by intense competition, the supervisors may seem less sensitive to the cost of unethical behavior. "Don't debate me; just do it."

Entrepreneurialism lured Yuppies with dreams of fast, big bucks translated into instant celebrity, huge financial returns, and retirement by 30. Undergraduate business students, members of an entrepreneurial club, stunned even their academic advisers. They wanted to talk, not of chips and webs, but of social entrepreneurialism—how to make Newark's social services work better, help the Bronx homeless, or tackle drugs.

Lifestyle—friends, novels, and career choices. In the author's classes many guest lecturers—operating executives, journalists, and public relations practitioners—are friends of many years. Without realizing it, they and she emphasized how, in the best of corporate times and the worst, a circle of compassionate, intelligent confidants makes the difference. One speaker, who particularly stressed friendship, was collared by several students, themselves largely bereft of friends in business, to ask how this unique idea worked. Compare that to a 40-something editor who during a similar discussion said: "we were too competitive, too selfish to find time for friends."

Novels. Yuppies consume the product. Quiddies find insight and refreshment. An illustration of each. An investment banker, just released from grueling merger negotiations into gorgeous resort sunshine, was consuming Tom Wolfe's *Bonfire of the Vanities*. Was he enjoying the sage and witty insights of our Dickens, our Dostoevski? Of course not. He was preparing to hold his own on "lemon tarts" and "masters of the universe" at his next power breakfast.

In contrast, the author assigned Heinrich Böll's *The Lost Honor of Katherina Blum*, a chilling, fictional account of press harassment. Many read it before classes began. All acted as if greatly appreciated cool water was being poured over intellectual sponges dried out by theories free-floating of reality and dull textbooks. Many graduate students yearn for more realism, breadth, and, yes, the fiction that illustrates facts sometimes better than the facts themselves.

Lifestyles of the rich and famous. Yuppies are legendary for addiction to work and money, leaving family, physical and mental restocking to some nebulous future that never seems to have time to arrive. A recent television sequence showed a career woman just told by her physician she cannot have children. Her husband rushes in late from a meeting. Wife says: "We can't have children. Goodbye. I'm late for a meeting. Doctor, you tell him why."

In contrast is a career decision made by a very bright, thoughtful accountant. He had interned in a Big Six firm, working long hours, traveling and commuting. As he looked toward graduation, career, and marriage, he chose a job certain never to give him the money, perks, and prestige of a Big Six firm. It would give him time to be a husband, father, and productive, hopefully long-lived human being. A similar choice was made by a male management counselor in a large firm. Though intrigued by politics, he opted out of public office at 30 to participate more fully in raising a child.

Students sometimes are ahead of their managers and professors in sensing shifts and changes in business today. For example, a speaker espoused the purely financial line: junk bonds are changing the face of America, providing access to capital markets for firms previously locked out, and displacing fat, incompetent managements—all without withering R and D funds or our global competitive edge.

Some in the audience questioned the social impact of $20,000-a-year workers being numbers-crunched out of jobs they can never hope to duplicate. Others recounted personal pain. Will we play this game for a short time and pay for it for a very long time?

Many additional trace-lines of change could be cited—occasional sharing of ideas rather than rampant competition, the gentleness with which some contest authority, the gasp of sadness and concern when a guest speaker, outlining the Singer Company takeover, said: "And the next day I walked into my office to learn the CEO had dropped dead two hours earlier."

The first fragile green shoots of change are there for those who look and are willing to encourage. Just as, a decade or more ago, corporate executives put the bloom and dollars on MBA Yuppie attitudes, now it behooves managers to cultivate the qualities of the Quiddies—questing, upwardly intelligent doers. They're a wonderful, tough yet tender, promising new breed.[19]

TRUST, WHAT'S THAT?

Downsizing, narrowing the stewardship for employees and communities, plus many communications misfires and mistakes, have seriously eroded management/employee relations. Daniel Yankelovich detailed these problems and prescriptions to correct them in a 1994 speech to senior public relations officers attending Page Society meetings.[20]

He noted many managements have strained to the breaking point their relationship with employees. How? Management's focus on shareholder value, reengineering, and TQM has transmitted a confusing mixed message to employees, not intended, but widely perceived. One tone is all uplift and promise: "Our corporate vision reveals an exciting path to future success in the new global economy." It can become a reality only "if you, our people, buy into it and give it every ounce of dedication and commitment you have.

Our success depends on you." Contradicting that is: "Our number one goal is to maximize shareholder value." "To achieve that goal, you, the employees, are expendable. We expect loyalty, dedication, and top performance . . . but understand we owe you nothing in return." Little wonder such mixed messages produce strain, confusion, and conflict. A classic symptom of a failing relationship, Yankelovich explains, is feeling "whipped around by contradictory signals."

These problems began in the 1980s when employers greatly narrowed the scope of their stewardship. Yankelovich noted that when he started his career in the early 1950s, he watched corporate clients broaden their view of stewardship and its responsibilities. By the early 1970s, it had evolved into balancing concerns of multiple constituencies: shareholders, employees, customers, suppliers, and the community, local and national. Now this outlook has narrowed, abruptly, to a single-minded focus on shareholders, which means creating shareholder value by cutting costs, through restructuring, downsizing, and slashing employee benefits.

Initially, employees did not respond. But, gradually, experiences with downsizing, chipping away at health care, retirement, and job security taught employees not to assume a secure job environment. Yankelovich's firm's annual Trend Tracking Study shows four patterns of employee response:

- No belief either in lifetime job security or in employer loyalty and concern
- Expecting rewards for learning and expanding skills has become vulnerability —a more expensive worker
- Recognition that TQM and other quality programs can be translated into downsizing, devaluating the employee and his job
- Work, to many, has become a less reliable source of satisfaction and rewards other than money.

These factors, accelerated by economic pressures, are revising downward "expectations about accumulating material wealth to achieve success." Yankelovich's studies found "less conviction that possessions equal status." Increasingly, success is being redefined as quality of life—"good relationships, less stress, being healthy and looking good, and living in a clean, healthy and safe environment—not what you own."

Another shift, surveys reveal, is away from working for large companies, toward working for small organizations. They may be no more secure, but offer rewards and satisfaction large companies don't. "The employees' contribution is seen and known; they are 'in the know,' and participate in decision-making."

Such values are one of very few common denominators that bridge the startling generation gap between Boomers and post-Boomers. Each is shaped by its own unique experience. Those in their 30s and 40s, raised when affluence dominated, produced four assumptions:

- Self-sacrifice is a thing of the past.
- Why choose, when "you can have everything"?
- Self-expression, self-fulfillment, self-satisfaction are moral rights.
- "Me and my needs" come first.

"These assumptions helped shape . . . the desire to do things 'my own way,' exercise maximum control, and manipulate other people for one's own ends. Characteristically, yuppies are needy and demanding people who crave attention and insist on their prerogatives."

While these unappealing traits only mildly irritate older people, they drive generation Xers to burn with resentment. "Their own shaping experience was not the presumption of affluence . . . plenty of everything for everyone, including jobs, security, money, parental attention, automatic raises, sex without AIDS, and a secure future." Now "the 20-somethings want these goodies, but fear the Boomer generation, like swarms of locusts, is devouring everything in sight."

MBA students discussing Yankelovich's point think Boomers not only ate their lunch, but dominated their music, icons, and fads. They resent following in their shadow. They are "very practical and less self-indulgent or ideological than Boomers." Most will do anything to succeed, but tend "to be cynical about large corporations and suspect it is suicidal to depend on them." "As workers they tend to be enigmatic—either hostile (chip-on-the-shoulder) or private, closed off, and reserved. Not an easy generation for employers to understand."

Often obscured by emphasis on a multi-cultural, multi-racial, global workplace is the challenge of managing three disparate generations—50 +, 30–50, and the 20-somethings. Pre-Boomers are resentful because the rules changed in mid-game. Boomers and Yuppies are shifting their ambitions and self-preoccupations from the workplace to cultivating their own "quality of life" garden. Post-Yuppies are mistrustful, resentful, practical, and desperately craving their piece of the action, but fearful Yuppies may have stolen it from them. Only good will and flexibility can bridge the gaps.

To Yankelovich, the question of will is particularly troubling. While some companies will develop the indispensable will to change, others may play ostrich when confronted by mixed corporate messages—"We don't need you; you are expendable," and simultaneously, "We desperately need you; you are indispensable." The contradiction is driven by two very different logics: the 1980s and the 1990s.

During the former, a period of brutal global competition, top management compensation depended on performance measured in share price. An ever-larger chunk of compensation was based on stock options. Raising the stock price demands greatly improved profitability. That means only one thing: cutting the fat to the bone or employing a large, mobile, less costly global labor force—not just unskilled labor: Top-notch Russian scientists can be hired for $35 a month. Such mobility lessens control, the point former Labor Secretary Robert Reich makes in his study *The Work of Nations*. As a result, the domestic labor market is weak and likely to remain so. The unions have lost much of their clout. With the downsizing of middle-management, experienced people are available to work part-time or freelance without benefits or raises. But restructuring and reengineering also broadcasts loud and painfully: "You are dispensable."

The newer logic of the '90s begins with similar words, according to Yankelovich, but reaches the opposite conclusions. "Brutal global competition . . . greater emphasis on performance . . . rich rewards that come only with outstanding profit performance." But profitability will come less from rapid growth in expanding markets than through strengthening market share at someone else's expense. This calls for a customer focus strategy, a superior level of knowing their product, and servicing needs better than the competition. That's possible only through highly motivated employees, not just those going through the motions and doing the minimum. Only employees motivated to share the vision and give their utmost in skill, dedication, and commitment can achieve this.

Attitudes of companies following the '80s logic, according to Yankelovich, "are wholly impersonal. . . . You manage people the same way you manage money." Wrong! People react; machines and money do not. When employees "feel expendable or exploited," they hold back as much as they can without risking their jobs. "They may sell their raw labor for capital, but not their dedication or loyalty or commitment." Even companies that talk the second logic haven't abandoned earlier attitudes. "Discretionary effort" may be a way out of this bind. This is the interest and initiative, motivation, creativity, responsibility, dedication, and loyalty individuals expend beyond the minimum needed to keep their jobs. Individuals themselves control this, not employers.

The amount of discretionary effort required varies greatly—partly in quantity of production, literally in quality and customer focus. In a world awash with bigness and technology, businesses who manage discretionary effort, whose employees care about the customer, have the competitive edge.

Finally, Yankelovich identified how managements must restore badly frayed bonds of trust with their employees.

1. *Treating people as considerately as dividends.*

Give the same care and attention to employees' job security as you give to dividends. As a director 20 years ago Yankelovich was impressed with the great time and effort management devoted to dividend policy. It outstripped time devoted to discussion of employee policy by a ratio of about 20 to 1. Corporate managements understand wide fluctuations in the dividend can undermine stockholder trust, but not the equally important swings in employment.

Differences in philosophy impinge upon this issue. Yankelovich cites differences in dividend policy as a reason for the breakdown in TCI and Bell Atlantic negotiations. John Malone of TCI urged that Bell Atlantic cut its dividend. He had other uses for the capital. Compelling business logic. Bell Atlantic's CEO recognized the harvest of stockholders' mistrust, confusion, and disillusionment that would result.

2. *Living the Jenkins Principle*

Yankelovich explained he stumbled on the Jenkins Principle while studying why a highly profitable and successful Florida supermarket chain paid its employees less than unionized chains, yet was totally immune to unionization. During the study, virtually every employee repeated one particular phrase when referring to the CEO, George Jenkins, "He didn't have to do that." One employee recounted when he was ill, Jenkins had visited him in the hospital twice.

What does "He didn't have to do that" mean? The unwritten contract that dominates employer-and-employee relations is more powerful than any written contract. "All employees develop, however inarticulate, a set of quid pro quos. As long as these expectations are met, the relationship is stable." If violated by restructuring, reengineering, and the use of TQM to cut jobs, the unwritten contract is threatened.

To compensate, management must apply the Jenkins Principle to job security for the survivors. There are many different ways. Sidney Harman, founder and CEO of Harman International, started a number of small ancillary businesses to absorb redundant employees. Workers at his manufacturing company not needed temporarily on the line can work with customers. Instead of outsourcing certain services, Harman lets his own people perform them. During business downturns, employees make parts instead of buying them from suppliers. Finally, the company has initiated a number of on-site training, retraining, and self-education programs, and experimented with "allowing workers to share in the proceeds of cost savings produced."[21] Harman International's 7,929 employees recognize this is something "the company didn't have to do." It is a measure of management concern with their well-being and security. In a crunch time, they are likely to trust such management and give it the benefit of the doubt.

3. Learning to dialogue

Management should accelerate the transition from the traditional command and control, which is rapidly losing favor to the new coaching/teamwork styles. Yet this transition is not only very difficult, but fatally prone to mistakes. "The single best way to make the transition is by cultivating dialogue, substituting it for the traditional top-down communications." "The fall-off of accurate communications among layers is huge," Yankelovich noted. A coaching/teamwork style flourishes only in corporate cultures of straight talk and truth-telling, autonomy and responsibility. It mobilizes people's discretionary effort. Without learning the art of dialogue, it is difficult, if not impossible. Both sides must modify their positions to accommodate the other. If successful, they can create common ground, acknowledge and accept differences, thus opening themselves to compromise.

This "is far different from selling, persuading, educating, or imparting information and far more intense than casual conversation. It is at once an act of empathy, listening, and communicating. It is the indispensable gift of seeing an issue from a variety of points of view." Yankelovich is concerned less with the creativity of management to develop sound ways to strengthen these bonds than with the will to implement and sustain them.

COMMUNICATING ACROSS OTHER CULTURES

Communicating to various generations and interest groups is challenging enough, but communicating across cultures that hardly know or care about one another is worse. Although a potential growth area for PR, it is viewed very warily, particularly by myopic U.S. counselors. Lack of knowledge, sensitivity, and caring stand in the way. Cuban-born Robert C. Goizueta, the late chairman and CEO of Coca-Cola, said if he didn't hear accents in executive suites, the company wasn't global. Some lapses are serious, other humorous, but all impede empathy and business. Just a few examples gathered from the author's experience and that of others.

During doctoral research in Sâo Paulo, Brazil, the author was asked to assess market potential for both PR and advertising services, and determine why associated firms were rather frosty and cooperated minimally. In a report circulated among the firm's senior management, she commented that Paulistas resented instructions from New York to have releases translated into Spanish for the local press or to hire a Spanish interpreter for visiting executives. "What the hell's wrong with that?" bellowed one executive. "Because they speak Portuguese," she replied. Lest anyone delude themselves that that problem is solved, she still must explain the joke. Even if an executive lacks the language of the land he's visiting, in-depth knowledge of the culture or history assuages the anger. A Rio de Janeiro television journalist was thoroughly annoyed by an English-only visitor. It all changed on the Avenida Rio Branco, when the visitor asked which Rio Branco it was named for. The journalist mellowed. "You mean you know there were two?"

Color, public shows of affection and gifts, when and what to give are details that matter. Starting a new venture in China with white boutonnieres displays ignorance. White signifies mourning, not celebrating. When the author once hugged a Japanese college classmate in Tokyo before some academics, she was first admonished that wasn't done, then asked how she knew a Japanese woman so well.

James Lane, who directed Hill and Knowlton operations around the Pacific Rim for many years, tells this story at the height of the Vietnam War. The Australian hosts of the cocktail party invited both U.S. and North Vietnamese guests. Novel in itself, then. Lane, being an inquisitive person, struck up a conversation with a North Vietnamese. It devolved around staying power and concept of time. Lane, a U.S. citizen, relates, "I knew we were in trouble because we wanted quick closure to the war. The Vietnamese time frame was years, decades." He warns, as do others experienced in working in and with other cultures, not to take too much of ourselves, our unexamined assumptions into situations. He uses baseball to illustrate. U.S. teams will—and do—play all night to reach a decision. Japanese teams after nine innings stop—win, lose, or tie.

Although many cultures are increasingly important to companies and communicators, an in-depth look at the Japanese market will illustrate essential points. Roy Sanada, president of Japanese Counselors, Inc., spoke in English to senior U.S. practitioners.[22] One must ask how many American executives could give a similar speech in Japanese, German, Russian? Few!

Following the theme "Globalization of Business and Its Impact on Communications," Sanada distinguished between international, which he felt Japan PR people were good at, and global. Being international means understanding things foreign—customs, characteristics, and values. Ever since the 1868 opening of Japan following the Meiji Restoration and ending of the feudal era, "Japanese have very diligently worked to understand different cultures" to "modernize" and "catch up" to the West, Sanada noted. This has entailed absorbing language, products, literature, art, science and medicine, legal and political practices, basically within Japan, rather than abroad.

When the yen's value rose greatly in the mid-1980s, many, many Japanese companies were forced to establish full-fledged operations off-shore. Coupled with a shrinking globe and an emerging world community, Japanese had to go global, requiring the "ability to adapt to different values, customs and characteristics." Just understanding is no longer enough. Once, NEC was "as Japanese" a company as one could find. Now it employs more than 7,000 Americans just at U.S. operations. "Even with superior products at competitive prices," NEC can succeed only by adapting to U.S. ways.

Although the art, science, and objectives of public relations in Japan are quite similar to those in the United States, practice and methodology vary substantially. For example, there are no Japanese words for communication or public relations. Promotion is based on seniority, not achievement, within a company rather than across trade labor unions. All require different approaches for the public relations practitioner, as do combating myths held by Americans, even those residing in Tokyo. Sanada cited three myths:

1. Japan runs a tremendous trade surplus with the United States. True, but the surplus actually comes from only two product categories, autos and electronics; also, trade figures do not include direct investment or the "invisible trade." All those Coca-Cola products, Schick safety razors, Proctor & Gamble health-care and toiletry goods, money spent by the 120 million Japanese who went to Tokyo Disneyland in 1991 do not show up in the trade figures.

2. Japan is a homogeneous society. Although the country may be a 99 per cent homogeneous race and speak one language, corporations and the generations vary greatly. Teenagers and young adults, who have not faced post-war hardships, are astoundingly different in customs and behavior from their predecessors. Not so much "westernized" as "modernized."

3. The Japanese woman's place is in the home. No longer—60 percent work.

However, Sanada noted nine cultural differences that do influence communication and public relations:

- *Mura-Ishiki* (The Village Mentality). As a densely populated, agrarian island country, Japanese tended to be less mobile than societies dependent on hunting or cattle; hence most relationships are long lasting. Identification and harmony among village members are more highly valued than an individual's personal desires. In corporations, group consciousness is not just loyalty, but reflects the need to establish one's identity based on the group, not individually.

- Social Rules *vs*. Morals. In contrast to Judeo-Christian moral-based societies, Japan is rule-based, rooted in the village mentality and the influence of Confucian and Buddhist values. Japanese aim to maintain social order and avoid shame; Western counterparts "do good" and avoid guilt. Rather than consider absolute rights and wrongs, Japanese obey social rules that change and vary according to the situation.

- *Tatama* and *Honne*. To create the appearance of social harmony, communication is often indirect or "grey." Even diverse opinions are expressed with "*tatamae*, truth for public consumption." "To express 'honne,' or one's 'true feelings' can lead to shaming someone or disrupting the social order."

- *Ishen Denshin* (feelings conveyed without words). Communication depends on situational social rules rather than individual principles. Hence, "Japanese are adept at reading each other's minds and true feelings without words." "Mood" commercials on television seem too indirect to most Westerners. But "Japanese have a great respect for the understated. "Silence Is Expression." "Symbols are very powerful."

- *Nemawashi* (consensus-building). Decision-making is based on consensus rather than majority or authority rule. To avoid shaming anyone, Japanese devote time and energy to laying the groundwork, a bottom-up process, to reach a decision. With each member given a sense of involvement, responsibility is collective, not the province of one authority.

- *Deru Kugi Wa Utareru* (The nail that sticks out gets hammered). An individual who disrupts the social harmony experiences *murahachibu* or village ostracism. "Self-promoters, even if not at the expense of others, are often labelled renegades and indirectly sabotaged by colleagues."

- Process Over Actual Results. For a samurai, winning or losing was important, but less so than dedication to effort and the way he won or lost. The process leading to a contract, not its wording, establishes the business relationship. How did the sides exchange ideas? Negotiate and arrive at an agreement? Mutual trust, faith, and understanding, not profitability, dictate the terms. A rush to litigation to resolve differences is rare in Japan. Normally, parties themselves attempt a compromise. If unsuccessful, a third party, perhaps a senior figure in the industry, tries. "Going to a lawyer is the absolute last resort and signifies that trust and the process . . . have broken down."

- Trusting Authority. Because Japanese "are brought up to trust authority to do the right thing," employers generally take a dim view of an employee who makes individual demands, even if warranted.
- Is there consumerism in Japan? Despite economic success in the '80's, Sanada still sees a "we are poor" mentality stemming from paucity of natural resources and post–World War II rebuilding. "Sacrifice for the country's economic well-being" was led by Japan, Inc., an "invisible coalition of bureaucracy, leading universities and the manufacturing sector." Can such success be sustained? "How long can Japan continue as a nation of savers and investors? Of the hard-working? Of the financially undemanding?" A generation of consumers, the first not to know hardship, is being exposed to other, "richer" lifestyles. Will traditional patterns hold? Maybe, maybe not. Whatever the pattern, it will vary from the U.S. and, hence, its public relations.

One could argue that PR illustrates a stage in a society's development and modernization. Often it lags advertising by some 20 years. PR often starts with a specific need or model. In Brazil the first thrust was integrating rural workers, minimally literate or less, into workplaces of the rapidly industrializing areas around Sâo Paulo and Belo Horizonte. Later, U.S. practice became the model.

Sanada sees the Japanese taking a low-key approach to self-advocacy, not formally interacting and communicating with publics to persuade. Even so, all the large "firms have some type of internal public relations department." The Public Relations Society of Japan has more than 500 members. Four elements affect their PR environment.

Freedom of Information. Freedom of speech and press are basic rights, but do not include freedom of information. Hence, public relations practitioners must be more careful than American counterparts. Because information is very much top-down, without cynical scrutiny, there is greater acceptance of media information as truth. However, "often the media is treated as no more than a 'house organ' of Japan, Inc."

A *National Mass Media.* Despite some local media, basically, news and editorial are national. The industrialized world's most widely circulated general newspaper, *Yomiuri,* has a circulation of more then

10 million, and the business/economic daily, *Nikkei*, more then 3 million.

Press Club System. "A unique (some would say primitive) system of press clubs are organized around industry-specific or government-specific functions." These clubs, begun as "information-sharing" circles following the war, "have grown into powerful, exclusionary organizations." Of the 76 Tokyo press clubs, 49 are government-related, 18 private industry–related, and 2 are for political parties. A new government trade policy would be announced at the Ministry of International Trade and Industry. Nissan would announce the launch of a new car or joint-venture at the Economic Federation Press Club. Newcomers or those who lack an established identity encounter difficulty using these clubs, even if their information is very newsworthy and they work with a public relations firm.

Press clubs neither are exclusive nor compete for information. A journalist, instead of running an exclusive story, will share the information with other press club members, who represent competing publications. Instead of aggressive investigative reporting, journalists wait for information to be provided. Members track government, police, or company announcements. An independent interview, contradicting the official announcement, is very risky. The journalist may not receive information or answers to his questions in the future—a type of "village ostracizing." Foreign companies, unable to make formal announcements at press clubs, can contact media individually. Although this is inefficient and reduces the chance for placement, Sanada sees this as the only solution for now. The 500-member Foreign Correspondents' Club of Japan, the world's second largest after Washington, is trying to secure "fair and equal" access to information announced at press clubs for non-Japanese, hence non-member journalists.

Perhaps this distinction actually is more apparent than real. "Herd journalism," litigation fears, and ostracizing, formal or functional, of "offending" journalists, make tough-questioning, scoop-seeking journalists much less a factor in the U.S. Did journalists question the milk-run safety messages of NASA's PR? Do they protect their best leakers even at the expense of a major story? Are they too supine and supportive of a media-savvy President? Too much linked by the reality or aspirations of elite education, income, and class to major politicians? The initial dismissal of Paula Jones's charges against

President Clinton because of "big hair" and "trailer trash" stereotypes raises questions of U.S. journalists going against the grain. Perhaps it is more self-editing than externally imposed, but is the result much different than in Japan?

Consultancies. External consultation—legal, accounting, and public relations—are less accepted in Japan. Prospecting business becomes very difficult even for firms offering a quality product at a reasonable price. "Getting in the door can be a long process." Once in and accepted as a trustworthy partner, practitioners can grow the business without constant competitive reviews. Consultants are oriented toward "hardware"—a message or a communication tool, such as a corporate profile—and largely excluded from strategic counseling or introducing new ideas.

Sounds like the bleat of many U.S. communicators who resist being restricted to projects, media, and tactics and being excluded from broad corporate strategies. They bear some blame by not thinking management strategy or being strong, effective advocates of their broader capabilities.

In conclusion, Sanada offered U.S. PR people some guidelines to successful practice in Japan:

Play Strong Defense and Smart Offense • Advocate a communication policy of speaking with "one consistent voice, respond efficiently and positively to inquiries." Credibility is based on deeds, not words. Once established, a company can take a smart offense—emphasizing its deeds and philosophy, but letting others say "you're number one." Non-Japanese companies may use aggressive messages. A Japanese firm establishes positive public identities through messages that balance subtlety and flair. In the United States brands establish the corporate identity. In Japan, products are measured primarily by trade customers and by the company's attributes, not the brand's. "The corporate logo and identity are the main focus of marketing communication."

An "invisible" collective unit makes decisions • Sanada advised patience, playing the *nemawashi* game when communicating to employees, clients, or external audiences. Misunderstandings are frequent. An oral "yes" less often means "I agree with your proposal" than "I understand it." This implies a review for a response at a later date—often much later.

Work to understand the Honne, *true feelings* • Unlike the bluntness and quick decisions of U.S. business meetings, much said at a Japanese meeting, be it internal, with a trading partner or even a government official, will not reflect true feelings. "After-hour, informal get-togethers are an excellent, if not only, way to communicate openly and honestly." Foreign clients experiencing "communication difficulties" might host "*nomyunication* get-togethers." "*Nomyunication*," a made-up word, consists of "*nomu*," to drink, and "communication." "Alcohol is a very heavy social lubricant in Japan."

Employees are your most important public • U.S. companies mouth this, but "in Japan, one must communicate often and empathically to employees, both on formal and [on] informal occasions." Management/labor relations are not adversarial, but structured for compromise and shared responsibility. A Japanese management "will take voluntary pay cuts in hard times to communicate their wish to maintain village harmony." Several foreign capital companies in Japan faced lawsuits after layoffs, based not on legal rights, but on breaking the social order.

Do not debate in public • An executive wanting to communicate an idea different from the consensus should do so during the *nemawashi* process, not publicly. "One who debates, even with logic on his side, is seen as [a] disrupter of social harmony." This accounts for the absence of comparative advertising. Pepsi-Cola ran a very controversial comparative ad campaign against Coca-Cola, which boosted Pepsi sales by double digits, but Coca-Cola's market share is still 10 times greater and its overall business 30 times larger than Pepsi's. Sanada assessed Pepsi-Cola's success with the comparative advertising: "if you are going to be the nail that sticks out, do so by so much that you cannot be hammered."

Take a long-term approach to media relations • Keep disseminating objective information even if it doesn't produce publicity short-term. Augment "standard press releases, media seminars, and interviews with informal measures such as year-end courtesy calls with gifts." Journalists, rotated about every two years to a different department or industry, come to rely on a company's information. Personal relationships facilitate the barter of information in return for media exposure.

Government lobbying is format as much as content • No matter how logical a position, it will not bear fruit without the right lobbyists—usually senior executives, sometimes from the home office, formally introduced by an insider. "Most big Japanese companies [employ] an ex-government official" as such an adviser.

Crisis management: Show Shame and Regret • During a crisis, "one must communicate regret and shame, regardless of the circumstances," then take corrective action. If an airliner crashes, the company president must call a press conference, apologize for the incident, and announce his resignation, even if the airline is not at fault. This indicates sincerity, not guilt, as it would in Western culture. Such behavior is exerted socially, not legally. "Retribution is often based on the culprit's attitude subsequent to the event, rather than the action itself."

Culture in Crashes

Seldom was such a cultural difference in crisis management revealed as starkly as the August 12, 1986, JAL crash and the December 21, 1988, Pan Am 103 explosion over Lockerbie, Scotland. Both achieved unenviable distinction: JAL's 524 fatalities was the worst until then in a single air crash; Pan Am's, the worst in its history and in Great Britain. All 259 aboard and 11 on the ground were killed. Both crises managements reflected the expectations of country and corporate cultures. Public information flow, CEO visibility, care for families, and the way multinational (Scotland, UK, West Germany, United States, Israel, Finland and several Middle Eastern) investigations were conducted reveal deep cultural differences. The striking contrast between JAL and Pan Am is meant to illuminate these differences, not to assess the humanness or effectiveness of one or the other.

In all crashes, the press immediately wants names and numbers of survivors and dead. JAL almost immediately reported the exact—and correct—number of passengers. Communicators appeared to have good control over information flows. Technical people gave detailed reports, including even conversations between the cockpit and the control center. Within minutes, the crash became a national crisis for the Japanese, who view themselves as a giant extended family. Throughout the night, television stations broadcast passengers' names. Buses loaded with relatives arrived at the small town nearest the crash sight that night; others were flown to Tokyo from Osaka the next morning so that they too could journey to Nagano. As each person deplaned in Tokyo's Haneda Airport, JAL's President Yasumoto Takagi stood at the foot of the stairs, bowing deeply. At a November news conference he said, "I cannot find appropriate words to express my apology." Not behavior expected of a United States executive.

This reaction reveals not only the Japanese tendency toward "group think," but the consciousness of equality for each member of the group as well. What is regarded as "just" or "moral" is what everyone in a particular group, at a particular place, at a particular time agrees is right. As a result, the spokesperson or president of an airline responds and behaves according to the way the majority defines "just and proper." News is received differently. JAL's president's visibility and his offer to resign responded to his deep thoughts and feelings. In a country where nonverbal communication is far more crucial and effective than the spoken, not only are live action reports relevant, but so are the images and aftershock of the crisis.

Despite JAL's best efforts, it could not successfully assuage the anger of all important families of the victims. Six families refused to participate in memorial services. None, however, filed lawsuits. Perhaps the airline's quick admission of responsibility and assistance to family members created a web of gratitude and obligation that discouraged legal remedies. Granted: the culture is far less litigious than the U.S.'s.

From the day of the accident, the airline had mobilized its staff, from the president down, to offer the gestures of apology and regret that Japanese require at such times. When family members had to travel to a small mountain village to identify bodies, airline staff accompanied them, paying all expenses, bringing them food, drink, and clean clothes. Later, airline staff members assisted each family in arranging funerals and blocking intrusive reporters. JAL spent $1.5 million on two elaborate memorial services. It dispatched executives to every victim's funeral although some were asked to leave. JAL also established a scholarship fund for children whose parents died in the crash.

At the last memorial service in Tokyo on October 24, 1985, airline employees stood in tribute as a JAL vice president approached the altar, holding a list of victims' names with both hands, a Japanese mark of respect, and bowing deeply to the families. He placed the list on the altar. President Takagi then delivered a short eulogy. "To the bereaved, all we can do is try our utmost to help you and ease your pain as best we can. To those who were lost, I cannot restrain my tears of sorrow in saying farewell to you now."

JAL appears to have gone above and beyond what Western survivors would expect. Given the Japanese milieu, it had no choice. To do otherwise would have prompted criticism and charges of being inhuman and irresponsible. What was the impact on the JAL corporation? Although it remained profitable, employees were shaken by the wrenching, extensive turnover of executives. The crash also unleashed an unusual torrent of government and press criticism directed at the airline.

The voluntary moratorium on advertising hobbled JAL's promotion of ski package tours. The new management also faced negotiating compensation to the victims' families, establishing harmony among JAL's four trade unions, and ensuring that strict repair and flight regulations were in place. However, despite government and press criticism, JAL communicators imparted the feeling of a caring and empathetic airline with impeccable service expected by that culture.[23]

BUILDING GOSSAMER WEBS: TRUST AND RELATIONSHIPS

All good stories should end happily. Likewise, all analyses are jejune—useless—without prescriptions for changes and cures.

Human communication networks are seemingly delicate, tenuous links that can be made lasting and productive only if they are constantly nourished by solid performance, by keeping promises and serving markets. Human networks are built upon trust and relationship. Rather than rigid institutional egos, actual customer/employee needs must be the driving force. To be successful, they cannot be cold superhighways, conceived to be all things to all people, but smaller, more personalized routes.[24] In this post-quantifying age, problems in communication can no longer be attributed solely to such easy-to-spot reasons as industry jargon and incompatible technologies. Other beguilingly softer, but tougher-to-solve communications concerns are ahead.

Trusting in turbulent times isn't easy. Business turbulence, particularly in the U.S., creates a demand for candid, honest communication. To steady troubled attitudes and sell services, turbulence must be positioned and muted by communications, services, and relationships more in tune with emerging demands and apprehensions. Traditional moorings and relations have been weakened, not gradually by a gentle ebb and flow, but by the crashing and pounding of relentless change. The good news, and the bad news, are that it's not over.

Long, expensively nurtured images fade if not backed by highly trained, sensitive people, candor, and trust. Companies will be judged by their deeds, not their talk. Companies, once perceived as solid, even boring, garnered highly visible criticism by major public mistakes, misdeeds, and misspeaks.

Burgeoning and increasingly vocal consumer sovereignty has consigned product-driven markets to insular obsolescence. This means opportunities must be assessed through the public's eyes, not through the executive's self-interest or institutional egos. The most effective communication is gathering, not spreading, information. Really listening, neither inattentively waiting to interrupt nor hearing minimally through a subjective screen.

The false security bred inside corporate cocoons, even those once highly successful, must be replaced by webs of relationships and communications quickly sensitive to troubles. But communications, no matter how convincing, cannot alone assure in the face of facts. Communications well handled can mitigate problems. Candor is key, but delivering is the acid test.

Relationship management involves communicating, trusting, understanding, responding, knowing. Cold, bureaucratic relations won't work anymore, anywhere, not even in adversarial or unequal power situations. A veteran professor, who has taught Ivy League students for 35 years, notices now that they want to know the professor, his or her attitudes, knowledge and, yes, ethics.

What then dams up communications and breaks those delicate, tenuous human links?

- *Spinning wishful ideas.* Hyperbole and pumped-up company images get mugged by reality every time. Quality and profits result from trust, delivering exactly when and what was promised. Failure cannot be explained away.

- *Distrust.* While trust may be earned the old-fashioned way—day by day, deal by deal, employee by employee—it can be destroyed by just one glitch or employee.
- *Telling them anything.* Executives, caught up in the euphoria of success or the panic of disaster, rashly make promises that return to haunt them.
- *Not listening.* Many employees lament that bosses talked to us, but didn't think with us. Or he listened merely through the hubris that only he knows what was right. Others say too many managers talk, talk, talk, assume, assume, assume, but rarely heed comments of those who live with the realities of markets and changing lifestyles.
- *Talking only during troubles.* Although the stereotype is that companies delight in bragging about good news, the reality is that advertising and public relations budgets rise with trouble. Often the aim then is more to manipulate than to communicate.
- *Becoming a dinosaur.* Some blind themselves through lethargy or fear; some are convinced of their invincibility and don't understand the innovation essential to a company's success. Making the absolutely best buggy whip means nothing when cars are whizzing by the factory. Conversely, others clutch innovation—computers, for example—uncritically as the panacea for all problems.

In a time of more words than understanding, in a time when large structures appear both dominant and dysfunctional, in a time when industries are crossing from old forms through the turbulence to newer ones, in a time when older organizational pyramids are pancaking into horizontal information clusters, candid, pragmatic communication flows are more vital to success than ever before.

NOTES

1. John Micklethwait and Adrian Wooldridge, *The Witch Doctors: Making Sense of Management Gurus* (New York: Times Books/Random House, 1996).

2. Scott Adams, "Dilbert's Management Handbook," *Fortune*, May 13, 1996, pp. 99–118.

3. Ibid., p. 104.

4. For more detail of the passing fads of communication technology,

see, "E-mail: Use It While It Works," *The Ragan Report Weekly Survey of Ideas and Methods for Communications Executives*, April 28, 1997, p. 6.

5. *Jack O'Dwyer's Newsletter*, January 10, 1993, p. 7.

6. Adams, "Dilbert's Management Handbook," p. 108.

7. Comments contained in essays from "The Individual and the Organization," *Focus*, November 20, 1997, p. 43.

8. Barbara S. Carmichael, vice president and executive director, corporate communications, Dow Corning Corporation, told this fable during "Managing Crisis: The Role of Real Time Response" at Fordham's Graduate School of Business, April 27, 1992.

9. *Jack O'Dwyer's Newsletter*, April 2, 1997, p. 2.

10. G. Bruce Knecht, "The Pen Is Mightier," *The Wall Street Journal*, December 23, 1996, pp. A1, 6.

11. *Jack O'Dwyer's Newsletter*, February 15, 1996, p. 2.

12. *Impact*, December 1996, p. 5.

13. Readers interested in Truman's explanation are referred to his memoirs, *Years of Trial and Hope, 1946–1952* (Garden City, N.Y.: Doubleday, 1956), pp. 440–450, or his post-presidency interviews, *Plain Speaking: An Oral Biography of Harry S. Truman*, by Merle Miller (New York: G. P. Putnam's Sons, 1973), pp. 287–306.

14. John Ezard, "Fifty Ways to Lose Your Work Force," *Manchester Guardian Weekly*, June 16, 1996, p. 3.

15. Ibid.

16. "You're Dehired," *Harper's Magazine*, March 1991, p. 22.

17. Stanley Bing, "Stepping Up to the Firing Line," *Fortune*, February 3, 1997, pp. 51–52.

18. "The MTV Wall," remarks by Robert L. Dilenschneider, The Dilenschneider Group, Inc., in a presentation to the International Association of Business Communicators in Kansas City, Missouri, November 10, 1995.

19. Marion K. Pinsdorf, "Quiddies: Post-Yuppie MBA's," *Executive Challenge: Issues, Strategies and Communications*, published by Hill and Knowlton Inc., Winter, 1989.

20. Daniel Yankelovich, "Corporate Logic in the 1990's," 1994 Arthur W. Page Society Spring Seminar in New York, New York.

21. Richard W. Stevenson, "Mending More than the Bottom Line," *The New York Times*, May 9, 1996, pp. D1, 21.

22. Roy Sanada, "How to Communicate Successfully in the Japanese Market," speech to Page Society, St. Amelia Island, Florida, September 1992.

23. The JAL–Pan Am comparison was abstracted from: Marion K. Pinsdorf, "Flying Different Skies: How Cultures Respond to Airline Disasters,"

given at the International Communications Association meetings at Trinity College, Dublin, June 1990 and subsequently published in *Public Relations Review*, Spring 1991, p. 37.

24. Excerpted from the author's article, "Gossamer Webs of Communications: Trust and Relationships," in *Focus*, published by Zurich Insurance.

10

Understanding the Janus[1] Manager

Communicators in Corporations

> God of openings and beginnings, the gateway, "sensitive
> to dualities and polarities."
>
> —WILLIAM SAFIRE

Wanted

CEO seeks corporate communications officer. Duties: keep media at
bay; explain company's prospect to financial community and individual shareholders; function as corporate undertaker to come in after
the fact to explain lapses and tout successes; motivate employees; feed
executive egos. Qualifications: communications/media background
desired but not required; legal, financial, or operating skills preferred;
must have informed world-view, but understand management and
marketing. Evaluation: based on personal chemistry and perception.
Prospects: large department budget and staff, subject to severe cutting
and dismemberment during downsizing; high visibility with other
members of senior management and public enhances career opportunities.

Who would answer this preposterous advertisement? Most communications officers for major corporations. They know, but usually
don't voice, that this description more pragmatically summarizes
their responsibilities than all the wishful mush written in trade jour-
nals and management guides or mouthed by company recruiting sergeants.

Denigration of corporate communicators is both great sport and
popular, but senior managers indulge in it at high risk. Many recent
disasters, damaging to companies in dollars, public support, employee loyalty, and product preference, have involved public percep-

tions, media relations, and communications. Dalkon Shield, companies hiding deleterious effects of new pharmaceuticals, Dow Corning's silicon breast implants, Bhopal, public fights among senior executives, even Tylenol, an image and marketing success—all cost dearly. When the public or media focus on an issue, such as toxic waste disposal, when it's a hot topic, only absolute honesty and complete correction succeed. Good communicators know this, but must demonstrate it again and again to naturally skeptical managements, often by recounting cautionary tales from corporate battlefields. Here's one from Waste Management, the nation's largest disposal firm. In March 1985, a former employee made front-page headlines by telling how the company had illegally disposed of toxic chemicals at an Ohio dump site. In two days, shares dropped 30 per cent. Waste Management feared its name was sullied forever, that government fines and extensive litigation would cut into its highly profitable 30 per cent operating margins.

It reacted aggressively in appearance and operations by creating an environmental compliance department, beefing up internal controls and lobbying efforts, and launching a $5 million television advertising campaign. These actions impressed investors. Even though executives admitted past lapses—significant reporting delays, mishandling, and storage problems—they wondered why the EPA seemed to deliberately scrutinize and penalize the company, to make it a public example. These executives had fallen into the classic trap of not understanding that when an industry leader or business sector is under suspicion, cosmetics can't conceal. Public relations, lobbying, even chopping executive heads are not enough. Nothing less than radical surgery, complete clean-up, will do.

No communications officer makes himself popular by bearing such tidings. Nor does he enhance his credibility by having to rely on projections, hunches, or soft reasoning. Tough-minded number crunchers and operations people don't want production mucked up by some might-bes. Many communicators further weaken their position by not even trying to think in terms of their peers. Unlike other managers, communicators do not have the force of established procedures, such as legal codes or production statistics, a power base, and substantiation. Rather, they must often rest their counsel on experience—usually only their own—plus opinions and judgments that are binding on absolutely no one. Even if they have a faultless track record, survival can be precarious.

Thoughtful, senior practitioners see the "Practitioner's Dilemma" very clearly:[2] "In a survey of 225 of the top U.S. business journalists, about 47 per cent of respondents believe PR people are more of a nuisance than a help." Why? Journalists often cavil that PR people impede their way to the truth by lying or blocking access to the corporate executives to whom PR people report. These executives enjoy greater credibility among journalists, but ego-tripping is an element, too: journalists seek to talk as high as they can. With their sights set on none less than the CEO, the journalists will dismiss the PR officer, wrongly, as merely a bothersome gatekeeper.

Employees, investors, and customers are skeptical that management, especially senior management, rarely tells them the real story about what's going on in the organization.

Public perceptions too often are formed by the most obvious activists, the hottest topics, and the most visible journalists, not strategy, documented facts and figures. Hence, the communicators' job is both precarious and difficult. To correct such perceptions, practitioners must become more convincing advocates, make judgment calls more emphatically and clearly. That's not easy. How far can practitioners go, for example, in telling employees about really serious changes next year in benefit plans? What's the best strategy for telling a major business publication why a company is selling a subsidiary for half what it was bought for five years ago? How best to explain to customers—or should they explain at all—why a product line, launched with great fanfare just a year before, is being discontinued? Every operating executive and communicator, faced with these and equally ambiguous situations knows there's no easy, quick, or pat answer.[3]

But the picture is not totally bleak. Senior management accepts value-added counsel, wherever the source. It's not a jurisdictional issue, but a matter of "intellectual horsepower" and a "methodology," a "risk saliency ration." "The degree of risk dictates the degree of disclosure. . . . You do this, this and this, or you're going to jail. . . . 'Here's our professional judgement. Here's what's going to happen in the broadcast and print media nationally and the trade press. Here are the consequences of Option A, of Option B.' " Transforming that "kind of risk assessment into a methodology" would allow practitioners "to bring something to the table besides opinions. . . . Reporting structure is not what this is about. Access is essential." Granted: the key issue of communicators is the value added and the methodology that focuses thinking, but if the best ideas are never heard or discounted, mistakes are made.[4]

As David Halberstam describes in *The Best and the Brightest*, quantifiers in the Pentagon documented, with apparently incontrovertible evidence, the effectiveness of bombing runs, body counts, and general Vietnam readiness. One querulous fellow, like Herman Melville's Bartleby, over in a corner recited a mantra: in my gut it seems wrong. He was discounted, fired, but eventually proven correct. Nay-sayers often are a nuisance, but listen. They may just be right. Critical decisions well based in statistics, marketing surveys, and legal considerations too often exclude or belatedly admit public perceptions, long-term ramifications, and communications considerations.

The communicator faces other difficulties unique to his function and background. While finance, law, operations, and marketing are venerated as fast internal tracks to the top, the communications officer often rises through liberal arts, media, and writing outside the company. Those with purely communications education may suffer from training that was either too nuts-and-bolts or too theoretical. A Conference Board survey of 300 CEOs of major companies showed that 60 per cent had been with their companies at least 21 years. The longevity customary among most executives is unusual in communications. While most other officers are Ivy League white males, the token woman or black often heads the communications department. It's also too often abused as the dumping ground for corporate losers, burn-outs easing into retirement, or badly trained liberal arts graduates who "like people" but are otherwise unfocused.

Insufficient information or candor from the top is another difficulty. Some practitioners depict themselves as mushrooms: kept in the dark and shoveled shit. The communicators' credo seems to be "Last to know; first to go." Even the most competent are excluded from the inner ring of information and influence, where secrecy produces great power. Many U.S. presidential press secretaries lament being out of the loop, with premature announcements, inconsistencies, leaks, and unwitting misstatements the result.

One street-smart woman officer lacked access to rumors regularly posted on the mirror in the executive men's room, until female cleaners leveled the advantage. Not being informed fosters whining and adamant ego-touting attitudes that irritate colleagues. Even well-trained communicators, unfortunately, adopt stand-offish, even elitist, stances or slight the guts and realities of the business. In one major company, the communications department, from the vice president down, made a point of professional pride never to attend a marketing meeting, talk over plans with brand managers, or come down from their lofty professional perches to walk a plant floor. When a tough, cost-conscious management took over, almost the entire department was fired—and they were not missed. Only those who demonstrated their value survived.

Communicators can be handicapped by a different sense of urgency, priorities, and timing from other executives'. To operating managers who are developing five-year business plans or writing twenty-year insurance policies, other deadlines seem rude and unrealistic. Break into a planning meeting on marketing for the next century when the press is clamoring for a statement on an oil spill and criticism is sure to follow. The statement will come only much later. Too late to be used, of course. And a journalist has been angered unnecessarily.

Unlike the corporate structure, the news room environment—media or company—allows little time to talk about strategic planning. A communicator faces what erupts. He must be prepared, organizationally and personally, for the single event, the one telephone call that can transform a company's relative normality into a maelstrom, a rush of events and tensions. This unique view can be excellent training for a business career. It was for this author. While many senior managers of large corporations were attending prep school and later prestigious universities and graduate schools, the author already was immersed in a demanding newspaper city room. No talk of strategic planning or latest management fads. Reporters faced what they were assigned: a church fire in the morning and a senator's speech in the evening sandwiching a lady-lady luncheon. Instead of cheering for the home team, the author was covering bloody highway accidents and sniffing out the shady backroom deals of small-town politicians. Abrupt change, adversarial situations, and searching out facts in mazes of contradictions were drilled into the author's journalistic psyche early and were put to good corporate use later.

Investigations and almost engulfing, microscopic media attention can magnify existing small fault-lines into deep crevices. They damage profitability, public image, and promising careers. Most executives, basically very private and highly organized individuals, are put off by the hurly-burly turbulence of the corporate city room and the media's uncontrollable demands and incessant deadlines. Even with insight and planning, a great deal of effort must be expended in responding to events that erupt suddenly. Some of these a novice will smile over incredulously. But any seasoned communicator can trade war stories about suicides, blackmail, expropriations or illegal payments; bailing out a homosexual executive; explaining why a boss died in the wrong bed with the wrong woman; cleaning up a publicly messy marital situation, or disclaiming any connection between an executive's falling downstairs, fatally breaking his neck, and major investigations of his company.

Business school graduates and fast-trackers to the contrary, no single recipe guarantees success. Communications officers, perhaps more than any others, must be sensitive, astute Januses—very much involved internally in the business, and consummately versed in marketing and general strategies. They must be able to translate the hard-knuckles world of media relations to colleagues, and to spot specks on the horizon potentially important to the company. They must be multidimensional thinkers who do not ape their peers, willing to tactfully ask the tough questions that others may be too political, polite, or uninformed to ask. Global business means communicators must work across and understand many cultures. It's not just the big issues that scuttle public relations effort. Details such as the use of the wrong color—white to signal beginnings in China where white signifies mourning—are important.

What is needed is not just a yeoman who can make a great media buy, create a zingy commercial, write a speech, or plant a favorable story in a hometown newspaper. That's expected and minor. More important are acute awareness of cross currents of public opinion, an understanding not just of the techniques of communications but of the overriding issues, and knowledge not just of short-range tactics but of strategies that may make or break the company. Such wide-vision thinkers must also be as adaptable as the character Dustin Hoffman played in *Tootsie*, who was desperate for any role.

FOUNDERS AND FOLLOWERS

The founders of public relations were as heterogeneous a collection of personalities as their heirs, today's practitioners. Edward Bernays, Sigmund Freud's nephew, introduced sociological and psychological tools to influence public opinion. Ivy Lee transformed the image of the Rockefeller family, damaged badly at Bloody Ludlow—a "ferocious conflict" between labor and industry in Colorado coal fields in 1913 and 1914. The scathing criticism following the deaths of more than 100 people, mostly miners, their wives, and children, during a ten-day war in April 1914 prompted the Rockefeller family to hire Lee. (John D. Rockefeller, Jr., was controlling director of the state's largest mine operator, Colorado Fuel and Iron Company.)

At the high tide of muckraking journalism and anti-trust "rampage" among politicians, Lee warned his client, if you don't do something, you and your family will be destroyed and your company broken up.[5] Lee, known as a skillful verbalist, succeeded in the "art of getting believed in." Through carefully crafted public statements, personal, caring appearances by Rockefeller, bulletins and pamphlets, some of dubious veracity—in short, "a broad educative campaign of publicity"—Lee dramatically changed the family image to generously philanthropic. It began with John D., Sr., giving away dimes to children and grew to gifts of hundreds of millions of dollars and funding of such New York City landmarks as Rockefeller Center, Riverside Church, and the World Trade Center. However, George S. McGovern, who wrote his doctoral dissertation on Ludlow, considers the Rockefeller image indeed restored not so much by a "publicity prodigy" as by changes in operations, driven mainly by Canadian labor expert William Lyon Mackenzie.[6]

Others fault it, although in the face of the surging political rage against monopolistic power, Lee's advice saved the family—for a while. The philanthropic strategy so weakened the Rockefellers' entrepreneurial spirit, critics note, that the great opportunities for future profit fell from their hands.[7]

John W. Hill was a canny Indiana farm boy with a genius for seeing the profitable niche and understanding current needs to build a worldwide counseling firm. Milton Fairman, a Chicago newspaper man, built one of the first major corporate departments at Borden, Inc. Harold Burson came north to New York from Memphis with newspaper and counseling skills to chair Burson-Marsteller. Chester Burger, a manager and counselor from Brooklyn, developed the unique role of confidential adviser to CEOs and leading public relations and advertising firms. None practiced public relations in the almost mindless, nitty-gritty manner of many fictional stereotypes.

Just as Bernays identified opportunities for publicity high-jinks, and Hill the importance of labor/management strife immediately following World War II, their progressive followers today are matching their efforts to the temper of new times. Astute practitioners understand how vital communications can be in an age of multinational labor forces and stiffer competition: the wider use of visual and electronic than print communication, particularly with employees—new techniques required by less management layering; downsizing of organizations; and greater participation by the people who actually make, assemble, or sell products. That said, communicators still must make managements realize how vital an accurate, respected public understanding is to corporate profitability, even to survival.

Public relations is a relatively new trade; many of the founders trained today's senior practitioners. Although the past is seldom any prologue today, a brief look at how counselors and companies worked in the past can enhance an understanding of how practitioners operate now.

No complex event can be satisfactorily pinpointed as starting at a precise moment or by a single pioneer, but it is generally agreed that Bernays and his work with the United States Committee on Public Information—essentially, a wartime propaganda machine— introduced press agentry. Those who first worked with Bernays were authors, newspaper and advertising men, and college professors, who scrambled for information wherever they could. Chief executives in both government and business were reluctant then, as some still are today, to court public opinion. Bernays repeatedly described the lost opportunity to gain support for the Treaty of Versailles. President Woodrow Wilson refused, despite prodding, to engage in popular activities that would delight American newspaper readers.

In the 1920s, as public relations began expanding rapidly, companies hired staff regardless of experience. Much was trial and error. Press gimmicks abounded. For one client Bernays countered the new fashion of shingled hair styles, which did away with hair nets, by publicizing appearance, safety, and health reasons for continuing to wear nets. He was convincing. For example, everyone cooking in a restaurant or working in a factory was required to wear a net regardless of hair length.

Another Bernays coup was Ivory soap recognition. He staged a cleanliness campaign and arranged publicity events like washing public statues and sculpturing soap. His most spectacular success, unthinkable today, was for the American Tobacco Company. To change the déclassé image of cigarette smoking, Bernays established a Tobacco Society of Voice Culture, Inc.: "So to improve the chords of the throat through cigarette smoking that the public will be able to express itself in songs of praise and more easily swallow anything. . . . Our ultimate goal: A smoking teacher for every singer."[8]

The publicist touted cigarettes not as a pleasure, but as medicine. He sought and got testimonials from physicians. Appealing to weight-conscious women, he urged, "Reach for a Lucky instead of a sweet." To enhance the female market—nice women then did not smoke freely and surely not publicly—he induced New York City debutantes to parade on Easter along Fifth Avenue obviously smoking. Discovering a female preference for green, he redesigned the packaging accordingly. Bernays understood his campaigns had to appeal to current values and interests, even if they are unconscious. If not, they are laughed at or ignored into failure.

Unfortunately, this early era left impressions that still plague public relations today: slick press agents, hidden persuaders, devious manipulators of dummy front organizations and golden livers, who expensively ply the power brokers and media with drinks and favors. But image lags behind the reality. Business is too serious and abstemious, and the media too sensitive, to accept even a token gift and too health-minded to indulge in drinking orgies.

USE AND ABUSE OF COMMUNICATIONS

The Great Depression boosted public relations. Responding to widespread criticism of capitalism, business realized it could no longer merely sell its goods and services. It had to explain its broader contribution to society. A book written in 1957 by John W. Hill, founder and long-time intellectual force behind Hill and Knowlton, expanded this mandate, setting the stage for a widening and professionalizing of communications.[9] To Hill, public relations had no mystical powers to work miracles, sway public opinion, or create lasting value where none existed. Rather, communications was a broad management function rooted in integrity, soundness of policies, decision making, and actions able to be viewed in the light of public interest.

Hill's counsel succeeded because it suited the times. As labor and management struggled, he told management that employees were its nearest and most important audience. Lukewarm communications with them, or any other public, was worse than none. Nor could smart publicity ever replace sound management policies and good financial results in building a lasting foundation of good will. To approve of its actions, people must know what a company is doing. If management refuses to tell its own story, someone else will, either incorrectly or to their detriment. Too many managements bestir themselves to tackle a problem only at its flash point, Hill continued. Then, confounded by slow-moving public attitudes and seemingly intractable problems, they grow frustrated and bored, leaving the field open to the unrelenting efforts of detractors. Hill espoused a different approach: once companies are sure that policies are right and decent, that their house is clean of payoffs and other possible embarrassments, then they should tell the story forthrightly and repeatedly. As George Cabot Lodge wrote later, Hill told private enterprise that it exists only under the franchise of public opinion.

Perhaps the best-known, although somewhat misleading, picture of public relations in its earlier years is *The Man in the Gray Flannel Suit*, which has passed into public consciousness as synonymous with conformity. Actually, the central figure of Sloan Wilson's novel was struggling to adapt himself from the relative security of olive drab to the quicksand world of late-1940s corporate public relations. In his interview for a public relations job at United Broadcasting Corporation, he gave expected, not truthful, answers: Why do you want to work for UBC? It's a good company, not for the money. Why PR? Not merely because the job is open, but because my previous experience at a foundation would be helpful. However, one question hasn't changed since then: Can you write?

Although he hated the work, he dredged up the expected enthusiasm, researching "nauseatingly noble" speeches for a mental health committee that his chairman sought to ride to fame. "If you want good publicity, do something good." Friends predicted a great future in publicity, because he was already defending his boss from all comers and criticism. "We don't write speeches for Mr. Hopkiss. We just help him with the research—take notes on the great man's thoughts and try to get something on paper for him to work with."

Ghostwriting still daunts communicators. Viewed as a specialized service, it is not a pathway to power unless the writer develops a unique rapport with senior officers or is perceived within the organization as having special entrée. Even the most skillful ghost finds it an intimidating, intimate exercise to catch an executive's thoughts exactly or coax them from him. The writer must phrase the thoughts comfortably, with appropriate allusions to golf, the military, or fishing, and avoid tongue-tangling phrases. If the writer has far different experiences and purview, the collaboration succeeds only if the officer shares his ideas initially, then works closely with the writer so the words and thoughts appear to be the officer's. The greatest abuse— and the most obvious—occurs when the speaker sees the material only when he presents it.

Public relations in the 1950s, the world in which Wilson's character operated, seems almost innocent and secretarial to us now. Checking out hotel arrangements: Was the mattress hard? Did long-stemmed roses grace the night table? Were the meeting room lectern and notebooks ready? Was the press alerted to receive the news release? The hacks, who give communications a menial image, still work on that level. However, even sophisticated, seasoned professionals get immersed in such ludicrous, time-consuming tasks. They always look deceptively easy, but never are.

Sloan Wilson's man learned early that whistle-blowing, or even less than the most robust support, is translated as disloyalty. "I'll always tend to agree, until I get big enough to be honest without being hurt. That's not being crooked, it's just being smart." Saying anything for pay. But as with petting a tiger, one must be very careful. Even today, liabilities for bearing bad news or disagreeing are still high, except with the most self-assured, progressive managers.

As a result of polite silence, many problems are hidden when nascent, only to blossom into major magnitude later. An ethicist recounts a meeting during which a manager explored his responsibility for red-flagging the dangers of a chemical spill. Everyone attending pooh-poohed its importance, saying it was neither ethical nor necessary to bring the matter to a superior's attention. The chemical was kepone, which, soon after the meeting, became a major environmental and publicity problem.[10]

Thomas McCann, for many years United Fruit's vice president of public relations, traces communications from the company's go-go years through its public meddling in Central American politics, and finally to the abuses by Chairman Eli Black.[11] Before his very public suicide in 1975, Black turned publicity into personal vanity and created financial Potemkin villages that even savvy newspaper men believed.[12]

Bernays began counseling the company by suggesting a Middle American Information Bureau, financed and run within United Fruit. To complement his work, an internal department was created in 1955; within a year its staff grew to 28, with a budget of $1.5 million. One highly visible project was an institutional advertising campaign, "The Living Circle," run in Spanish-language publications. The great wheel was superimposed on a map of America. From the north came an endless supply of all good things: cars, refrigerators, radios, television sets, tires, and other manufactured products. From the south came all the materials and agricultural products one could take from the land: raw rubber, minerals, lumber, and, especially, bananas—a graphic although unwitting representation of colonialism. Even in that less-sensitized time, the campaign created resentment and rancor in Central America. Typically, the company was so isolated from the impact of its actions and attitudes that it continued the advertising for almost five years, inflaming its audiences and working counter to any conceivable self-interest.

Other weaknesses illustrated by United Fruit's efforts—a cautionary tale for any practitioner—involved erecting façades, inspiring chimeras, and attempting to maneuver public figures for self-interest. When problems arose with union activist César Chávez, for example, corporate managers insisted on a public stance of cooperation with the United Fruit Workers Union, despite earlier animosity. Black tried maladroitly to "handle Chavez" by inviting him to participate in a well-attended religious service. "That's PR," crowed Black. But all the publicity and fellowship in the world are worthless when each side must represent its constituencies.

Despite United Fruit's well-known record in Central America, company films attempted to position it as the hemisphere's most enlightened benefactor. But the incongruity of photographs showing freshly laundered T-shirts on exuberantly happy workers and faked blow-ups of the plantations mocked the accuracy. When a more honest attempt was aimed at college students, Black tried to kill it.

Such public relations efforts featured many techniques accepted then by company, press, and public. Junkets to the tropics were conducted for reporters, who saw only company-staged events. United Fruit sponsored newspapers, circulated free to employees, often their only source of information. Here, too, the company misjudged. Many employees were illiterate; others railed at the refusal to discuss issues and the paper's portrayal of life on a banana plantation as an idyllic, happy holiday. Soon the newspapers were supplanted by inexpensive transistor radios even the poorest employee could afford. Radios provided more information than company-sponsored publications. No reporter, CEO, or communications officer with a smattering of brains would even attempt any of these tactics today.

Crazing the Communicator

No corporate officer is as vulnerable to executive ego, to foibles and excesses, as the communicator. Personal chemistry is vital not only because of the communicator's responsibilities, but also because of the nature of the working relationship. Yet crazy bosses, like ego, are usually ignored, or at best smiled over sympathetically, when recounted to the battle-wise. At worst, corporate novices may greet such tales with disbelief, or even question the teller's balance. Pathological superiors, workaholics, those who wishfully indulge in appearances rather than reality, those who operate and judge according to religious and sexual prejudices, those who suffer serious but overlooked or unrecognized personality flaws, those who focus on unimportant details rather than crux issues, wreak great damage, especially on communicators. Every executive has his own stock of Captain Queeg-like yarns. The stories that follow all actually happened; each illustrates a liability particular to corporate communications.

Appearances • In a time when packaging is paramount, when snap judgments are made on appearance and office alone, a typewriter can be dangerous to success. One highly respected communicator was ruled out of a promotion to officer because he had a typewriter in his office and, worse yet, actually used it. The successful candidate, whose office in another company also housed a typewriter, was very careful not to move one into the executive suite. Initially, women executives are reluctant to have a word processor or anything roughly resembling a typewriter around: too close to the secretarial stigma.

Incidentals That Win • Every communicator knows that he may stand or fall on whether he gets an executive's daughter's wedding announcement in *The New York Times* or *The Washington Post* society page, secures scarce tickets for the Superbowl, knows the "in" restaurants or plays, or arranges an honorary degree or a coveted speaking engagement. One chairman, very skeptical about communications, finally warmed up. His great idea—and it was—was to strike a commemorative plate with an attractive annual report cover design.

Illegalities • During the height of sensitive, intense national investigations of a company, a corporate loser sought to regain power by controlling media relations. Talking to reporters looks like great fun, power, and visibility to the uninitiated executive who has never been backed into a corner by a smart reporter or misquoted in headlines and then had to explain them. To accomplish his aims, the executive had to defeat and/or neutralize the press chief. What better means than taping, secretly, a planted incriminating interview? However, the communicator defended himself long and comprehensively enough that the hidden tape buzzed its presence.

Prejudice • Even today, when management should be objective, communicators attract unsolicited, prejudiced advice. Be a journalist from New York City and read books and you'll be cautioned about the local difficulties of being Jewish. He wasn't. Sign a pro-abortion petition published in a newspaper and be counseled about how serious it is for a Roman Catholic to go public against church teaching. She wasn't. Have lunch with a long-time friend in an eating club frequented by officer peers and be counseled against being seen there again with a black. He was.

Yes, But • Communicators are charged with understanding how the media works. But the media's demand for information may be at cross purposes with legal counsel. Even the most convincing communicator may lose his case until the next day's headlines. One company under intense scrutiny by investigative reporters wanted to stonewall them. Lawyers won; communicators lost. The next day, when management was wooing financial analysts, a long, uncomplimentary story written without company input ran on page one.

Women, Still a Special Case • The first senior management opportunity for many women frequently comes in communications or human resources, often perceived as soft areas by machismo management. This poses additional difficulties, particularly if the woman has more street smarts than her male peers.[13] She is in a vulnerable post at best: she must bear bad news and counsel against some of the firmest-held ideas of others. This was *one* factor in Mary Cunningham's troubles at Bendix. When a woman appears with males at a meeting, even today, she is assumed to be a subordinate, never the boss, although only dolts still assume automatically that she is a secretary. One woman officer and a male who reported to her visited a corporate subsidiary. The guide assigned to them concentrated on the male; she was invisible. Finally, he asked very confidentially, "How does it feel to work for a broad?" "Meet her," the subordinate responded.

Another woman, the first on a posh executive floor, was barred one weekend from her office. The guards just knew no woman had an office there, and secretaries were not allowed up on weekends without special permission. Later, when her secretary asked for a key to the ladies' room for her, the response was ribald.

Accreditation and Degree • Non-degree–holders may not be hired to push cheese in supermarkets, or a non-high school graduate who is a member of Mensa may not be considered for an audiovisual position he handled elsewhere successfully. But too many credentials are problems, too. APR, the sign of accreditation so important to public relations practitioners, means little or may even be negative to others. Ph.D.s are particularly suspect. What can a theoretically trained Ph.D. know about corporations, business, even communications? Lots. If a woman has a doctorate and her male superior does not, she should be ready for not-too-subtle suggestions to drop it.

LYING TO THE SPOKESPERSON

If executives as a group don't trust their spokesperson to present their position prudently, they should find another. Not confiding in the spokesperson, telling her what can be made public and what cannot, or, worse, treating her like a mushroom, kept in the dark, causes serious lapses and mistakes. An obvious instance was Larry Speakes, President Reagan's press spokesman at the time of the Grenada invasion. As Speakes explains in his book *Speaking Out*: "Rear Admiral John Poindexter had hung me out to dry, and I didn't even know it."[14]

On October 24, 1983, a television reporter asked Speakes privately if U.S. forces were assembling in the Caribbean to invade Grenada. The island nation had been flirting with Fidel Castro and was in political turmoil internally. Speakes writes, "I was blissfully unaware about the impending invasion." Even after 2½ years on the job he was "still out of the loop" and "not completely trusted." When Speakes queried Poindexter, his response was "preposterous." "Knock it down." Speakes repeated "preposterous." Twelve hours later, "Operation Urgent Fury," the invasion of Grenada, was launched. So too were four basic PR mistakes:

- Never lie to or keep the spokesperson in the dark
- Use more neutral language, not a word as strong as "preposterous," when the speaker knows full well the opposite is evident. (Gathering an invasion force can hardly be hidden)
- Had Speakes known the situation, he would not have repeated "preposterous." One could question whether he should have used it under any circumstances
- Never lie to the press.

Even as rumors flew, media queries persisted, and leaders gathered; Speakes could only speculate. Next morning, a fifth PR principle was breached: give the spokesman time to prepare. Speakes had little more than an hour to digest an inch-thick packet of materials and announce the invasion. A good recipe for mistakes. One administration official's attitude was: "we give them [the press office] just enough to do these foolish daily briefings." Speakes's position was: "Tell me everything so I'll know not only what to say, but what not to say."

Communication snafus were not over. Some reporters were kept incommunicado. Others risked being fired upon if they attempted to land to cover operations. Even military systems didn't talk to each other, resulting in "friendly" bombing of elements of the 82nd Airborne. Watching all these communications follies was the Deputy Commander, who vowed never again. And in the Gulf War, he, H. Norman Schwarzkopf, handled the press masterfully.

FICTION ILLUMINATES REALITY

James Baar, a sardonic and witty public relations man, gives very realistic insights into press and corporate information-sources in his spoof *The Great Free Enterprise Gambit*. Business writers sit in a three-row semicircle in plush oversized conference chairs. Some, "dressed like bankers, carry pocket calculators, gold pencils and attaché cases"; they assume the mien of senior loan officers. "Others are rumpled and openly pugnacious. A few in business gray fawn nervously in hopes of future employment." Most smell trouble, happily anticipating their claims to major space for particularly nasty stories.

The CEO, expectedly, wants to cut a couple of those bastards off at the pockets. The vice president of corporate information, also typically, attempts to allay his boss's worries following a press conference with the canard of canards: "We can handle them. Believe me, I know those guys." Famous last words, uttered before the deluge of truth; the next day's headlines. One, reading "IC Rents Mercenary Troops to Latin American Dictators," produced a nightmare, a saturation attack of press calls. Predictably, hauling out a cannon to kill a gnat, the vice president of public information devised "operation integrity," to show up those crazy press sharpshooters who are printing all that rotten stuff. Usually, public relations people delight in seeing their company's name in headlines; in this instance it was depressing. To show "them" that the company was moving forward in the old IC spirit, a massive campaign was unfurled with great fanfare and at great expense. It was just ineffectual, laughable boilerplate.

In Baar's novel, the CEO explains away the company's difficult financial condition, saying that what looks today like major setbacks tomorrow will be regarded as minor blips on the curve—an attitude that makes the Rock of Gibraltar look spongy and arouses the worst possible suspicions. Fiscal fairy tales will return to haunt a company if financial performance does not fulfill public promises.

GOOD COUNSELORS LISTEN UP

Public relations counselors pride themselves on being good listeners, sizing up problems and personalities quickly, and dealing with lots of strange situations. Few have made as dramatic a career switch as Richard E. Cheney, formerly Hill and Knowlton's chairman. In his lecture to the Institute for Public Relations Research and Education, "How I Went From the Corporate War Room to a Seat Behind the Analyst's Couch: Is There a Lesson Here for Public Relations?" Cheney recreated the 1980s. He was reigning financial public relations guru then:

> Investment bankers were picking up briefcases stuffed with money from furtive messengers on downtown street corners as a pay-off for giving arbitragers inside information. Greedy chief executives were plotting surreptitiously to take over companies run, say, by somebody they bumped into around the country club.

Cheney began leading a double life. "During the day I was working with people like the late Mad Dog Beck . . . an investment banker who was trying to get hired to engineer a takeover by the CEO of a pet food manufacturer who [had] a half opened box of dog food on his desk. Mad Dog snarled, grabbed a dog biscuit and bit it in two to show how fierce he was."

Was Cheney's second life that different? Several nights a week he was studying to be a psychoanalyst at the Center for Modern Psychoanalytic Studies. On Saturdays, he worked in a locked ward of a New Jersey mental hospital. "It was full of men who talked "word salad." I "may have been leading two lives . . . but it struck me I was living in one world." Why did he "turn away from a lucrative crap game run for jackals and open my own psychoanalytic office?" Partly because "I felt I had missed the boat. During my career, before I worked in investor relations . . . I had a public relations job in the oil business. . . . Being gender insensitive and with our minds violated by an idea, we proudly called ourselves oil men fighting for percentage depletion. At the American Iron and Steel Institute we called ourselves Steel men and tried to teach the unions it was only common sense to settle for less money. . . . Surely being alive was for more than this. The universe was a big and extravagantly wide place, but I was missing almost all of it, too often dealing with appearances rather than underlying feelings, emotions and realities."

The career switch wasn't clear-cut for Cheney. "Good public relations can make or break companies." Save jobs and lots of money. And so do good. Cheney cited the example of his work on a polyvinyl chloride disaster. A Midwestern company discovered employees in its PVC plants were dying of liver cancer. "The company's public relations man would have liked advice from me on how to hunker down." Instead, Cheney asked the right question at the right time: What would the CEO do if his mother was in the plant? His response? He "studied employee death records for the last 10 years, paid off relatives of any employee who had died with even a suspicion of liver cancer, gave plant employees respirators and never kept them in the plant for more than half an hour at a time." He reassigned employees with "even an irregularity in their liver tests." Finally, he embarked on a research program to redesign the plant machinery to prevent PVC emissions altogether. It must be noted that Cheney's experience and the CEO's action was unusually open and swift.

The CEO also questioned and disproved the conventional wisdom. The industry said eliminating emissions completely was impossible. Within a few months Cheney's client announced company researchers had reduced emissions to zero. This produced lots of positive press: a New York news conference, favorable stories in New York papers and the national media. A *New York Times* editorial praised the accomplishment. Not only did the company save itself a great deal of trouble and money but, far more important, lives. Everyone was proud. Cheney also suffered defeats. "Nothing gnaws at you like losing a proxy fight to a crowing competitor who is working for a scoundrel."

But triumphs didn't satisfy Cheney's curiosity. Even in the turmoil of proxy fights, usually very revealing of personal motives and flaws, Cheney felt he had only a superficial understanding of what made people the way they were. "I found myself dealing with appearances and not the source of clients' troubles, which often arose from their personalities and the way organizations were run." Gradually, he saw skills that made him a successful counselor applied to analysis as well. The goal: to get client or patient to say everything. Listening is vital, but asking the right questions or reflecting on the answers is involved also.

The power of the right question at the right time can be astonishing. Some are obvious; others, not so simple. They reveal complexity of motives and spur surprising action. Sometimes, the practical business mentality conflicts. Objectives are important. People get ahead by taking and giving orders. Having goals for a patient, however, is tempting but unwise. "Get the patient to say everything and he'll figure out what to do." Often a client, by simply organizing the problem to explain to his PR counselor, also figures out the problem or solution.

Patience is a virtue not prevalent in business. We want to show how smart we are. "We think coming up with the right answer right away will impress and keep our client." Analysts must listen. Not a bad PR nostrum either.

Cheney concluded by detailing the relevance of his work in public relations and in psychotherapy. First, he noted drastic changes in public relations. Firms were acquired by advertising agencies and by hard-boiled conglomerates. The bottom line dominates. Increasingly, practitioners are pressured "to sell themselves and their services." Counseling and long-term relationships with clients are supplanted—gone. Once a troubled client who wanted to change his reputation (now sheer image) sought advice. Reputation was more apt to be based on actions; image, on appearances, like the quick distortion when a flash bulb goes off. Reputation is changed by actions, by reality; images, by ideas from a focus group or poll. Image may vary greatly from the truth, but if it works short-term, that seems enough.

The MBA candidates the author teaches are frequently bewildered and bothered, sometimes angered, by events and people not being what they seem. U.S. Presidents look vigorous, healthy, recovering quickly. Then the students see the photo-ops, spinning of the truth, and the imaging to create the illusion. Marshall McLuhan's analysis in *The Mechanical Bride* of how ads sell and bilk and beguile arouses the same ire.

Once public relations leaders such as John Hill just sat down with a potential client CEO and talked bluntly. Today, it's more competitive. A potential client asks for a presentation. Tell us why we should hire you, not another firm. A team studies the company and cranks up a beauty contest or dog-and-pony show complete with slides, music, whatever to win favor. Conversely, a chief executive under great pressure or in big trouble, after a limited consultation, seeks a quick fix. What PR person will admit there aren't any? PR is incremental. Inside the Beltway, a counselor may suggest ways to put spin on his story so the client "won't be condemned by the public for what was essentially egregious behavior." "The infatuation with spin and black magic largely has supplanted the notion that public relations is doing good and getting credit for it."

Fads increasingly infect public relations and business thinking generally. But they must be rooted in public attitudes or they'll quickly prove dysfunctional. *Mea culpa* sighs of regret and desire to make amends worked for a time; overexposure weakened its usefulness. "Now brazen confrontation is the first public defense of rascals—I did it and I'm glad." One need only think of Al Dunlap's public bragging about employees and expenses cut, justifying his own handsome reward, to underscore Cheney's point.

He cited the example of once Louisiana Governor Earl Long. A lobbyist for the theater exhibitors told him that he would make campaign contributions if Long removed the state tax on movie admission. Long assured the lobbyist the tax would go if he got the contributions and was reelected. After Long was, the lobbyist asked "Governor, how soon can I tell my clients that you're getting rid of the theater tax?" Long reneged. When the lobbyist asked Long what he should tell his clients, the governor replied, "Tell them I lied."

Clearly, staring down critics is nothing new, but it is arguably more prevalent since Watergate. "Admittedly, it is easy to distort the past when comparing between then and now, but I can't recall any incident in the past comparable to a foot fetishist bringing his wife onto the cover of *Time* to stand behind him after he passed presidential secrets to a hooker." Cheney also noted that the tobacco industry's determined defiance of public health "seems to dwarf the labor strife and the broken heads of the thirties."

"Borrowing from the therapeutic talking cure, I believe [those] who work in public relations can . . . help clients by asking more of the right questions at the right time." It's not easy. Clients are impatient. They want a quick fix. That's the way executives are taught to run operations. Why should the public or media be any different? "You can't impose your public relation goals on them, any more than I can impose my own ideas on my patients."

"The competent public relations person . . . should not rush to come up with the big idea to advance a client's fortunes. Even if you are being hammered for a presentation." Slow down. Help your client figure out what he really wants. Take the time to gather all the facts—especially unpleasant ones. Listen attentively. Talk only when you are on sure ground. A shot from the hip more often than not winds up in your foot. Instead, keep the potential client talking. How does he see the public? How does he think the public perceives him?[15]

Most PR counselors would argue that stopping a client hell-bent for trouble is no easy task, especially if you want to keep the account and your own reputation. A clinical psychologist friend once wisely said during great corporate stress, only a healthy sense of the absurd will keep you sane. Most battle-tested in public fights and client foibles would say "Amen."

WHAT CEOS SHOULD EXPECT OF COMMUNICATORS

Many senior managers, fully confident when evaluating other subordinates, puzzle over what to demand of the communications officer and how to assess his performance. Communications is a staff not an operating function; a cost rather than a profit center; and difficult to quantify in a numbers-dominated corporate culture. Most important, personalities vary greatly. Harry Gray of United Technologies to the contrary, most CEOs come to major responsibilities with modest contact with media or communications. The straddling of spheres—finding the commonality between communications and business strategy—is akin to bridging the gap between techies and more traditional managers. Communicators must know the business well enough to devise the most effective public positions. The CEO who knows operations intimately must understand enough about communications to view it as a valuable management tool. Complicating this equation is a growing tendency to appoint communicators who are unschooled in their trade and unable to write well. (One concerned veteran writer, baffled by this trend, foresees sign language and semaphore.)

Ronald E. Rhody, a respected senior practitioner and former executive vice president of the Bank of America, offered a public relations primer to young presidents.[16] No single group, he pointed out, gets as much sheer hokum thrown at them as CEOs, especially the newly appointed. Consultants, experts, professional ego-salvers, and many Monday morning quarterbacks, all of whom enjoy perfect 20/20 hindsight, second-guess decisions and offer advice for fancy fees.

The worst, however, are the fuzzy futurists, infected with rampant over-optimism bred of never having carried profit-and-loss responsibilities, who encourage expensive, extensive, but nonproductive studies. The logic is impeccable, but not profitable. Many consultants mouth hot management fads—spin-off, merger, going private, leveraged buy-out, reengineering, rightsizing and entrapreneurial—then shoe-horn them into any situation, regardless of applicability. All these off-target experts afflict the CEO more than any other corporate officer because he is viewed as being so powerful and yet much more susceptible to outside pressures.

Many CEOs, Rhody pointed out, stumble through the socioeconomic landscape in happy ignorance, bruising and sometimes even savaging customers, shareholders, and employees. This creates negative public perceptions that can result in lost markets, unproductive employees, restrictive if not punitive laws and regulations, and recruitment difficulties.

To be successful, Rhody advised managers to integrate all the forces operating in their environment, dealing with the emotions, fears, and expectations of all the publics they touch, not just those they choose to reach or are even aware of.[17] The surprises in business will not come from the closely monitored, well-known corporate heartlands, but from the rim lands: universities; social activists; previously silent, aggrieved *Rolling Stone* readers; patriotic but resentful rust-belt towns; a lumpen proletariat who are seldom given a voice until a news event erupts in their midst. Often trouble brews outside the experience or purview of inwardly directed senior management.

It should not surprise a broadly trained and interested public relations manager, although it does.

Rhody urged business leaders to manage in the future by consent and consensus, not command and control. To accomplish this, a CEO should expect his communications people to have these basic qualities:

- Skills in mass communications and interpersonal relations
- Media expertise
- A creative discipline
- Standard and shared techniques in social science and political affairs[18] (a standard budget for a well-rounded program relates to company size and needs, but a sound yardstick is one-tenth to one-quarter of one per cent of sales for larger established corporations)

Publics act on their perceptions. How they view a company and its leaders, rightly or wrongly, is almost as important as what the company actually does. Short-term communications programs can help mitigate and preempt misleading information on issues important to the company. But over the long haul it is important to build a climate of public opinion and understanding that will allow legislators, regulators, and the general public to support operations and positions vital to the company.

Corporate performance, no matter how stellar, never speaks loudly and accurately enough to cut through the cacophony and competition of noise from disparate sources. To make a persuasive or competitive difference, officers must be bold enough to tell of achievements aggressively and often.

In all this the CEO plays a critical role:

- He must be marketed skillfully. Although he may shrink from the unfamiliar and uncongenial public spokesman role, it is essential to project the corporate personality and to become a public asset with constituencies. As public image becomes increasingly determinant in executive success, it is essential that CEOs, in particular, be trained in media relations and other aspects of communications.
- Personal communications. Leaders must project confidence—be persuasive, authoritative, and articulate, speaking in the lingo of the constituencies. However, these appearances must be rationed to complement strategies and conserve executive time.
- Few CEOs have the time, and perhaps not even the talent, to write

speeches, position papers, and testimony. Here an articulate writer
can assist, but never take over.

- Communications policy. Rhody concludes that the media's all-per-
vasiveness, the instantaneousness of information, and the fish-bowl
business environment make one point abundantly clear: nothing is
secret. The only safe policy for senior executives is to tell all the
truth as fast and as accurately as possible.

Later, in the fall of 1996, Rhody offered personal observations on
public relations, "Of Woolly Buggers, Managers and Time to Come,"
to senior communications officers of the Arthur W. Page Society: It
is still the best game in town, the most challenging, demanding,
rewarding in psychic income and increasingly in financial terms.
And, as he sees it, getting even better.

"The savvy CEOs are realizing they stand no chance at all of
reaching their goals unless they can create buy-in." "Most senior
managements—sometimes nudged by their board of directors—are
realizing they badly need the counsel," abilities, and experience only
first-rate professionals can provide. Rhody cited two examples. If a
company, at one of the most important junctures in its history, takes
the right action, it becomes a world-beater. "If it takes the wrong
one, or, worse, no action at all, it will be an also-ran." The key: can
management convincingly and persuasively make its case? The CEO
needs help, but if his PR staff consider themselves part of marketing,
they are totally unequipped, by mindset, inclination, or experience,
to handle major gut issues.

That's not "wholly the CEO's fault." He'd been told, wrongly,
public relations is a marketing function. Rather, it's a "reputation—an existence—function . . . involved with all the corporation's
challenges," PR can support sales and marketing, but that is only a
part of its charter. When the CEO is up to his knees in alligators, he
understands this. Increasingly, corporations are turning over their
entire public relations, governmental affairs, and internal communications operations to a lawyer, totally lacking experience. Neophytes
generally know what they don't know. "But, like almost everyone
else, they think they [know] what public relations is, [are] certain
any quite reasonably competent manager can manage the function
well." Events sink that idea often.

A lawyer often gains the top PR position, Rhody noted, because
the CEO and other senior management know and trust him, feel

comfortable with him. "He's intelligent, knows the company, and has good judgement, so what's the big deal?" Conversely, senior management too often doesn't really know or have much faith in the head of PR, or the function. "When the barbarians are at the gate, a first-rate staff under first-rate leadership is absolutely necessary to the corporation's success and growth."

Two other reasons non-PR communications executives are selected. First, the management myth. "We get away from the hands-on activities that built our reputation and got us our promotions in the first place. We 'delegate' and 'supervise' and don't like to get our hands dirty writing speeches, or releases, or dealing face-to-face with the hostile media."

Although "superior management skills are critical to running a successful public relations operation, the CEO has managers running out his ears." "When we stop plying our trade, we lose our edge and our value diminishes."

The CEO expects communicators to know what to do and how to do it, and to be able to do it themselves—"whether it's handle the tough media, write the critical policy speech, fashion the persuasive communications strategy, talk with the Congressman, sooth the irate customer . . . but just get the job done."

Second, "we do such an awful job of marketing ourselves." Why are those whose stock in trade is creating, articulating, packaging, and merchandising of ideas and concepts so bad at selling themselves? "We're just wrong to think performance will speak for itself, or the value of accomplishments is obvious, or there will be automatic appreciation for our work."

"Real pros make the job look easy. . . . The press isn't on your back, employees aren't picketing, special interest groups aren't burning you in effigy, shareholders aren't yelling for management's hide, Congress and the regulators aren't panting at the door—what could be so demanding about managing the public relations function?" What, indeed? Finally, simple incompetence—a job done so poorly management figures how much worse can a non-PR person screw up.

"Perhaps the most traumatic decade PR has ever experienced—takeovers, mergers, downsizings, rightsizings—produced many casualties. Budgets were slashed, staffs were cut, in some cases whole departments disappeared. A lot of people got bloodied. There are still a lot of walking wounded out there, and a lot of apprehension still among the survivors."

It has been a time of mixed blessings, he continued. Compensation packages, responsibilities, and authority have increased "quite nicely." The downside is: "reduced staffs and the wounds associated with cuts, a personal workload that is sometimes murderous, with no prospect of easing soon. A rapid turnover among senior practitioners, known, respected, and trusted, largely defined PR for their managements, industry, and the profession. "They knew their company's business as well as the line managers, they were damn good at what they did, they delivered when it counted, but perhaps most important, they all had synergistic relationships with top management."

Rhody doubts that "it is possible to build the same relationships today, with corporate management playing musical chairs." But new senior managers "are less media shy, much more sensitive to their constituents' expectations and standards, and far more understanding of the value of buy-in."[19]

GAZING AHEAD

A wide-ranging communications officer should be an early warning system for troubles and opportunities ahead. Miners and soldiers in World War I trenches used canaries to sense trouble early. In the spirit of communicators as corporate canaries, let's look ahead.

Thomas E. Eidson, in 1992 Hill and Knowlton's president and chief executive; shared with the Counselors Academy six trends changing public relations.[20] Citing Edward Bernays, he explained that public relations, "perhaps more than any other activity, continuously reinvents itself to reflect and serve our ever changing society." "It is clear a new era of regional competition is upon us." No longer is one company pitted against another, but against regional economic interests.

To manage global and competitive changes, Eidson noted Hill and Knowlton adapted total client service—essentially a shift from being a process to being client-driven. Written standards, established for every professional, and most aspects of the business aimed critiques not through the firm's eyes, but through those of the clients. Actually, this is a return to an absolute priority on client service that was the keystone of the firm's founder, John W. Hill. Externally, "the final globalization of business" drove practice shifts, such as more overseas offices and investment counselors who must understand and explain the new borderless economies.

Eidson cited the example of Hyundai, a Korean company best known for its automobiles, which also manufactures personal computers. Hyundai's PC market share is very small, so it moved the entire operation out of Korea—not to Singapore or Hong Kong—but to San Jose to be close to the leading edge of microchip technology.

Trend number two: Public relations is a major marketing player—every bit the equal of advertising and sales promotion firms. Unaided by advertising or any other communications device, PR is moving product at a greatly reduced cost. Why? How? According to Eidson, "A dozen years ago, spending for measured media advertising accounted for 54 percent of the advertising and sales promotion budgets of major U.S. corporations. The rest was spent on couponing, sponsored events, advertising novelties, and publicity. Now, only 30 percent of total spending goes toward measured media advertising. A full 70 percent goes for sales promotion, including public relations."

The high cost of network time is one reason for this dramatic reversal. A single one-minute network commercial can fund a public relations program for a month, even a year. Also, the increasing number of cable television channels and special interest publications permit marketers to spend less, yet better target their audiences. Brand proliferation is a factor, too. Marketing alone cannot effectively promote and differentiate products. Corporate image is reemerging as critical.

Eidson's third trend: "In the past, image-building was the most important mission of advertising and public relations. Not only did companies sell products, they sold themselves—first. For many reasons that strategy changed. Consumers became extremely price-conscious. Old-line corporations merged, were acquired, or went out of business. Technological advances made products outdated before they wore out. In a throw-away society, corporate image meant little to some manufacturers. They were very, very wrong."

Also some image-building was sullied by ego-tripping CEOs—all public presence was in their image or puffed their woolly ideas. Skeptics questioned not only the cost, but whether image was a smoke screen. Nasty proxy and merger fights further darkened reputations.

Now corporate image, also called reputation management, is being used to promote professional services such as lawyers, and to distinguish products amid a proliferation of choices.

A fourth trend—continuing major changes in the new media—heightens that challenge. Most cities are one-newspaper towns. Broadcast networks and magazines, once considered immune from acquisition, are becoming pieces of larger diverse companies. When American Express attempted to take over McGraw-Hill some years ago, many persons were shocked. (Not all was driven by the takeover of a large, important publishing company. The maladroit public actions of then AmEx chairman James Robinson "helped.") Eidson contrasted that to the reaction of the Time-Warner merger. "The biggest controversy involved the price of the stock, not the fact that one of the most distinguished names in print journalism was being submerged into a company famous for making gangster movies." His point was validated anew with the Turner merger, Disney and Viacom, and more to come. Nary a contentious word.

The problem for both PR and the public? First, "Profitability issues. No longer will the owners of news media view themselves operating primarily with the public interest at heart and with profitability as a secondary issue." "We already have seen what this can mean: Happy faces on television and cotton candy in print. Dismissal of highly skilled, highly paid veteran newscasters from networks and stations . . . early retirement of senior writers and editors at newspaper and magazines . . . the downsizing of news staffs almost everywhere . . . and a growing emphasis on sex, scandal and superficiality among even our most respected news media."

Eidson expects the "problem to get worse, not better. Many survivors of media downsizing are baby-boomers with more enthusiasm than experience, more energy than knowledge, . . . cynical and exceedingly self-protective." Time and cost pressures will deplete the time and resources to check out facts on controversial stories or initiate stories on complex issues or those that might offend advertisers. The summer of 1998 bore out Eidson's warning. The Boston Globe was faced with one columnist, Patricia Smith, faking information, and another, Mike Barnicle, repeating jokes sans attribution. And there was CNN's chemical gas debacle.

Eidson noted other lapses. "A noted compensation specialist unceremoniously broke ties with *Fortune* after identifying the CEO of

Time Warner as the most overpaid executive in America. Automobile dealers are beginning to pressure newspapers not to run articles telling consumers how to bargain for a new car." These plus court decisions against ABC's "Prime Time" will chill aggressive reporting, even that done thoroughly and fairly. Given the small profit margins of smaller news outlets, even a suit won may be fatally expensive.

The fifth trend—agency of record—alters the traditional firm–client relationship dramatically, according to Eidson. Twenty years ago, single agencies served a client's needs—contracting, subcontracting, either bringing in specialist firms or participating in their selection. Under the retainer structure, many clients stayed in-house for decades. Most agencies would not prospect a corporation if they knew a competing agency was in place. Large agencies flourished. They developed new and exciting communications techniques, all in a very, very helpful and benign environment. Genuine partnerships were formed between agencies and clients. Both sides invested time and money to ensure communications products and counsel were valid and valuable. To Eidson, "this was the golden age of public relations." In the late 1970s, things became unstuck. "Large agencies began to go at one another competitively."

The key question became not how to serve a client, but how to win a new one. "The impact on the industry, I suggest, was severe and negative. Tough and bitter agency shoot-outs for new clients became commonplace. Price cuts and huge expenditures on presentations to prospects were made." The average new business proposal for a $250,000 prospect rose in a decade from about $2,000 to between $10,000 and $15,000. Simultaneously, costs of special services—speeches and video news releases—as well as PR budgets generally rose. Increasingly, budget-driven clients began questioning dollar value and shopping for agency services ad hoc. 'Agency-of-record' and all it positives for both agency and client began to break up. Now it is more customary for "corporations [to be] served by as many public relations agencies as they have law firms—with often the same result, large fees with doubtful results." Eidson opposed this trend as ineffective. "It undercuts the . . . building of effective partnerships, in terms of trust, understanding, familiarity, investments in time, loyalty, responsibility, etc. . . . Serving ad hoc client relationships is a little bit like a surgeon trying to operate under a strobe light. You are in, you are out, you are in, you are out, and you never get a long-term picture." "We did this to ourselves. Clients did not do it to us."

Despite some corporate willingness toward agency-of-record, Eidson doubts a return to those golden years of a single agency/client relationship. Renewed focus on the quality of counsel, service and value, not price and quality of presentation, will benefit all. "But it will only happen if we . . . believe that long-term is better than short-term."

Finally, he addressed the "disturbing and growing tendency of the court system and regulatory agencies to allow, if not actually encourage, misplacement of responsibility. . . . Not laxity in taking law or regulation breakers to task; quite the contrary. It has everything to do with overzealous, punitive activity, . . . a growing belief that to deal with criminal and civil offenders, we need to hang everybody in sight." For example, public relations agencies are held responsible for the accuracy of all client information they distribute, "even when the client supplies the information, and the agency acted in good faith and met professional standards. Responsibility is portioned out to those who commit the crime as well as to those who unknowingly are associated with it." The effect on the PR industry will be devastating. "Agencies will be swimming in a chill, fog-shrouded sea."

This is not just a question of refusing to represent highly controversial clients, no matter how legitimate the cause, but of representing major social issues. Will we "shy away from clients with any potential liabilities for fear of being made legally part of the problem"?

Other practitioners argue that, like defendants in court, every PR client has a right to counsel. That only escalates the risks Eidson fears. For example, in the early 1990s for six months before the brouhaha over BCCI broke in the English courts, H&K handled some media relations work for the then relatively unknown international bank. When it became the hot news topic worldwide, both trade and general media charged that H&K should have checked out the client more closely. Eidson countered forcefully: "I must confess, professionals can barely fill out their time sheets properly. They are not competent to conduct legal and accounting reviews of an organization such as BCCI—reviews that large numbers of accounting, legal, management consulting firms and governments failed to carry out effectively. The idea of account executives and supervisors conducting an investigation of BCCI beyond the normal checks of Dun & Bradstreet, standard data banks and references—an investigation that would have ferreted out the criminal activities of this bank— conjures up for me visions of the Three Stooges. I'd laugh if it were not something that was actually raised, insinuated and pointed out publicly."

Battle-like pressure hones principles about crisis-coping and communications. The best, most valuable communicators must keep saying, "Look out that window to a wider world." And do it all, while understanding the corporate culture well enough to keep their jobs.

NOTES

1. Janus is an ancient Roman deity who presided over doors and gates, and beginnings and endings. He was commonly represented with two faces looking in opposite directions. Translated to communications, Janus represents the corporate officer who, to be effective, must face outward to the world, yet inward to his peers and the business. *New York Times* columnist William Safire writes that "Janus Lives" in words that mean both the original and the changed sense. This diminishes Janus words because they communicate confusion. Also, the doors to Janus's temple were open in wartime, closed when Rome was at peace See William Safire, "Janus Lives," *The New York Times Magazine*, April 27, 1997, p. 22. Sounds like the door to the CEO? The chief communicator? There's the rub, the problem.

2. William Oliver, "Practitioner's Dilemma," *TJFR*, May 1996.

3. Based on remarks made by William Oliver, vice president for public relations, AT&T, to the Thirteenth Annual Meeting, Arthur W. Page Society, September 29, 1996, Sundance, Utah, pp. 3–4 of the report.

4. Ibid., pp. 19–20.

5. Clay Felker, "The End of a Dynasty," *Manhattan, Inc.* March 1995, p. 8.

6. Readers interested in public relations during labor strife and the involvement of Ivy Lee are referred to George S. McGovern and Leonard F. Guttridge, *The Great Coalfield War* (Boston: Houghton Mifflin, 1972), p. 383.

7. Felker, "End of a Dynasty," p. 8.

8. Edward L. Bernays, *Biography of an Idea: Memoirs of PR Counsel* (New York: Simon & Schuster, 1965), p. 374.

9. John W. Hill wrote two books. The first, *Corporate Public Relations: Arm of Modern Management* (New York: Harper & Brothers, 1958), details

the concept—more valid today than when Hill wrote—that communications must be in the matrix of its times, meeting needs. The second work is somewhat autobiographical; *The Making of a Public Relations Man* (New York: David McKay, 1963).

10. Kepone is an unremembered historical footnote today. In 1975, tremors, headaches, and sterility were reported by residents in Virginia. Allied Chemical Company (now Allied Signal) was reported to be dumping the insecticide into the James River. Allied reacted by investing heavily in antipollution and safety equipment. The malaise disappeared. The kepone incident illustrates, once again, a very public, costly problem that could have been avoided by thinking publicly.

11. Readers interested in the startling transformations in United Fruit's public relations, which in many ways track corporate communications itself, are directed to McCann's book *An American Company: The Tragedy of United Fruit* (New York: Crown, 1976).

12. Prince Gregori Alexsandrovich Potemkin, a Russian statesman and favorite of Catherine the Great's, constructed sham villages along the banks of the Dneiper River. He marshaled the peasantry to create the illusion of progress. Although these façades may have totally impressed foreign diplomats, Catherine understood that behind the sham was some sound prosperity and progress.

13. Men want to endow women with all the noble, good, and kind instincts that many men wish they could display openly in corporate life. When a women not only eschews this basically peripheral role but also demonstrates greater realism than her male colleagues toward the hard-knuckled world outside the corporation, she is in for trouble—no matter how capable she is.

14. Larry Speakes, with Robert Pack, *Speaking Out: Inside the Reagan White House* (New York: Charles Scribner's Sons, 1988), pp.150–163.

15. Ideas attributed to Richard Cheney come from his address "How I Went From the Corporate War Room to a Seat Behind the Analyst's Couch," The Institute for Public Relations Research and Education 35th Annual Distinguished Lecture Series, October 9, 1996.

16. Ronald E. Rhody, "Public Relations for the CEO," Bank of America Reprint of remarks to the Young Presidents Organization, Palo Alto, California, September 20, 1984.

17. Circumscribed *Literary Digest*-type thinking is dangerous and misleading. Poll only those who have telephones, as *Literary Digest* did in 1932, and of course Herbert Hoover will be predicted to win the presidency. That's akin to taking a poll at a private eating club, the country club, or the Business Roundtable.

18. These activities traditionally translate into: employee and financial

communications; media, government, and community relations; public information; external publications; contributions; product publicity; corporate advertising (usually image-oriented rather than product-oriented); and issues management.

19. Ronald E. Rhody, "Of Woolly Buggers, Managers and Times to Come," Arthur W. Page Society, Thirteenth Annual Meeting, September 29–October 2, 1996, Sundance, Utah, p. 32.

20. "Six Trends That are Changing Public Relations" remarks by Thomas E. Eidson, President and Chief Executive, Hill and Knowlton, Inc. Public Relations Counsellors Academy, San Diego,California, April 28, 1992.

11

Paths Around Pitfalls
Avoiding Communications Disasters

> "Public opinion will always believe the worst about you unless you tell your side honestly, completely and very quickly."
>
> —Chester Burger

Each communications crisis is different. None has a set pattern or a desired quick and easy resolution. As the cases commented on in this book indicate, sometimes the CEO can be too visible or too noticeably absent. Detailed advanced planning is almost sufficient in some instances, but in sudden disasters can be just an incomplete, outdated road map. Some aggrieved executives benefit from public protest; for others, it merely drags the story out and makes the executive sound like the proverbial misquoted politician. Some companies suffer by speaking out boldly; others have been hurt by being too quiet and defensive, even when basically in the right.

Just as managers thirst after the latest recipes for success, rather than selectively adapting the most useful ideas, managers under public pressure or in the throes of major turmoil, particularly for the first time, may seek the one quick fix. Be assured: there isn't any. Essential are intelligent general planning, developing personal survival techniques, and making sure operations and people don't fall into classic traps. Here are paths around pitfalls:

First, scope the environment honestly, not wishfully. Trace-lines, in retrospect, are always so obvious. The challenge is to spot in advance those that will affect a company, then plan to minimize their impact. Learning from the best analytical work of government intelligence agencies or simply tapping sources not normally used by competitors can yield advantages. For example, letters of protest in *The New York Review of Books* indicated the Shah of Iran's shakiness long before it was evident in business or general publications. Another useful technique is borrowing from disciplines not usually applied to business problems. Historians, particularly of the *Annales* school, point out that the easily seen and understood surface events seldom are the most important. By the time an event cracks through the surface, it may already be less powerful and significant than the glacially moving, difficult to detect and understand events hidden under many layers. Often such events are simply overlooked.

Dramatic changes often spring from unexpected sources. It behooves a manager to study the lines of change and power at the periphery as an indication of the future at the center. American historian Francis Parkman saw early on that the French empire in the New World was coming unstuck in the forest: first in the rimland, then at the heart. Remember the blind spot is the one you don't see.

Second, attempt to view the company as others do, particularly important audiences and the media. Adopt their mindset. Internal assumptions and procedures, the necessary concentration of senior management on immediate, pressing business concerns, dulls or delays the need to consider how an action will look to the public. This author has sensitized communicators to this by telling them to write a news release, then to literally walk around to the other side of their desks and ask as an editor or reporter (most had been) what they would believe or find newsworthy. Almost all the releases were reworked; some were just scrapped. That's advice for the press as well as business.

Third, attempt to appreciate the extreme pressures on the media: relentless deadlines, particularly on television, cable, and wire services; an equally relentless appetite for dramatic news and photographs; and fierce competition. Media people may be coming to your story tired, having just covered a totally different subject. Business people and journalists share tough, exacting work in a high-pressure world where mistakes are dealt with harshly. Too often this common condition is overlooked.

Fourth, hire a pragmatic, wide-vision thinker as the communications officer, then let him operate. Appreciate that, more than others reporting to the CEO, he must be a hybrid—very much a business, internal type, consummately versed in market and business realities, but also able to translate for colleagues the hard-knuckled needs of media relations and the less controllable public arena. If he is excluded from the loop of information, but still expected to front for the company, he is sure to transmit that lack to a vigilant press. To succeed, as executive or department, communications must be part of the corporation's total activities: built into long-range strategic plans, not patched in as an afterthought or peripheral activity. Some communicators call themselves corporate undertakers, people who are invited in after the death or damage, or firemen to put out public firestorms.

Fifth, consider the human toll of corporate turmoil. Too often it's overlooked. A popular, upbeat, and machismo attitude may leave the individual unprepared. Sound, pragmatic management skills that got the executive promoted to senior management will help him succeed in time of crisis—if he hasn't forgotten them. He must devise a psychological gyroscope, individual ways of keeping his footing and balance, his humor and perspective, while the maelstrom whirls about him. Theoreticians in stress management have their nostrums. Those who have been in the trenches themselves have ones of greater utility. A circle of confidants, people one can truly trust and who have shared roughly similar experiences, spells survival. Talking to the most intelligent, most well-intentioned family or friends is akin to the experience of soldiers on home leave from the Western Front during World War I. Despite the gunfire occasionally heard booming in the distance, despite the awesome losses, the soldiers' tales of battlefield horror were met with incredulity. Even several years after the Armistice, Vera Brittain, a front-line nurse, was treated as a little eccentric by students who were unscathed.

Experienced observers can assure the executive under public fire that others have survived such plights, and that his, too, will end eventually. He may not totally believe them. Some surprises in events and people will be nasty, but others will be unexpectedly pleasant. The personal qualities most essential to survival are patience, doggedness, and the willingness to go on day by weary day, nasty revelation by nasty revelation, leak by leak, misstatement by misstatement. Console yourself, the best communicators and best executives are not always the winners.

Three of the most common pitfalls—so obvious until you find yourself making them—are:

First, running operations as if the public were not interested. It is a pitfall for several reasons. Aggressive reporters and lawyers, increasingly activist boards of directors and pension-fund managers, vocal "victims" let few deeds, good or bad, pass unnoticed. Greater interest in business news and in personalities perceived to be powerful, successful, and exciting, government investigations, and general distrust of institutions leave nothing private for very long. Expecting that even a relatively routine action by a major company, particularly if it involves jobs, product safety, or the environment, will not arouse media interest is foolhardy. Secrets always surface at the most damaging, inconvenient, and embarrassing times.

When in doubt about an action, do as Dick Cheney did at Hill and Knowlton: suggest writing a release explaining why it was taken. Often that is convincing enough. Or, be just a bit more dramatic— but not much. If you are a defense contractor or chemical company, ask how that operational lapse, decision-making process, or product weakness would look on the front page of *The Washington Post* or on network television night after night. What is the cost analysis of public prudence beforehand compared with staggering costs later?

The second obvious pitfall is poisoning the in-box. Bad news gets strained out as it goes up the chain of command. This was tragically demonstrated by the *Challenger* disaster. No one wants to tell the boss it won't work, or it's dangerous, or even to consider a worst-case scenario. Strong language blurs into compromising weasel words easily misunderstood and interpreted for one's own purpose. To counter this, sincerely encourage a management milieu open to loyal, intelligent disagreement. Ask for dissenting or minority opinions, for the reasoning on which a decision was based. Accepting a bland, optimistic consensus conceals major questions and disagreements. Among communicators there is a saying: They're rearranging the deck chairs on the *Titanic*, but no one's on iceberg watch. Any iceberg they spot is dismissed as as dangerous as an ice cube.

Encouraging a trusted devil's advocate to hone thoughts also depoisons the in-box. No one is smart enough to be his own devil's advocate. More intensive supervision and investigation by shoe leather balance the staff-generated information on which decisions are based. Unconventional means may be the most rewarding, but also the most disconcerting and overlooked. One health-care executive thought that it would be flaky to visit pioneering storefront health maintenance operations. Hospice was suspect, too. He closed his mind to the visits and, unfortunately for his company, to a substantial piece of future business.

The third common pitfall is unrehearsed spokespeople. They are perilous, particularly at a press conference or in times of crises, if an executive is prepared only with his untested self-confidence and enthusiasm for a project or point of view. Lacking precision of expression, he may oversell a solution or a product. An ill-chosen word or two cannot be recalled or "spun" away. It is also perilous to the job security of the communicator who tries to forewarn the uncooperative spokesperson about the tough, embarrassing corners he might talk himself into. Such efforts are not always appreciated before, or even after, the event. The once-burned understand. One very sophisticated, polished CEO, despite meticulous preparation, allowed himself to be snared by financial analysts into speculating on a worst possible case: one possible flat quarter after years of earnings increases. Of course, the comment was purely speculative, but it caused the stock to drop several points—unfairly and unnecessarily. Federal Reserve Board Chairman Alan Greenspan's "irrational exuberance" rattled and depressed stock prices around the world.

What can an executive, an operating manager, or one isolated from the hurly-burly pressure of communicating during times of corporate upheaval and tension learn from the turmoil-tested?

- First, a manager ultimately must be his own director of intelligence, gathering information skeptically and objectively. He must insist on exact description, on accurate and detailed verification of claims and assumptions. Then he must analyze the data with intuition as well as intelligence.
- He must jettison the hubris that everything can be controlled, or at least strategically planned for. Things usually go awry. A unique cluster of misperceptions, volatile events, and mistaken decisions often produce results that no one intended and few probably even foresaw. Anticipate the law of unintended consequences.
- Conversely, explaining everything as an accident or systemic lets managers off the hook too easily. No lessons are learned. Purposeful human decisions or responsibilities are too easily discounted.
- The best way to win a conflict may be to avoid it. Particularly in communications, prevention often succeeds where cures fail.
- Narrow, atavistic patterns and practices won't work. Changes and the pressures they produce strip away protective hypocrisies and

make shortsightedness, cultural blindness, and narcissism danger-ous. There is no safety—only danger—in relying on old habits and proven talents. As one historian cautions, those who remember the past uncritically may be the ones condemned to repeat it.

- Disciplined, intelligent intuition may be the key. Winston Church-ill's life illustrates the value of this and of studying and understand-ing defeat. He had a great intuitive feeling for the next lurch of history. He also accepted humiliating defeats, such as Gallipoli, as episodes natural to wielding power. But then, he was an uncommon man out of his time.

- A manager who restricts himself to linear thinking—a straight line to a solution or career success—robs himself of the subtlety and wisdom of cyclical patterns. And is ill prepared for the gathering cluster of change. Thinking chaos theory alerts the executive to seemingly random events which may coalesce to help or harm the company.

- Alexander Haig views the press in the ancient role of humbling the great. When a Roman emperor or general triumphantly returned to the city after a great victory, lest he be made drunk by glory and the cheers of the citizens, he was accompanied in his chariot by a dwarf/jester, who whispered into his ear, "Remember you are mortal."

In her career this author has worked for profane city editors, forever infected by *Front Page* stereotypes, and for wizards of ooze; for overly confident managers in the fat years, who felt they could do no wrong; and for the hand-wringers of bleaker years, who sought instant reci-pes for success. In the change and chaos that many companies and individuals are experiencing lies great opportunity to manage differ-ently: more analytically and participatively, with longer-range vision and greater personal balance, and ultimately with communications playing a much more integrated, decisive role. But this means not looking inward or backward, but realistically reading the fever charts of corporate change, the symptoms of corporate turmoil, and then communicating about it honestly.

For, just when you think everything is running smoothly, and under control . . . that one telephone call zings in, and you find yourself communicating with the whole world watching—again.

Glossary

BRIEFING

Used more by political spokespeople than corporate. Usually orchestrated daily to update or announce news, but also to "advance" the story, make it news, add color and urgency—all to influence the story to the principal's advantage.[1]

BUCKRAKER

A celebrity journalist usually associated with a T.V. talk show who speaks frequently for large fees, but balks at any public disclosure.[2]

DANCING

Defined by Marlin Fitzwater as a spokesperson not fully sure of the facts but who must sound authoritative and give explanations that will hold up under critical examination. State one clear fact, "then qualify it forty-seven different ways."

DIRTY QUESTIONS BOOK

Before any executive meets the press or financial analysts, his/her staff should research the major important questions likely to be asked, rank them in importance or potential danger, then either suggest answers or rehearse the executive before appearance. A misspoken word cannot be recalled, but can cause damage to stock price, image, objectives.

DISINFORMATION

Spreading untruthful information about a competitor, product, or rival political leader with intent to damage or defeat. Illustrated in politics by Arnaud de Borchgrave's and Robert Moss' novel *Spike* and the American Express campaign against banker Edmond Safra. Veteran PR man

John F. Budd, Jr., offers this definition: Disinformation is characterized as either a statement or a report that contains a kernel of fact, extrapolated to make a conclusion that is *not* factual, or a completely fabricated story, planted in a friendly media, then circulated elsewhere as authoritative.

HERD JOURNALISM

Rather than "dig for the scoop," reporters paraphrase the leads of important publications and writers. Originally described by Timothy Crouse in *Boys on the Bus* as the physical herding of reporters on a campaign bus.[3]

HOT TOPIC

An issue often highly emotional, such as the environment, AIDS, or downsizing, widely covered by the media. If a public relations exposure includes such a subject, the likelihood of wider, continuing, even biased coverage is increased.

HOUSE ORGAN

A somewhat passé and pejorative term for an internal, company-produced publication; usually a newsletter or magazine.

INTERNAL COMMUNICTIONS

A generic term used widely to cover all communications within an organization: printed, voice, and e-mail memos, and, increasingly, widely distributed videos. Considered a major tool of management particularly now to motivate and create loyalty in the work force.

LEAKS

Information, either damaging or self-aggrandizing, given clandestinely to the media. In business, leakers can be disgruntled employees, proselytizers, or whistle-blowers.

NEWS CYCLE

Either deadlines, becoming less important as news is instantaneously transmitted on CNN, or the five-day sequence from hard-news, through editorializing and talking heads, to news magazines. The latter usually operates with major news events.

PRESS CONFERENCE — The first option of novices. Imagine the embarrassment if a press conference is called and no one comes. Even worse, if reporters come and there's no news. Reporters loath a vacuum, so fill it often to a company's detriment. Press conferences should be reserved for major news important to the media, not merely to corporations or executives.

RUNNING OR DEVELOPING STORY — News that unfolds as more is learned about an event such as a large plant fire or major airline crisis.

SOUND-BITING — Journalists work through material everyone else has culled until they can produce a brief formulation cleverer and more quotable than everyone else's.[4]

SPIN — Nuancing a subject to put it in the most positive possible light. A subtle but complete change. Former presidential press secretary Marlin Fitzwater defines spin as "Weaving of basic truth into the fabric of a lie; the production of a cover garment that protects, or obscures, or deflects public attention." He, like many others, accords David Gergen the accolade of "spin master."[5]

TICK-TOCK — The press's demand for minute-by-minute accounting of events. The danger in this demand for instantaneous details is a mistake or speculation bound to return and haunt.

NOTES

1. Marlin Fitzwater, *Call the Briefing!* (Holbrook, Mass: Adams Media Corp., 1996), p. 92.

2. James M. Fallows, *Breaking the News* (New York: Vintage Books, 1997), p. 84

3. Timothy Crouse, *The Boys on the Bus* (New York, Ballantine, 1972).

4. Fallows, *Breaking the News*, p. 119.

5. Fitzwater, *Call the Briefing!* pp. 220–221.

6. Ibid., p. 282.

Bibliography

ARTICLES

Adams, James Ring. "How Ohio's Home State Beat the Examiners." *The Wall Street Journal*, September 15, 1985, p. 5.

Adams, Scott. "Dilbert's Management Handbook." *Fortune*, May 13, 1996, pp. 99–118.

Aldrich, Gary. "The 'Character Issue' and the FBI." *The Wall Street Journal*, October 11, 1996, p. A12.

Altman, Lawrence K., M.D. "Faith in Multiple-Drug Aids Trail Shaken by Report of Error in Lab." *The New York Times*, July 27, 1993, p. C3.

———. "No More Could Be Done, Mrs. Onassis Was Told." *The New York Times*, March 28, 1995, p. B10.

———. "Reagan and Alzheimer's: Following Path His Mother Traveled." *The New York Times*, November 4, 1994, p. C3.

———. "Skin Lesions Were Removed During President's Checkup." *The New York Times*, March 25, 1995, p. B10.

Annual Reports, Union Carbide Corporation.

"Apple, Part 2: The No-Nonsense Era of John Sculley." *Business Week*, January 27, 1986, pp. 96–97.

Archdeacon, Thomas J. "The High Cost of Living." Review of *The Great Wave: Price Revolutions and the Rhythm of History* by David Hackett Fischer. *The New York Times Book Review*, January 5, 1997, p. 29.

"At Upjohn, A Grim Changing of the Guard." *Business Week*, May 3, 1993, p. 36.

Bagli, Charles V. "Goodbye, Takeover Pain: The Spin Doctor Is In Merger Messengers Have Plenty to Do." *The New York Times*, March 2, 1997, Section 3, pp. 1, 12–13.

"Bank of Boston: A Public Relations Nightmare." *Business Week*, March 4, 1985, p. 78.

Bennahum, David S. "Just Gaming: Three days in the Desert with Joan Baud-Rillard, PJ Spooky, and the Chance Band." *Lingua Franca*, February 1997, pp. 59–63.

Bennett, Amanda. "CEO's Illness May Endanger Company's Health As Well." *The Wall Street Journal*, January 21, 1993, p. B1.

Berger, Joseph. "Goodbye Tickle Me Elmo; Hello Beanie Babies." *The New York Times*, March 13, 1997, pp. B1, 6.

"Bhopal Has American Demanding the 'Right to Know.' " *Business Week*, February 18, 1985, pp. 36–37.

Biddle, Wayne. "Lester Crown Blames the System." *The New York Times*, June 16, 1985, Section 3, pp. 1, 26.

Bing, Stanley. "Stepping Up to the Firing Line." *Fortune*, February 3, 1997, pp. 51–52.

Bissinger, H. G. "The Detective's Story." *Vanity Fair*, February 1997, pp. 114–119, 140–146.

Blumenthal, Sidney. "In Retrospect: The Tragedy and Lesson of Vietnam." *The New York Review of Books*, March 1995, pp. 66–69.

Blumenthal, W. Michael. "Candid Reflections of a Businessman in Washington." *Fortune*, January 29, 1979, pp. 36–46.

"Borg Family Member Is Richest New Jerseyan." *UPI*, December 11, 1988.

Bowman, Edward, and Howard Kunreuther. "Post-Bhopal Behavior at a Chemical Company." *Journal of Management Studies*, 25 (July 1988), 4.

Brauchli, Marcus W. "Aging Leaders Spark Questions in Asia, Health of Nations and Their Rulers Become Linked." *The Wall Street Journal*, July 16, 1996, p. A8.

Brenner, Marie. "American Nightmare: The Ballad of Richard Jewell." *Vanity Fair*, February 1997, pp. 100–107, 150–165.

Brooke, James. "Despite Toxic Waste, 350 Seek Love Canal Homes." *The New York Times*, September 22, 1985, p. 54.

Burrelle's Clipping Analyst, July 1984.

Bussey, John. "Wise Guys—and Newspapers—Still Bedevil P&G About Its Infamous Corporate Logo." *The Wall Street Journal*, May 29, 1985, p. 21.

Buzzota, V. R. "A Quiet Crisis in the Work Place." *The New York Times*, September 4, 1985, p. A27.

Carley, William M. "CEO's Heart Surgery Is Giving GE a Case of Succession Jitters." *The Wall Street Journal*, May 24, 1995, pp. A1, 5.

"Cellular Telephone Health Threat Suit Dismissed." *Reuters Business Report*, August 16, 1993.

"Chairman Had Cancer Surgery, AT&T Discloses." *Los Angeles Times*, April 12, 1988, Section 4, p. 3.

Chapelle, Tony. "Time to Take the Spotlight at TLC." *The New York Times*, November 27, 1994, Business Section, pp. 1, 6.

Charland, Bernard. "No Comment: Moving Toward a Measured and Managed Media Response." *Journal of Corporate Public Relations*, 1996–1997, pp. 91–115.

Cheney, Richard E. "Playing Defense." In *Crosscurrents in Corporate Communications*, No. 12. New York: Fortune, 1983.

Chera, Susan. "JAL's Post-Crash Troubles." *The New York Times*, November 8, 1985, p. D1.

Cohen, Roger. "A Divorce in the Executive Suite." *The New York Times*, February 24, 1992, p. D1.

———. "Steven Ross Defends His Paycheck." *The New York Times*, March 27, 1992, p. 28.

Coleman, Jennifer, and Merrie Spaeth. "Transplanting the Mick's Liver." *The Public Relations Strategist*, September 1996, pp. 51–55.

Crutchfield, James. "German-American Yesteryears: The Philadelphia Elite." *German Life*, February–March 1997, p. 50.

D'Argenio, Raymond. "How to Conduct a Takeover." In *Crosscurrents in Corporate Communications*, No. 12. New York: Fortune, 1983. Pp. 17–23.

Darlin, Damon, and Melinda Grenier Guiles. "Whose Takeover? Some GM People Feel Auto Firm, Not EDS Was the One Acquired." *The Wall Street Journal*, December 19, 1984, pp. 1, 20.

Diamond, Stuart. "Warren Anderson: A Public Crisis, a Personal Ordeal." *The New York Times*, May 19, 1985, Section 3, pp. 1, 8, 9.

Dickson, Martin. "McGowan, MCI Chairman and Telecom Visionary, Dies." *Financial Times*, June 9, 1992, p. 26.

———. "When A Fatal Illness Is a Public Affair—The Executive's Duty When Serious Illness Strikes." *Financial Times*, January 25, 1995, p. 8.

Dobbs, Lou. "Moneyline." CNN, April 26, 1994.

"Doctor Calls for More Research on Cellular Phones." *Business Week*, February 17, 1993.

Dunne, John Gregory. "Your Time Is My Time." *The New York Review of Books*, April 23, 1992, pp. 49–55.

Eckhouse, John. "Apple Parties, Unveils Strategy." *San Francisco Examiner*, February 4, 1986, p. 4.

Eckhouse, John, and Vlae Kershner. "Apple Settles Case Against Steven Jobs." *San Francisco Chronicle*, February 4, 1986, p. 7.

Edelman, Lawrence. "AT&T Chairman James Olson Dead At 62." *Reuters*, April 18, 1988.

Edmond, Alfred, Jr. "Another Lewis Heads TLC." *Black Enterprise*, March 1994, p. 13.

"E-Mail: Use It While Works." *The Ragan Report Weekly Survey and Methods for Communications Executives*, April 28, 1997, p. 6.

Erlanger, Steven. "Russians Ask if Illness Is Eroding Yeltsin's Political Judgment." *The New York Times*, February 16, 1995, p. A12.

———. "Speculation Rises About the State of Yeltsin's Health." *The New York Times*, July 15, 1995. p. 3.

Ezard, John. "Fifty Ways to Lose Your Workforce." *Manchester Guardian Weekly*, June 16, 1996, p. 3.

Fabrikant, Geraldine. "Heir Apparent at Time-Warner Is Out Amid Signs of Dissention." *The New York Times*, February 21, 1992, pp. D1, 5.

————. "The Media Business: Building a Future for Cable TV Via the Telephone: Time-Warner Chief Proves Deal Maker." *The New York Times*, May 18, 1993, p. D1.

————. "Settlement From Time Warner." *The New York Times*, February 22, 1992, pp. 37, 51.

Farhi, Paul. "Is Time Finally on Time-Warner's Side?" *The Washington Post National Weekly Edition*, July 3–9, 1995, p. 20.

Felker, Clay. "The End of a Dynasty." *Manhattan, Inc.*, March 1995, p. 8.

Fenner, Austin Evans. "Lewis's Widow Takes Over At TLC Beatrice." *New York Daily News*, January 6, 1994, pp. 1, 64.

Forbes. October 26, 1987, p. 70.

Fortune report on 1983 Corporate Communications Seminar.

Frankel, Max. "An Olympian Injustice." *The New York Times Magazine*, October 20, 1996, pp. 60–61.

————. "Something Doesn't Like a Wall." *The New York Times Magazine*, January 19, 1997, pp. 18, 20.

Freudenheim, Milt. "Upjohn's Chief Getting Treatments for Cancer." *The New York Times*, February 2, 1994, p. D2.

"GE's Chief Undergoes Angioplasty." *USA Today*, May 4, 1995, p. 18.

"General Dynamics Under Fire, as the Circle Widens, Indictment May Be Under Way." *Business Week*, March 25, 1985, pp. 70–76.

Glabuson, William. "At Knight-Ridder, a Struggle of Illness, not Power . . . and a Protector of Profits Takes the Helm." *The New York Times*, April 3, 1995, p. D8.

Goldberg, Carey. "As Sugar Fades, Hawaii Seeks a New Cash Crop." *The New York Times*, August 9, 1996, pp. A1, 6.

Gopnik, Adam. "Elvis of the Elysée: How François Mitterand Orchestrated His Own Afterlife." *The New Yorker*, November 7, 1996, pp. 40–45.

"The Gotcha that Backfired." *The New York Times*, News in Review, January 26, 1997, p. 2.

Greenstein, Irwin. "Allen Takes AT&T Reign." *MIS Week*, 9, No. 17 (April 25, 1988), 1.

Grove, Andy. "Taking on Prostate Cancer." *Fortune*, May 13, 1996, p. 8.

Gruson, Lindsay. "Home to Some Is Still Love Canal to Others." *The New York Times*, December 3, 1991, pp. B1, 6.

Guardian Weekly, May 9, 1993, p. 10.

Guzzardi, Walter, Jr. "The Politics of the Press: How to Deal With It." *Crosscurrents in Corporate Communications*, No. 14. New York: Fortune, 1985. Pp. 68–70.

Harris, Marilyn, and Judith H. Dobrzynski. "Judgement Day May Be at

Hand for Pierre Gousseland: Amax's Financial Crisis and His Controversial Decisions Could Cost Him His Job." *Business Week*, September 30, 1985, p. B5.

Harris, Roy J., Jr., and Damon Darlin. "GM, Hughes Face Culture Clash, Mixing Opposite Corporate Styles." *The Wall Street Journal*, June 6, 1985, p. 14.

Hawthorne, Mary. "Light and Shadows." *The New Yorker*, August 14, 1995, pp. 79–81.

Hayes, Thomas C. "Taking on Big Oil." *The New York Times*, April 12, 1992, Section 3, p. 14.

———. "Tennaco Chief Has Brain Cancer." *The New York Times*, January 21, 1993, pp. D1, 20.

Henninger, Daniel. "Keeping Cool About Environmental Disaster." Review of *Toxic Terror* by Elizabeth Whelan. *The Wall Street Journal*, November 1, 1985, p. 34.

Herring, Hubert B. "Elmo Black Market Goes On-Line." *The New York Times*, December 23, 1996, p. D5.

Hicks, Jonathan P. "Reginald F. Lewis, 50, Is Dead: Financier Led Beatrice Takeover." *The New York Times*, January 23, 1993. p. 4.

Hinds, Michael De Courcy. "Pennsylvania Governor Faces Health Questions." *The New York Times*, July 18, 1993, p. 24.

Hoffman, Andrew J. "An Uneasy Rebirth at Love Canal." *Environment*, March 1995, pp. 26–27.

Hoge, Warren. "Prince Phillip Angers Britons on Gun Control." *The New York Times*, December 20, 1996, p. A12.

Honolulu Bulletin and Star Advertiser.

Huey, John W., Jr., "Mike Walsh Takes on Brain Cancer." *Fortune*, February 1993, pp. 76–77.

———. "Our Reluctant Author Comes Forward." *Fortune*, May 13, 1996, p. 8.

Hylton, Richard D. "Salomon's Remaining Challenges." *The New York Times*, August 19, 1991, p. 41.

Impact, December 1996, p. 5.

"The Individual and the Organization." *Focus*, November 20, 1997, p. 43.

Jack O'Dwyer's Newsletter.

Jack O'Dwyer's Newsletter, December 14, 1983, p. 1.

Jack O'Dwyer's Newsletter, January 10, 1993, p. 7.

Jack O'Dwyer's Newsletter, February 15, 1996, p. 2.

Jack O'Dwyer's Newsletter, April 2, 1997, p. 7.

Jenkins, Holman W., Jr. "Hope vs. Experience: The Rematch." *The Wall Street Journal*, January 14, 1997, p. A23.

Jones, Kathryn. "E-Systems Head Reports Illness." *The New York Times*, April 28, 1993, p. D2.

Joyce, Edward J. "To Stop Another Bhopal." *Datamation*, 32 (March 1, 1986), 5.

Keller, John J. "FDA Officials Faults Cellular Group for Its Confidence That Phones Are Safe." *The Wall Street Journal*, September 28, 1993, p. B9.

Kilkenborg, Varlyn. "Back to Love Canal." *Harper's*, March 1991, pp. 72–78.

Klein, Anne. "Historical Events: Metro Marketing." *Focus*, June 15, 1992, pp. 66–67.

Kleinfield, N. R. "Coleco Moves out of the Cabbage Patch." *The New York Times*, July 21, 1985, p. F4.

———. "When Scandal Haunts the Corridors." *The New York Times*, June 16, 1985, Section 3, pp. 17, 26.

Koenig, Fredrick. "Rumors That Follow the Sun." *Across the Board*, February 1985, pp. 25–30.

Kupfer, Andrew, and Kate Ballen. "Bob Allen Rattles the Cages at AT&T." *Time*, June 19, 1989, pp. 58–72.

Lauder, David. "Upjohn Chairman Theodore Cooper Dies." *Reuter's Asia-Pacific Business Report*, April 22, 1993.

Lennox, Donald D. "Reckless Reporting: The International Harvester Ordeal." *Crosscurrents in Corporate Communications*, No. 14. New York: Fortune, 1985. Pp. 60–64.

Lewis, Michael. "Naughty But Nice: In Praise of Cynicism, Humor." *The New Republic*, March 8, 1993, p. 14.

Light, Larry, with Mark Lander. "Killing a Rumor Before It Kills a Company." *Business Week*, December 24, 1990, p. 23.

"Lilco Is Praised by Its Chairman for Storm Effort." *The New York Times*, October 8, 1985, B4.

Lipton, Martin. "Takeovers and Communication." *Crosscurrents in Corporate Communications*, No. 12. New York: Fortune, 1983. Pp. 00–00.

Loomis, Carol. "Six Handy Rules for Dealing with the Media." *Crosscurrents in Corporate Communications*, No. 14. New York: Fortune, 1985. Pp. 65–68.

"Loss Leader." *Financial Times*, May 12, 1987, p. 24.

"Love Canal." *The Facts (1892–1982)*, Occidental Chemical Fact Line, No. 13 (September 1982).

Lueck, Thomas J. "Chief's Post Given Up by Gray, Technologies Names Daniell." *The New York Times*, September 24, 1985, p. D1.

Magnet, Myron. "Is ITT Fighting Shadows—or Raiders?" *Fortune*, November 11, 1985, pp. 25–28.

"Managing Innovation." *Daedalus: Journal of The American Academy of Arts and Sciences*, Spring 1996.

Mankowski, Cal. "U.S. Rules on Reporting Executive Illness." *Reuters*, April 26, 1988.

"Mattel Profits Lowered by Hair-Chewing Doll." *The New York Times*, February 6, 1997, D4.

May, Clifford D. "Shoreham Plant Opponents Pressing for State Takeover of Lilco." *The New York Times*, December 28, 1985, p. B5.

McClintick, David. "The Man Who Swallowed Time Inc." *The New York Times Book Review*, April 10, 1994, pp. 1, 32, 33, 37–38.

McGough, Robert. "My Son, I Brought Him Up Like An Immigrant." Great Wealth in America, *Forbes*, October 26, 1987, p. 70.

McGrath, Dan. "As Two Mikes Return, Recall How They Left." *Sacramento Bee*, March 26, 1995, p. A2.

"MCI's McGowan Recovering From Heart Transplant." *Los Angeles Times*, May 8, 1987, Section 4, p. 3.

Milhill, Chris. "Low-Paid Most at Risk From Heart Attacks." *Manchester Guardian Weekly*, September 3, 1995, p. 1.

Monroe, Tony. "Union Pacific's Lewis at Alcohol Abuse Unit." *The Washington Times*, January 24, 1994, p. A19.

Morias, Richard C. "The Banana Skin Factor: Standard Charter Is a Cheap Bank Stock." *Forbes*, July 19, 1993, pp. 73–75.

Mutchler, Megan. "Roosevelt's Disability at Issue at Memorial." *The New York Times*, April 10, 1995, p. A10.

Myerson, Allen R. "Michael Walsh, Executive, Dead at 51." *The New York Times*, May 7, 1994, p. 30.

———. "Top Tenneco Official Quits to Fight Effects of Illness." *The New York Times*, September 25, 1994, p. D1.

———. "West Pointer Commands at Tenneco." *The New York Times*, May 15, 1994, p. B4.

The New York Times, editorial, June 20, 1981.

The New York Times, August 13, 1985, p. B9.

The New York Times, October 30, 1985, p. A13.

The New York Times, January 24, 1993, p. B2.

The New York Times, Week in Review, February 2, 1997, Section 4, p. 2.

O'Brien, Thomas F., and Mark Russel. "Troubled Marriage: Steel Giants Merger Brings Big Headaches, J&L and Republic Find." *The Wall Street Journal*, November 30, 1984, pp. 1, 20.

O'Dwyer, Jack. *Jack O'Dwyer's Newsletter*, March 12, 1997, p. 2.

O'Reilly, Brian. "Agee in Exile." *Fortune*, May 29, 1995, pp. 50–74.

Oliver, William. "Practitioner's Dilemma." *TJFR*, May, 1996.

Pace, Eric. "Kenneth R. Crispell, 79, Dean and Health Expert on Presidents" (an obituary). *The New York Times*, August 26, 1996, p. 8.

Pagan, Rafael D., Jr. "Carrying the Fight to the Critics of Multinational Capitalism: Think and Act Politically." *Vital Speeches*, July 15, 1982, pp. 589–591.

Parish, Andy. "Antenna Exorcises TV Ghosts." *Houston Chronicle*, February 26, 1994, p. 2.

Pereira, Joseph. "Toy Story: How Shrewd Marketing Made Elmo a Hit." *The Wall Street Journal*, December 20, 1996, pp. B1, 7.

Philadelphia Inquirer.

Pimitel, Torres Minton Ben. "Maria Group Battles Cellular Phone Giant." *San Francisco Chronicle*, October 15, 1993, p. A23.

Pinsdorf, Marion K. "Flying Different Skies: How Cultures Respond to Airline Disasters." *Public Relations Review*, Spring 1991, pp. 37–56.

———. "Gossamer Webs of Communications: Trust and Relationships." *Focus*, July, 1993, pp. 18–21.

———. "Quiddies: Post Yuppie MBA's." *Executive Challenge: Issues Strategies and Communications*, published by Hill and Knowlton, Winter, 1989.

Pires, Mary Ann. "Time to Cultivate Real 'Influentials.'" *Impact*, December 1996, p. 1.

Pollack, Andrew. "Morita, Sony Founder, Hospitalized." *The New York Times*, December 3, 1993, p. D2.

Power, Thomas. "No Laughing Matter." *The New York Review of Books*, August 10, 1995, pp. 4–6.

PR News, Case Study no. 1963.

Proxmire, William. "Why Military Contracting Is Corrupt: Cleaning Up Procurement." *The New York Times*, December 15, 1985, Section 3, p. 3.

"Return to Job Questioned: MCI Chairman McGowan Receives Heart Transplants." *Communications Daily*, May 8, 1987, p. 2.

Richards, Rhonda. "TLC Beatrice's No-Nonsense Boss: Lewis Ends Mourning, Takes Helm." *Money*, January 11, 1994. p. 58.

Ringer, Richard. "Shareholders Hail Changes at Beatrice." *The New York Times*, January 7, 1995, p. D5.

Rosett, Claudia, and Steve Liesman. "Yeltsin Takes Sick, But Russia Stays Calm; Constitutional Septem Appears to Have Taken Hold." *The Wall Street Journal*, July 12, 1995. p. A11.

Ross, Thomas. "RCA's Comeback, Communicating the Story." *Crosscurrents in Corporate Communications*, No. 14. New York: Fortune, 1985. Pp. 28–31.

Royster, Vermont. "End of a Chapter." *The Wall Street Journal*, March 5, 1986, p. 30.

Sack, Kevin. "A Man's Life Turned Inside Out by Government and Media." *The New York Times*, October 28, 1996, pp. A1, B7.

Safire, William. "Janus Lives." *The New York Times Magazine*, April 27, 1997, p. 22.

Sancton, Thomas. "A Lunch with France's James Bond." *Time*, April 4, 1994, p. 16.

San Francisco Examiner, October 29, 1985, pp. 1, 6.

"Saul Steinberg, Chief of Insurer Reliance, Had Stroke in June." *The Wall Street Journal*, August 10, 1995, p. B10.

Schemo, Diana Jean. "Hidden and Haunted Behind the Headlines." *The New York Times*, June 12, 1992, pp. B1, 7.

Science, June 1981.

Sease, Douglas R. "GE's Image Makes Conviction More Jarring; Fraud Case Illustrates Difficulty of Enforcing Standards." *The Wall Street Journal*, July 5, 1985, p. 4.

Seitz, Robert. "Corporate Conundrum: Disclosing Illness in the Corner Office." *The New York Times*, May 2, 1993, p. 9.

Sellers, Patricia. "When Tragedy Faces Change." *Fortune*, January 10, 1994, p. 114.

Sen, Falguni, and William G. Egelhoff. "Six Years and Counting—Learning from Crisis Management at Bhopal." *PR Review*, November 20, 1990. Pp. 69–83.

Sharkey, Joe. "Elmo: The Spirit of Christmas." *The New York Times*, New Jersey section, December 21, 1996.

Sheeline, William A. "The Quiet Passing of a Star." *Fortune*, February 8, 1993, p. 32.

"Slowdown in Silicon Valley." *Newsweek*, September 30, 1985, pp. 46–57.

Smart, Tim. "Who Could Replace Jack Welch?" *Business Week*, May 29, 1995, p. 32.

Solomon, Caleb, and Robert Johnson. "Tenneco's Walsh Gives Up CEO's Post, Remains Chairman; Mead is Successor." *The Wall Street Journal*, February 25, 1994, p. A3.

"Some Cabbage Patch Dolls to Carry Warning Labels." *The Wall Street Journal*, January 2, 1997, p. 13.

Spaeth, Merrie. "What You Can Learn from Brokaw & Co." *The Wall Street Journal*, January 6, 1997, p. A12.

Specter, Michael. "Yeltsin Taken to Hospital Suffering Heart Pain." *The New York Times*, July 12, 1995, p. A3.

Stanley, Allesandra. "Issue of Yeltsin's Health Bungled, Kremlin Admits." *The New York Times*, September 5, 1996, p. A8.

———. "Yeltsin Displays His Health on TV." *The New York Times*, July 19, 1995, pp. Al, 4.

Sterngold, James. "The Undoing of Robert Fomon." *The New York Times*, September 29, 1985, Section 3, pp. 1, 10, 11.

Stevenson, Richard W. "Mending More than the Bottom Line." *The New York Times*, May 9, 1996, pp. D1, 21.

Stodghill, Ron. "At Upjohn, A Grim Changing of the Guard." *Business Week*, May 3, 1993, p. 36.

————. "TLC Beatrice Could Use More Than TLC." *Business Week*, January 24, 1994, p. 35.

Suskind, Ron. "Deadly Silence: How the Inner Circles of Medicine and Sports Failed a Stricken Star." *The Wall Street Journal*, March 9, 1995. pp. A1, 12, 13.

"Tennaco Says Walsh's Condition Not Improved." *Financial Report*, April 26, 1994.

"Texas Official Resigns Over Falsified Résumé." The *New York Times*, September 26, 1992, p. A5.

Thompson, Rachel W. "No Quick Changes Seen After Ross' Death." *Los Angeles Times*, November 11, 1992, Business Section, p. 2.

"TLC Beatrice's No-Nonsense Boss." *USA Today*, January 11, 1994, p. 5B.

Toobin, Jeffrey. "Courtroom vs. Newsroom." *The New Yorker*, January 21, 1997, pp. 5–6.

Trost, Cathy. "OSHA Plans to Fine Carbide $1.4 Million: Alleges Violation at West Va. Plant." *The Wall Street Journal*, April 2, 1986, p. 2.

Trotter, Clayton R., Susan G. Day, and Amy E. Love, "Bhopal, India, and Union Carbide: The Second Tragedy." *Journal of Business Ethics*, 8 (1989), 439–454.

"Union Pacific Announces Increase in Price of Proposal to Negotiate with Santa Fe; Lewis Takes Short-Term Medical Leave." *PR Newswire*, October 30, 1994.

"Union Pacific Chairman Takes Medical Leave." *Reuters Business Report*, October 30, 1994.

Uttal, Bro. "Behind the Fall." *Fortune*, August 5, 1985, pp. 20–24.

Verhouek, Sam Howe. "A Store Manager Interrupts a Theft, and His Career." *The New York Times*, December 18, 1996, p. A16.

Vickers, Marcia. "After Tripping on Its Laces, Reebok Is Focused Again." *The New York Times*, March 2, 1997, Section 3, p. 3.

Vidal, Gore. "Love on the Hudson." *The New York Review of Books*, May 19, 1995, pp. 4–6.

Walker, Blair S. "CEOs Who Fell to Illness." *USA Today*, January 25, 1993, p. 2B.

————. "How Healthy Are CEOs? Illness Often Treated as Private Issue." *USA Today*, January 25, 1993, p. 1B.

Walker, Jerry. "J-Prof Picks Best Newspapers in the World." *Jack O'Dwyer's Newsletter*, May 8, 1991, p. 5.

The Wall Street Journal, August 21, 1985, p. 1.

The Wall Street Journal, August 10, 1995, p. B10.

Wells, Ken, and Carol Hymowitz. "Takeover Trauma: Gulf's Managers Find Merger into Chevron Forces Many Changes." *The Wall Street Journal*, December 5, 1984, pp. 1, 24.

"Widow of Reginald Lewis Becomes TLC's Chairman; Founder's Brother Resigns." *Jet*, January 24, 1994, p. 38.

"William McGowan." *Financial Times*, June 17, 1992.

Wills, Garry. "What Makes a Good Leader." *The Atlantic Monthly*, April 1994, pp. 71–76.

Wise, Deborah C. "Can John Sculley Clean Up the Mess at Apple?" *Business Week*, July 29, 1985, pp. 70–72.

Wise, Mike. "Celtics Deny Reports About Lewis." *The New York Times*, March 10, 1995, p. B12.

Young, Lewis H. "The Distorted Image." *Financial Executive*, April 1985, p. 18.

"You're Dehired." *Harper's Magazine*, March 1991, 22.

Zellner, Wendy. "The Fight of His Life: Michael Walsh's Battle Against Cancer." *Business Week*, September 20, 1993, pp. 55–57, 62.

Zuesse, Eric. "Love Canal: The Truth Seeps Out." *Reason*, February 1981, pp. 17–33.

BOOKS

Abodaher, David. *Iacocca: A Biography*. New York: William Morrow, 1987.

Aldrich, Gary. *Unlimited Access: An FBI Agent Inside the Clinton White House*. Washington, D.C.: Regnery, 1996.

Angell, Marcia, M.D. *Science on Trial: The Clash of Medical Evidence and the Law in the Breast Implant Case*. New York: W. W. Norton, 1996.

Baar, James. *The Great Free Enterprise Gambit*. Boston: Houghton Mifflin, 1980.

Baltzell, E. Digby. *Philadelphia Gentlemen: The Making of a National Upper Class*. Philadelphia: University of Pennsylvania Press, 1979.

Baritz, Loren. *A History of How American Culture Led Us into Vietnam and Made Us Fight the Way We Did*. New York: William Morrow, 1985.

Barret, Marvin, and Zachary Sklar. *The Eye of the Storm*. New York: Lippincott & Crowell, 1908.

Behrens, John C. *The Typewriter Guerrillas: Closeups of Twenty Top Investigative Reporters*. Chicago: Nelson-Hall, 1997.

Bell, Daniel. *The Coming of Post-Industrial Society: Adventure in Social Forecasting*. New York: Basic Books, 1973.

Bernays, Edward L. *Biography of an Idea: Memoirs of Public Relations Counsel*. New York: Simon & Schuster, 1965.

Bernstein, Carl, and Bob Woodward. *All the President's Men*. New York: Simon & Schuster, 1974.

Blyskal, Jeff, and Marie Blyska. PR: How the Public Relations Industry Writes the News. New York: William Morrow, 1985.

Böll, Heinrich. The Lost Honor of Katharina Blum. New York: McGraw-Hill, 1975.

Broder, Paul. Outrageous Misconduct: The Asbestos Industry on Trial. New York: Pantheon, 1985.

Brown, Michael. Laying Waste: The Poisoning of America by Toxic Chemicals. New York: Pantheon, 1979.

Bruck, Connie. Master of the Game: Steven Ross and the Creation of Time-Warner. New York: Simon & Schuster, 1994.

Burrough, Bryan, and John Helyar. Barbarians at the Gate. New York: Harper & Row, 1990.

Carroll, James. An American Requiem: God, My Father, and the War That Came Between Us. Boston: Houghton Mifflin, 1996.

Carter, William C. Conversations with Shelby Foote. Jackson: University of Mississippi Press, 1990.

Clurman, Richard M. To the End of Time: The Seduction and Conquest of a Media Empire. New York: Simon & Schuster, 1992.

Cramer, Richard Ben. What It Takes: The Way to the White House. New York: Random House, 1992.

Crispell, Kenneth R., M.D., and Carlos F. Gomez. Hidden Illness in the White House. Durham, N.C.: Duke University Press, 1988.

Crouse, Timothy. The Boys on the Bus. New York: Ballantine, 1972.

Cunningham, Mary, with Fran Schumer. Powerplay: What Really Happened at Bendix. New York: Linden Press/Simon & Schuster, 1984.

Deaver, Michael K., with Mickey Herskowitz. Behind the Scenes, in Which the Author Talks About Ronald and Nancy Reagan and Himself. New York: William Morrow, 1987.

De Borchgrave, Arnuad, and Robert Moss. The Spike. New York: Avon, 1980.

Dilenschneider, Robert L., ed. Dartnell's Public Relations Handbook. 4th ed. Chicago: Dartnell Corporation, 1996.

Donald, David Herbert. Lincoln. New York: Simon & Schuster, 1995.

Drucker, Peter. Innovation and Entrepreneurship: Practice and Principles. New York: Harper & Row, 1985.

———. Managing in a Time of Great Change. New York: Dutton, 1995.

Epstein, Edward Jay. Dossier: The Secret History of Armand Hammer. New York: Random House, 1996.

Erikson, Kai. A New Species of Trouble: Explorations in Disaster, Trauma, and Community. New York: W. W. Norton, 1994.

Fallaci, Oriana. Interview with History. Trans. John Sheply. Boston: Houghton Mifflin, 1976.

Fallows, James. Breaking the News: How the Media Undermine American Democracy. New York: Pantheon, 1996.

Ferguson, Marilyn. *The Aquarian Conspiracy: Personal and Social Transformation in the 1980s.* Los Angeles: J. P. Tarcher, 1980.

Fitzwater, Marlin. *Call the Briefing: Reagan and Bush, Sam and Helen—A Decade with Presidents and the Press.* New York: Times Books/Random House, 1995.

Fox, Stephen. *A History of American Advertising and Its Creators.* New York: Vintage, 1984.

Gallagher, Hugh Gregory. *FDR's Splendid Deception.* New York: Dodd, Mead, 1985.

Garreau, Joel. *The Nine Nations of North America.* Boston: Houghton Mifflin, 1981.

Geneen, Harold, with Alvin Moscow. *Managing.* New York: Avon, 1984.

Geyer, Georgie Anne. *Buying the Night Flight: The Autobiography of a Woman Foreign Correspondent.* New York: Dell Laurel/Merloyd Lawrence, 1983.

Gilbert, Robert E. *The Mortal Presidency: Illness, and Anguish in The White House.* 2nd ed. New York: Fordham University Press, 1998.

Ginzberg, Eli, and George Vojta. *Beyond Human Scale: The Large Corporations at Risk.* New York: Basic Books, 1985.

Goldstein, Tom. *The News at Any Cost: How Journalists Compromise Their Ethics to Shape the News.* New York: Simon & Schuster, 1985.

Goodwin, Doris Kearns. *No Ordinary Time: Franklin and Eleanor Roosevelt—The Home in World War II.* New York: Simon & Schuster, 1994.

Gordon, Michael, and Bernard E. Trainor. *The Generals' War: The Inside Story of Conflict in the Gulf.* Boston: Little, Brown, 1995.

Green, Mark, and Robert Massie, Jr., eds. *The Big Business Reader: Essays on Corporate America.* New York: The Pilgrim Press, 1980.

Greenstein, Fred I. *The Hidden-Hand Presidency: Eisenhower as Leader.* New York: Basic Books, 1982.

Grove, Andrew S. *High Output Management.* New York: Random House, 1983.

Haig, Alexander M., Jr., *Caveat: Realism, Reagan, and Foreign Policy.* New York: Macmillan, 1984.

Harr, Jonathan. *A Civil Action.* New York: Vintage, 1995.

Hartz, Peter F. *Merger: The Exclusive Story of the Bendix–Martin Marietta Takeover War.* New York: William Morrow, 1985.

Hill, John W. *Corporate Public Relations: Arm of Modern Management.* New York: Harper & Brothers, 1958.

———. *The Making of a Public Relations Man.* New York: David McKay, 1963.

Hobsbaurn, Eric. *The Age of Extremes: A History of the World, 1914–1991.* New York: Vintage, 1996.

Hoopes, Townsend, and Douglas Brinkley. *Driven Patriot: The Life and Times of James Forrestal.* New York: Vintage/Random House, 1993.

Iacocca, Lee, with William Novak. *Iacocca: An Autobiography.* New York: Bantam, 1984.

Ivins, Molly. *Molly Ivins Can't Say That, Can She?* New York: Random House, 1991.

Johnson, Paul. *Modern Times: The World from the Twenties to the Eighties.* New York: Harper & Row, 1983.

Kanter, Rosabeth Moss. *The Change Masters: Innovation and Entrepreneurship in the American Corporation.* New York: Simon & Schuster, 1983.

Karlen, Arno. *Napoleon's Glands and Other Ventures in Biohistory.* New York: Warner Books, 1984.

Karnow, Stanley. *Vietnam: A History—The First Complete Account of the Vietnam War.* New York: Viking, 1983.

Kindleberger, Charles P. *Maniacs, Panics, and Crashes: A History of Financial Crisis.* New York: Basic Books, 1978.

Kingwell, Mark. *Dreams of Millenium: Report from a Culture on the Brink.* Toronto: Viking Penguin, 1996.

Levin, Hillel. *Grand Delusions: The Cosmic Career of John DeLorean.* New York: Viking, 1983.

Levy, Steven. *Hackers: Heroes of the Computer Revolution.* Garden City, N.Y.: Anchor/Doubleday, 1984.

Lewis, Michael. *Liar's Poker: Rising Through the Wreckage on Wall Street.* New York: W. W. Norton, 1989.

Lewis, Reginald F., and Blair S. Walker. *Why Should White Guys Have All the Fun? How Reginald Lewis Created a Billion-Dollar Business Empire.-* New York: John Wiley, 1995.

Little, Roy. *How to Lose $100,000,000, and Other Valuable Advice.* Boston: Little, Brown, 1979.

Louv, Richard. *America II.* New York: Viking Penguin, 1973.

MacMahon, Edward B., and Leonard Curry. *Medical Cover-Ups in the White House.* Washington, D.C.: Farragut, 1987.

Manchester, William. *American Caesar: Douglas MacArthur, 1880–1964.* Boston: Little, Brown, 1978.

Mangold, Tom, and John Penycate. *The Tunnels of CuChi.* New York: Random House, 1985.

Martinez, Thomas Eloy. *Santa Evita.* Trans. Helen Lane. New York: Alfred A. Knopf, 1996.

May, Rollo. *The Courage to Create.* New York: W. W. Norton, 1975.

Mayer, Martin. *The Money Bazaars: Understanding the Banking Revolution Around Us.* New York: Dutton, 1984.

McCain, Thomas A., and Leonard Shyles, eds. *The 1000-Hour War: Communication in the Gulf.* Westport, Conn: Greenwood, 1994.

McCann, Thomas. *An American Company: The Tragedy of United Fruit.* New York: Crown, 1976.

McClintock, David. *Indecent Exposure: A True Story of Hollywood and Wall Street.* New York: Dell, 1982.

McGovern, George S., and Leonard F. Guttridge. *The Great Coalfield War.* Boston: Houghton Mifflin, 1972.

McNeil, William H. *Plagues and People.* Garden City, N.Y.: Anchor/Doubleday, 1976.

Micklethwait, John, and Adrian Wooldridge. *The Witch Doctors: Making Sense of Management Gurus.* New York: Times Books/Random House, 1996.

Miller, Merle. *Plain Speaking: An Oral Biography of Harry S Truman.* New York: G. P. Putnam's Sons, 1973.

Morris, Celia. *Storming the State House: Running for Governor with Ann Richards and Diane Feinstein.* New York: Charles Scribner's Sons, 1992.

Morrow, Lance. *The Chief: A Memoir of Fathers and Sons.* New York: Random House, 1984.

Nance, John J. *Blind Trust: How Deregulation Has Jeopardized Airline Safety and What You Can Do About It.* New York: William Morrow, 1986.

Nessen, Ron. *It Sure Looks Different from the Inside.* New York: Playboy Press, 1978.

Novak, Michael. *The Spirit of Democratic Capitalism.* New York: American Enterprise Institute/Simon & Schuster, 1982.

Ortiz, Alicia Dujovne. *Eva Perón.* Trans. Sharon Fields. New York: St. Martin's, 1996.

Overly, Richard. *Why the Allies Won.* New York: W. W. Norton, 1995.

Page, Joseph. *Perón.* New York: Random House, 1983.

Parkinson, C. Northcote. *Big Business.* Boston: Little, Brown, 1974.

Parkinson, C. Northcote, and Nigel Rowe. *Communicate: Parkinson's Formula for Business Survival.* Englewood Cliffs, N.J.: Prentice-Hall, 1978.

Peck, M. Scott, M.D. *People of the Lie: The Hope for Healing Human Evil.* New York: Simon & Schuster, 1983.

The People and the Press: A Times-Mirror Investigation of Public Attitudes Toward the News Media Conducted by the Gallup Organization. Los Angeles: Times-Mirror, 1986.

Perry, Susan, and Dawson Perry. *Nightmare: Women and the Dalkon Shield.* New York: MacMillian, 1985.

Peters, Tom, and Nancy Austin. *A Passion for Excellence: The Leadership Difference.* New York: Random House, 1985.

Peters, Thomas J., and Robert H. Waterman, Jr. *In Search of Excellence: Lessons from America's Best-Run Companies.* New York: Harper & Row, 1982.

Phillips, Kevin. *The Politics of Rich and Poor: Wealth and the American Electorate in the Reagan Aftermath*. New York: Random House, 1990.

Polmar, Norman, and Thomas B. Allen. *Rickover*. New York: Simon & Schuster, 1982.

Pratt, John Clark. *Vietnam Voices: Perspectives on the War Years, 1941–1982*. New York: Penguin, 1984.

Rather, Dan, with Mickey Herskowitz. *The Camera Never Blinks: Adventures of a T.V. Journalist*.New York: Ballantine, 1977.

Reedy, George E. *Lyndon B. Johnson: A Memoir*. New York: Andrews & McMeel, 1982.

———. *The Twilight of the Presidency*. New York: Mentor/New American Library, 1970.

Rogow, Arnold A. *James Forrestal: A Study of Personality, Politics, and Policy*. New York: Macmillan, 1963.

Safire, William. *Before the Fall: An Inside View of the Pre-Watergate White House*. Garden City, N.Y.: Doubleday, 1975.

Salsbury, Stephen. *No Way to Run a Railroad: The Untold Story of the Penn Central Crisis*. New York: McGraw-Hill, 1982.

Schoenberg, Robert J. *Geneen*. New York: Warner Books, 1985.

Schroeder, Eric James, ed. *Vietnam, We've All Been There: Interviews with American Writers*. Westport, Conn.: Praeger, 1992.

Schwarzkopf, H. Norman, with Peter Petre. *It Doesn't Take a Hero*. New York: Bantam, 1992.

Sevasy, Alicia. *Soap Opera: An Inside Story of Procter & Gamble*. New York: Touchstone, 1993.

Shapely, Deborah. *Promise and Power: The Life and Times of Robert McNamara*. Boston: Little, Brown, 1993.

Sherlock, Patricia. *On and Off the Record*. Hackensack, N.J.: Bergen Evening Record Corporation, 1995.

Sigafoos, Robert A. *Absolutely Positively Overnight: The Story of Federal Express*. New York: New American Library/Mentor, 1983.

Simons, Howard, and Joseph A. Califano, Jr., eds. *The Media and Business*. New York: Vintage, 1979.

Simpson, Alan K. *Right on the Old Gazoo: A Lifetime of Scrapping with the Press*. New York: William Morrow, 1997.

Speakes, Larry, with Robert Pack. *Speaking Out: Inside the Reagan White House*. New York: Charles Scribner's Sons, 1988.

Spector, Robert, and Patrick D. McCarthy. *The Nordstrom Way: The Inside Story of America's #1 Customer Service Company*. New York: John Wiley, 1995.

Thurow, Lester C. *The Future of Capitalism: How Today's Economic Forces Shape Tomorrow's World*. New York: William Morrow, 1996.

Timberg, Robert. *The Nightingale's Song*. New York: Simon & Schuster, 1995.

Toffler, Alvin. *Previews and Premises*. New York: William Morrow, 1983.

Truman, Harry S. *Years of Trial and Hope, 1946–1952*. Garden City, N.Y.: Doubleday, 1956.

Tuchman, Barbara. *The Distant Mirror: The Calamitous Fourteenth Century*. New York: Alfred A. Knopf, 1978.

Tzu Sun. *The Art of War*. Trans. Samuel B. Griffith. London: Oxford University Press, 1963.

Vested, I. M. *The Confidential Memos of I. M. Vested*. New York: Harcourt Brace Jovanovitch, 1981.

Wallace, Mike, and Gary Paul Gates. *Close Encounters: Mike Wallace's Own Story*. New York: William Morrow, 1984.

Watson, Thomas, Jr. *Father, Son & Co.: My Life at IBM and Beyond*. New York: Bantam, 1991.

Wilson, Sloan. *The Man in the Gray Flannel Suit*. New York: Simon & Schuster, 1955.

Wolfe, Tom. *Bonfire of the Vanities*. New York: Farrar, Straus, Giroux, 1987.

Wouk, Herman. *The Caine Mutiny*. Garden City, N.Y.: Doubleday, 1951.

Wyden, Peter. *The Unknown Iacocca*. New York: William Morrow, 1987.

Yates, JoAnne. *The American Disease*. New York: Alfred A. Knopf, 1984.

———. *Control Through Communication: The Rise of System in American Management*. Baltimore and London: The John Hopkins University Press, 1989.

SPEECHES

Burger, Chester. Untitled, The Vern C. Schranz Distinguished Lectureship in Public Relations at Ball State University, Muncie, Indiana, November 10, 1983.

Burson, Harold. "A Decent Respect to the Opinions of Mankind." Given at the IPRA World Congress, Amsterdam, June 1985.

Carmichael, Barbara S. Allegory of the sea told during "Managing Crisis: The Role of Real Time Response," Fordham University, Graduate School of Business, April 27, 1992.

Cheney, Richard E. "How I Went From the Corporate Boardroom to a Seat Behind the Analyst's Couch," The Institute for Public Relations Research and Education 35th Annual Distinguished Lecture Series, October 9, 1996.

———. "What to Do When the Plant Blows Up and the CEO Steals Company Money and Runs Off with His or Her Secretary." Presented at the

Negative News Seminar, Practicing Law Institute, New York, October 16, 1984.

Dilenschneider, Robert L., and Richard C. Hyde. "Crisis Communications: Planning the Unplanned," published by Hill and Knowlton, Inc.

———. "The MTV Wall." Remarks made to the International Association of Business Communicators, in Kansas City, Missouri, November 10, 1995.

Eidson, Thomas E. "Six Trends That are Changing Public Relations." Remarks to the Public Relations Counselors Academy, San Diego, California, April 28, 1992.

Hyde, Richard C. Untitled remarks to the Counselor's Section of the Public Relations Society of America in Chicago, October 9, 1979.

Lavine, Gary. "Is PR Too Important to be Left to PR People?" Remarks to the Page Society, April 1991.

Madden, Richard B. "A Key to Management in the 1990s." Given at the *Business Week* Conference on the Future, White Plains, New York, April 30, 1985.

Occidental Petroleum executives, "The Other Side of Love Canal." Presentation Before the Financial Community Representatives from New York, Philadelphia, Boston, and Hartford. New York City, July 31, 1980.

Oliver, William. Remarks at the Thirteenth Annual Meeting, Arthur W. Page Society, September 29, 1996, Sundance, Utah. Pp. 3–20 of the report.

Pinsdorf, Marion K. "The Corporate City Room." Given to the New England Section of Public Relations Society of America, Providence, Rhode Island, April 1980.

———. "The New PR Pros: The Generals and Pols." Given at International Communications Association, Miami, Florida, May 22, 1992.

Rhody, Ronald E. "Nobody Told Me It'd Be Like This." Bank of America Reprint of remarks made at the Public Relations Roundtable, San Francisco, May 28, 1985.

———. "Of Wooly Buggers, Managers, and Times to Come." Remarks to the Arthur W. Page Society, Thirteenth Annual Meeting, Sundancee, Utah, September 29–October 2, 1996.

———. "Public Relations for the CEO." Bank of America Reprint of remarks to the Young Presidents Organization, Palo Alto, California, September 20, 1984. Sanada, Roy. "How to Communicate Successfully in the Japanese Market." Speech to Page Society, St. Amelia Island, Florida, September 1992.

Steinberg, Saul P. "Maximizing Investment Decisions." The Wharton School, University of Pennsylvania, March 28, 1984.

———. "Mergers and Acquisitions: Realities of a Drastically Changing

Marketplace." The Wharton School, University of Pennsylvania, February 19, 1985.

Yankelovich, Daniel. "Corporate Logic in the 1990's." Arthur W. Page spring Seminar, New York City, 1994.

Young, Lewis H. Various published speeches.

Unpublished Materials

Dugan, George M. "The Role of Public Relations in the Recovery of Chrysler Corporation," written as partial requirement for an MBA at the Graduate School of Business, Fordham University, Winter 1996.

Lattime, Jeffrey. "Love Canal Today," written as partial requirement for an MBA at the Graduate School of Business, Fordham University, April 1996.

Rush, Barbara. "Playing in the Middle of the Court: The Salomon Treasury Scandal," written as partial requirement for an MBA, Graduate School of Business, Fordham University, December 1992.

About the Author

MARION K. PINSDORF uniquely combines experience as a journalist, corporate officer, and director with a Ph.D. in economic history. Currently Senior Fellow in Communications at Fordham's Graduate School of Business, Dr. Pinsdorf has served on Amfac's Board of Directors, taught in the department of Portuguese and Brazilian Studies at Brown University, and been a partner of a New York–based consulting firm. Previously, she was a vice president of Hill and Knowlton, of Textron while William G. Miller served in two U.S. presidential appointments, and of INA during its merger with Connecticut General into CIGNA. In addition to numerous articles, she has authored *German-Speaking Entrepreneurs: Builders of Business in Brazil*. Her counsel in this book has been battle-tested over more than twenty years in the trenches of communications counseling and managing public crises.

Index

422

INDEX

press conference, definition, 389
Prince Philip, 106–107
process vs. results, and Japanese culture, 334–335
Procter & Gamble, 285–287
product disasters, 256–267
products, saving through PR campaigns, 301–305
Promise and Power: The Life and Times of Robert McNamara (Shapley), 109
prostate enlargement treatment, saving of as product, 304–305
publicity, danger of believing one's own, 63
public relations: and appeal to current values, 354; and Chrysler, 57–59; and elitist attitude, 350; and fads, 366, 368; future of, 372–377; historical development of, 335; and image building, 373–374; journalists' view of, 248; as major marketing player, 373; *The Man in the Gray Flannel Suit*, 355–357; and mergers/acquisitions, 233–235; mistakes in dealing with, 361–362; need for, 13–16; and quantification, responsibility and, 376; 322–323; and role of agencies, 375–376; and saving products, 301–305; and success in Japan, 337–339. *See also* communicators, communications
Public Relations Society of America, 14
Publix Supermarkets, 330
Puna Sugar, 297–301
Purolator Courier, 289

quantification, insufficiency of, 322–323
Queeg, Philip F. (fictional character), 126, 190, 202–204
Quezon, Manuel Luis, 217–219
"Quiddies," 322–325; lifestyle of, 324–325. *See also* "Baby Boomers," "Generation X," "Yuppies"

rabies vaccine, saving of as product, 301–304
racism, 171–172; 359
Ramsey family, 31
RCA, 132
Reagan, Nancy, 123, 293
Reagan, Ronald, 136–137, 146, 189–

190, 195, 204, 361; visit to Bitburg Cemetery, 136–137
Reebok, 95
Reed, Joseph, 177
Reedy, George, 121
Reich, Robert, 328
relationships, building, 341–342
Reliance Group Holdings, 179
removal of executives, 128–133
reporters. *See* journalists, journalism, media
Republic Steel, 232
reputation vs. image, 365–366, 374
responsibility, and public relations, 376
Rhody, Ronald E., 280–282, 368–372
Rice, Donna, 106
Richard & Edwards, 292
Richards, Ann, 102, 104
Ridder, P. Anthony, 180
Ridgeway, Matthew B., 137
rightsizing, and executive truthfulness, 102–103
Rittereiser, Robert, 258
RJR Nabisco, 123
Roberts, Bob (fictional character), 153, 161, 217
Roberts, Xavier, 292
Robins, A. H. (company) 265–267
Robinson, James, 374
Robinson, Lake & Montgomery, 235
Rockefeller, David, 177
Rockefeller, John D., Jr., 352
Rockefeller family, 352
Rogow, Arnold A., 144, 192, 196
Roosevelt, Franklin D., 42, 61, 147, 169, 189, 204, 217
Rose law firm, 108
Ross, Steven J., 146, 148–149, 179, 183–187
Royster, Vermont, 42
rumors: countering of, 283–285; effects of, 278–287; of satanism, 285–287
Rumsfeld, Donald, 8
running or developing story, definition, 389

Safire, William, 17, 263, 346, 387
Safra, Edmond, 387
Salomon Brothers, 99–101
Sanada, Roy, 332–339